P9-EMB-786

DISCARDED

The Productive High School

Joseph Murphy
Lynn G. Beck
Marilyn Crawford
Amy Hodges
Charis L. McGaughy

The Productive High School

Creating Personalized Academic Communities

CORWIN PRESS, INC.
A Sage Publications Company
Thousand Oaks, California

Copyright © 2001 by Corwin Press, Inc.

All rights reserved. When forms and sample documents are included, their use is authorized only by educators, local school sites, and/or noncommercial entities who have purchased the book. Except for that usage, no part of this book may be reproduced or utilized in any form or by any means, electronic or mechanical, including photocopying, recording, or by any information storage and retrieval system, without permission in writing from the publisher.

For information:

Corwin Press, Inc.
A Sage Publications Company
2455 Teller Road
Thousand Oaks, California 91320
E-mail: order@corwinpress.com

Sage Publications Ltd.
6 Bonhill Street
London EC2A 4PU
United Kingdom

Sage Publications India Pvt. Ltd.
M-32 Market
Greater Kailash I
New Delhi 110 048 India

Printed in the United States of America

Library of Congress Cataloging-in-Publication Data

Main entry under title:
    The productive high school: Creating personalized academic communities /
by Joseph Murphy . . . [et al.].
        p.   cm.
    Includes bibliographical references and index.
    ISBN 0-7619-7777-5 (cloth) — ISBN 0-7619-7778-3 (pbk.)
    1. High schools—United States—Administration.   2. School improvement
programs—United States.   3. Classroom environment—United States.
I. Murphy, Joseph, 1949–   . II. Title.
LB2822.2 .P76   2001
373—dc21   00-011048

This book is printed on acid-free paper.

01   02   03   04   05   06   07   7   6   5   4   3   2   1

Acquiring Editor:	Rachel Livsey
Editorial Assistant:	Kristen Gibson
Production Editor:	Diane S. Foster
Editorial Assistant:	Victoria Cheng
Designer/Typesetter:	Lynn Miyata
Indexer:	Kathy Paparchontis
Cover Designer:	Michelle Lee

Contents

Preface

This volume is designed to inform the educational community about the empirical foundations of productive high schools. The work grew out of three important conclusions drawn from our research on school improvement over the last decade. First, only a very small proportion of the reform literature addresses the high school. Most writing here is either generic in nature (addressed to all levels of schooling) or consciously focused on elementary education. Second, most of the reform agenda relating to high schools is untethered to research—its architecture is primarily conceptual and philosophical. Finally, much of the work on change and improvement at the high school level is unanchored in any meaningful way to the development of the high school as an institution.

The design of the volume is based on an adaptation of a model of organizations originally developed by Parsons (1960). In Part I, we focus our analysis on: (a) the core technology (learning and teaching), (b) the organizational systems in which the core functions are nested (the ecology of the institution), and (c) the institutional linkages between the school and its environment, especially the immediate school community. In the opening section of the book, we place the notion of *the productive high school* in historical context, especially in the light of shifting organizational aims and evolving theories of learning. In Part II, we turn our attention to the research on productive high school classrooms, sketching out a portrait of a productive core technology while clarifying the factors responsible for effective classroom learning environments. Part III of the volume examines the empirical evidence linking organizational structures and routines with enhanced learning. The lone chapter in Part IV of the book explores the theoretical underpinnings of the research on productive high schools. The foundation we cobble together from all the material in the book is captured in the construct of a personalized, academic, organizational infrastructure.

As noted above, Part I exposes the historical footings of the American high school. Our approach is to describe the broad periods of the development of secondary education in the United States (e.g., 1820-1890, "The Formation of the Public

High School," in Chapter 1). Within each of these major phases or stages of development, we begin by analyzing the institutional contexts that provided the blueprints for the construction and renovation of the high school. The framework is the same for each evolutionary period. For each time period, we review the dominant trends in the economic, political, and social domains around schooling. We also examine the dominant ideology in education in each period of development. We focus that discussion in four areas—the prevailing aims of education, theories of learning and teaching, views of school organization, and beliefs about institutional linkages. In this way, our organizing framework mirrors the overall design of the volume. We are particularly attentive to the intersection between educational ideology and conceptions of organizational productivity.

Part II, on productive classrooms, begins by analyzing the web of relationships at the heart of learning and teaching. We develop an understanding of the individual learner-teacher relationship as central and then expose the two faces of that relationship: cognitive-intellectual connection and social-emotional connection. A critical understanding of teacher-teacher relationships and student-student relationships that add communal context for learning is also provided. Together, these early sections of Part II shed new light on our knowledge of the network of responsive human relationships that ground learning in productive schools. The web of relationships provides context for high expectations, the second dominant classroom theme that emerges from the literature. The analysis here refines understanding of high expectations and paints a portrait of excellence in learning and teaching. The last section of Part II explores the final major classroom theme: the fluid, responsive nature of the productive high school learning environment. Students learn in a wide variety of ways, and effective teachers and schools provide flexible paths to excellence that nurture learner individuality and autonomy. One subtheme here focuses on teacher knowledge of how different students learn. Another addresses the wide variety of teaching strategies that constitute effective response to learner diversity. A third situates the flexible learning environment in a larger context, developing understanding of the many ways effective classrooms connect to the world outside school and link to students' futures.

Part III focuses on the organizational structure of high schools. It emphasizes the importance of the organizational structure being built around the core technology of learning and teaching. Three main themes emerge as important considerations for high school organization: (a) It must be anchored on a clearly defined learning imperative; (b) it must be built on humanized, intellectual relationships for learning; and (c) it must be nested in a dynamic, adaptive culture for change situated in a local context.

Our analysis reveals that successful high schools focus on academic success for all students and that this is the anchor around which organizational and managerial decisions are made. One important theme is a schoolwide focus on an explicit, powerful educational agenda. We explore what it means for a high school to have a clear vision of learning and teaching goals as well as planning that focuses on those goals. The review also highlights the importance of community commitment to success. We discuss the need for the school to have high standards of success for all students as well as the importance of shared responsibility for student learning.

The middle section of Part III provides evidence that a cardinal factor in success for high school students is relationships with adults involved in the school community. An important dimension here is the idea of creating a cohesive, nurturing culture for students. This involves designing activities for inclusion of all students. A nurturing culture also involves a school's viewing students as individuals and recognizing their needs. Still another key dimension is found in the concept of teachers operating in a positive, professionally oriented community. For this to happen, research reveals that the school organization and administration must support the professionalization of teachers, involving them in decision making and problem solving as well as giving them some control over their work. And the school structure must increase capacity for teachers' success and growth by providing professional development focused on the needs of the staff, necessary resources for effective teaching, and evaluations that assist teachers in their growth. Another dimension focuses on the student-adult relationships that drive the community of commitment in productive high schools. This is achieved by organizing programs and by adopting structures that facilitate relationships.

The third section of the organizational part of the volume underscores the need for the high school community to understand change and to learn to manage it within the local context of the school. Evidence is marshaled about the need for school staff to be engaged in improvement-oriented behavior, which includes schools' removing of barriers to change, adding achievement-focused innovations and resources, and recognizing responsibility to the local community. An interesting finding is the consideration of local community and local context in program planning, and examples are provided of high schools that tailor programs for students. In this way, schools are responsive to changes in culture both inside and outside the school. Evidence is also provided about the importance of schools operating from an organic, evolutionary mindset. This requires the school culture to enhance the capacity for change as well as to create the will to change. Schools with a culture of inquiry for both students and staff and an environment that supports trying new things are critical factors in creating a climate conducive to change. A cardinal principle is a passionate desire within the adults involved in the high school to help students succeed.

After reviewing research on communal features of productive high schools, we see four themes that recur in this scholarship:

1. In successful high schools, people feel *special.* Students have a strong sense of their own identities and believe that they are known and respected as individuals.

2. In high schools in which students succeed, young people also have a sense of belonging. They believe that they matter to others who care about them.

3. In high schools that work for young people, students believe that they are contributing to the success of the school (or of some group within it) and to the success

of their fellow students. They identify with some group and feel a sense of mutual responsibility for the well-being of others.

4. In successful secondary schools, there is shared activity aimed at promoting meaningful learning. Although the literature, at times, contrasts schools that are focused on academic achievement with those that foster a strong sense of community, a large body of research suggests that high schools in which students achieve academically tend to have a communal organization that is bolstered by focused, collaborative activities that intentionally promote learning.

In Parts II and III of the book, our focus is on characteristics of productive high schools. We report on research exploring a range of factors that correlate with high levels of student achievement. In the course of this work, we touch on theories offered by scholars to explain the links between a host of structural, curricular, social, cultural, and pedagogical features and powerful learning within young men and women. In Part IV, we concentrate on these theories in an effort to highlight likely and possible connections between the development of adolescents' academic and life skills and factors such as small-size, heterogeneous classes, a limited and focused curriculum, caring relationships, and teacher collegiality. We begin by creating a framework within which we review both explicit and implicit theories that attempt to explain links between correlates of student achievement and actual learning. We then synthesize or integrate these explanations. That is, we explore themes and patterns that cut across and link the various theories.

Our conclusion, based on our historical analysis and review of the empirical evidence, is that if we wish to have productive high schools, then researchers, practicing educators, parents, policymakers, and citizens must create institutions very different from most that inhabit our communities. We must strive to create models of learning-driven school communities that allow for and encourage excellence, and we must support and implement these models. Such efforts will challenge us intellectually, emotionally, and interpersonally. They will require resources, energy, and patience. Our perspective is that we must undertake these efforts, drawing strength and encouragement from the reality that an impressive body of empirical evidence and a robust set of theories support this work.

About the Authors

Lynn G. Beck is Dean of the School of Education at Pacific Lutheran University. Her research and teaching focuses on administrative ethics, principalship, and leadership preparation. Her recent publications include *Understanding the Principalship: Metaphorical Themes, 1920s to 1990s* (with Joseph Murphy, 1993), *Ethics in Educational Leadership Programs: An Expanding Role* (with Joseph Murphy, 1994), *Reclaiming Educational Administration as a Caring Profession* (1994), and *The Four Imperatives of Successful Schools* (with Joseph Murphy, 1996).

Marilyn Crawford is a career educator who has spent thirty years working in the public schools both in teaching and leadership roles. As a national participant in school reform efforts, she focuses on developing secondary schools that demand high performance of all students while providing a wide range of paths for achieving what is required of them. She is currently serving as Director of the Office of Teaching and Learning in the School District of Lancaster, Pennsylvania, as well as continuing her work as a national consultant for middle and high school reform.

Amy Hodges is the House Principal in charge of Curriculum, Instruction, and Assessment at McCaskey East High School in Lancaster, Pennsylvania. Her work involves implementation of a district-wide standards-based reform at the high school level. Formerly, she was a mathematics and science teacher in public schools in Alabama and at a private boarding school in Kenya. Her primary area of interest is high school personalization.

Charis L. McGaughy is a Research Associate in the Department of Leadership and Organizations at Peabody College of Vanderbilt University. She is a former third grade teacher. She has also served as an interagency liaison with the Texas Education Agency and as an accountancy manager with the Tennessee Department of Children's Services.

Joseph Murphy is a Professor in the School of Leadership and Policy in the College of Education at Ohio State University and President of the Ohio Principals' Leadership Academy. He also chairs the Interstate School Leaders Licensure Consortium. Prior to moving to Ohio State, he was an Associate Professor at the University of Illinois and Professor and Chair of the Department of Leadership and Organizations at Peabody College of Vanderbilt University. He is a former Vice President of the American Educational Research Association (Division A, Administration). Earlier in his career, he served as a school administrator at the school, district, and state levels.

Epigram

We stand at a point in time when we need to examine those educational institutions and values we have taken for granted. We need to turn facts into puzzles to perceive alternatives both in the past and in the present.

—Tyack (1974, p. 4)

Knowledge of and respect for an institution's historical record is indispensable for the reformer or policy maker intent on charting new paths into the future, and . . . the interplay of historical tendencies and contemporary circumstances will continue largely to shape the particular forms that institutions display at each stage of their history.

—Herbst (1996, p. xv)

Perhaps the best one can do is to take heart from successes of the past and hope that as the citizenry and the profession journey into uncharted pedagogical seas, a vision of the high school will emerge which both profits from the wisdom of prior generations and yet boldly reaches toward new goals.

—Cremin (1955, p. 308)

I

Lessons Learned

Perhaps the greatest idea that America has given the world is the idea of education for all. The world is entitled to know whether this idea means that everybody can be educated or only that everybody must go to school.

—Robert M. Hutchins,
cited in Ravitch (1983, p. 75)

1

The Formation of the American High School

1635-1890

There is a sense in which history is treated as arcane, esoteric, and of little import to the concerns of practice and policy. I am convinced that precisely the opposite is true. Carefully conducted historical inquiry may well provide us with the most powerful guides available.

—Shulman (1984, p. vii)

The success of any current attempt to provide an adequate secondary-school program depends in no small measure on an appreciation of the course traversed by the school to date.

—Spears (1941, p. 24)

The way we understand that past profoundly shapes how we make choices today.

—Tyack (1974, p. 4)

In this introductory part of the book, we construct the historical footings and expose the contextual perspectives that help ground the empirical analysis that follows in later chapters. To be consistent with the best scholarship we reviewed, this section is organized by historical periods. We begin by examining the central political, economic, and social forces that helped shape conceptions of schooling within each era. We then illuminate the tapestry known as schooling in each time frame, paying particular attention to the ways that prevailing educational goals and dominant theories of learning were woven into distinct patterns.

In the initial chapter, we follow the evolution of the American public high school through three phases of development, showing how each gave rise to a unique form of schooling. In so doing, we explore the development of the high school as a quasi-private enterprise and review its transformation into a public institution. Specifically, we provide a brief overview of the Latin grammar school era (1635-1780), describe the academy movement (1751-1875), and expose the initial foundations of the public high school (1821-1890). In later chapters, we trace the development of the comprehensive public high school from 1891 to 1980 and examine the forces that are reshaping that institution at the dawn of the 21st century.

Precursors to the American Public High School

> An understanding of the secondary schools which served American youth of past generations is essential to any study of the secondary school as it exists in the United States today.
>
> —Anderson and Gruhn (1962, p. 24)

The Latin Grammar School Era

Secondary education in the United States began in Boston in 1635 with the establishment of the Latin grammar school, a form of schooling that continued for nearly two centuries. Although the grammar school was almost exclusively a New England phenomenon (Spears, 1941) and "can scarcely properly be ever said to have flourished" (Odell, 1939, p. 67), it did provide a useful function for the small number of students served and did raise the issue of secondary schooling in the national consciousness for the first time—and in the process "helped to produce a leadership that carved national independence out of almost unyielding odds" (Latimer, 1958, p. 114).

By 1700, there were at least 27 Latin grammar schools in New England (Stiles, McCleary, & Turnbaugh, 1962, p. 25), and according to Odell (1939), by the time of the American Revolution, every colony except Georgia had at least one grammar school. At the peak of their popularity, the total number of academies in existence fell somewhat short of 100 (Odell, 1939). In New England, the institutions were public in nature, meaning that they were authorized by and subject to control by the government, not that they were heavily supported by public funds. In the other colonies, Latin grammar schools were largely a private affair. Tuition was a common feature of nearly all these early schools.

The Latin grammar school was patterned on the English version of secondary education—the only form with which the early colonists were familiar. Attendance was limited to males and, although democratic in design, because of tuition charges, primarily to boys from more prosperous homes (Anderson & Gruhn, 1962).

> Colonial public schools were not created as potential avenues of opportunity for poorer boys or *any* girls or people of color. Education largely confirmed

one's status or enabled young men with family advantages to gain the skills to compete more favorably in a world of supply and demand. (Reese, 1995, p. 6)

They were day rather than boarding schools and had longer hours and a longer school year than is the norm today. Grammar schools had a quite limited purpose. The goal was to prepare for college and "ultimately for positions of leadership in church and state" (Cuban, 1984, p. 25) or "to prepare members of the landed aristocracy for their roles as country gentlemen or squires" (Latimer, 1958, p. 1).

The curriculum was equally circumscribed, directed exclusively to the prerequisites for college (Koos, 1927; Spears, 1941). Or as Latimer (1958) captures it: "Latin and Greek constituted the twin suns around which the rest of the curriculum revolved. They were the be-all and know-all and almost end-all of the schoolboy's existence" (p. 25). Consistent with the accepted educational philosophy of the time, this classical training was "cherished more for the discipline it exacted on body and mind then for its curricular content" (Herbst, 1996, p. 13). As we explain more fully below, the prime objective was the development of important facilities of the mind such as observation and persistence. The quality of instruction depended on schoolmasters who "varied much in their abilities and attainments" (Odell, 1939, p. 72). Perhaps the best that can be said is that it was uneven.

Odell (1939) and others have revealed that Latin grammar schools were never especially popular. Indeed, by the end of the 18th century, they were nearly extinct (Herbst, 1996; Spears, 1941), a victim largely of their limited mission and narrow curriculum. As Latimer (1958) explains, "The curriculum was the greatest factor in the grammar school's decline. As population and wealth increased and social distinctions became less important, dissatisfaction with this type of education and its narrow curriculum became stronger and stronger" (p. 4). Although "classical education remained the gateway to Harvard, . . . an important segment of the town wanted to offer children more practical education" (Reese, 1995, p. 4).

The Academy Era

It is clear, nevertheless, that the restriction of educational opportunities and consequent dissatisfaction with a curriculum geared so exclusively to the past ushered in the next phase—the founding of private academies and the introduction of subjects conceivably of more immediate and practical use. (Latimer, 1958, p. 114)

In closing the last section, we pointed out the growing dissatisfaction with the limited aims of the Latin grammar schools. It was this unrest and the changing social conditions that led to the second revolution in high school education in the United States, the rise of the academy (Koos, 1927; Spears, 1941). The first academy was established by Benjamin Franklin in Philadelphia in 1751. The movement took root in New England a dozen years later. By 1800, this new form of secondary education was appearing throughout the territories. By 1830, there were 950 academies in the United States. By 1850, that number had ballooned to nearly 6,100 schools employing approximately 12,250 teachers and serving more than 263,000 pupils (Anderson & Gruhn, 1962; Odell, 1939; Spears, 1941). From its dominant position around 1860, the academy has experienced a significant decline in importance, although, unlike the Latin grammar schools, numerous academies survive today.

In their early stages of development, academies became defined by a number of key elements. As was the case with the Latin grammar schools, they relied heavily on student tuition. Unlike most of the earlier schools, however, they were privately sponsored; although, because of the infusion of some government support, they often assumed a quasi-public form. Paradoxically, although private, they were more democratic in character than the publicly sponsored grammar schools they replaced. As Koos (1927) explains, the academy was "an institution committed to a more generous service, inclusive of both sexes and of college-going and non-college-going groups" (p. 45). They were much more attentive to the interests of the middle class than the grammar schools had been (Spears, 1941). They offered practical subjects as well as preparation for college and were "much less distinctly denominational than the Latin grammar school[s]" (Koos, 1927, p. 24).

During the heyday of the academy movement, the typical school enrolled 40-45 students and employed two teachers (Koos, 1927; Odell, 1939). The original purpose of the academy was to address the needs of non-college-bound pupils. However, as the Latin schools fell into disfavor, academies developed a more diverse mission—training for life and preparation for college: "To the more practical subjects, . . . public opinion compelled them to add those required for college preparation" (Latimer, 1958, p. 58). It is not surprising, then, that the curriculum of the academies was much broader than that found in the grammar schools. In addition to the classical subjects of Latin and Greek, "academies were noted for the breadth and variety of their offerings in the *moderns,* that is, science, history, modern languages (German and French), and literature in English" (Krug, 1964, p. 4). The academy introduced and provided legitimacy to practical subjects such as bookkeeping and navigation that were largely absent from the grammar school (Anderson & Gruhn, 1962; Odell, 1939). They made English rather than Latin the primary language of instruction (Anderson & Gruhn, 1962), and their "emphasis on history, including United States history and modern history, was also a distinct departure from the curriculum offered in the Latin grammar school" (p. 30). Finally, the academies introduced the extracurricular activities that would become such a central part of the comprehensive public high school of the 20th century (Anderson & Gruhn, 1962).

Shortly after the Civil War, the academy was displaced by the public high school as the dominant form of secondary education. Although we say more about this issue in the next section, it appears that the private nature of the academy was largely responsible for its decline. Leaders of the universal public education coalition were quick to suggest that the private school was "less responsive to the general need and less well adapted to . . . democratic institutions than its successor, the public high school" (Koos, 1927, p. 45). As they declined in number in the face of growing support for publicly supported high schools, the academies often became more classical in nature, focusing primarily on the college preparatory function (Odell, 1939). Or, as Spears (1941) ironically records, by 1885, "the institution that had originated as a popular protest to the college preparatory character of the grammar school was sentenced to become the type of school against which it had made its original protest" (pp. 41-42).

The Public High School: The Formative Era

The transition period between 1821 and 1890 marked the high point of the academies, ended their dominance in the field, and brought secondary education largely under public control.

—Latimer (1958, p. 59)

The Context

Economic, social, and political upheavals transformed everyday life, challenging urban leaders to redefine the nature of private and public responsibility for education and schooling. (Reese, 1995, p. 3)

Before exploring the advent of public secondary education, it is instructive to reemphasize a theme introduced earlier, namely, that larger societal forces play a significant role in legitimizing prevalent forms of schooling (Murphy, 1996). In terms of the public high school, the economic dimensions of this phenomenon can be traced to "the new economic order" (Reese, 1995, p. 20) taking root in the mid-to-late 1800s. One aspect of the new economy forming in the 1800s was the decay of the older system, including the twin pillars of the barter economy and economic self-sufficiency. The other aspect was the emergence of a "new economic structure" (p. 95), specifically, the evolution of the United States into a "commercial republic" (p. 39) with a market economy. With the advent of this new order and, with it, "the struggle for survival and preferment in an individualistic and complicated commercial world" (p. 18), the connections between schooling and the economy became more robust, and higher levels of education more important. Education now provided a competitive edge in the world outside the pulpit and the university classroom. School was seen increasingly as "a gateway to opportunities in the free market" (p. 19), and "the high school diploma per se began to have value in the marketplace for employment in a way it had not previously" (Sizer, 1964, p. 9). Demand for schooling was on the rise (Anderson & Gruhn, 1962; Sizer, 1964).

Concomitantly—and often in response to changes underway in the economy— powerful social and political forces also began to influence the transformation of secondary schooling. Specifically, Reese (1995) avers that bedrock shifts in the economy eroded "familiar social patterns and relationships" (p. 167), widened class divisions, and "generated new questions about social relationships and the place of schools in society" (p. 2). He suggests that schooling increasingly came to be seen as a solution for these "profound social changes" (p. 20) and "grave social ills" (p. 19). In particular, Reese holds that the following key ideas about the role of schooling in relation to society's needs flowered in the mid to late 1890s—all of which promoted the development of public secondary education: (a) The well-being of the nation depended on the knowledge of its citizens; (b) an extensive middle class was essential to the prosperity of the country; (c) education provided the key for the creation of productive workers for the new economy; and (d) education was directly linked to social harmony or, alternatively, "schools produced politically safe individuals for the new commercial, increasingly industrialized order" (p. 40)—in other words, schools could help socialize workers into accepting the emerging changes associated with industrialization (Vinovskis, 1985).

Development and Growth

The formation of the public high school—the third revolution in secondary schooling—can be traced to a number of dynamics in the educational sector as well. As noted above, many leaders argued that the existing system of private academies was inconsistent with what Ravitch (1983) has described as the "great struggle of the 19th century" (p. 15)—the fight by professional educators to "establish the principle of free universal education" (p. 15; see also Cremin, 1961). Herbst's (1996) review shows how this "democratic imperative . . . targeted the private academies or 'select schools' as the greatest enemy" (p. 67). Indeed, Reese (1995) reported that by the 1820s and 1830s, a "growing network of reformers" (p. 17) was at work, laboring to discredit past and current practices and to lobby for a common system of tax-supported high schools" (p. 15).[1]

A second "step in the direction of the public high school was the extension of the elementary schools by the addition of higher subjects" (Koos, 1927, p. 29)—a trend Koos saw as "a clear example of the natural upward extension of the public school system" (p. 29). A third factor promoting the establishment of the public high school was the development of union schools—a movement that consolidated teachers and pupils in a single building and made it easier to cluster students who desired extended education beyond the elementary grades (Koos, 1927; Odell, 1939).

In addition to the conditions chronicled above, Anderson and Gruhn (1962) suggest that the increased capacity of communities to support public schools—especially in the cities (Sizer, 1964)—and court cases such as the famous Kalamazoo decision of 1874, which affirmed the power of townships to levy taxes in support of public high schools, also help account for the dominance attained by the public high school by the end of the 19th century.

Demand for change was sufficiently powerful that it "led to the third period of development—the creation in 1821 of a new instrument of democratic education, the public high school" (Latimer, 1958, p. 115). Over the next 70 years, the academy and the public school both vied for dominance on the landscape of secondary education. By the time of the Civil War, "the academy had reached the height of its development, and thereafter declined rapidly in both numbers and influence" (Anderson & Gruhn, 1962, p. 31). "By the 1880s, especially in the North, public high schools stood triumphant" (Reese, 1995, p. xiii). By 1890, roughly 60% of the secondary schools in the nation were public high schools. By 1900, 75% were public in nature (Odell, 1939).

The development of the high school as a free, tax-supported institution can be traced to the establishment of the Boston English Classical School in 1821. The school was open to boys only, matriculation was dependent on passing entrance examinations, and the course of study was for three years (Odell, 1939). Important mile markers in the expansion of secondary public education included legislation in 1827 in Massachusetts requiring towns of 500 or more families to establish public high schools and the provision of state aid to high schools in Maine in 1871 (Odell, 1939; Sizer, 1964).

Although a number of fully tax-supported public high schools opened in the 1830s and 1840s, the public high school movement was slow in picking up speed (Anderson & Gruhn, 1962; Latimer, 1958; Reese, 1995), with the number chartered remaining relatively small until around 1860. Although probably understated, figures provided by the United States Bureau of Education provide a snapshot of this growth pattern: 11 schools in 1850, 33 schools in 1860, 160 schools in 1870, 800 schools in 1880, and 2,526 schools in 1890 (Odell, 1939, p. 87), with approximately 8,000 teachers and 200,000 students in the system in that final year (Krug, 1964). By 1890, "the public high school had clearly become the dominant feature on the secondary education landscape" (Latimer, 1958, p. 14). Yet by the close of the formative era, there were very few separate high school buildings (Reese, 1995).

Although the typical high school of this era enrolled "one or two dozen pupils taught by a 'principal' teacher and perhaps a lesser paid assistant" (Reese, 1995, p. 128), it is also clear is that there was a good deal of diversity in the structure and operation of public high schools during this formative period (Sizer, 1964). As Reese (1995) has uncovered, "There was really no such thing as *the* American high school" (p. 208); citizens "lacked a coherent definition of a high school or a high school student" (p. 217; see also Herbst, 1996). Although there was a growing supply of public secondary schools, "they were hardly cast from a single mold" (p. 208).

> From community to community, the length of a period varied widely as did the years needed to complete the work of the high school, and the curricular offerings. Thus considerable confusion existed as to the number of years the high school should include, the nature of its offerings, and what should constitute a year of credit in a given subject. (Taylor, McMahill, & Taylor, 1960, p. 76)

Before the 1880s, however, contemporaries realized that high schools in rural, village, and city systems differed tremendously. High school scholars included those who read one or two advanced subjects in a rural school, those who enjoyed richer academic fare in a union graded school, and those who imbibed a full curriculum in America's cities. (Reese, 1995, pp. 208, 221)

Indeed, Sizer (1964) goes so far as to suggest that as the formative era of the public high school drew to a close, "secondary education was in chaotic condition" (p. 18).

Learning Infrastructure

Students

In terms of students served by public high schools in their formative years, a few patterns emerge. First, over the years, there was a gradual increase in the age of the students attending. Although it was not unusual to find 12-year-olds in the high school before 1840, "by the 1850s and 1860s the majority of pupils admitted were 14 or 15; . . . 'youth' between 14 and 16 predominated" (Reese, 1995, p. 172). Second, as the numbers below reveal, only a small percentage of eligible students were served by these schools, and of those who attended, very few graduated (Krug, 1964). The roughly 203,000 students in public high school in 1890 represented only 1.0% of the total population of the nation. Only about 20,000 of these students would graduate (Tyack, 1974). Looked at in another way, at the close of the formative period of the American public high school, only 6.7% of the nation's 14- to 17-year-olds were being served (Rothstein, 1994). Approximately 5.0% of students enrolled in public education were in high school (Reese, 1995). One rough algorithm by which to picture high school enrollments is the following: Of 10,000 students who entered public school in the first grade, 1,000 completed the elementary grades. Of these 1,000, 100 entered high school. Of these 100, 10 graduated from high school. Of these 10 graduates, 1 went on to college. Not unexpectedly, according to Sizer (1964), until 1890, public high school "remained outside the main stream of American life. The secondary school counted for little as the social sorting device that the 19th century American used" (p. 6). Tyack (1974) concurs; he argues that "the great majority of the population acted as if the high school was superfluous" (p. 59).

We know that the student body was predominately female: 58% of secondary pupils and 65% of graduates were female (Tyack, 1974, p. 58). According to analysts of the era, this imbalance was largely a response to labor market opportunities and economic needs that "forced many pupils, especially boys, to leave school prematurely" (Reese, 1995, p. 238). In addition, because of rigorous entrance examinations, pupils who attended high school represented "an aristocracy of the intellect" (p. 152). Finally, the available data suggest that the public high school of the era also "served mostly the upper reaches of the middle class" (Tyack, 1974, p. 58). "Most high school pupils by midcentury came from the relatively privileged native born. . . . Children of the poorest families and even skilled workers . . . were consistently under represented in high schools" (Reese, 1995, pp. 180, 178).

Purpose and Goals

Issues of purpose and aim dominated discourse and activity during the formative era of the American public high school. What was the function of the public high school—to prepare students for life or for college? The early answer was clear—to provide youngsters who would not be attending college with "a good English education to fit them for active life and to qualify them for eminence in private or public station" (Regulations of the School Committee, cited in Anderson & Gruhn, 1962, p. 33). Within this framework, a trilogy of goals or "a tripartite definition of school achievement" (Reese, 1995, p. 184) was underscored: attendance, deportment, and scholarship (Tyack, 1974). "Most educators in the 19th century assumed that character development, religiosity, and intellectual achievement were inseparable. Knowledge was always embedded in a moral framework" (Reese, 1995, p. 166). Historical scholars are quick to note, however, that the portfolio of aims for this emerging institution quickly broadened. Although the "original function was to prepare students for practical life, . . . under the pressure of diverse needs in a democratic society this function was gradually enlarged to include preparation for college" (Latimer, 1958, p. 16). Indeed, the rebalancing of goals was so dramatic that:

> By 1890, the high school had largely repeated the history of the academy in that after beginning as a practical, non-college preparatory institution, it had come to be dominated by higher institutions and the college preparatory aim. This was true even though the majority of those who entered it did not continue their education further. Thus high school was failing to meet the needs of a large portion of adolescent youth who desired a secondary education. (Odell, 1939, pp. 86-87)

Theories of Learning

The scientific bedrock on which theories of learning and methods of teaching were built during this era was known as *faculty psychology* a foundation laid out most fully in the United States in the Yale University report of 1829. According to Krug (1964), faculty psychology, as described in that document, "proclaimed the two great points of 'intellectual culture' to be the discipline and the furniture of the mind, with discipline considered 'perhaps, the more important of the two' " (p. 205). The development of the ability to think as opposed to the acquisition of knowledge "was by far the more significant function of education" (Kliebard, 1995, p. 5). Adherents of the theory "saw the mind as something to be trained rather than furnished" (Krug, 1964, p. 208). More concretely, according to the theory of faculty psychology, the mind was believed to be divided into several domains or areas, "each of which controlled different faculties, such as judgment, will, memory, reason, imagination, and feelings" (Latimer, 1958, p. 65), and each of which could be trained and later engaged when needed (Odell, 1939).

For high schools, "faculty psychology manifested itself primarily in the emphasis on mental discipline" (Herbst, 1996, p. 30)—a focus that shaped all of the major dimensions of learning and teaching during the formative era of this unique institution. At the beginning, the theory established a purpose for classroom activity—"to furnish mental training" (Krug, 1964, p. 445). "Having a 'well- disciplined mind' was an important goal of secondary instruction" (Reese, 1995, p. 101). The emphasis of the theory on the development of the full portfolio of faculties led to an educational system that underscored the moral (character) as well as the reasoning dimensions of the mind (Odell, 1939; Spring, 1990). The theory provided a conception of knowledge—"something scholars memorized and recited to their teachers" (Reese, 1995, p. 261); a picture of intellectual development—"the recalling of facts in many subjects" (p. 261); and a portrait of the educated person—one "who knew the most facts" (p. 148). Faculty psychology catapulted the concept of transfer to the foreground of schooling. Subjects were studied and learned less for their own sake than for the development of faculties (e.g., of observation) that could then be engaged across a spectrum of academic and practical problems (Spears, 1941). The theory also nurtured an emerging understanding of student failure not as a consequence of the inability of teachers "but as evidence of the students' personal and moral recalcitrance" (Tyack, 1974, p. 55).

Instruction

Not surprisingly, the theory of faculty psychology heavily colored emerging perspectives on instruction and curriculum in these nascent educational institutions. Or as Kliebard (1995) expresses it, "The mind-as-a-muscle metaphor [became] the basis for explaining to future teachers what they ought to teach and how they ought to go about it" (p. 5). On the instructional side of the equation, it firmly "placed the teacher in control of the pupil's education by making him the expert who knew which of the pupil's faculties needed special training and who could adjust his tutorial labors to the greatest advantage of the pupil" (Herbst, 1996, p. 31). Under this intellectual framework, "what mattered was [that which was] contained in textbooks, stored in one's mind, and recited to teachers. Little wonder, then, that one pedagogical primer called recitation 'the *summa summarium* of teaching'" (Reese, 1995, p. 135).

In general, instruction during the formative era of the public high school left a good deal to be desired. According to Kliebard (1995), faculty psychology with its "belief that the mind was in fact, or at least like, a muscle provided the backdrop for a regime in school of monotonous drill, harsh discipline and mindless verbatim recitation" (p. 5). Analysts of the era describe a "bleak picture" (Sizer, 1964, p. 47) of instruction in the public high school. They establish a story line of "dull and deadly teaching" (Reese, 1995, p. 137). "All the evidence about teacher classroom work in the late 19th century suggests that it was regularly bad and frequently horrible" (Powell, Farrar, & Cohen, 1985, p. 253). The teachers were generally young, inexperienced, and poorly trained (Kliebard, 1995; Sizer, 1964). Each teacher was often responsible for a variety of subjects. Conformity was prized (Reese, 1995), and classrooms were expected to "be run with military discipline" (Tyack, 1974, p. 97).

Again, faculty psychology and "mental discipline provided them [teachers] with an authoritative justification" (Kliebard, 1995, p. 5) for this model of tedious pedagogy.

The prevailing system of pedagogy emphasized "passive students whose education consisted of memorizing facts" (Reese, 1995, p. 137). The trilogy of classroom instruction consisted of textbooks, memorization, and recitation. Textbooks "reigned supreme" (Reese, 1995, p. 105). They provided "the central source of information and authority in the curriculum" (Tyack, 1974, p. 47). They defined acceptable knowledge and established acceptable methods of instruction (Reese, 1995). It was mastery of textbooks rather than completion of courses that determined progress through school. In every subject, students were required to memorize large numbers of rules and facts from these textbooks. Indeed, "memorizing knowledge was the hallmark of education" (p. 134). Recitation, in turn, made up the third pattern in the pedagogical mosaic of the early high school. Students regularly were expected to enumerate material that they had memorized from their textbooks. Accountability for learning was measured by successful recitation and rested squarely on the shoulders of the pupils. The entire process unfolded in a competitive environment. Written work, on the other hand, was not heavily underscored in the public high schools of this era (Reese, 1995).

An interesting dimension of schooling during this time was the fact that entrance to high school was dependent not on completion of the elementary grades but rather on passing admissions tests, most of which were written. According to Reese (1995), these early "systematic attempts to measure educational progress" (p. 143) served to confirm the type of education valued at the time—a focus on factual information, a lack of emphasis on analysis and interpretation, and the spotlighting of "mechanical pedagogy" (p. 161). These entrance tests were designed to carry considerable freight. They were expected: (a) to lift standards throughout the elementary grades; (b) to define the content of the elementary grades, "thereby promoting a better sequenced, graduated system of instruction" (p. 152); and (c) to provide ways to assess the quality of elementary schools and their teachers (Reese, 1995).

Curriculum

The birth of the public high school was in some sense a reaction to the narrow curriculum that grew from the intellectual taproot known as mental discipline, especially the nearly exclusive focus on instruction in the classical subjects. In time, however, as was the case with the academy, the public high school would also be drawn into the orbit of faculty psychology—so much so, in fact, that Kliebard (1995) argues that the curriculum status quo at the close of the formative era of the public high school "was represented by the doctrine of mental discipline and its adherents" (p. 4).

The first public high schools were primarily concerned with the practical side of life—"preparation of youth for practical life was their slogan" (Latimer, 1958, p. 8). High schools were known both for what they did not emphasize—the traditions of the Latin school (Reese, 1995)—and what they did spotlight—youngsters who did not plan to attend college, a concern with a modern or a practical as opposed to a classical education (Anderson & Gruhn, 1962; Odell, 1939), and with "intimate ties between the curriculum and business life in a general sense" (Reese, 1995, p. 92). Thus "in keeping with its initial purpose—to prepare youth for the practical affairs of contemporary life—the curricula of the early high schools were broadly vocational in context and scope" (Latimer, 1958, p. 115). According to scholars in this area, "the curriculum centered around English [with] the next heaviest concentration in mathematics" (p. 8). Science was generally limited to the final year of the high school program.

> Three years of work were offered in English composition and literature. The other subjects were arithmetic, geography, and declamation in the first year; algebra, geometry, trigonometry, navigation, surveying, mensuration, history, and oratory in the second; and further mathematics and history, astronomy, logic, natural philosophy, moral and political philosophy, and declamation in the third year. The school was definitely not college preparatory. (Odell, 1939, p. 83)

Shortly after their formation, however, pressure was brought to bear to expand the aims of the public high school and, consequently, its curriculum. Analysts such as Latimer (1958) document how "the original intent was gradually enlarged" (p. 115) and reveal how "public sentiment compelled high schools, as it had compelled the academies before them, to add college preparatory subjects to their curricula" (p. 115). What began to emerge by the close of the Civil War were high schools with two distinct *courses* or *departments*—an English and a classical course of study, with the former intended primarily for youngsters seeking employment after completing high school and the later intended for those whose objective was college attendance (Anderson & Gruhn, 1962; Krug, 1964). Public high schools with dual aims and differentiated curricula had become part of the fabric of the educational tapestry. The outcome was "a high school that ceased to have clearly defined objectives and repudiated its emergence from a tradition of common schooling by trying to serve all members of its varied clientele with differentiated course offerings" (Herbst, 1996, p. 95). As we will explore in later sections of the book, this dual function placed a heavy burden on the public high school—one that would continue to bedevil educators for the next century.

The focus on mental discipline and faculty psychology influenced the curriculum in this formative era in a number of ways. First, because "mastering basic information was the essence of learning" (Reese, 1995, p. 149), collecting facts was underscored but understanding and analysis were not. Second, as noted earlier, strengthening the memory was more significant than was understanding of the course (Reese, 1995). Third, because "it was assumed that mastery of certain subjects trained the separate faculties and that the mental discipline thus acquired was transferred for mastery of other subjects" (Latimer, 1958, p. 65), within each of the major departments, the educational process and the educational curriculum was the same for all students. Once a student selected "one or the other of these [departments] his choice was ended" (Odell, 1939, p. 80).

Governance

Reese (1995) and Tyack (1974) have uncovered the roots of important governance issues in this formative era, which have occupied a central place in the development of the public high school for nearly two centuries. According to these scholars, the key governance issues were forged on the anvil of control. Their work exposes two major points.

First, throughout the formative era, a rather robust struggle was taking place between two divergent ideologies. One side was populated by reformers who believed that centralized control was imperative for fostering the widespread implementation of the public high school and for strengthening the quality of the educational system. These progressive reformers were guided by the values of centralization of power, specialization, and professional expertise (Reese, 1995). They supported a larger role for the state, especially in the area of financial support for secondary education. Decentralized or local control infuriated these reformers. For them, a system of local governance was "archaic, unprofessional, and too decentralized" (p. 26). They regularly "highlighted the foibles of local school politics . . . before professional educators set things straight" (p. 26). The local control advocates were, according to the reform crowd, "drags on social progress" (p. 70).

On the other side of the debate were citizens who were leery of the ideas and the initiatives of the reformers. For some, attempts to expand the public high school were seen as efforts by the wealthy to use the tax system to benefit their children at the expense of the poor, who were not using the schools. Citizens on this side of the case argued that those who benefited from the high schools should pay for the advantage. Many others simply did not accept the values of the reformers, especially notions of professional control and expert knowledge. They believed in citizen control and self-governance. They emphasized personal liberty and family responsibility (Reese, 1995). Not surprisingly, and unlike the reformers, they "chafed at state intrusiveness in education" (p. 75), believing that "centralization undermined democracy" (p. 78). For them, decentralized school control was viewed as an asset not a liability.

Second, by the close of the formative era of high school development, the local-control camp was ascendant. The efforts of the progressives had largely "foundered on the shoals of localism" (Reese, 1995, p. 215). A pattern of decentralization was visible across the nation, and local control became the dominant form of governance, or as Tyack (1974) reports, "the whole mode of lay management was diffuse" (p. 127).

Summary

In the first of the chapters that unpack the development of secondary education in the United States, we explored the creation of three distinct forms of the high school: the Latin grammar school, the academy, and the public high school. We paid particular attention to the forces that propelled the public high school onto education's center stage. We also revealed the educational and governance ideologies that provided the blueprints for the construction of this unique institution. In the following chapters, we examine how this nascent organization, limited in scope and serving less than 10% of school-aged youth at the dawn of the 20th century, grew into a comprehensive institution providing nearly universal education to youths aged 14 to 18.

Note

1. Although it is beyond our charge to discuss this in detail, it is important to note that there was considerable opposition to the creation of tax-supported public high schools (Dorn, 1996). Not surprisingly, a good deal of animosity emanated from the supporters of academies who feared the effects public high schools would have on their privately financed schools. Additional opposition arose from citizens who, because these new high schools were likely to over-enroll the children of the well-to-do, saw the tax system being used to transfer income from the poor to the wealthy.

2

The Development of the Comprehensive High School

1890-1920

Schools do change; but they seem to change only when the gap between schools and society is extreme and at the same time the demand for formal education is growing. In 1892, the pressures that inevitably affected education clearly were great; change was inevitable.

—Sizer (1964, p. 17)

During the first two decades of the new century, high school administrators . . . were aware that a momentous, revolutionary change was in the offing and that they were engaged in a debate that would determine the course of American secondary education for decades.

—Herbst (1996, p. 117)

The blueprint for the comprehensive model of secondary education emerged from social, political, and economic developments that took place during the quarter century following the release in 1893 of the famous Committee of Ten Report.

—Wraga (1994, p. xiii)

In Chapter 1, we traced the evolution of the high school through its first three phases of development, from its birth in 1635 to the point at which it had "struck its roots deep in the American soul" (Philbrick, cited in Reese, 1995, p. 61). In the next few chapters, we examine "the fourth stage of the high school's development" (Latimer, 1958, p. 116), the emergence of the comprehensive high school, the model that would define secondary education in the United States throughout the 20th century. Here, we focus on the formation during the last decade of the 19th century and the first two decades of the 20th century of the distinguishing scaffolding of the comprehensive high school. We begin by charting some of the contextual issues that "contributed to a growing awareness that the old conception of school no longer suited the needs of the modern day" (Wraga, 1994, p. 3). We then expose the foundations of the comprehensive high school that were laid during the seminal period between 1890 and 1920. To accomplish that task, we describe the aims of secondary education, theories of learning, and conceptions of curriculum that were welded together to form the infrastructure of the comprehensive high school—an infrastructure that shaped almost every aspect of secondary education for nearly a century.

The Context

The sweeping economic and social changes set in motion by scientific and industrial advance[s] necessitate[d] a complete transformation of the school.
—Cremin (1961, p. 218)

The mass public secondary school as we know it has its roots in the transformation of the economy and society that took place after the civil war.
—Trow (1961, p. 145)

It was this emphasis on education to serve economic and social needs that shaped the development of the modern high school.
—Spring (1990, p. 197)

In our discussion of the formation of the public high school, especially its ascendancy as the prevailing form of secondary education after 1870, we explored the contextual forces that fueled "the ideal of universal secondary education—the grand experiment of the [20th] century" (Anderson & Gruhn, 1962, p. 83). Our intention here is simply to reinforce that analysis and to establish the fact that these fundamental political, social, and economic changes provided much of the impetus for the construction of the comprehensive high school—as well as many of the elements of the emerging blueprint.

On the political front, the change with the most impact on education was the use of progressivism and the development of the liberal democratic state (Murphy, 1996, 1999). Rooted in discontent with political corruption and an expanded recognition of government as too limited for the new industrial era, the political landscape was noticeably recontoured in the late 19th and early 20th centuries. Direct citizen control and machine politics gave way to bureaucratized institutions led by a cadre of educational experts.

The social tapestry was also being rewoven during the period from 1890 to 1920. The central dynamic was "the transformation of American society from one characterized by relatively isolated self-contained communities into an urban, industrial nation" (Kliebard, 1995, p. 2). "Industrialization, demographic shifts, and urbanism were altering country life" (Tyack, 1974, p. 22). Most important from our perspective here is the fact that these "marked changes in social conditions [resulted in] marked changes in schools" (Willing, 1942, p. 41). As Cremin (1961), Kliebard (1995), Tyack (1974), and Wraga (1994) have all demonstrated, "With the recognition of social change came a radically altered vision of the role of schooling" (Kliebard, 1995, p. 1).

Turning to the economy, we see a confirmation of the story we chronicled in Chapter 1, the emergence of "new economic realities brought on by the industrial revolution" (Wraga, 1994, p. 2). At the core of the matter was the transformation from an agricultural to an industrial economy, or perhaps more accurately, given the social changes outlined above, to an industrial society (Cremin, 1955). The nation was witnessing the "advent of machine production and its accompanying specialization of occupation" (Koos, 1927, p. 310). Stated in language that eerily would be reintroduced nearly a century later in reshaping the high school to the realities of a postindustrial world, it could be said that by 1890 "national concerns about international economic competition" (Spring, 1990, p. 220) and the demands of "advancing technology" (Krug, 1964, p. 209) began to influence the design of the blueprints being used to shape the foundations of the newly emerging model of secondary education. In ways that were not previously evident (Sizer, 1964), schools became "directly linked . . . to the needs of the economic system" (Spring, 1990, p. 220). "In effect, some saw the school as a critical means of transforming the preindustrial culture—values and attitudes, work habits, time orientation, even recreations—of citizens in a modernizing society" (Tyack, 1974, p. 29). And the high school became the preferred venue for this transformation process.

Development and Growth

As professional educators saw it, the great struggle of the 19th century had been the fight to establish the principle of free universal public schooling; the great struggle of the first half of the 20th century had been to make secondary schooling universal.

—Ravitch (1983, p. 15)

In the early part of the 20th century, a complex set of social, economic, and educational conditions shaped the modern high school for service to a broader range of the population.

—Spring (1990, p. 196)

Each decade between 1890 and 1920 witnessed a doubling or near doubling in the enrollment of public high school students. In 1890, there were 202,963 students; in 1900, there were 519,251; in 1910, there were 915,061; and in 1920, there were

1,857,155 (Koos, 1927, p. 2). In terms of the percentage of youths of secondary-school age (ages 14-17) in public high schools, the figures are equally impressive, with 4% enrolled in 1890, 8% in 1900, 13% in 1910, and 24% in 1920 (p. 5)—although it is important to emphasize, as Dorn (1996) has noted, that "despite growing attendance . . . high schools were [still] the realm of relatively few students" (p. 39). Graduation rates were also on the rise. Using number graduated per 1,000 persons 17 years of age, Taylor, McMahill, and Taylor (1960) document the following pattern: 3.5% in 1890, 6.4% in 1900, 8.8% in 1910, and 16.8% in 1920 (p. 89). Between 1900 and 1920, a youngster's chance of graduating from high school increased from 16 to 45 out of 100 (Latimer, 1958, p. 74). In 1890, the average high school student attended school 86 days a year (Cuban, 1984, p. 25).

The period between 1890 and 1920 also experienced a fairly dramatic increase in the number of teachers and the number of available high schools. In 1890, there were 9,120 instructors; 20,372 in 1900; 41,667 in 1910; and 63,258 in 1920 (Koos, 1927, p. 2). Tyack (1974) reveals that from 1890 to 1918, more than one new high school was constructed every day of the year (p. 25). In 1890, there were 2,526 public high schools; by 1900, that number had increased to 6,005; in 1910, it stood at 10,213; and by 1920, 14,326 public high schools were operating throughout the nation (Odell, 1939, p. 92).

Koos (1927) also portrays the "increasing public high school dominance of the era" (p. 7). The percentage of secondary pupils in public schools increased each decade, from 68.1% in 1890 to 82.4% in 1900 to 88.6% in 1910 to 91.0 in 1920 (p. 7). Analysis of the proportion of public high schools among all secondary schools reveals a similar pattern, rising from 60.0% in 1890 to 87.3% in 1920 (p. 7).

High schools throughout this period remained relatively small, predominately rural, and universally coeducational (Koos, 1927). In 1904, for example, 30% of 7,199 public high schools had only one teacher; another 19% employed only two instructors (Krug, 1964, p. 183). In 1903, Indiana's 580 township high schools "averaged 23 pupils and one and one-half teachers per school" (p. 182). In the 1917-1918 school year,

> . . . almost a fourth of the high schools [in the United States] enrolled 25 pupils or less, and an even larger proportion enrolled from 26 to 50. This means that *more than half of all the high schools* of the country that year were serving 50 pupils or less. (Koos, 1927, p. 202)

Seventy-five percent of the high schools served 100 or fewer students (p. 203). In the same year, 85% of the high schools in the nation were rural, and 10% were classified as city. Setting a pattern that we would see throughout the 20th century, however, the city schools enrolled 50% of students attending high school (p. 207).

Although a number of factors account for the rapid expansion of public secondary education during this period, some of the most important include: (a) immigration, which "facilitated the exclusion of teenagers from work as employers could turn to adult immigrants for cheap labor" (Dorn, 1996, p. 39); (b) a mushrooming concern about the need to socialize the flood of these immigrants and the growing number of urban poor, to "counterbalance the lack of industrial skills and poor attitudes" (Rothstein, 1994, p. 98); and (c) a newly forming recognition of the connections between education and economic well-being.

Learning Infrastructure

> *By the turn of the century a revolution was already at hand.*
> —Cremin (1961, p. 91)

> *The most fundamental question that industrialization posed for American education: Was there a change for the American common school to survive into the 20th century and extend its reach into the high school years, or would industrialization with its attendant specialization create new, and deepen existing, social divisions in the body politic?*
> —Herbst (1996, p. 116)

The period between 1890 and 1920 began with the publication of one of what were perhaps the two most important reports on secondary education ever produced in the United States and ended with the publication of the other—the 1893 *Report of the Committee on Secondary School Studies,* commonly referred to as the *Report of the Committee of Ten,* and the 1918 report from the National Education Association titled *Cardinal Principles of Secondary Education.* It was the time when the learning and teaching foundations that have defined the comprehensive high school for nearly a century were poured. It was here that the educational response to the new industrial world that would define the 20th century was forged. More specifically, it was during this era that the ideology that would define the comprehensive high school was developed and implanted in secondary education. Nowhere are these ideological pillars more important and more visible than in the core dimensions of the educational industry, in the formation of educational aims, and in the drafting of pedagogical blueprints.

Purpose

As the public high school began its rapid growth in American communities, the inevitable questions of its function and design came very much into prominence. Increasingly and for ill-defined reasons, Americans began to see education beyond the rudiments as something desirable. As the high school thus became more important to a more representative group of citizens, its purpose needed clarification. (Sizer, 1964, p. 1)

Discussions among educators and laypeople alike revealed conflicts of purpose and confusions of aim. One could quickly enough gain agreement that the goal of the high school was "preparation for life"; but, like agreements on *motherhood* and *sin,* what this meant in practice was not entirely clear. (Cremin, 1955, p. 296)

For most Americans, the battle over the high school was not one of the classics versus the modern sciences but one of academic culture versus practical training—the well-known confrontation between those who wanted to prepare for college and those who wanted to prepare for life. (Herbst, 1996, p. 115)

As noted in Chapter 1, although the public high school started out, as did its predecessor the academy, as a "practical, non-college preparatory institution" (Odell, 1939, p. 86), by the end of the 19th century, it was dominated by college interests. Preparation for college largely determined what was taught. Agreement on the central aim of public secondary education was short-lived, however. By 1920, the purpose of secondary schooling would be radically redefined.

In their famous 1893 report, the Committee of Ten attempted to resolve the question of purpose by "merging the high school's two functions into one" (Herbst, 1996, p. 109). The perspective of the Committee was that there was no difference in these two aims and that preparation for life should lead naturally to preparation for college.

There was to be no difference between them. Life and college were both best prepared for by a mental discipline developed through the study of the academic subjects. What the colleges required and what life demanded were not, in the Committee's view, different or contradictory. (Sizer, 1964, p. 132)

As Cremin (1955) and others have highlighted, it was the Committee's belief in the primacy of "improving intellectual ability by disciplining the mind" (p. 297) that allowed them to arrive at this resolution: "The best preparation for life was to strengthen the intellect. . . . The discipline-centered college preparatory curriculum was viewed as the program best suited for all youth" (Wraga, 1994, p. 2). "Practical knowledge would follow later, on the job in 'life' " (Sizer, 1964, p. 143).

Although most graduates of secondary school were not destined for college, the secondary school was to remain, as it had been for centuries, a downward extension of the college. In the words of the day, it was to be truly the university of the people. (Cremin, 1955, p. 297)

Analysts have concluded that "the report of the Committee reflected the crossroad between an educational system designed to provide everyone with a common education and an educational system organized to provide everyone with a specific education based on a future social destination" (Spring, 1990, p. 200). The signals provided by the Committee—that "the purpose of secondary schools was to train minds" (Sizer, 1964, p. 197) and that "mental discipline was the chief criterion of the curriculum" (Willing, 1942, p. 60)—pointed the high school in a direction that urban, industrialized America of the 20th century was unwilling to follow. "The Committee had in fact written an epitaph instead of a blueprint for the future" (Herbst, 1996, p. 108). "The Committee did not see the vast scope of the issues facing American secondary schools and thus did not prescribe for them in any way. As a result, the suggestions in the *Report* became obsolete within two decades" (Sizer, 1964, p. 170).

Those who believed that the aim of education was mental training and intellectual development were not able to hold the high ground. Between 1890 and 1920, a new agenda, "education for social control" (Krug, 1964, p. 250), buttressed by a new science of learning known as social efficiency, gradually came to dominate secondary education. This newly forming purpose rested on a rejection of what critics labeled "a medieval concept of high schools" (Spring, 1990, p. 203)—"the idea that fitting for college was the same as fitting for life" (Sizer, 1964, p. 196). According to many analysts of secondary education during the early years of the 20th century, "Intellectual development, the great purpose of schooling according to the mental disciplinarians, was of course vital, but it had to be reconciled with the school as a social institution and its place in the larger social order" (Kliebard, 1995, p. 54).

Subject to the pull of the contextual conditions described earlier, a focus on individualism, the "goal of individual development of intellectual powers" (Kliebard, 1995, p. 54) and the goal of "individual success" (p. 80), began to give way to the social purposes of schooling. Although some viewed the social function of schooling in terms of social reform (Cremin, 1961), the dominant leitmotif was that of "schools as an instrument of social control" (Kliebard, 1995, p. 81). Social efficiency, in turn, became the "predominant school of thought in influencing the development of the high school" (Spring, 1990, p. 201) or, as the great historian of the American high school Edward Krug (1972) concluded, the comprehensive high school became "the cathedral of social efficiency" (p. 150).

> Of the varied and sometimes frenetic responses to industrialism and to the consequent transformation of American social institutions, there was one response that emerged as clearly dominant, both as a social ideal and as an educational doctrine. It was social efficiency that, for most people, held out the promise of social stability in the face of cries for massive social change, and that doctrine claimed the now potent backing of science to ensure it. (Kliebard, 1995, p. 77)

Education for social control included the introduction of new ideas, such as specialization, and a reformulation of older ones, such as equality of opportunity (Spring, 1990). It represented a rejection of the prevailing position on the academic function of the high school and provided an affirmation of the practical aims of schooling (Powell, Farrar, & Cohen, 1985; Spears, 1941). It acknowledged the role of the high school in addressing new socially anchored responsibilities. In language that sounds a good deal like the reformist ideology at the end of the 20th century, analysts argued that "educational functions traditionally carried on by family, neighborhood, or shop are no longer being performed; somehow they must get done; like it or not, the school must take them on" (Cremin, 1961, p. 117). Social efficiency meant fundamentally that the function of high schools would be to prepare students for the new industrial world that was redefining American society—for what Spears (1941) called "the great and real business of living" (p. 56). Advocates of the new goal of social control "wanted education to produce individuals who were trained for a specific role in society and who were willing to work cooperatively in that role" (Spring, 1990, p. 201). "High schools would fit the young for their niches in that structure" (Powell et al., 1985, p. 247).

Theories of Learning

> Two men, William James and Edward L. Thorndike, tried not one but many experiments to test the theory of formal discipline. The evidence uncovered disproved this theory on which much of the work of the elementary and the secondary school had been based prior to the 20th century. (Taylor et al., 1960, p. 82)

Two significant elements combined to form the learning foundations that were laid during the construction of the comprehensive high school. The first was the undermining of the pillars supporting faculty psychology and the rejection of the accompanying theory of mental discipline (Ravitch, 1983). Early critiques by scholars, such as Small and Hinsdale (Kliebard, 1995; Sizer, 1964), were supplemented by experimental studies that seriously weakened the concept of transfer that was at the heart of the doctrine of formal discipline and that "cast doubt on even the existence of such mental operations as memory, perception, reasoning, and observation" (Kliebard, 1995, p. 92). Under the scrutiny of this newly emerging science of learning, "the whole value of general education was cast into doubt" (p. 92) and with it, as we shall see below, the rationale for what was to be taught. Linked with the "changing social order that brought with it a different conception of what knowledge is most worth" (p. 6), these studies were instrumental in "the collapse of mental discipline" (p. 6).

A second significant development was the formation of a new "science of pedagogy" (Cremin, 1961, p. 186)—"the rise of experimental psychology" in the place of faculty psychology (Kliebard, 1995, p. 34)—and the formulation of "a new theory of learning and a new 'law' founded on that theory" in the place of the theory of formal discipline (Cremin, 1961, p. 111). The heart of the new approach was "cast[ing] aside older notions of faculty psychology in favor of an essentially behaviorist outlook" (Cremin, 1961, p. 109).

Thorndike's theory maintained that learning involves the wedding of a specific response to a specific stimulus through a physiological bond in the neural system, so that the stimulus regularly calls forth the response. In Thorndike's words, the *bond* between S and R is "stamped in" by being continually rewarded. And from this follows what Thorndike called the "law of effect"—namely, that a satisfactory outcome of any response tends to "stamp in" its connection with a given situation, and conversely, that an unsatisfactory outcome tends to stamp out the bond or connection. Whereas previous theories had emphasized practice, or repetition, Thorndike gave equal weight to outcomes—to success or failure, reward or punishment, satisfaction or annoyance to the learner. (Cremin, 1961, p. 19)

Equally important, his work illustrated a "new theory of the mind" (Kliebard, 1995, p. 111):

In place of a concept of mind comprising a limited number of discrete faculties, Thorndike and other psychologists in the early 20th century sought to construct something more consistent with their experimental evidence. The mind that Thorndike envisioned was a machine in which there were thousands—millions—of individual connections each one bearing a message having little in common with the next. The mind in his view consisted not of large capacities such as memory and reasoning waiting there to be developed, but of "multitudinous separate individual functions" (Thorndike & Woodworth, 1901, p. 249), a kind of switchboard with innumerable wires (bonds) connecting discrete points. (p. 92)

Combined with emerging work in the area of child development, ideas from experimental psychology helped produce a new understanding of pedagogy. Together, they "shattered time-honored assumptions about the disciplinary value of certain subjects and thereby accelerated utilitarian tendencies already gaining in the schools" (Cremin, 1961, p. 113). At the same time, they helped ensure that "the needs and purposes of the individual student were endorsed as a proper approach to instruction" (Spears, 1941, p. 214); that is, they helped "shift the educational center of gravity back to the child" (Cremin, 1961, p. 118). Finally, they nourished, both directly and indirectly, the belief that children's ability to succeed in school differed radically. All of these changes combined to pull the curriculum of the comprehensive high school into a new orbit.

Curriculum

By the 1890s, the forces that were to struggle for control of the American curriculum were in place, and the early part of the 20th century became the battleground for that struggle. (Kliebard, 1995, p. 1)

High schools would serve democracy by offering usable studies to everyone rather than dwelling on academic abstractions that would interest only a few. (Powell et al., 1985, p. 260)

Framing the Question

With the possible exception of the topic of expanding student enrollment, the formation of the comprehensive high school, or what Dewey called "the 'reorganization' of the academic high school into 'the wider-high school' " (Wraga, 1994, p. 12), is best understood through an examination of curriculum development. The most salient question in 1890 was "whether the curriculum that had been so ardently defended in the Yale Report [of 1828] and had remained essentially intact ever since could continue to serve a new population of students and, for all intents and purposes, a new society" (Kliebard, 1995, p. 8). If "function determines curriculum" (Anderson & Gruhn, 1962, p. 85), and if society was being transformed and the purpose of secondary education was being recast, what were the implications for the high school curriculum?

What history teaches us is that the answers to this question were heavily debated at the dawn of the 20th century. We also know that the dispute crystallized core issues that would shape our understanding of curriculum. Finally, we know that although not formed for all times, specific conceptions of these core issues were forged and were then welded together to form the curriculum framework for the comprehensive high school—a model that would define secondary schooling in the United States for the next century.[1]

On one front, the debate about the nature of curriculum took place around the issue of purpose discussed above, specifically around the great dualism of whether high school should prepare youngsters for life or educate them for college. A second element of the struggle to shape the curriculum "on which positions both intersected and ran parallel to the college-preparatory controversy was whether training or information was the proper object of schooling" (Krug, 1964, p. 203). As the public high school moved from its formative era, information studies, which focused on knowledge accumulation and understanding of the subject at hand, were still being "written off as inferior vehicles of education . . . [Mental] training remained the standard by which the worth of studies was judged" (p. 204).

Where to seed the curriculum represented a third element of the quest to define what was to be taught in the newly forming comprehensive high school. Should the core technology be defined by "academic conceptions of subject matter" (Powell et al., 1985, p. 242), as was the case as the 19th century drew to a close, or should it be seeded in newer ground? The two emerging alternatives were the abilities, needs, and interests of the learner, that is, the idea that "the key to the curriculum lay in child study" (Kliebard, 1995, p. 35), and the needs of the larger society, that is, the idea that the key to the curriculum lay in "community interests" (Herbst, 1996, p. 115).

A fourth facet of the debate centered on the topic of sameness versus variation in the curriculum—should all students be exposed to the same material or should they be provided with distinct learning experiences? As we revealed in Chapter 1, given the prevailing logic on the purpose of the high school, the theories of learning in play at the time, and the general domination of the high school by pro-college forces, at the dawn of the 20th century, the standard was similar curriculum for all students. A fifth sphere of the curriculum puzzle, perhaps best thought of as a subarea of the topic of curricular differentiation, was the matter of elective versus required courses (Krug, 1964). If students were to experience diverse curriculum opportunities, would they be free to select these offerings and, if so, on what basis—by course of study or by individual subject. The resolution of these five issues would help define educational quality and educational equity in American high schools for all of the 20th century.

Response From the Committee of Ten

The first systemic resolution to these issues was provided by the Committee of Ten, although, as noted earlier, the framework of answers they cobbled together provided a model of the past rather than a blueprint for the future (Herbst, 1996). On the first three issues in particular, they threw down clearly on the side of tradition. Because education for life should be the same as education for college, the Committee maintained, everyone who graduated from high school should be able to pursue a college degree (Sizer, 1964). The "humanist ideal of a liberal education for all" (Kliebard, 1995, p. 14) held. That is, although the Committee "recognized varying purposes of students going through the secondary school, [they] saw no distinction in subject needs between college-bound and noncollege-bound students" (Spears, 1941, p. 212). More specifically, this meant that "there should be no difference made in the teaching of any subject on the grounds of whether or not a pupil was going to college" (Krug, 1964, p. 65). In like fashion, the Committee showed little "enthusiasm for information or content. The purpose of subjects was to develop power, particularly in observation, expression, and reasoning" (p. 63). Finally, and consistent with their belief in a liberal education for everyone, the Committee proposed a curriculum constructed on academic subjects.

Where the Committee did begin to break with tradition was on the topics of curricular differentiation and electives. On the issue of diverse offerings, they suggested the creation of four courses of study—classical, Latin-scientific, modern language, and English. Each course of study required

> Study in five subject-matter fields: English, mathematics, foreign languages, history and government, and science. The four courses of study differed from each other mainly in two ways: in the foreign language designated (ancient or modern), and in the number of periods per week devoted to various subjects. (Latimer, 1958, p. 117)

> Because of the students' continuation in school and because sound educational planning suggested it, the Committee believed that choice of a particular curriculum should not be made until after the first, or better still, after

the second year in high school. Accordingly, most of the subjects for the first two years were the same in all four curricula. (Latimer, 1958, p. 66)

All subjects, as expected given our discussion above, were academically grounded. To adhere to the belief in a lack of distinction between preparation for life and education for college, all subjects taught were to be of equal status for entrance to college (Krug, 1964). On the matter of electives, the Committee proposed a system linking choice to courses of study, although once a choice was made, little additional freedom was offered. Elective subjects were not an option.

Answers Framed for the Comprehensive High School

Under an onslaught of criticism—for their infatuation with the conservative ways of a former time, their adherence to the prescientific doctrines of faculty psychology and mental discipline, and their unwillingness to bring the high school into line with the changing nature of American society and a rapidly changing student population—the resolution to the curriculum debate proposed by the Committee of Ten was unable to hold the high ground. Indeed, the quarter century after the release of the report was marked by "a vigorous drive to replace what was commonly regarded as a curriculum unsuited for the new industrial age and for the new population of students entering . . . secondary school in larger numbers" (Kliebard, 1995, p. 156). The curriculum blueprint for the comprehensive high school would be developed from quite different designs from those sketched out by the Committee of Ten.

One change was that academics would be illuminated much less brightly in the comprehensive high school than they had been before the turn of the century (Ravitch, 1983). As the belief "that the high school was too academic, too exclusive, [and] too tied to the preparation of the college bound" (Reese, 1995, p. 260) became ingrained in the American culture, the curricular spotlight was redirected elsewhere (Latimer, 1958). At its worst, this refocusing signified a "denigration of intellect" (Kliebard, 1995, p. 43). At the middle point of the continuum, it was simply a reaction to the ideology of academic intelligence that had occupied court for so long in education. At its best, the change recognized a legitimate critique of "curriculum removed from any prospect of reward in occupational terms" (p. 87) and honored a call for "subject matter . . . to be functional in the practical affairs of life" (Krug, 1964, p. xiv).

As the academic scaffolding supporting the high school of the 19th century was dismantled, a new infrastructure rose up to take its place—one constructed more from the raw materials of personal and practical experiences than from the frameworks of the academic disciplines: "Practical education was needed most" (Powell et al., 1985, p. 264), and the "potential for a practical and especially an occupational payoff" (Kliebard, 1995, p. 114) took on added significance.[2] In addition, academic subjects would now have to "prove their right to existence in the school program" (Krug, 1964, p. xiv). Schooling for life was no longer education for college but rather "preparation for earning a living" (Kliebard, 1995, p. 86). When social control as the foundation for schooling, and social efficiency as the theory of learning, became dominant threads in the tapestry known as secondary education, a diminished—and continually decreasing—role for academics would also be woven into the fabric. These trends would, unfortunately, dictate defining themes of the comprehensive high school (Angus & Mirel, 1995; Latimer, 1958; Powell et al., 1985).

We have now depicted fundamental alterations in three of the five dimensions of the framework we outlined earlier: (a) a shift "in the school's distinctive and central function [from the] development of the intellect" (Kliebard, 1995, p. 40) toward earning a living; (b) a revision in the objective of the curriculum, from training of the mind to gathering information; and (c) a recentering of the curriculum, with the academic disciplines being overshadowed by an amalgam of student and societal needs and interests.

The pieces that would complete the pedagogical core[3] of the comprehensive high school focus on the organization of the curriculum and on student access to subject matter. In the comprehensive high school, students would no longer be educated alike, with similar, or at least equivalent, curricular experiences. Instead, a number of new ideas would emerge to help reground the curriculum and to shape the variety of learning experiences available to students. One of these perspectives, "the nature and needs of the adolescent" (Krug, 1964, p. 120)—or what has been described nicely by Spears (1941) as "a campaign for the recognition of the individual pupil" (p. 211)— grew directly from the incipient body of knowledge being codified by child development psychologists (Tyack, 1974). Indeed, although not quite pushed into ascendancy, based on the belief "that the natural order of development in the child was the most significant and scientifically defensible basis for determining what should be taught" (Kliebard, 1995, p. 11), "the idea of adolescence as the determiner of the secondary school curriculum was vigorously advanced" (Krug, 1964, p. 117) during this era. This viewpoint maintained "that children, not books and teachers, ought to be the schools' starting place" (Powell et al., 1985, p. 261) and "that the child's own natural impulses could be used as a way of addressing the question of what to teach" (Kliebard, 1995, p. 37). This doctrine "called for [curricular] adjustments in accordance with individual capacities and interests" (Spears, 1941, p. 213). It also argued for greater diversity in curricular offerings.

A second perspective, social efficiency, would hold even greater influence over the organization of the curriculum during the formation of the comprehensive high school. The vision of the social efficiency group "included a sense that the new technological society needed a far greater specialization of skills, and therefore, a far greater differentiation in the curriculum than had heretofore prevailed" (Kliebard, 1995, p. 24) and "a much wider sphere of studies" (Cremin, 1961, p. 125). Thus like their colleagues who saw adolescent needs as the appropriate ground for curriculum development, social efficiency advocates clamored for greater variety in the learning menu. Unlike their colleagues, however, they saw the landmarks on the new curricular frontier defined not by individual interests and the "individual development of students" (Tyack, 1974, p. 196) but by societal needs and "aggregate goals" (p. 196). Students were viewed not as individuals but as members of groups. Subject matter would be "organized in differentiated programs of study designed for pupils categorized in [these] groups" (Krug, 1964, p. xiv)—or for "different classes of pupils" (Tyack, 1974, p. 191). As Kliebard (1995) documents, "Predicting future destination as the basis for adapting the curriculum to different segments of the school population became a major feature of curriculum planning" (p. 13) during the period from 1890-1920. What was called for was "an educational regime that would fit students into their 'proper' social roles" (Wraga, 1994, p. 10) and a "curriculum tied to the destined roles that future citizens were to perform" (Kliebard, 1995, p. 93), through which roles translated directly into careers (Tyack, 1974).

Thus the ideas of differentiated curriculum and the function of "differentiation [to] prepare the student for a particular place in society" (Spring, 1990, p. 220)—homogeneous clustering and tracking—became central beams in the construction of the comprehensive high school. Unfortunately, so also did a strong strand of economic determinism. Under the mantle of the *scientific theories* of learning, the curriculum was allocated or students were matched to the curriculum on the basis of questionable scientific claims that reinforced class distinctions (Tyack, 1974). Immigrants, youngsters from lower socioeconomic homes, and *finishing students* (those completing their education during or at the end of the high school years) were banded together into curricular tracks offering quite distinct educational opportunities. As Spring (1990) has observed, with the advent of the comprehensive high school, "the race for social position was no longer to be a function of the marketplace but of the selection process in the school instead" (p. 221).

All three of these aspects of the curriculum—differentiation, differentiation linked to one's place in society, and differentiation defined by class distinctions—would become welded together in ways that would determine the educational experiences of youngsters in the United States for nearly all of the 20th century. Collectively—whether based on individual capacities and needs or on social efficiency—they helped establish the reality that there would be easier curricular programs "for the children of workers and merchants [based] on the grounds that their minds couldn't manage intellectual work or that their careers would not require it" (Powell et al., 1985, p. 243).

Although proponents for election by subjects (e.g., a core of six or seven units and rather open freedom about other subjects to complete) were heard from in the early part of the 20th century, consistent with the storyline developed above, the *elective principle* (Krug, 1964, p. 190) came to mean primarily the choice of a course of study. Or as Krug (1964) relates the development, "In the 1890s and early 1900s . . . there was beginning to develop an idea of election by courses more closely related to the occupational futures of the finishing pupils" (p. 200).

In closing our discussion of curriculum, we note that the period between 1890 and 1920 also witnessed what Krug (1964) described as a "drive toward standardization" (p. 162). In particular, efforts were undertaken to more clearly distinguish the boundaries of high schools from those of the elementary schools and the colleges. A key dimension of this later effort was to get "secondary school administrators to accept the notion of uniform college entrance requirements that could serve as yardsticks for academic standards across the nation" (Herbst, 1996, p. 114). It was during this period that a common curricular measure, the Carnegie Unit, was established as "a course five periods weekly throughout the academic year" (Krug, 1964, p. 161) and that a standard for a high school program was fixed as fourteen Carnegie units.

Instruction

Harnessed to an infant science of educational psychology and reinforced by the scientific knowledge of the day about learning, teacher-centered instruction [became] deeply [anchored] in the minds of teachers and administrators at the turn of the century. (Cuban, 1984, p. 31)

In the instructional realm, conditions in the early part of the 20th century were not much different from those we described in Chapter 1. The overall level of instructional quality left a good deal to be desired. Indeed, one major reviewer of the era, Joseph Rice, concluded that "it was the quality of teaching that seemed to be most responsible for the catastrophic state of American education" (Kliebard, 1995, p. 19). Although they received more training than their elementary school counterparts (Cuban, 1984), high school teachers were still often ill prepared for the task that confronted them (Sizer, 1964).

An assortment of other factors combined to dilute instructional quality in American high school classrooms during this era. To begin with, because high schools were often quite small, teachers were required to teach a multitude of subjects (Cuban, 1984; Sizer, 1964). Because teaching was largely a woman's job and "women often tended to view teaching as a stopgap before marriage rather than as a career, the large turnover that resulted led inevitably to lower standards" (Sizer, 1964, p. 44). In addition, many high school teachers were drawn from the lower grades, and many of them failed to adapt their instruction to the needs of adolescents. The political nature of hiring (and firing) in locally controlled schools also tended to dampen quality. Poor pay simply exacerbated the portfolio of problems already outlined.

Throughout the era, instruction tended to be teacher centered and, as was the case throughout much of the 19th century, textbooks dominated (Cuban, 1984). Both of these dimensions of pedagogy would be tightly woven into the still forming tapestry known as the comprehensive high school.

Organizational Scaffolding

The writings of schoolmen at the turn of the century bristled with apprehension and hope. They knew what was wrong: . . . when they talked about solutions, characteristically, they saw them in the form of better organization.
—Tyack (1974, p. 96)

The revolutionary changes underway in schooling from 1890 to 1920 were not confined to classrooms. The methods used to govern education and the designs employed to structure schools were also undergoing significant alterations, which were, again, in directions heavily shaped by powerful political, social, and economic currents. The defining element of the organizational revolution was the shift from lay control, which dominated the governance landscape before 1890, to a "corporate bureaucratic model" of governance (Tyack, 1974, p. 6). As was the case in the construction of the learning infrastructure, the new scientific models of school organization and governance provided some of the defining components of the comprehensive high school.

The organizational transformation that marked the evolution of the high school within the industrial world was laced with two central ideologies, a "corporate form of external school governance and internal control by experts" (Tyack, 1974, p. 146). Both elements drew freely from models supporting the development of the postagricultural business sector (Callahan, 1962; Newlon, 1934). The external dimension focused on the transfer of power and control from lay citizens to elite decision makers (Tyack, 1974). "Working under the banner of the depoliticalization of schooling and eliminating political corruption, reformers sought to remove the control of schools as far as possible from the people" (Tyack, 1974, p. 167), to eliminate community control. As was the case with the development of the differentiated curriculum, the struggle to separate education from politics was powered in part by both antidemocratic ideology and class prejudice. In terms of influence, we know that this movement accomplished much of its goal, "for it destroyed the decentralized power which had sustained a grass roots lay influence in the schools" (p. 3), dramatically reducing the size of governing boards and radically changing their composition, from membership that reflected the occupations of the community to elite representatives of the business world and of professional organizations. By 1920, throughout the nation, a closed system of governance had replaced much of the more open system that had prevailed at the end of the 19th century.

Shifts in the basic governance equation during the early decades of the 20th century were accompanied by a reconfiguration in the way schools were managed and structured (Callahan, 1962). One distinctive development was the appearance of a class of administrative experts to whom governance elites delegated control for the management of schools (Tyack, 1974). Borrowing from the new models of organization and management being forged in the corporate sector, reformers began to draw a "strict parallel" (p. 143) between the leadership of business enterprises and the management of schools (Callahan, 1962; Tyack, 1974). They argued that "to change schools, . . . one first needed to concentrate power at the top so experts could take over" (p. 3).

In order to facilitate the use of this centralized power and to maximize its potential to effect change, reformers drew up blueprints for a new structure for their institution (bureaucracy) and cobbled together a new philosophy of leadership (scientific management)—again borrowing freely from materials originally crafted in the corporate sector (Callahan, 1962; Newlon, 1934). In so doing, they brought forth the array of operating principles that would form the organizational backbone for the comprehensive high school for most of the 20th century, principles that collectively represent a distinct break with the model of organization in play before 1890: authority vested in office, differentiation and specialization of roles, professionalism, separation of management from labor, chain of command, and so forth.

Summary

In this chapter, we examined the formative period in the development of that uniquely American institution known as the comprehensive high school. We explored the larger political, social, and economic forces that produced the transformation of the 19th century secondary school. We also chronicled the development and growth of the public high school during this era, attending primarily to expansion in terms of students served.

The bulk of the chapter was devoted to an analysis of the learning infrastructure that gave shape to much of what was to emerge as the comprehensive high school. We charted how powerful ideologies that had guided the formation of the public high school in the 19th century fell from favor and were supplanted by the powerful forces of social control and social efficiency. We closed by examining important curricular design principles that were drafted during this era and that came in many ways to define what we would come to call the comprehensive high school.

Notes

1. It is important to underscore the point, as Krug (1964) carefully documents, that although the overall pattern of change was transformational in nature, revisions did not occur overnight. It took much of the 30-year period for particular perspectives to gain ascendancy and then to be melded together to form the framework of the comprehensive high school.

2. Although the issue is beyond our ability to tackle in this brief review, "the vocational education movement during the first 15 years of the 20th century was a crucial development" (Wraga, 1994, p. 6) in shaping the model of the comprehensive high school.

3. Other parts of the infrastructure that we do not examine here include the rise of extracurricular programs and the struggle to maintain all aspects of the high school in one place rather than developing specialized secondary schools. On the first issue, Powell et al. (1985) note that boys' sports defined the first wave of extracurricular activities between 1890 and 1910. The authors go on to reveal that "between 1910 and 1930, public high schools welcomed a veritable avalanche of nonacademic activities" (p. 257). As we show later, the introduction of extracurricular activities was to have a deleterious influence on academic influence in the comprehensive high school.

3

Institutionalization of the Comprehensive High School

1920-1980

The creation of a mass terminal system, with functions and orientations quite different from that of the traditional college preparatory system it succeeded, forced not merely certain changes in the curriculum but a drastic shift in the basic assumptions underlying secondary education.

—Trow (1961, p. 149)

The heart of this revolution was a shift in the conception of the school, of what could be and should be its primary goals and responsibilities.

—Cremin (1955, p. 296)

In the stew that became the American curriculum in the 20th century, social efficiency emerged as the principle ingredient.

—Kliebard (1995, p. 189)

In Chapter 2, we uncovered the foundations of the modern high school. In the last chapter of this part of the book, we undertake two additional assignments. First, we expose the pillars built on these foundations that gave added shape to the comprehensive high school. Second, we explore emerging educational thinking about the role of secondary education in a postindustrial world, building, in the process, the foundations for high school education in the 21st century. To accomplish the first task in a reasonable amount of space, we focus the analysis on the dimension of development, building the superstructure, most directly linked to the material in later parts of this volume—what we labeled in earlier chapters as *the learning infrastructure*.

Building the Superstructure: 1920-1980

*After early arguments, a remarkably broad consensus was quickly forged
about what the purposes of a mass system would be, about how schools should
be organized, and about what sorts of work students and teachers should do.*
                    —Powell, Farrar, and Cohen (1985, p. 234)

*Once drawn . . . the blueprints for the comprehensive model awaited
implementation.*
                              —Wraga (1994, p. 29)

*From an institution conceived for the few, the high school became an insti-
tution conceived for all. From an adjunct to the college, the high school
became the pivotal point in the public school system, one which carried
forward objectives yet unfinished by the elementary school and opened new
vistas leading on to the college. And from an institution restrictively concerned with the intellectual, the high school became an agency with no less a
goal than the progressive amelioration of every individual and social need.
Such was the grand design of this Commission [on the Reorganization of
Secondary Education]. It was one, which, in weaving a multitude of new
and pressing demands into an integral view of the school, was able to face
squarely toward the future and thereby to usher in a whole new age in
American secondary education.*
                              —Cremin (1955, p. 307)

Before turning to the core technology, a few notes on the connection between the
external environment and secondary education are in order. First, throughout the
20th century the world around education continued to strongly influence the aims
and designs of the comprehensive high school (James & Tyack, 1983). Nearly every
outline for educational reform is anchored on an assessment of the need to change
schools because of "the demands placed on them by a democratic polity in an industrial society" (Herbst, 1996, p. 206). For example, here is Krug's (1964) analysis of
the connection between context and the major high school reform document of the
century, the *Cardinal Principles:*

> Still another point of view is that the report described the kind of reorganiza-
> tion of secondary education demanded by over-all social and economic
> change, presumably either ignored by the Committee of Ten or taking place
> after its time. Among the changes mentioned have been the new immigra-
> tion, the expansion of industry, the population shift from rural to urban
> areas, and the decline of apprenticeship. (p. 404)

> "These changes in American life," said the report, "call for extensive
> modifications in secondary education." (p. 380)

Second, although the line of influence generally flows more powerfully from context to school, it is still a recursive relationship. There is a good deal of literature during the history of the comprehensive high school about education's role in helping shape rather than simply adapting to these environmental forces (Cremin, 1961; Kliebard, 1995). Third, even though context shifted throughout the 1900s, nearly all the calls for educational change reflect the dominant patterns described in Chapters 1 and 2, that is, the development of a modern industrial nation and the creation of a democratic welfare state. Most of the contextual analyses within this period are variations on these themes.

Growth and Development

The central concept around which the structure centered seemed to be the obligation of the school to take, retain, and instruct all possible adolescents. (Cusick, 1983, p. 105)

Progressive concepts proved to be particularly appropriate in easing the transition to mass secondary education. At the opening of the century, about half a million students (about 10% of the age-group) attended high schools, where the curriculum was strongly academic, though only a minority graduated or went on to college; by midcentury, high school enrollment was over five million (65% of the age-group), and the secondary curriculum was remarkably diverse. (Ravitch, 1983, p. 45)

In terms of its development, the comprehensive high school continued for much of the century on the trajectory pictured in Chapter 2, with "the 1920s [being the decade] that the high school truly became an institution serving the masses" (Spring, 1990, p. 197) and the 1930s being the time when the "high school began to serve the majority of youth" (p. 198). Enrollments by decade are as follows: 1890—203,000; 1900—519,000; 1910—915,000; 1920—2,200,000; 1930—4,399,000; 1940—6,601,000; 1950—5,725,000; 1960—8,485,000; 1970—13,336,000; 1980—13,327,000; and 1990—11,336,000 (Alexander, Saylor, & Williams, 1971, p. 84; Sonnenberg, 1993, pp. 36-37). In 1910, 14.5% of the youth aged 14-17 were in high school (public and private), in 1920, the percentage was 31.2, in 1930, the percentage was 51.1, in 1940, it was 71.3, in 1950, it was 74.5, by 1960, it had climbed to 86.9, and by 1970, to 92.2, at which time it leveled off (Sonnenberg, 1993, pp. 36-37).

In Chapter 1, we noted that for each 1,000 students who entered the first grade, 100 graduated from elementary school, 10 enrolled in high school, and 1 graduated from the 12th grade. In 1917-1918 the numbers had jumped dramatically: For 1,000 in the first grade, 634 graduated from elementary school, 342 enrolled in high school, and 139 graduated from 12th grade (Koos, 1927, p. 115). By 1929-1930, those numbers increased again: For 1,000 in the fifth grade, 825 graduated from elementary school, 760 enrolled in high school, and 403 graduated from 12th grade (Spears, 1941, p. 376). Embedded in the analysis is a steady increase in graduation rates, from 16.8% of youngsters aged 17 in 1920, to 29.0% in 1930, to 41.3% in 1935, to 50.8% in 1940, to 59.0% in 1950, to 69.5% in 1960, to 76.9% in 1970—the high point of the last two decades (Sonnenberg, 1993, p. 55).

Not surprisingly, given the numbers presented above, before being overwhelmed by the consolidation movement, the nation experienced a fairly dramatic increase in the number of high school facilities. In 1920, there were 14,326 public high schools; by 1930, there were 22,237 (Odell, 1939; Krug, 1972). The number of schools peaked in the 1967-1968 school year at 27,011 and has since fallen back to 1930s levels—22,639 in 1990 (Sonnenberg, 1993, p. 56)—still far short of the reduction to 9,000 called for in *The American High School Today* report of 1959 (Conant, 1959).

High schools remained relatively small throughout much of the nation well into the middle part of the century. In the last chapter, we reported that in the 1917-1918 school year, more than half of all high schools enrolled 50 or fewer students and only 12% had more than 200 pupils. Twenty years later, although only 18% of the public high schools enrolled fewer than 50 students, two thirds of them continued to serve fewer than 200 youngsters, and 41% enrolled fewer than 100 pupils. Only 15% of the nation's high schools enrolled in excess of 500 students (Spears, 1941). An average high school at the end of the 1930s was a "10-teacher institution with 250 pupils" (Odell, 1939, p. 93), although it is important to note that rural schools continued to be quite small whereas city schools were growing in enrollments. Although enrollments continued to grow over the next 20 years, as we approached the 1960s, small schools were still the norm. In 1958-1959, for example, the median size of the American high school was less than 300, and 70% of the high schools had an enrollment of fewer than 500 students (Anderson & Gruhn, 1962, p. 80). More than one third of all high schools had fewer than 200 students (Hampel, 1986, p. 74). Indeed, in his famous report on the American high school, Conant (1959) maintained that "the prevalence of high schools with graduation classes of less than 100 students consti-tute[d] one of the serious obstacles to good secondary education throughout most of the United States" (p. 77). According to Conant, in 1957, nearly 3 in 4 high schools (73.9%) graduated fewer than 100 students, whereas more than 1 in 3 students (38.8%) attended one of these high schools of "inadequate size" (p. 80).

As was true since its inception, through the first six decades of the 20th century, high school enrollments did not align perfectly with national demographics (Hampel, 1986; James & Tyack, 1983; Krug, 1972; Odell, 1939). Girls were overrepresented in initial 9th grade enrollments and were even more of a presence at high school grad-uation ceremonies. On the other hand, youngsters from families of unskilled laborers, from rural communities, and from lower socioeconomic groups were underrepre-sented, as were students of color (Cohen & Neufeld, 1981; Odell, 1939; Krug, 1972): "The rhetoric of democracy notwithstanding, access to secondary education . . . was contingent on social and economic standing" (Kliebard, 1995, p. 159).

The rationale for the growth in high school attendance has been explored in part in earlier chapters. To that framework we add the following explanations:

1. "The emphasis on schooling as a force of unity and cohesion" (Krug, 1972, p. 9) after World War I

2. The passage of compulsory attendance laws after 1920

3. The growing belief that "educational attainment [was] a crucial step in the race for economic and social position" (Cohen & Neufeld, 1981, p. 72)—and "that secondary education counted in obtaining a good job" (James & Tyack, 1983, p. 401)

4. The development of a modern economy that offered fewer opportunities for adolescents to participate (Hampel, 1986; James & Tyack, 1983; Krug, 1972)

5. The devastating loss of employment opportunities resulting from the Great Depression (Krug, 1972)

6. An expanding commitment to the high school as the prime institution for socializing adolescents (Powell et al., 1985)

7. The growth of "vocational and technical courses" (Hampel, 1986, p. 15) that had more immediate payoff for students

8. An increase in "education requirements for white-collar jobs" (Hampel, 1986, p. 15)

9. A decline in the number of children per family, which "made it easier for parents to support their children for more years of schooling and to defer the children's earnings" (James & Tyack, 1983, p. 401).

In closing this section on growth and development, we would be remiss if we failed to make explicit the cornerstone of the modern high school—unitary, universal education. The formative era of the public high school during the final 50 years of the 19th century was marked by the battle for legitimacy of public—as opposed to private—education. Consistent with the prevailing ideology of the modern era (Wells, Lopez, Scott, & Holme, 1999), the 20th century would witness the construction of the comprehensive high school and the struggle for universal—as opposed to selective—education. The resolution, as would be the case with most of the major doctrines of the comprehensive high school, was heavily influenced by the seminal report in 1918 from the Commission on the Reorganization of Secondary Education (CRSE). Building on the idea of "secondary schooling as a necessary extension of universal elementary schooling" (Krug, 1964, p. 393), the Commission advocated a tightly linked elementary-secondary educational program, with compulsory schooling to the age of 18, although not on a full-time basis (Krug, 1964). Although it took some time to capture the prize (Dorn, 1996), "an achievement quite distinct in human history" (Cohen & Neufeld, 1981, p. 69), advocates for universality quickly gained the high ground (James & Tyack, 1983). The "egalitarian ideal" (Cusick, 1983, p. 25) of extending "the offer of education to as many people as possible regardless of their background, ambitions, or abilities" (p. 25) became firmly ingrained in the American secondary education system. In the process, however, as we discuss more fully below, "serving all youth in the community was to take precedence over serving scholarship and high standards" (Krug, 1972, pp. 8-9), and "the democratic impulse . . . turned the high schools into mass custodial holding tanks" (Herbst, 1996, p. 203).

> Universal secondary education in the United States was achieved through a system of comprehensive high schools, devoted primarily to the education of the great mass of its students for work and life, and secondarily to the preparation of a small minority for higher education. (Trow, 1961, p. 165)

The second face of the cornerstone features a relief depicting the "unitary" nature of the high school, and "the incorporation of American youth within a single institution" (Westbury, 1988, p. 291)—"an inclusive trajectory that has been the hallmark of the American secondary school" (p. 302). When the design for the modern high school was being drawn, some support arose for the position that "one way to give both mass education and train the gifted proportionate to their abilities would be to have secondary education distributed among separate and parallel institutions above the elementary school" (Spears, 1941, p. 82). In particular, some analysts argued for modeling secondary schooling "on the dual European system of education, with separate academic and vocational schools" (Tanner & Tanner, cited in Wraga, 1994, p. xiv). They based their assessments "mainly on the greater efficiency of such schools in giving vocational training" (Odell, 1939, p. 95).

> Concentration of interest and effort on one general field results [, they maintained,] in more effective work than that done in comprehensive schools, with their more widely divided energies. (pp. 94-95)

As suggested above, the battle of unitary *versus* specialized high schools was brought to a head with the birth of vocational education (Herbst, 1996). Anchored again in the work of the Commission on the Reorganization of Secondary Education, the benefits of a composite high school that promoted unifying activities among students of all classes and backgrounds was trumpeted in the face of the efficiency gains of separate institutions (Krug, 1964). The idea of the high school as a crucible of democracy was heavily underscored in the Commission's report (Cremin, 1955; Spring, 1990), and in the end it carried the day: "By the beginning of the 1920s, the die was cast" (Herbst, 1996, p. 119), the "incorporative mission" (Westbury, 1988, p. 302) was firmly grounded—all students would attend a unitary high school, completing separate courses of study within the composite institution (Cusick, 1983; Krug, 1964). Diversification, individualization, specialization, and fragmentation of structure and program would quickly grow up from these seeds of inclusion, openness, and comprehensiveness (Cusick, 1983).

The Learning Infrastructure

In 1890 general education was obviously an education which was suited to the few who had brains and money, but in 1930 it was an education which was needed by the many who might or might not have brains and money. The first was an education for leadership; the second, an education for efficient living. The first was uniform and disciplinary; the second was differentiated and socializing. The first was indirect, and the second was direct. The first was an education designed to prepare the chosen for anything, but nothing in special; the second to prepare all for everything, but nothing in general. The first permitted a stable, coherent curriculum; the second enforced a changing, divided curriculum. This first had a method, in fact, was a method. The second had no method, in fact, was all methods. The product of the first was predictable; the product of the second was of the nature of things hoped for. (Willing, 1942, p. 81)

Conant's conception of the comprehensive high school was therefore not a substantial deviation from what educators had proposed for decades. His starting assumptions—that everyone should attend a comprehensive high school, that some should take an academic curriculum but most would not, and that the schools had the responsibility to guide students into the proper curriculum—were, in outline, what the *Cardinal Principles* report had described [40 years earlier]. (Dorn, 1996, p. 49)

Purpose

The *Cardinal Principles* report established the two fundamental functions of the comprehensive high school model: to provide an educational program suitable to the needs of all youth and to unify students of diverse backgrounds, abilities, and aspirations. The report named these the specializing and unifying functions, respectively. (Wraga, 1994, p. xiv)

The three main objectives of a comprehensive high school are: *first,* to provide a general education for all the future citizens; *second,* to provide good elective programs for those who wish to use their acquired skills immediately on graduation; *third,* to provide satisfactory programs for those whose vocations will depend on their subsequent education in a college or university. (Conant, 1959, p. 17)

Advocates of a differentiated, universal high school had won the fight over the purpose of high schools. (Dorn, 1996, p. 49)

In Chapter 2, we uncovered the still-developing roots of a new vision of secondary education, one in which the goals of social control and preparation for life's tasks began to choke out the earlier aim of intellectual development. These new purposes or functions were to be fully transported to the American high school through the influence of two of the most significant reform efforts in secondary education in the 20th century: (a) the work to implement the report of the Commission on the Reorganization of Secondary Education, titled *The Cardinal Principles of Secondary Education*—"a major landmark in secondary education in the United States" (Kliebard, 1995, p. 96), and "the seminal document in the emergence of the comprehensive high school model" (Wraga, 1994, p. xiii), and (b) the life adjustment movement, which was anchored by two important reports—the 1940 document from the American Youth Commission, titled *What the High Schools Ought to Teach,* and the 1944 report commissioned by the Educational Policies Commission, titled *Education for ALL American Youth*—that provided "a ringing reaffirmation of the ideals of the Cardinal Principles" (Angus & Mirel, 1995, p. 297). These were the documents that provided the framework allowing the public high school to meet the criterion of social control—to "help students accommodate to an industrial world and their presumed place in it" (Dorn, 1996, p. 39), to put into operation scientific learning theories supporting the doctrine of social efficiency, to achieve the goal of "developing socially efficient men and women" (Willing, 1942, p. 55), and to define what preparation for work and for living actually meant in a post-mental-discipline era.

In the era of faculty psychology, "preparation for life meant developing and training for the powers of the mind. By 1920 it meant explicit, comprehensive, and contemporaneous fitting for the approved activities of adults in their daily living" (Willing, 1942, p. 56). Social efficiency became "the guiding star for the redirection of secondary education" (p. 56). By the 1940s, the ideal of social efficiency "had become so widely accepted as to appear traditional itself" (Krug, 1972, p. 271), a tradition that has held the high ground—although not always alone—for most of the 20th century (Kliebard, 1995). In the process, "schools increasingly sloughed off academic tradition in favor of producing good workers and efficient citizens" (Krug, 1972, p. 178): "Vocation . . . moved from being a curricular sideline to a major *raison d'être* of the school" (Herbst, 1996, p. 145).

> The comprehensive high school became a mixture of planned social activities and a variety of curricula, all of which were attempts to prepare a new generation for a society based on large organizations and occupational specialization. In this context, the development of human capital meant selection and training for a specialized task and socialization for a society based on cooperation. (Spring, 1990, pp. 210-211)

At the heart of the new ideology were new aims for secondary education, a focus that represented

> . . . a pronounced shift in the stated goals of schooling, away from concern with intellectual development and mastery of subject matter to concern for social and emotional development and to the adoption of "functional" objectives related to areas such as vocation, health, and family life. (Ravitch, 1983, p. 55)

In the transition to the goal of "fit[ting] pupils for their probable future destinies" (James & Tyack, 1983, p. 403) and to "the demands of modern society" (Kliebard, 1995, p. 90), social goals were highlighted. More important, "the idea that schools should derive their goals from the life activities of adults in society" (Ravitch, 1983, p. 48)—"that educational objectives should be determined by analyzing the normal out-of-school life and activities of individuals as members of families and of various civic and social groups, as wage-earners, as users of leisure, and so forth" (Odell, 1939, p. 167)—became a defining element of the comprehensive high school.

The most powerful statement of preparation for life's activities during the first part of the century was contained in the *Cardinal Principles*. This highly influential report promulgated seven "objectives" (Anderson & Gruhn, 1962, p. 41), "aims" (Krug, 1972, p. 25), or "distinct principles" (Ravitch, 1983, p. 48) that were to define the curricular framework of the comprehensive high school: "1. Health. 2. Command of fundamental processes. 3. Worthy home-membership. 4. Vocation. 5. Citizenship. 6. Worthy use of leisure. 7. Ethical character" (cited in Krug, 1964, p. 388). "Intellectual education" (Krug, 1972, p. 5) was considered to be inadequate—a throwback to a previous time and, as a goal, hopelessly out of step with the demands of an industrial society. The focus on "the assimilation of subject matter and mental equipment" (Spears, 1941, p. 125) dimmed considerably. Indeed, as Dorn (1996) notes, "Only as an aside did the commission acknowledge academics" (p. 42). The important function of school was to prepare the student "to play his part as a producer, as a husband or wife, a father or mother, a friend and neighbor, a creator of public opinion and a servant of the public will" (Ellwood, cited in Krug, 1972, p. 5). New purposes and objectives were welded together to support the comprehensive high school: "civic-social-moral responsibility, recreational and aesthetic participation and enjoyment, occupational efficiency, and physical efficiency" (Koos, 1927, pp. 156-157).

> By 1940, high school teachers worked in institutions with vastly inflated purposes: They sought to meet students' psychic needs, their needs for practical education including but ranging far beyond the vocational, and their social needs. Academic learning had expanded greatly, but it had become a much less important feature of high schools. (Powell et al., 1985, p. 277)

The social and practical aims of the comprehensive high school that found expression in the *Cardinal Principles* were "justified and rationalized" (Angus & Mirel, 1995, p. 303) and deepened by the later work of the American Youth Commission and the Educational Policy Commission of the National Education Association. First, the spotlight on functional education and social adjustment was turned up even more brightly. Second, the academic role of high schools—"the dead hand of preparation for college" (Krug, 1972, p. 346)—came under even greater criticism. Third, even more than in the 1920s and 1930s, "adolescent priorities" (Hampel, 1986, p. 45) were featured in the goals algorithm—and the emerging curricular frameworks. Fourth, "the doctrine of practicality" (Powell et al., 1985, p. 278) or the definition of usefulness was reformulated to provide "plain living equal educational status with work" (p. 275)—"to give the small details of life as much place as vocational training" (p. 274). Finally, there was a greater push not simply to reorient existing courses on the practical-social axes but to have these new "aims representing areas of living . . . become the subjects" (Kliebard, 1995, pp. 185-186).

Schools would now be charged with the "all-around development" (Spears, 1941, p. 223) of youngsters—"social, physical, emotional, as well as mental" (p. 147). "All will secure the experiences necessary for the development of effective, well-rounded, democratic citizens" (Mackenzie, 1942, p. 85), and all should be "educate[d] for the activities of citizenship, homemaking, health, and leisure" (Willing, 1942, pp. 71-72). As we reveal more fully below, this new set of purposes would take on concrete meaning "through measures such as providing 'a wide range of subjects,' 'exploration and guidance,' adaption of curriculum and instruction to individual capacities, 'flexibility of organization and administration,' and 'differentiated curriculums' " (*Cardinal Principles,* pp. 21-22, cited in Wraga, 1994, p. 23).

In sum, the *Cardinal Principles* and the life adjustment movement brought to secondary education "a significantly broadened mission" (James & Tyack, 1983, p. 402), an expanded set of purposes, and a revaluing of these component aims—reformulations that heavily influenced the development of the comprehensive high school and our understanding of secondary education throughout most of the 20th century. In the process, educators "extend[ed] into the secondary school the traditional function of unification" (Krug, 1964, p. 403) that had characterized elementary school education. Social cohesion was emphasized, and socialization activities became more visible in the mosaic known as secondary education. Individualism and pluralism were downplayed (Tyack, 1974). Education into "group consciousness, group intelligence and group services" (Smith, cited in Krug, 1964, p. 422) were valued: "So much emphasis was placed on the social side of life that the result was a massive shift away from individualistic school purposes" (Krug, 1964, p. 274). The aim of schooling, according to Poland (cited in Krug, 1964), was

> . . . not individuality but social unity. In a political and social democracy such as ours, children must be taught to live and to work together cooperatively; to submit their individual wills to the will of the majority; and to conform to social requirements whether they approve of them or not. (pp. 275-276)

Theories of Learning

> A nationwide examination of learning activities, teaching activities, and plans for the organization of instruction reveals more than a change in the aims of the high school; a new conception of the nature of the learning process is also evident. (Mackenzie, 1942, p. 87)

Two closely interrelated movements were to emerge in the 20th century. One was the development of a psychological theory to replace the moribund faculty psychology, one which fit in neatly with the basic presuppositions of social efficiency; and the other was the mental measurement movement which provided the technology necessary for the kind of assessment and prediction that a curriculum based on social efficiency doctrine required. These two movements, both flowering in the first quarter of the 20th century, in effect, created a new psychology. (Kliebard, 1995, p. 90)

The mold for the learning philosophy that was to be used to build the modern high school had already been forged by the time of the report from the Commission on the Reorganization of Secondary Education. What the *Cardinal Principles* document accomplished was to take the poured products and to cement those learning pillars firmly into the superstructure that would become the comprehensive high school. At the risk of oversimplification, the new learning scaffolding might best be labeled "behavior psychology" (Spears, 1941, p. 256), and the architecture that it replaced "mind psychology" (p. 256). As we observed in Chapter 2, the transformation from philosophies of learning anchoring agricultural-era high schools to theories supporting education in the industrial era unfolded in the context of "the scientific movement in the schools" (Willing, 1942, p. 47), especially in "the quest for a science of education" (Cremin, 1961, p. 199) and "the beginnings of educational psychology" (Cremin, 1955, pp. 303-304). The development of experimental psychology, in turn, provided the major portal to the new scientific world of education (Spears, 1941) and the blueprints for the reformulation of curriculum in the comprehensive high school (Cremin, 1961): "A purposeful effort was made by the Commission on the Reorganization of Secondary Education to base the new design for the secondary school on the best available knowledge in social and behavioral science" (Wraga, 1994, p. 28). Material from the new science of child development was also welded into the learning framework of the high school taking shape in the 1920s and 1930s (Cremin, 1955; Krug, 1964).

Curriculum

The *Cardinal Principles* has been the experiment's [the comprehensive high school's] blueprint. For the past eighty years it has supplied the high schools' curricular guidelines. (Herbst, 1996, p. 206)

The high school curriculum that we have, or at least had until the mid-1980s [, represents] a slow but steady working out of the ideas first clearly enunciated in the *Cardinal Principles of Secondary Education*. (Angus & Mirel, 1995, p. 320)

The scope of the curriculum needed to be broadened beyond the development of intelligence to nothing less than the full scope of life activities, and the content of the curriculum had to be changed so that a taut connection could be maintained between what was taught in school and the adult activities that one would later be called on to perform. (Kliebard, 1995, p. 87)

As we have documented over the last two chapters, the aim of social control and the educational philosophy of social efficiency combined to create a remarkably firm framework for the construction of the comprehensive high school. United, they exerted considerable influence over the shape and texture of the secondary school curriculum (Spring, 1990). Below, we examine the central dynamics of that molding process as well as the resulting form that the curriculum in the comprehensive high school has taken. Our goal is not so much to provide a history of curriculum in the high school as it is to expose the defining elements of the core technology in this uniquely American institution. We organize our analysis into the general categories of curriculum foundations and curricular frameworks.

Curriculum Foundations

Such an approach to providing an educational program implies an appreciation of (1) the youth, his needs and interests . . . and (2) the American life in which he moves and grows, its problems, mores, democratic ways, etc. From these two the curriculum designer takes his cue for the school. (Spears, 1941, p. 108)

Not only was mental discipline dead as a formal theory, but the new scientific curriculum-makers . . . were developing a theory of curriculum entirely consistent with the concept of mind inherent in the new psychology. If transfer from one task to another was much less than had been commonly believed, then the curriculum had to be so designed as to teach people specifically and directly those exact skills required for the tasks that lay before them in life. (Kliebard, 1995, p. 93)

Schools that revised their curriculum reported agreement that . . . education must embrace the total life experience of the child; that the goal of education must be to achieve effective living for all; that curriculum objectives had to be stated in terms of useful activities; that the focus of instruction had to shift from subject matter to the experience of the child; that college-preparatory studies were narrow and aristocratic, and that the curriculum had to embrace the interests of all children, not just the college-bound. (Ravitch, 1983, p. 53)

The comprehensive high school curriculum was built with three load-bearing walls: practical concerns, social needs, and student needs and interests.

Practical Concerns. The first wall—practical concerns—was crafted not from the designs of the academic disciplines, as had been the case in the 19th century, but from the blueprints of functioning in adult society. As we describe more fully below, in conjunction with "vigorous assaults on the academic traditions" (Krug, 1964, p. 280), a profound shift occurred from the earlier perspective laid out by the Committee of Ten that equated preparation for higher education with preparation for life: "Educators began to move the focus of high school studies away from traditional academic work toward what they judged to be the 'practical' needs of . . . students" (Cohen & Neufeld, 1981, p. 79). "The high schools' true mission [became] helping students to learn about the practical realities of everyday life, rather than teaching academic subjects" (Powell et al., 1985, p. 289). Analysts came to "doubt the strength of the connection between academics and 'the real demands of living' " (Hampel, 1986, p. 43). In a sharp "break with the academic tradition of the past" (Herbst, 1996, p. 146), a firewall was built between these two domains, to the point that academic education became viewed as the province of a select few whereas practical education was to serve the needs of the masses (Cohen & Neufeld, 1981). As the final pieces were added to the dividing wall, it became increasingly obvious that the extant high school "curriculum was inappropriate" (Kliebard, 1995, p. 208) and "lagged badly in its eternally professed function of preparing for life" (Willing, 1942, p. 50). People examined the American high school and concluded that it was not "sufficiently practical" (Krug, 1972, p. 322) or "relevant" (Alexander et al., 1971, p. 202). Not surprisingly, the attention of curriculum developers was turned toward the education of those who were preparing not for college but for the responsibilities of life.

The result was the establishment of the belief that students "were entitled to some new kind of education, one that was presumably practical rather than traditional or classical" (Krug, 1964, p. 322) and an extended 40-year reformulation of the knowledge anchoring the curriculum, "with the substitution of content that had a much more utilitarian and less academic character" (Kliebard, 1995, p. 143)—a shift in "the focus of secondary education from the question of democratic support to that of utilitarian purpose" (Dorn, 1996, p. 39). In the process, the curriculum of the modern high school "was firmly linked to [a] sort of social utilitarianism" (Ravitch, 1983, p. 50) or "social functionalism" (Mackenzie, 1942, p. 84) in which educators set about "to devise programs of study that prepared individuals specifically and directly for the role they would play as adult members of the social order" (Kliebard, 1995, pp. 77-78). As opposed to being grounded on academic subjects, the curriculum was built up from: an "analysis of contemporary society" (Cremin, 1961, p. 199); "the current practices of society . . . and the tasks of everyday life" (Herbst, 1996, p. 141); the " 'life needs' of pupils" (Latimer, 1958, p. 72); "the full range of human experiences" (Cremin, 1961, p. 199); "the learner's ongoing stream of life situations" (Spears, 1941, p. 105); "the ascertainable uses and needs of social living outside of the school" (Willing, 1942, p. 50); "the standards of adult living" (Kliebard, 1995, p. 158); "effective living in all areas of life" (Mackenzie, 1942, p. 84); "vocational matters" (Powell et al., 1985, p. 303), "vocational training" (Sizer, 1964, p. 200), "work and social service" (Herbst, 1996, p. 145); "functional needs and significant life problems" (Krug, 1972, p. 263); "youth problems" (Mackenzie, 1942, p. 86); and "lines of probable destination [and] efficient performance in a future social role" (Kliebard, 1995, pp. 129, 102)—in short, on the basis of "human needs" (Spears, 1941, p. 233) rather than "subject requirements" (p. 233). Curriculum became "defined as a series of guided experiences paralleling present and future out-of-school experiences" (Krug, 1972, p. 269), and "the scientific curriculum-makers' conception of education as preparation for what lies ahead [was] thoroughly infused into contemporary educational thought" (Kliebard, 1995, p. 104).

Social Needs. The second wall of the triangular base of the modern high school curriculum—social needs—or what Krug (1964) describes as "an explicit social mission for the schools" (p. 249), can be seen in the conception of curriculum as the full set of experiences students receive at school and in the content of the individual courses in which they enroll. Developing a little later than the functional aspects of the curriculum, "socialized aims" (Spring, 1990, p. 218) "lent unmatched support to the comprehensive high school model" (Wraga, 1994, p. 86). They supported a curriculum designed to build in individual students the social skills necessary to participate successfully in society—what Spears (1941) described as "individual growth in and adjustment to social situations" (p. 32), to adapt to the "corporate structure" (Spring, 1990, p. 217), and "to create a stable and smoothly functioning society" (Kliebard, 1995, p. 83).

A focus on social needs ensured that "attitudes, understanding, appreciation, and socially accepted actions [began to] take their place beside facts and skills as instructional outcomes" (Spears, 1941, p. 147), that attitudes and beliefs would become important educational aims (Krug, 1972), and that "social skills" (Hampel, 1986, p. 198) would, along with practical skills, become more important than academic proficiencies. It also helped energize what the authors of the *Cardinal Principles* labeled the unifying function of secondary education, especially the integration of collective curricular experiences, such as assemblies and extracurricular activities, into the infrastructure of the comprehensive high school.

Students' Needs and Interests. The final building block in the curricular triangle of the modern high school is a composite of students' needs and interests (Cohen & Neufeld, 1981; Cusick, 1983). "As the high school was experiencing rapid growth in the 20th century and as it was increasingly being suggested that the traditional subjects were . . . unsuitable for the 'masses' . . . invading the high school" (Krug, 1964, p. 285), critics argued that the needs of more and more pupils were not being addressed. A common, prescribed academic curriculum, they held, "cannot stand as evidence of similarity in interests, capacities, and destination of the pupils enrolled. Instead, it stands as evidence of maladjustment" (Spears, 1941, p. 86). The reformers took the "immediate life of the child" (Kliebard, 1995, p. 158) or "an appreciation of the nature of personal development as the point of departure in proper curricular provision" (Spears, 1941, p. 205). The " 'needs of youth' became a catechetical slogan [in the] fundamental reconstruction of the secondary school program" (Ravitch, 1983, p. 62) as did the belief that "the child rather than what he studies should be the center of all educational effort" (Cremin, 1961, p. 258). High school teachers "embarked on an endless search for something that would interest each of their students" (Cusick, 1983, p. 44).

> The focal point of secondary education was definitely shifting from emphasis on subject matter to emphasis on the pupils and their life adjustment needs. The old idea that pupils should conform to the curriculum was giving way to the new concept of adapting the curriculum to fit the wide divergence of student interests and capacities. (Latimer, 1958, p. 72)

Certain principles stand out as signposts in curricular provision:

1. Learning situations cannot be rigidly set in advance but must flexibly provide for the purposes of pupils.

2. So closely must the curriculum be tied into the needs of the students at hand, it is impossible to conceive a curriculum without doing so in connection with the particular individuals to be served through it. (Spears, 1941, p. 109)

In the process, "the importance of the child and adolescent interests and their sense of purpose" (Kliebard, 1995, p. 145), the "problems of youth" (Krug, 1972, p. 312), the "identifiable needs and interests of students" (Ravitch, 1983, p. 45), and the "activities of youth" (Wraga, 1994, p. 34) were welded into the scaffolding of the comprehensive high school, generally displacing traditional subject matter at the same time (Kliebard, 1995; Krug, 1964, 1972). In the 1960s and 1970s, a concern for students' "rights and feelings" (Hampel, 1986, p. 141) was added to the infrastructure (Powell et al., 1985).

It is important to point out that three somewhat distinct tributaries fed the central channel of student needs and interests. The oldest of these might best be thought of as the psychological stream or, perhaps more specifically, the stream of developmental psychology. It represented the movement to develop a child-centered core technology based on the belief "that somewhere in the child lay the key to a revitalized curriculum" (Kliebard, 1995, pp. 137-138)—"that certain natural laws govern the development of human beings, that these can be scientifically determined, and that knowledge of these laws is the only solid basis for pedagogical theory and practice" (Cremin, 1955, p. 302). The second tributary was formed not from scientific endeavors but from a growing sense that as enrollments skyrocketed and more and more of these new students were unsuccessful, something was required to make the curriculum more attractive to adolescents, something in particular that would hold their attention (Kliebard, 1995). Finally, the curriculum river of student needs and interests was fed in part by an offshoot of the social functionalism stream described earlier. This was especially evident as the somewhat pure social efficiency ideology of the *Cardinal Principles* gave way to the hybrid version that characterized the life adjustment movement of the 1940s and 1950s. Efficiency was extended beyond the central dynamic of fitting youngsters to the needs of society. In an interesting twist of logic, focusing on the needs of youngsters became an accepted corollary of social efficiency.

All of this, of course, strengthened the central place of student interests in the curriculum of the comprehensive high school. Equally important:

1. It helped unify the three lines of work that occupied distinct spheres of the student interest playing field—the developmentalists who were no more fond of functionalism than they were of classical studies, and the

other two groups who built their concern for students' interests on sociological and utilitarian moorings.

2. It fused the traditions of social functionalism and student interests.

What emerged in the comprehensive high school was a "curriculum tied directly to the needs of students as well as the duties of life" (Kliebard, 1995, p. 190)—"a fusion of the social efficiency concern that the schools prepare directly and specifically for the duties of life and the activity curriculum's overriding emphasis on the needs and interests of the learner as the basis of the curriculum" (p. 187). The curriculum that took hold in the comprehensive high school was one of "human experiences rather than one of subjects to be taught" (Spears, 1941, p. 110).

Curricular Frameworks

> The four programs recommended by the Ten still had great appeal for college-bound students, but for the vast majority, new curricula based on new goals were designed. (Sizer, 1964, p. 205)

> The definition of a high school education is . . . open to as many interpretations as there are combinations of courses. (Cusick, 1983, p. 4)

Curricular forms that would collectively characterize education in the comprehensive high school for most of the 20th century were molded on the foundations of practicality, social needs, and student interests. Although these forms overlap to a significant extent, for purposes of analysis we separate them into differentiated curricula and expanded subject offerings, with special privileges granted to practical courses.

Differentiated Curriculum. As Dorn (1996) reminds us, in the early years of the public high school, the norm was "standardization of academic subjects and equal treatment of all students in the context of limited high school enrollment" (p. 42). As the idea of universality took root and the number of students of high school age continued to grow, so too did the belief in the need for differentiated education to handle the new masses being dumped into America's high schools (Cusick, 1983)—a belief solidly buttressed by the new science of learning, especially the growth of intelligence testing (Cohen & Neufeld, 1981; James & Tyack, 1983). Tradeoffs "in the structure of [high] schools . . . particularly their curricula" (Westbury, 1988, p. 302) followed as "high schools continually diversified and fragmented their structures as far as they could to accommodate particular groups and individuals" (Cusick, 1983, p. 118). There were two sides to the ideological coin of differentiation—the belief that a "uniform curriculum . . . represented the 'idealism' of an earlier time and was quite out of place under modern economic conditions" (Tyack, 1974, p. 192) and the need for "tailoring instruction more and more to the different kinds and classes of children who were brought within the purview of the school" (Cremin, 1961, pp. viii-ix).

Central to the formation of this pillar of the comprehensive high school, that is, "a stratified conception of the high school" (Westbury, 1988, p. 307) and a differentiated curriculum designed for all students, was the belief that growing numbers of adolescents were incapable of serious academic work or, even if capable, largely uninterested in academic subject matter[1] (Cohen & Neufeld, 1981). Conant (1959) captured this belief in numerical terms as follows. "The normal pattern of distribution of academic talent is such that a class of one hundred will have between fifteen and twenty academically talented students" (Conant, 1959, p. 78). In either case—inability or lack of interest—the viewpoint that "a college preparatory curriculum . . . was unsuited to the masses of students" (Krug, 1972, p. 126) had gained the high ground as the comprehensive high school curriculum was being formed. The result, not surprisingly, was that "the practice of tracking emerged in the schools during the decade following the release of the *Cardinal Principles* report" (Wraga, 1994, p. 53) and "differentiation by course of study" (Krug, 1972, p. 280) became the keystone of the curriculum in the modern high school—"a cheap way to manage diversity among secondary students . . . [but] a poor way to protect or expand quality" (Powell et al., 1985, p. 300).

The effects included:

1. The creation in the comprehensive high school of a dualism "between the academic and the practical" (Krug, 1964, p. 294), "between those who were presumed to be academically able and those who were not" (Powell et al., 1985, p. 254)—a solidification of the belief that academic subjects were "appropriate only for that segment of the high school population that was destined to go on to college" (Kliebard, 1995, p. 13), and a reinforcement of "the divergence between college preparatory and non-college-preparatory programs" (Krug, 1964, p. 303) and "a pervasive differentiation between the curriculum considered appropriate to those who are college bound and those who are not" (Westbury, 1988, p. 310).

2. The infusion of anti-intellectual design principles into the modern secondary school curriculum and "the creation of a climate that discouraged serious academic work" (Powell et al., 1985, p. 254).

3. A reformulation of the definition of equal educational opportunity. In the formative era of the public high school, "equality of opportunity meant giving everyone the same education so that they could compete on equal terms in the labor market" (Spring, 1990, p. 214). In the comprehensive high school, "equality of opportunity meant giving students different types of education based on the individual's future occupation" (p. 214) and on "the abilities and needs of the learners" (Spears, 1941, p. 372). *Equality* of educational opportunity calls for just such adjustments . . . in experiences, standards, and expectations, . . . and was never supposed to have been *identity* of educational opportunity. . . . Equality of educational opportunity means that each boy and girl should have the chance to make the most of his [or her] particular potentialities" (p. 372). Equal opportunity in the comprehensive high school "now meant simply the right of all who came to be offered something of value, and it

was the school's obligation to offer it. The magnitude of this shift cannot be overestimated; it was truly Copernican in character" (Cremin, 1961, p. 303; see also Cusick, 1983, p. 119).

Given the discussion to date, it will come as little surprise that differentiation was formed on the foundational triangle of "the varied needs of society" (Krug, 1964, p. 389), the "future social needs of the students" (Spring, 1990, p. 201), and "the individual differences in pupils" (Krug, 1964, p. 389). The most visible threads in the design were those highlighting differentiation based on "the future social destination of the student" (Spring, 1990, p. 201), "vocational needs" (Wraga, 1994, p. 214), and "a specific social and occupational role" (Kliebard, 1995, p. 130)—a differentiated curriculum tightly tethered to the dominant ideology of social efficiency (Kliebard, 1995) and one "planned with reference, not to each pupil's personal needs primarily, but with reference to the different educational requirements of special groups of pupils—curriculums based on social rather than necessarily vague psychological considerations" (Johnston, cited in Krug, 1964, p. 320). Less prevalent but growing in importance in the 1930s and 1940s were differentiation patterns woven from "the doctrine of individual differences" (Spears, 1941, p. 372). These individual differences break out into three clusters: different tastes or interests, different needs, and different abilities or capacities—as determined by the rapidly developing field of educational measurement.

The modern high school, in striving to attend to these various viewpoints, ended up with a "proliferation of courses" (Wraga, 1994, p. xv) as well as with a whole new set of separate "paths toward the accumulation of the necessary credits" (Cusick, 1983, p. 10) to graduate. We report in detail on the proliferation issue in the next section. Here we highlight the growth of curriculum tracks. During the early years of the differentiation movement, schools prided themselves on the creation of a plethora of narrow curricular channels (Koos, 1927). The work of Robert and Helen Lynd, as discussed in Dorn (1996), is informative here. In their study of "Middletown" high school, the Lynds revealed that in 1890, the students had only 2 curricular options; by 1924, they had 12 tracks from which to select. George Counts documented a similar pattern. In 1923-1924, when he studied high school curriculum, "the wide acceptance of different curricula for different segments of the high school population was clearly evident. He reported 18 different curricula in Los Angeles secondary schools and 15 in Newton, Massachusetts" (Kliebard, 1995, p. 97). Powell and his colleagues (1985) provide a nice summary of the curricular differentiation storyline:

> In 1906-11 and in 1929-30, nearly all the schools studied had at least one college-preparatory curriculum. Some had two, one to prepare students in the classical subjects and another to prepare those with a taste for science and math. The real changes came in the other courses of study. Early in the century, only about one school in six offered a general curriculum, but by 1930, more than five of every six schools had installed a course of study for the uncertain or unspecial student. In 1906-11, half of the schools offered a commercial course of study; by the beginning of the Great Depression, all

schools offered such work, and several had more than one. In the earlier period, only one school in six offered an industrial arts diploma, but by 1930,
nearly five in every six offered such a curriculum.

By 1930, then, almost all the schools in this study were offering quite ex-
tensively differentiated curricula. The average number of curricula in the
schools studied had more than doubled in 20 years. The practical arts curricula (home economics, industrial, and commercial arts) had the largest
growth—they increased threefold—and the general curricula multiplied by
nearly as much. But the average number of college-preparatory curricula had
increased only slightly. (p. 246)

Over the years, these varied options collapsed so that by 1960, the comprehensive
high school was generally defined by four broad curricula—the academic, the commercial, the general, and the vocational (Hampel, 1986; Powell et al., 1985)—that
offered quite different educational experiences.

Tracking the emergence of differentiation as the central component of the comprehensive high school curriculum does not provide the full picture, however. To
complete the portrait, it is necessary to examine the other side of the reciprocal relationship between students and curricula. That means looking not at the side of the
equation focusing on the creation of subjects in response to student interests and capabilities but rather at the ways that students, individually and in groups, were chan-
neled or sorted into curricular tracks—what Spears in 1941 labeled as "the adjustment of pupils to courses" (p. 118) and Tyack (1974) described nearly a quarter of
a century later as "the assignment of students to lanes leading to different careers"
(p. 205). The key issue on this side of the formula was fitting students to the appropriate curriculum (Ravitch, 1983). This, of course, necessitated a "proper classifica-
tion of pupils" (Tyack, 1974, p. 45). The starting point here was "the growing emphasis on individual differences" (Spears, 1941, p. 372) that was surfacing in the
newly emerging science of mental measurement (i.e., IQ testing)—a movement that
"swept over the nation as an educational crusade" (Tyack, 1974, p. 207) and was to
have a profound effect on "the ordering of the school" (Willing, 1942, p. 44) by providing the key to the student side of the curricular differentiation equation. Through
such a system, "The needs of the student, the needs of the educational system, and
the needs of the larger society could be more precisely calibrated and the connecting
parts more smoothly meshed" (Tyack, 1974, p. 199).

As Taylor, McMahill, and Taylor (1960) captured it, the central point is that the
work of psychologists at the dawn of the modern high school "revealed a way to identify individual differences and show[ed] us how to adjust our programs to students of
varied abilities" (p. 83)—to ensure "better adaptation of the work of the school to
the widening distribution of mentalities represented" (Koos, 1927, p. 543). The goal
of educators became to determine the mental abilities of students and then to place
them where they belonged in a curriculum stratified by intelligence (Tyack, 1974).
Bright students were fitted to the academic curriculum, whereas students who were
believed to be less intelligent were assigned to the vocational, commercial, and general streams. And, given the reciprocal student-curricular relationship noted above, as

more and more presumably inferior pupils had to be accommodated in the nation's high schools, considerably more less-challenging, nonacademic work was built into the overall curriculum framework. Within tracks, there was a second *fitting* as students were clustered into sections of courses differentiated by intelligence or ability (e.g., high-, middle-, and low-level Algebra I classes) (Conant, 1959; Koos, 1927).

It is important to underscore the fact that as the modern high school took form, assessments of individual differences—or measures of intelligence—were explicitly linked to social class. The connection was facilitated by a number of dynamics. One of these was the fact that "the use of testing to track students was influenced in powerful ways by widespread social passions and prejudices" (Wraga, 1994, p. 56), especially "the old social efficiency notion that the so-called masses were incapable of handling academic schooling" (Krug, 1972, p. 304). A second factor was the penchant for ranking occupations by required intelligence (Koos, 1927). A third force was the tendency to think of meeting the needs of individuals not one person at a time but as members of groups, especially class-based groups (Krug, 1964). The result was the hardwiring into the comprehensive high school of "programs for pupils of the different social or economic groups" (p. 276) and thus a differentiation process that was considerably less objective than the cloak of educational science might lead one to believe (Wells et al., 1999). In the process, intelligence "became not just a diagnostic device, but a powerful tool by which society could be regulated" (Kliebard, 1995, p. 93).

In closing the discussion of curricular differentiation, it is necessary to underscore the role that the guidance systems being crafted in the modern high school played in fitting students to curricular programs and in nurturing the type of educational determinism touched on above. A reasonable assertion is that, next to mental measurement, "vocational guidance" (Willing, 1942, p. 78) was the major force animating the process of sorting and fitting students in secondary education for much of the 20th century. In the comprehensive high school:

> Educational guidance was defined as helping students select educational programs that matched their interests, abilities, and future occupations. Within this framework, the curriculum was to be subservient to the occupational goals of the students. Ideally, the school counselor would match a student to an occupation and then to a course of study that would prepare the student for his or her vocation. (Spring, 1990, p. 218)

According to Spears (1941), "a better selection of school courses in accordance with a possible future occupation" (p. 220) was the heart of the guidance program— holding in mind our earlier note that occupations could be ranked by required intelligence scores. In this manner, guidance personnel did much to solidify the central role of differentiated curriculum in the comprehensive high school.

Expanded Course Offerings. If differentiation formed one strand of the curriculum DNA of the comprehensive high school, then expanded course offerings comprised the second—or as Alexander and his colleagues penned it (1971), "The most obvious change in the program of studies during the 20th century has been its steady expansion as more and more subjects have been added by schools seeking to provide a comprehensive program" (p. 195). As Wraga (1994) has observed, "In the two decades following the *Cardinal Principles* report, commitment to the [comprehensive] model was most apparent in the proliferation of courses offered by high schools in the United States" (p. xv)—a phenomenon Koos (1927) "considered almost if not fully as significant as the numerical and proportionate increase in schools and enrollment" (p. 34). In an effort to accommodate a rapidly expanding enrollment (Alexander et al., 1971); "to have the curriculum fit the students' needs" (Cusick, 1983, p. 69); "to provide something of value for young people of widely different ability, background, and interests" (Ravitch, 1983, p. 11); and to "serve many institutional (if not intellectual) needs" (Hampel, 1986, p. 148), the modern high school was transformed into a veritable "department store in education" (Magruder, cited in Wraga, 1994, p. 15) offering "a smorgasbord of courses" (Westbury, 1988, p. 307)—a movement marked by an almost "indefinite expansion of the scope of the curriculum" (Kliebard, 1995, p. 216) and "a significant shift in the variety and range of courses offered in the American high school" (Wraga, 1994, p. 33).

One way to highlight curricular expansion is to describe changes from the formative era of the public high school in which most students completed a uniform course of study. In their investigation of Middletown, the Lynds described that whereas in 1890, the high school offered 20 separate courses, by 1925, the number had grown to 102 (Wraga, 1994, p. 36). In a study using 1890 and 1934 as the end points, Jessen reported an expansion in the curriculum from 16 to 206 courses (cited in Wraga, 1994, p. 34). Taking 1890 and 1949 as comparison points, Latimer (1958) observed that the curriculum had experienced "phenomenal growth" (p. 21). He concluded that "at the rate of six courses each academic year it would take a student almost 46 years to complete all of the 274 courses offered by the high schools in 15 or more states in 1948-49! At the same rate, a student could have finished all the courses offered in 1889-90 in a maximum of six years" (p. 21). Finally, Angus and Mirel (1995) documented that the number of high school courses logged by the Department of Education rose from 175 in 1922 to 2100 in 1973 (pp. 301-302). Between 1961 and 1963 alone, the number of courses nearly doubled, growing from 1,100 to 2,100 (Powell et al., 1985, p. 295). Angus and Mirel (1995) concluded that it is "difficult to avoid the impression of curricular expansion running amok" (p. 302), a pattern that defined "the real foundation of our educational house" (Latimer, 1958, p. 21).

Accompanying the great expansion in "the breadth and diversity of curriculum" (Cusick, 1983, p. 114) and "the rapid multiplication of the number and kinds of courses" (Ravitch, 1983, p. 11) that came to represent the modern high school was a new sense of what was to be valued in secondary schools—a not surprising turn of events given that expansion was built on the foundations of practicality, social needs, and student interests discussed earlier. In addition to aligning with these new foundations, the establishment of new courses also progressed by discrediting what had been esteemed previously: "With the slow triumph of efficiency advocates . . . academic disciplines faced an onslaught of criticism" (Dorn, 1996, p. 43). Thus social utilitarianism was promulgated not only as an important end in its own right but also as an antidote to the dead hand of academics—to "high schools . . . dominated by a college preparatory curriculum" (Krug, 1972, p. 318), or what Spears (1941) referred to derogatorily as "the scholar's curriculum" (p. 19)—and as an alternative to the practice of "sacrificing students on the altar of academic formalism" (p. 386). Increasingly the argument was made that the "predominately academic . . . equipment brought over into the 20th century" (p. 58) was ill-suited for secondary education in the new century and that it was becoming "increasingly obsolete" (Kliebard, 1995, p. 180) with the passage of each new decade.

As the comprehensive high school took form, this meant that "the so-called 'academic subjects' no longer commanded first attention" (Krug, 1964, p. 225). By 1920, "the humanist position reflected in [the] Committee of Ten report was forced to go on the defensive, no longer playing the dominant role it once did in the battle for the American curriculum" (Kliebard, 1995, p. 99). By the early 1950s, academic focus had become equated with the "discredited ideal of scholarship" (p. 219). "Disillusionment and in some cases outright antagonism to the traditional course of study" (p. 194) characterized the educational culture of the high school. There was "a conscious attempt to denigrate the traditional notion of 'knowledge for its own sake' as useless and possibly worthless" (Ravitch, 1983, p. 55). "Academic tradition clearly remained the object of attack" (Krug, 1972, p. 288).

> By some, the traditional curriculum was seen as ignoring the natural course of development in children and youth as well as their interests and penchant for activity; by others it was regarded as supremely nonfunctional, dangerously ignoring the actual activities that adults are called on to play in our society, leaving society bereft of the trained individuals that would make it work; and by still others, it was [judged] clearly lacking in social direction, particularly irrelevant to issues of social justice and social renewal. (Kliebard, 1995, pp. 194-195)

The expanded course of study that gave shape and texture to the modern secondary school transformed the school from "a source of learning [to] a site for individual fulfillment" (Cusick, 1983, p. 115). It was marked by the following dynamics: (a) a nucleus of utilitarianism—or a "change . . . in the direction of more functional education" (Alexander et al., 1971, p. 197); (b) "a widespread bias against the so-called academic side of schoolwork" (Krug, 1964, p. 243)—a "general disrepute attached to the academic tradition" (p. 253), and the "explication of [an] anti-intellectual idea" (Krug, 1972, p. 316); (c) the acceptance of a "sharp conflict between the academic and the practical" (Krug, 1964, p. 244); (d) the "debase[ment of] the content of secondary education" (Cohen & Neufeld, 1981, p. 81); and (e) the substitution of good relations between teachers and students for academic content (Sedlak, Wheeler, Pullin, & Cusick, 1986; Sizer, 1984)—a situation in which "cordiality or 'liking and getting along with kids' was more important than any agreed-on body of knowledge"

(Cusick, 1983, p. 71). On both the academic and practical sides of the curriculum equation, these dynamics ensured that a number of course-taking patterns were woven deeply into the fabric of the comprehensive high school, all of which grew from the high schools' "forsaking their own distinctive function: intellectual training" (Cremin, 1961, p. 346) and, consequently, "relegat[ing] the school's role in intellectual development to an inferior status" (Kliebard, 1995, p. 224)—making "the strengthen[ing] of young minds . . . a secondary consideration" (Hampel, 1986, p. 17) and resulting in the development of a "low-achievement system" (Westbury, 1988, p. 81) that had "a corrosive effect on academic performance" (Cohen & Neufeld, 1981, p. 81).

On the academic front, all of these forces led to a limited and stunted role for traditional subject matter in the comprehensive high school—to "the dilution of academic standards" (Cohen & Neufeld, 1981, p. 86). To begin with, they produced a curricular portfolio heavily weighted with nonacademic courses and a subsequent shift away from academic course taking (Angus & Mirel, 1995; Latimer, 1958). They nurtured the growth of the belief that "the academic subjects were appropriate only for a narrow segment of the school population" (Kliebard, 1995, p. 209; see also Conant, 1959), with the resulting concentration of academic subjects in a small number of curricular tracks serving "only a limited proportion of students" (Dorn, 1996, p. 38). Finally, at the individual course level, these dynamics led to a radical redefinition of academic subjects and the infusion of courses with nonintellectual aims. On the practical side of the curricular ledger, prevailing forces resulted in the introduction of myriad new courses, especially vocational, personal-social, and practical subjects. They also helped to redefine traditional academic courses in terms of functional and social objectives. In forging the curriculum of the comprehensive high school in this fashion, "educators . . . managed to build a system of secondary schools in which the popular passion for education and the popular contempt for intellectual work were woven tightly together" (Powell et al., 1985, p. 273) and in which "a watered-down program aimed at the lowest common denominator of the entire population" (Herbst, 1996, p. 178) gained the high ground. They created "the American high school as an institution asking too little of its students and offering them too little" (Westbury, 1988, p. 292).

> A new system of secondary studies had been installed, in which a small minority of college-bound students were expected to pursue intellectually serious work whereas everyone else was taking courses explicitly designed for those less able, less willing, or less interested. American educators quickly built a system around the assumption that most students didn't have what it took to be serious about the great issues of human life, and that even if they had the wit, they had neither the will nor the futures that would support heavy-duty study. (Powell et al., 1985, p. 245)

Below we briefly track these curricular trends, providing first a numerical portrait and then a short description of the key patterns that define curricular expansion in the comprehensive high school.

In developing the numerical sketch, we rely on analyses provided by Koos (1927), Latimer (1958), Alexander et al. (1971), Sonnenberg (1993), Angus and Mirel (1995), and Herbst (1996). To the extent possible, we use 1910 as the date preceding the formation of the comprehensive high school. We start by examining academic coursework. Using percentage of high school students enrolled[2] as our frame, two discernable patterns emerge: (a) a decrease in overall enrollments across the academic domains and (b) a fairly dramatic decrease in enrollments in some of the traditional subjects within academic domains, accompanied by a sharp increase in participation in less academically vigorous subjects.

On the first issue—overall enrollments—we note that in 1910, fully 89.7% of the students were enrolled in mathematics classes. By 1949, only 55.0% of students were taking mathematics classes (Koos, 1927, p. 359; Latimer, 1958, p. 23). Other enrollments were: In foreign languages—84.1% in 1910 and 22.0% in 1949; in science—81.7% in 1910 and 54.1% in 1949; and in English—114.2% in 1910 and 103.1% in 1949. Only in the area of social studies was there an increase in enrollment, from 71.6% in 1910 to 99.4% in 1949 (Koos 1927, p. 359; Latimer, 1958, pp. 26, 28, 30, 33). In the final 30 years of the comprehensive high school (1950-1980), as determined by "percentage distribution of subject field enrollments," the total academic package remained fairly stable—59.3% in 1949 and 60.7% in 1982 (Angus & Mirel, 1995, p. 303).

Turning to within-domain analyses for the three areas of significant decline recorded above (mathematics, foreign language, and science), between 1910 and 1982, the high school experienced the following changes in enrollments.

Mathematics: algebra from 56.9% in 1910 to 26.8% in 1949 to 29.5% in 1982; geometry from 30.9% in 1910 to 12.8% in 1949 to 11.4% in 1982; trigonometry from 1.9% in 1910 to 2.0% in 1949 to 3.5% in 1982 (Herbst, 1996, p. 136; Latimer, 1958, p. 23; Sonnenberg, 1993, p. 50).

Foreign Languages: Latin from 49.0% in 1910 to 7.8% in 1949 to 1.1% in 1982; French from 9.9% in 1910 to 4.7% in 1949 to 6.6% in 1982; German from 23.7% in 1910 to 0.8% in 1949 to 2.1% in 1982; Spanish from 0.7% in 1910 to 8.2% in 1949 to 12.3% in 1982 (Alexander et al., 1971, p. 136; Latimer, 1958, p. 26; Sonnenberg, 1993, p. 50). At mid century, "nearly half of [the] . . . high schools offered no foreign languages at all" (Latimer, 1958, p. 131).

Science: physics from 14.6% in 1910 to 5.4% in 1949 to 1.0% in 1982; chemistry from 6.9% in 1910 to 7.6% in 1949 to 9.8% in 1982; biology from 1.1% in 1910 to 18.4% in 1949 to 23.2% in 1982; physiology from 15.3% in 1910 to 1.0% in 1949 to 1.2% in 1982; earth science from 21.0% in 1910 to 0.4% in 1949 to 0.2% in 1982 (Alexander et al., 1971, p. 196; Sonnenberg, 1993, p. 50).

Staying within domain analyses but moving on to the growth of less academically oriented courses, the following examples are illustrative: general mathematics from 0.0% in 1910 to 13.1% in 1949 to 21.7% in 1982; general science from 0.0% in 1910 to 20.8% in 1949 to 23.0% in 1982 (Latimer, 1958, pp. 23, 28). Although Algebra I enrollments increased 80% between 1922 and 1955 and geometry enrollments jumped 96%, participation in general mathematics rose 190%. Although chemistry enrollments increased 192% over the same time frame and participation in physics moved up 52%, general science enrollments skyrocketed 257% (Latimer, 1958, p. 94).

When the numerical spotlight is thrown onto the nonacademic areas of the curriculum, fairly dramatic patterns again emerge. In 1910, 11.0% of high school students enrolled in business education courses; by 1949, 58.8% did so (Latimer, 1958, p. 36). The percentages for other subjects are: vocational education—8.6% in 1910 and 27.9% in 1948 (p. 38); home economics—3.8% in 1910 and 24.3% in 1949 (p. 41); physical education—0.0% in 1910, 69.4% in 1949, and 59.0% in 1982 (Sonnenberg, 1993, p. 50); art—14.7% in 1910, 9.0% in 1949, and 24.2% in 1982 (p. 50). Agricultural enrollments fell about 30% between 1910 and 1982, whereas music enrollments fell nearly as much between 1949 and 1982 (p. 50).

We have already devoted considerable space to the forces underway in society in general and in the educational sphere specifically that explain the central curricular pattern described above—a decline in academic rigor with a concomitant expansion of the practical dimensions of schooling. Most critical was the implanting of two beliefs at the very point that the comprehensive high school was being formed in the service of more and more American youngsters attending school for longer and longer periods of time: (a) that high schools needed to assume a greatly expanded role, one that carried them well beyond their traditional focus on academic coursework, and (b) that most students were unsuited for or uninterested in academic endeavors—because of low ability, because they would not go to college, or because the life and the workplace for which they were being fitted did not require much in the way of intellectual skills.

In the academic sphere of the ballooning curriculum framework, a number of changes grew directly from the ideology just outlined. The first was a reduced place for academic subjects under the onslaught of demands for more practical courses:

> Each of the major life areas identified under social efficiency secured the support of a special group of schoolmen during the 20s. Thus some of the professionals worked mightily to promote the cause of citizenship in the school, others to advance the interests of family and homemaking, others to develop health education, others to ensure training for the worthy use of leisure, and many others indeed to increase the attention given to vocations. Thus a new competition for curricular place was added to the old one of the subject specialists. And, of course, both competitive systems competed with each other. (Willing, 1942, p. 56)

As the comprehensive high school took shape, the idea that academic content would be the mainstay of the expanding curricular portfolio was abandoned—as the scholarship of Latimer, Angus and Mirel, and Herbst confirm.

The increasing proportion of enrollments they [nonacademic subjects] attracted showed up significantly between 1910 and 1922, when the distribution and concentration of high school studies gave unmistakable evidence of decided changes. These changes became even more evident in the period between 1922 and 1949. (Latimer, 1958, p. 68)

It is quite clear that the proportion of the high school curriculum claimed by the academic subjects, whether measured by course enrollments or credits, declined significantly from the late 1920s until some time in the late 1960s or early 1970s. (Angus & Mirel, 1995, p. 309)

The proportion of students taking a general program increased from 12% in 1964 to 42% in 1979. (Herbst, 1996, p. 198)

These changes reflected the forging of a new curricular architecture within the modern high school:

The high schools' center of gravity changed radically and quickly. In the period 1906-11, nearly 60% of high school curricula were of the standard academic sort; two decades later the academic curricula had fallen to one third of all the curricula offered. Two thirds of the curricula were commercial, general, and trade. The academic sector of high school studies had been cut in half in only 20 years. (Powell et al., 1985, p. 252)

Traditional academic subjects were significantly reduced or jettisoned outright (Powell et al., 1985; Rothstein, 1994).

The "radical revision of academic requirements" (Powell et al., 1985, p. 249) in the comprehensive high school encompassed more than a reduced place for academic coursework in the burgeoning curricular framework. It also included a de-emphasis of academic content at both the macro (across the curriculum and within subject areas) and micro (within specific courses) levels of the curriculum. Across the curriculum, the following patterns of course taking reflect a reduction in academic focus: fewer students enrolling in higher level academic courses (e.g., a third year of a specific foreign language), fewer pupils completing sequences of academic courses (e.g., biology, chemistry, physics), more electives, and more participation in semester-length as opposed to full-year courses of study (Angus & Mirel, 1995; Cusick, 1983; Hampel, 1986; Latimer, 1958; Powell et al., 1985)—trends that reveal a truncated pattern of academic course-taking, in which students terminated their intellectual studies very early in their high school careers. The "dominant trend was toward less challenging classes" (Angus & Mirel, 1995, p. 316; see also Conant, 1959).

Within subject areas, the undercutting of academics was most noticeable in the substitution of general survey courses for more specific and more robust disciplinary offerings (Alexander et al., 1971, p. 197):

> Schools did away with the old system of requiring all students to take courses in specific academic subspecialties, like physics or history, that built on each other and led, at least in principle, to deeper command of a subject. Instead, most of the new students were given general survey courses. They might have had meat but got pabulum; not algebra but general math; not history but social studies; not physics and chemistry but general science. The new surveys were both introductory and terminal. They were not a first step toward deeper knowledge but a passing glance on the way to other, more practical matters. (Powell et al., 1985, p. 251)

Also prevalent was the creation of applied sections of traditional academic subjects, such as "applied chemistry" (Krug, 1964, p. 377), "practical physics" (Conant, 1959, p. 73), and "household chemistry [and] household physics" (Koos, 1927, p. 415). Remedial classes also began to overshadow more traditional academic offerings (Cusick, 1983; Herbst, 1996). For example, between 1961 and 1973, "remedial English grew at more than six times the rate of overall enrollments" (Powell et al., 1985, p. 295), as courses such as "Girl Talk," "What's Happening," and "Developmental English" (Cusick, 1983, pp. 45-46) displaced more traditional academic fare. And as Powell and his colleagues (1985) note, "These courses were not preliminaries to required English courses but replacements for them" (p. 295).

At the micro level, "courses were also undergoing internal transformations" (Kleibard, 1995, p. 110) as "changes [were] made to this same end in existing subjects" (Willing, 1942, pp. 76-77). Old "courses [were] broadened tremendously to ensure training in all of the major areas of human living" (Mackenzie, 1942, p. 84). Disciplinary standards gave way to those based on "commercial uses" (Kliebard, 1995, p. 110), and academic goals receded in favor of social and personal objectives. The "criterion of social reality and utility" (Willing, 1942, p. 76) moved front and center in the reformulation of traditional academic coursework: "The objectives of 'self-realization,' 'human relationships,' 'economic efficiency,' and 'civic responsibility' " (Carr, cited in Ravitch, 1983, p. 61) crowded out disciplinary aims in many academic courses.

To find a home in the rapidly expanding curricular framework, school subjects were called on "to prove their right to exist" (Krug, 1964, p. 336), employing the criteria outlined above—not an easy task for traditional academic classes. Two ways out from under this "cloud" (p. 318) presented themselves to high school educators, however. First, each academic subject was melted down and recast not in a disciplinary mold but in terms of experiences "meant to be good for something other than itself" (Krug, 1972, p. 82). In the reformulation, academic subject matter became a means to an end and was judged not on the basis of a match with the relevant disciplinary framework but "in terms of criteria outside the subjects themselves" (Krug, 1964, p. 389). Second, there was a widespread attempt "to introduce an element of practicality into the traditional humanist curriculum" (Kliebard, 1995, p. 111) while encouraging "secondary school people . . . [to] dig their wagon out from the academic sands that [had] covered the wheels" (Spears, 1941, p. 382). Subjects were "not designed primarily and solely for academic purposes, but that they may be used for the purpose of practical life" (Massachusetts Commission on Industrial and Technical Education, cited in Krug, 1964, p. 220). Academic subjects were reformed to be of "practical and immediate value" (Latimer, 1958, p. 76). They were made "easier, more practical, and more relevant" (Powell et al., 1985, p. 266). In the process, academic subjects experienced a "demotion from discipline to be acquired to skill to be performed at the level of one's ability" (Herbst, 1996, p. 146).

Under this new design,

> The subject-matter content and the skills that [had] so long been the backbone of the curriculum [were] shifted from ends to means. . . . English, for instance, in this view of learning, [was] not taught as a subject for its own sake, but the values it [contained might] be called up by the learning experience at hand. (Spears, 1941, p. 255)

English classes began to focus less on the teaching of the classics and more on such issues as "conducting polite conversations with one's friends" (Powell et al., 1985, p. 275) and "the ability to write a concise business letter" (Krug, 1964, p. 380). In general, English classes were to "be organized with reference to basic social needs rather than with reference to college-entrance requirements" (CRSE Committee on English, cited in Krug, 1964, p. 366). They were "reorganized to relate 'literature to life' " (Angus & Mirel, 1995, p. 302) as "English literature in the high school began to make good its claim as a paramount means of educating for leisure" (Willing, 1942, p. 75).

During the early stages of the development of the modern high school, curriculum analysts concluded that mathematics and "science as taught in schools [were] not related to life" (Krug, 1964, p. 369). For example, it was argued that "algebra and geometry as traditionally taught . . . were intolerable failures and out of keeping with the legitimate demands of the time" (Krug, 1964, p. 94). Educators were quick to respond to the critique. In mathematics, practical and business applications were infused into the curriculum. In both mathematics and science, "material introduced from consideration of theory rather than intelligent practical mastery" (CRSE Committee on Mathematics, cited in Krug, 1964, p. 351) was de-emphasized. For example, "future housewives [were] taught how to sew, prepare meals, and keep house, bringing science and mathematics usefully down to earth for girls" (Powell et al., 1985, p. 275).

The domain of social studies began with the construction of the comprehensive high school as government and history courses that characterized secondary education prior to 1900 but gave way to new subjects highlighting the seven aims of the *Cardinal Principles* (Angus & Mirel, 1995): "History, for example, was gradually . . . replaced, or at least supplemented, by other social studies, some of which were aimed directly at the development of efficient citizenship" (Kliebard, 1995, p. 108). Many of these newer courses such as "high school psychology [were] decidedly more social than scientific" (Hampel, 1986, p. 48). The "culturally accumulative" (Spears, 1941,

p. 205) and "the old academic study" (Kliebard, 1995, p. 110) receded in the face of the goal "of direct[ing] youth toward the democratic way of life" (Spears, 1941, p. 205). "The bodies of knowledge conception of the social studies" (p. 193) were dismantled. The curriculum as "a program of citizenship training" (p. 193) emerged from the rubble. The central "objective of the social studies program [became] training in living with others" (p. 200), and "the primary aim of teaching history was to make good citizens" (Krug, 1972, p. 81).

Turning to the topic of curricular expansion from the viewpoint of the non-academic courses, three lines dominate the facade of the comprehensive high school superstructure—vocational material, personal-social courses, and traditional extra-curricular subjects:

> In 1910, there were proportionately more students studying foreign languages or mathematics or science or English or social studies than were studying all of the nonacademic subjects combined. . . . The seven nonacademic fields had the equivalent of 28%. . . . All of the subjects in the seven fields [had] the equivalent of 130% of the total high school enrollment. . . . [In 1949] enrollments in nonacademic subjects . . . were now equivalent to 211% of the high school enrollments and considerably larger than those in mathematics, science, and foreign languages combined. (Latimer, 1958, pp. 118-119)

Given the conditions that we have been describing, especially demands for practical education that would fit youngsters to occupations, it is hardly surprising that "many schools understood the spirit of curriculum revision as a mandate to expand vocational education" (Ravitch, 1983, p. 56). In many ways, vocational education came to be viewed as the answer to what many educators saw as "an overly bookish program which overemphasized the accumulation of useless knowledge" (Cremin, 1961, p. 48). Designed to meet the needs of: (a) "unscholarly pupils" (Krug, 1964, p. 227) and the "concrete-minded students" (Spring, 1990, p. 213), who were thought to be ill-served by the traditional academic curriculum; (b) young women who were headed to lives as homemakers and who made up the majority of high school students (Herbst, 1996); (c) "certain social and economic classes of society" (Krug, 1964, p. 228)—the masses, if you will; (d) "the 95% of students who did not intend to go to college" (Herbst, 1996, p. 128); and (e) all students who, it was believed, would benefit from "occupational adjustment" (Spears, 1941, p. 241) and "practical fitting . . . for their calling" (Spring, 1990, p. 213), vocational education became "the most successful curricular innovation of the 20th century" (Kliebard, 1995, p. 124).

What is important to hold in mind here is that "vocational education represented a revolution in the role of schooling" (Spring, 1990, p. 211) and that "it gave secondary schooling a new mission" (Herbst, 1996, p. 139)—"developments whose consequences are still being played out" (p. 140) in the comprehensive high school. Vocational training "challenged centuries of tradition" (p. 117) and "broke in fundamental ways with what until then had been a common Western tradition of secondary schooling as exclusively a general training" (p. 139). It "supplied the crucial element that enabled the comprehensive American high school to usher in a new age of secondary education" (p. 139):

> A movement that had begun as a simple response to a perceived demand for practical education and as an attempt to shore up and enlarge the role of secondary schooling and the power of its managers had radically transformed conceptions of secondary education. It undermined the high school's historical mission to ground all of its students in the basic skills of the liberal arts. . . . It served as a catalyst to redefine the meaning and to redesign the institutions of public secondary education. (pp. 205-206)

The introduction of vocational education had a profound effect on the high school curriculum. It pulled time, energy, and focus away from academics (Cusick, 1983; Murphy, Hull, & Walker, 1987) and reinforced the gap between academic and practical education that we described earlier (Spring, 1990). It "opened the door for a class-based education" (Spring, 1990, p. 215) and forced colleges, however reluctantly, to recognize vocational courses as part of their entrance requirements (Krug, 1964; Willing, 1942). The most important legacy, however, has been vocational education's

> Effect on the American curriculum as a whole. Preparation for a particular occupational role, including attending college as a form of occupation, has permeated the justifications for virtually all school subjects. These justifications, in turn, profoundly affect the selection of materials to be studied and the manner in which they are organized for instruction. (Kliebard, 1995, p. 129)

The vocational education movement also added considerable impetus to the development of the differentiated curricular framework being implanted at the founding of the modern high school, or, in the words of Wraga (1994), it "expand[ed] the specializing function of the comprehensive high school" (p. 14). As we documented in the earlier numerical analyses, the favored device of high school educators "was to add vocational and semivocational courses of study to the already overloaded course structure of the general high school" (Krug, 1964, p. 237). In so doing, it provided "extended opportunities for work in trades, agriculture, [and] home economics" (Cremin, 1961, p. 306).

Initiatives to infuse vocational content into the general curriculum and to bundle together practical content into specific vocational courses were augmented by efforts to expand the curriculum with an assortment of personal and social courses that downplayed mastery of academic content in favor of "socio-personal adjustment" (Ravitch, 1983, p. 73) and a focus on "social . . . matters and personal development" (Powell et al., 1985, p. 303). Two interconnecting forces buttressed this dimension of curricular proliferation: (a) the growing commitment to the expanded aims of secondary education outlined in the *Cardinal Principles* and (b) the developing belief that the educational program should be "designed to serve any and all needs of children" (Cremin, 1961, p. 65). Based on a belief "that schools had new functions arising from changes in home, community, and church" (Krug, 1972, p. 227) and on a societal mandate for schools to assume "full responsibility to train not only their students' intellects but also their social . . . selves" (Sizer, 1964, p. 201), "an expanded view of education" (Cremin, 1961, p. 65) took form—the view of education as "a custodial agency for all youth" (Krug, 1972, p. 311). This, in turn, meant high schools "assuming responsibility for all the needed education of adolescents that [was] not being otherwise provided" (Odell, 1939, p. 150), particularly, "education functions classically assigned to home and neighborhood" (Cremin, 1955, p. 300), and a "broadening of the program and function of the school to include direct concern for health . . . and the quality of family and community life" (Cremin, cited in Wraga, 1994, p. 28).

In the most general sense, this expansion helped produce a reconceptualization of schools from places in which young people gathered to be educated to "schools as social or community centers" (Krug, 1964, p. 255)—"a shift in purpose to social service" (p. 258), in which each school would become "dedicated to the improvement of community life in all its forms" (Cremin, 1955, p. 299). Turning specifically to the burgeoning conception of curriculum, expansion took a variety of forms. It resulted in the addition of new personnel in schools, for example, doctors, nurses, and psychologists, and of new functions, such as providing bathing for youngsters (Cremin, 1961) and "the feeding of hungry school children" (Krug, 1964, p. 263). It also fostered the infusion of subject matter "aimed at the development of skills and attitudes needed for cooperative effort both in school and in society" (p. 259). It meant that issues such as "manners, cleanliness, dress, and the simple business of getting along in the classroom . . . [were] taught more insistently and self-consciously than ever" (Cremin, 1961, p. 72).

Socially grounded curricular expansion also threw the spotlight on the unifying function of the curriculum in new ways. General education courses that mixed students "with different abilities and different vocational interests" (Conant, 1959, p. 74) in the pursuit of social aims appeared in secondary schools between the two World Wars (Kliebard, 1995) and became a defining feature of the comprehensive high school (Conant, 1959). The homeroom period or advisory class was introduced as "an integrating force" (Spears, 1941, p. 18) and "a center for social activity" (Spring, 1990, p. 219)—"a time and a place for teaching personal-social matters, and other topics such as school spirit and citizenship" (Krug, 1972, p. 138) to "a cross section of the school in terms of ability and vocational interest" (Conant, 1959, p. 74). The assembly was rejuvenated and "drawn into the doctrine of social aims" (p. 139). Social how-to courses with titles like "Personal Development," "Social Personal Relationships" (Kliebard, 1995, p. 187), and "Basic Living" (p. 220) began to cover more and more of the curricular landscape and move closer and closer to the center of importance and activity (Kliebard, 1995). So, too, did functional classes. For example, by midcentury, "physical education was the second leading subject matter field in the high school curriculum" (Latimer, 1958, p. 46), enrolling 69.4% of secondary school students, up from 5.7% in 1922 (Sonnenberg, 1993, p. 50). By 1960, fully half of all ninth-grade students were enrolled in a class on typing (Alexander et al., 1971).

Finally, the rapid development of the nonacademic curriculum in the comprehensive high school can be traced to the "granting of credit for courses that were once noncredit or even extracurricular" (Angus & Mirel, 1995, p. 320). Under this development, "activities once offered purely on a voluntary, noncredit, after-school basis [became] credit courses included in the program of studies" (Alexander et al., 1971, p. 194). According to Spears (1941), "the story of the extracurricular movement is one of phenomenal growth" (p. 151) in the evolution of the comprehensive high school, or, as Cremin (1961) characterized it, "along with the proliferation . . . of the formal curriculum, there came a concomitant expansion of extracurricular activities" (p. 306). For our purposes here, three aspects of this proliferation are most salient. First, as was the case with most of the other nonacademic growth, the development of extracurricular subject matter represented an orientation toward the practical and "a revolt against the traditional curriculum . . . in favor of life activities nearer . . . here-and-now existence" (Spears, 1941, p. 154). These experiences aligned particularly well with the broadened goals of the *Cardinal Principles,* especially in "contributing to the unification of the school and the preparation of students for participation in a cooperative democracy" (Spring, 1990, p. 208). Second, as time went on, these extracurricular experiences began to be "accepted as an important part of the total program of secondary education" (Anderson & Gruhn, 1962, p. 38). "They came to be regarded as more than desirable adjuncts to the academic program, as of equal, possibly even greater importance" (Krug, 1972, p. 136). Third, they started to encroach on the traditional school program as "what were formerly school activities and sports [were] turned into credit classes" (Cusick, 1983, p. 55). This in itself was a two-step process. To begin with, they were "incorporated into the regular school day with special periods" (p. 137). Next, through the extension of credit, "transplantings [were] made from the extracurricular to the curricular field" (Spears, 1941, p. 157).

> Schools were showing a marked disposition to incorporate them more closely with what was still regarded as the real curriculum. Many were allowing them to operate in school time and to count in some fashion or other toward the requirements for graduation. (Willing, 1942, p. 74)

For example, most courses "in music, dramatics, speech, journalism, and physical education came into the program of studies as extracurricular activities" (Alexander et al., 1971, p. 208). Eventually, "the line of demarcation" (Spears, 1941, p. 155) between the two areas became blurred.

The Changing Face of High School: 1980 →

> *Another way to put the point is to say that most of the foundation work of decent secondary education still remains to be done, seven or eight decades after the system began to take shape. High schools seem unlikely to make marked improvement, especially for the many students and teachers now drifting around the malls, until there is a much clearer sense of what is most important to teach and learn, and why and how it can best be done.*
>
> —Powell et al. (1985, p. 306)

> *Late 20th-century high schools deserve a more appropriate purpose than a warmed-over version of principles promulgated in 1918.*
>
> —Sizer (1984, p. 84)

> *It is time for a reformulation of the purposes and means of secondary education for youth of senior high school age in the 21st century.*
>
> —Herbst (1996, p. 208)

A central premise of our work over the last decade is that public education is in the process of being dramatically overhauled—that a change parallel to the one that led to the birth of the comprehensive high school at the dawn of the 20th century is underway as we move into the postindustrial world of the 21st century. The dimensions of that change and the difficulties of the challenge were foreshadowed by Trow (1961):

> Secondary education in the United States began as an elite preparatory system; during its great years of growth, it became a mass terminal system; and it is now having to make a second painful transition on its way to becoming a mass preparatory system. But this transition is a good deal more difficult than the first, because while the first involved the *creation* of the necessary institutions, the second is requiring the *transformation* of a huge existing institutional complex. (p. 154)

Similarly, Powell and his colleagues (1985) have documented that the long series of reforms throughout the 20th century have not led to a significant overhaul of secondary education but have been accommodated "within the organization and ideology that were adopted seven or eight decades earlier" (p. 301). Our position is that the high school of the future will be formed to a significant degree by the changing environment in which education operates and by emerging knowledge about appropriate models of schooling for the 21st century.

The Changing Nature of the Educational Environment

The schools have to operate in an environment of declining social and political cohesion. (Consortium on Productivity in the Schools, 1995, p. 3)

About the middle of the 20th century, we entered the postindustrial age, a new stage in the human evolution. This new age requires new thinking . . . and a new vision of education. (Banathy, 1988, p. 51)

As has been the case throughout our history, the forces propelling the reformation of schooling and the redefinition of high school education are located primarily in the educational environment—in the web of economic, social, and political dynamics in which the educational system is ensconced. Each of these dynamics is outlined below.

Economic Forces

On the economic front, there is a shift from an industrial to a service economy. (Murphy, 1998, p. 159)

Over the last 15 years, the defining element of the economic environment for schooling has changed—from a sense of crises in the economy and from a sense of deterioration of the nation's well-being that dominated the reform reports of the 1980s to a focus on preparedness for the global economy of the 21st century.

One side of the problem discussed by critics is the belief that systems that hold steady in today's world are actually in decline. Whereas others see stability, these critics see "increasing obsolescence of the education provided by most United States schools" (Murnane & Levy, 1996, p. 6). The other side of the productivity issue raised by these reviewers is the claim that because of the changing nature of the economy, as outlined above, the level of outcomes that students need to reach must be significantly increased.

Today's schools look much like Ford in 1926. The products they produce—student achievement levels—are not worse than they were 20 years ago; in most respects they are slightly better. But in those 20 years, the job market has changed radically. Just as the Model T that was good enough in 1921 was not good enough in 1926, the education that was adequate for high-wage employers in 1970 is no longer adequate today. (Murnane & Levy, 1996, p. 77)

Reviewers find that the schools are not meeting this new standard for productivity. They argue that "American schools are not providing students with the learning that they will need to function effectively in the 21st Century" (Consortium on Productivity in the Schools, 1995, p. 3). The press to redefine the educational system to address these concerns is palpable.

Social Forces

> The dismantling of the welfare state is on the agenda everywhere. (Dahrendorf, 1995, p. 26)

Understanding of education for the 21st century is also formed by the documented need to address the changing social dynamics of American society and to repair an ever widening tear in the social fabric of the nation. The first issue is concerned with a reweaving of the social fabric—with demographic shifts that threaten "our national standard of living and democratic foundations" (Carnegie Council on Adolescent Development, 1989, p. 27) and that promise to overwhelm schools as they are now constituted. Minority enrollment in United States schools is rising as is the proportion of less advantaged youngsters. There is a rapid increase in the number of students whose primary language is not English. The traditional two-parent family, with one parent employed and the other at home to care for the children, has become an anomaly.

The second force might best be described as an unraveling of the social fabric. The number of social ills confronting society appears to be expanding exponentially. Ever increasing numbers of families are falling into poverty. As the gap between the rich and the poor grows, many are sinking even deeper into poverty. Children are disproportionately represented among the ranks of the poor, and the number of children in poverty—currently one in five—continues to grow. At the same time, we are bombarded with news of alarming increases in measures of dysfunction and ill health among youth and their families: unemployment, unwanted pregnancies, alcohol and drug abuse, and violence. Indexes of physical, mental, and moral well-being are declining. The stock of social capital is decreasing as well.

As with the economy, analysts believe that schools offer a solution strategy to confront these forces and to alleviate accompanying problems. Once again, there is considerable pressure to address environmental dynamics by reshaping the educational system, especially the comprehensive high school that defined secondary education for most of the 20th century.

Political Forces

> The political . . . concepts that have traditionally given legitimacy to government actions have come under growing criticism. (President's Commission on Privatization, 1988, p. 229)

At the same time, new bundles of ideas are emerging in the political environment that are both fueling and shaping our understandings of schooling. One of the key elements involves recalibration of the locus of control, based on a reconfiguration of functions among levels of government. Originally called *democratic localism,* it has more recently come to be known simply as localization or more commonly, as decentralization. However it is labeled, it represents a backlash against centralized and bureaucratic forms of education organizations. A second emerging political force can best be thought of as a recasting of democracy, a replacement of representative governance with more populist conceptions, especially direct democracy. A third shift encompasses a rebalancing of the governance equation in favor of lay citizens while diminishing the power of the state and (in some ways) educational professionals. This line of ideas emphasizes parental empowerment by recognizing their historic rights in the lives of their children. Choice is a fourth element of the reconfigured political environment, one that shares a good deal of space with the concepts of localism, direct democracy, and lay control. Finally, it seems likely that something that might best be thought of as democratic professionalism will form a central part of the infrastructure of the political landscape in the postindustrial world. What this means is the gradual decline of control by elite professionals—by professional managers and more recently by teacher unions—that characterized education for most of the 20th century (Murphy, 1999, 2000).

Rebuilding the Learning Infrastructure

From these collective efforts emerges a vision of education quite unlike "the center of production" . . . image that . . . shaped schooling throughout the industrial age. (Murphy, 1992a, p. 114)

Purpose

After visiting schools from coast to coast, we are left with the distinct impression that high schools lack a clear and vital mission. They are unable to find common purposes or establish educational priorities that are widely shared. They seem unable to put it all together. The institution is adrift. (Boyer, 1983, p. 63)

If educators could agree on . . . purposes, they would be better armed for debating education and for deciding that some things cannot be done because others are more important. In addition, they would be in a position to think seriously about pedagogy. (Powell et al., 1985, p. 307)

The theme of the 1980s rang clear and loud: Bring the academic standard of students graduating from American high schools back to that of 90 years ago, the years of the Committee of Ten report. (Herbst, 1996, p. 198)

As we have already chronicled, while the comprehensive high school took form and expanded, goals for secondary education multiplied. What had been, at its inception, an institution charged primarily with training the mind had over time "accumulated purposes like barnacles on a weathered ship" (Boyer, 1983, p. 57). As the portfolio of aims grew, the academic function moved down several notches in the goals hierarchy and in the process became fuzzier and more circumscribed. By the dawn of the technological age, the high school had become "a troubled institution" (p. 9), and school people had "lost their bearings" (Herbst, 1996, p. 200).

Over the last 20 years, under an onslaught of criticism about the dysfunctional dynamics of the comprehensive high school and its less than salutary influence on students (Powell et al., 1985; Sedlak et al., 1986; Sizer, 1984), reformers have succeeded in reenergizing the academic mission of secondary education. Educators in the past have responded to demands for academic excellence in ways that have interfered little with the basic design features of the comprehensive high school. As a matter of fact, they have been able to use some design features—differentiated curriculum, for example—"to subvert or contain the reforms" (Angus & Mirel, 1995, p. 319). Or as Powell and his colleagues (1985) nicely phrase it, whereas the academic reformers got some of what they wanted, "the schools managed to arrange these bargains within the organization and ideology that were adopted seven or eight decades earlier" (p. 301). There are some suggestions and emerging evidence, however, that a reformulation of purpose that highlights academics will be much more systemic than has been the case in the past—that returning academic training to center stage may lead to a redefinition of the architecture of the comprehensive high school. As Angus and Mirel (1995) argue, if this academic press takes root and

> . . . reaches more deeply into the ranks of high school administrators, counselors, and teachers, and continues to influence course-taking patterns, it will constitute by far the most significant shift in educational values and behaviors since the 1930s. It will also represent the ultimate vindication of the Committee of Ten. (p. 319)

Theories of Learning

> The development of the comprehensive high school took place in a milieu very different from the present and was responsive to social assumptions about the distribution of ability and aptitude very different from those of the present. (Westbury, 1988, p. 307)

> The advocates of adventurous instruction may be working near the beginning of a great, slow change in conceptions of knowledge, learning and teaching. (Cohen, 1988, p. 22)

There is some evidence that a more robust understanding of the education-production function is beginning to be translated into new ways of thinking about learning and teaching. The strongest theoretical and disciplinary influence on education—behavioral psychology—is being pushed off center stage by constructivist psychology and newer sociological perspectives on learning—in much the same way that behavioral psychology pushed mind psychology aside at the dawn of the 20th century. This shift toward "research on cognition as a basis for understanding how people learn casts an entirely different perspective on how the schooling process should be redesigned" (Hutchins, 1988, p. 47). Underlying this change are radically different ways of thinking about the educability of children. Those who are at the forefront of transforming schools that were historically organized to produce results consistent with the normal curve, to sort youth into the various strata needed to fuel the economy, see education being transformed around a new definition of equal opportunity for learners—equal access to high-status knowledge.

At the center of this newly forming vision about schooling for tomorrow are fairly radical changes in assumptions about intelligence and knowledge. Intelligence is viewed as multifaceted and learnable rather than as unitary, innate, and fixed. The prevailing conception of knowledge—the view that "knowledge can be assumed to be an external entity existing independently of human thought and action and hence, something about which one can be objective" (Fisher, 1990, p. 82)—"dominant for so long in classroom practice, has begun to be critically examined in a new way" (p. 84). A new view, one that holds that knowledge is internal and subjective, that it "depends on the values of the persons working with it and the context within which that work is conducted" (p. 82), is receiving serious consideration. Thus the new educational design considers "knowledge not as somehow in the possession of the teacher, waiting to be transmitted to the student or to be used to treat the students' problems but as mutually constructed by teacher and student to make sense of human experience" (Petrie, 1990, pp. 17-18). Learning is seen as a social phenomenon, and considerable attention is devoted to the social origins of cognition.

Curriculum

> Our analysis of the many reports on student course-taking has indicated that the grip of this educational ideology may have weakened since the mid-1980s. Serious attention is being given to the old idea that all students should follow the same curriculum, whatever their career goals may be, and that to fail to require this is to deny equal educational opportunity. Supporters of this notion do not deny that there are educationally relevant differences between individuals in interests and abilities. But they argue that such differences should challenge educators to explore a host of alternative instructional methods and approaches rather than adopt the long-standing policy of split-level education. (Angus & Mirel, 1995, p. 320)

A constructivist philosophy of learning was being put forth as a way to rebuild high school curriculum in the last part of the 20th century in much the same way that social efficiency theories were employed to form the curricular frameworks of the comprehensive high school in early- to mid-20th century. Vigorous attacks on differentiated curriculum and the practice of tracking are accompanied by calls for a core curriculum for all students. Reformers involved in the redesign of secondary education are also fighting to restore the academic backbone to the high school curriculum. They promulgate an alternative image of a core technology that (a) reflects an interdisciplinary vision, (b) features a curriculum that is more vertical and less horizontal—that covers fewer topics in more depth, (c) emphasizes robust standards and highlights a higher order of thinking skills for all students, (d) spotlights the use of technology and original-source documents in lieu of textbooks, (e) and underscores the use of a broadened evaluation system that highlights authentic measures of assessment.

In the constructivist-anchored high school, a learner-centered pedagogy replaces the more traditional model of teacher-centered instruction. The model of the teacher as the *sage on a stage,* the model in which instructors are viewed as specialists in content who possess relevant knowledge that they transmit to students through telling, is replaced by an approach in which teaching is more of a guiding function. The student becomes the primary actor—the constructor of knowledge, if you will. Substantive conversation replaces conventional classroom talk and didactic instruction. Analysts believe that in the 21st century, high schools will be conceived of as knowledge-work organizations, learning will be seen as the construction of understanding, and teaching will be viewed as facilitating this development. Students are seen as "producers of knowledge" and teachers "as managers of learning experiences" (Hawley, 1989, p. 23). The focus is on learning, not on the delivery system.

The Evolving Nature of Organization and Governance

Organization

> Existing structures for schooling cannot produce the kind of changes necessary to make a substantial difference. (Mojkowski & Fleming, 1988, p. 1)

In recent years, reformers have also begun to call into question the operant organizational and management models and structures of America's high schools. There is a growing sentiment that the existing administrative structure is failing, that the reformers of the last century have produced "bureaucratic arteriosclerosis, insulation from parents and patrons, and the low productivity of a declining industry protected as a quasi monopoly" (Tyack, 1993, p. 3). It is increasingly being concluded that the existing bureaucratic system of administration is incapable of addressing the problems of the secondary education system.

In particular, the current bureaucratic system of management and governance has come under sharp criticism from: (a) those who argue that schools are so covered with bureaucratic sediment that initiative, creativity, and professional judgment have all been paralyzed and the likely success of reforms has been neutralized; (b) critics who maintain that the "bureaucratic management practices have been causing unacceptable distortions in educational process" (Wise, 1989, p. 301), that they are paralyzing

American secondary education and interfering with learning; (c) analysts who believe that bureaucracy is counterproductive to the needs and interests of educators within the schools; (d) critics who suggest that bureaucratic management is inconsistent with the sacred values of education, who question "fundamental ideological issues pertaining to bureaucracy's meaning in a democratic society" (Campbell, Fleming, Newell, & Bennion, 1987, p. 73); (e) scholars who view bureaucracy as a form of operation that inherently forces attention away from the core technology of schooling; (f) reform proponents who hold that the existing organizational structure of schools is neither sufficiently flexible nor sufficiently robust to meet the needs of high school students in a postindustrial society; and (g) analysts who believe that the rigidities of bureaucracy impede the ability of parents and citizens to govern and reform schooling.

This tremendous attack on the bureaucratic infrastructure of schools has led to demands to develop alternative methods of operating that are grounded on new values and principles. Concomitantly, new forms of school organization and management are emerging. The basic organizing and management principles of schooling are giving way to more proactive attempts to govern educational systems. In addition, a new "social physics" (Bell, cited in Campbell et al., 1987, p. 26) that promises to significantly change the nature of social relationships in schools is emerging. The hierarchical, bureaucratic organizational structures that have defined schools since the onslaught of scientific management at the inception of the comprehensive high school are giving way to more decentralized and more professionally controlled systems that create new designs for school management. In these new postindustrial organizations, there are important shifts in roles, relationships, and responsibilities: Traditional patterns of relationships are altered, authority flows are less hierarchical, role definitions are both more general and more flexible, leadership is connected to competence for needed tasks rather than to formal position, and independence and isolation are replaced by cooperative work. Furthermore, the structural orientation implanted during the reign of scientific management is being overshadowed by a focus on the human element. The operant goal is no longer maintenance of the organizational infrastructure but rather the development of human resources. Learning climates and organizational adaptivity are being substituted for the more traditional emphasis on uncovering and applying the one best model of performance. The changed role definitions applied to these new high school designs, for example, not principal as manager but principal as facilitator and not teacher as worker but teacher as leader, nicely portray these fundamental revisions in our understanding of social relationships and in our views of organizations and conceptions of management. They reveal a reorientation in transformed secondary schools from control to empowerment.

Institutional Level

> Furthermore, the best avenue for reform is one that replaces the bureaucratic and democratic control of the school with elements of market control. (Beers & Ellig, 1994, p. 21)

> During the latter part of the 1980s . . . reformers advanced a case for public schools of choice based largely on free-market idealism. Under this scheme, the comprehensive high school would disintegrate further as parents sent their children to narrow specialty schools. (Wraga, 1994, p. xv)

Most analysts of the institutional level of schooling—the interface of the school with its larger (generally immediate) environment—have concluded that the public monopoly approach to education led to "the belief in almost complete separation of schools from the community and, in turn, discouragement of local community involvement in decision making related to the administration of schools" (Burke, 1992, p. 33). Indeed, a considerable body of literature suggests that one of the major functions of bureaucracy is the buffering of the school from the environment, especially from parents and community members (Meyer & Rowan, 1975).

Many chroniclers of the changing institutional arrangements envision the demise of schooling as a sheltered government monopoly heavily controlled by professionals. In its stead, they forecast the emergence of a system of secondary schooling and improvement designs driven by economic and political forces that substantially increase the saliency of the market. Embedded in this conception are a number of interesting dynamics, all of which gain force from a realignment of power and influence between professional educators and consumers. The most important is that the traditional dominant relationship—with professional educators on the playing field and parents on the sidelines acting as cheerleaders or agitators or, more likely, passive spectators—is replaced by rules that advantage the consumer.

Four elements of this emerging portrait of transformed governance for consumers are most prevalent: choice in selecting a school, voice in school governance, partnership in the education of their children, and enhanced membership in the school community. Central to all four is a blurring of the boundaries between the home and the school, between the school and the community, and between professional staff and lay constituents. Collectively, these components lend support to the grassroots political and competitive economic arguments that support the calls for more locally controlled organizations and to market-anchored conceptions of secondary education.

Summary

In this chapter, we completed our brief analysis of the history of secondary education. Specifically, we examined the construction of the comprehensive high school that defined secondary education for nearly all of the 20th century. We saw how the scaffolding for the superstructure was built up from the foundations poured in the early 1900s—foundations that we explored in the previous chapter. In particular, we exposed the learning infrastructure that formed the core of the design known as the comprehensive high school, revealing the purposes, learning theories, and curriculum patterns that were welded into that framework.

We also highlighted forces that may be reshaping the high school as we move into the 21st century. Our argument is that major social, economic, and political forces are at work that suggest a reformulation of secondary education. At the same time, new perspectives on learning and organizations are being proposed as principles to be employed in developing blueprints for the post comprehensive-era high school. We closed the chapter by examining some of these emerging principles.

Notes

1. Although we cannot attend to the issue in detail, it should be noted that a plethora of critics over the years have addressed the negative aspects of curriculum differentiation and tracking. The major complaints are that curricular differentiation: produces dysfunctional fragmentation; leads to the segregation of students by race and class, and sometimes gender; promotes the inappropriate labeling of students; and results in a much reduced educational experience for certain groups of students (Oakes, 1985).

2. If one focuses on *percentage of total youth of high school age* enrolled in academic subjects, then the picture is much brighter than that provided by looking at *percentage of high school students enrolled*. Since 1900 when only 8% of the high school population attended high school until 1950 when nearly two-thirds (64%) were participating, the numbers have skyrocketed—from 3.3% to 60.9% in English, from 6.2% to 12.8% in foreign languages, from 7.2% to 33.5% in mathematics, and from 5.2% to 43.5% in social studies (Stiles, McCleary, & Turnbaugh, 1962, pp. 215-216).

PART II

The Classroom Dynamics of Engaged Learning and Teaching

One area that has received considerable attention in the secondary reform literature is the concept of personalization of high schools, and the empirical literature supports a strong connection between personalization of the high school learning environment and student success (Bryk & Driscoll, 1988; Lee, Bryk, & Smith, 1993; Louis & Miles, 1990; Meier, 1995; Newmann, 1996; Sizer, 1984).

In this section, we examine dynamics that affect high-performance relationships between teachers and learners. In Chapter 4, "High Expectations," we follow paths of socially constructed expectations for achievement that wash through high school classrooms, strongly affecting both learner and teacher. In Chapter 5, "Personal Support," we examine the dynamics that affect creation of school community, a source of strong personal support for both learner and teacher. Finally, in Chapter 6, "Academic Autonomy," we explore the role of the individual, examining teacher and student academic autonomy as essential to successful learning and teaching at the high school level.

Together, these three dimensions create an empirical portrait of effective teaching and learning that is similar to effective, high-performance parenting (Steinberg, 1996; Steinberg, Elmen, & Mounts, 1989; Steinberg & Silverberg, 1986; Steinberg, Lamborn, Dornbusch, & Darling, 1992). In combination, these powerful dynamics—high expectations, personal support, and academic autonomy—inform our understanding of effective teaching and learning at the secondary level.

4

High Expectations

To an important extent, people tend to live up (or down) to what is expected of them.

—Rutter, Maughan, Mortimore, Ouston,
and Smith (1979, p. 187)

The importance of teachers' holding high expectations for student achievement is well established in the literature (Rutter et al., 1979; Wilson & Corcoran, 1988), and "a certain amount of stress in the form of high expectations (combined with . . . other factors) serves to improve performance" (Fullan, 1988, p. 11). Thus "in a school with high levels of academic press, all students are expected to meet high academic standards and to devote substantial effort to their schoolwork. This message is delivered clearly and consistently to students by all faculty and staff" (Lee, Smith, & Croninger, 1995, p. 5).

Although there is agreement that expecting students to achieve at high levels is fundamental to learning, the literature varies in regard to teacher ability to affect achievement. Socially and politically, a sea of strong demands washes daily through high school classrooms. Pressures from parents, community, school, and district stream through classrooms, providing teachers with a turbulent backdrop of conflicting demands, power inequalities, changing innovations, and resource dependencies (Fullan, 1988; Louis & Miles, 1990; Metz, 1990a; Page, 1991; Sedlak et al., 1986). If all students are to achieve at high levels, who is responsible and where is the locus of control?

Societal, Individual, and Collective Forces Affect Expectations for High Achievement

According to one perspective, secondary teachers routinely straddle many worlds and juggle many priorities as "brokers who construct educational arrangements that acknowledge the goals of society, the characteristics of the students with whom they work, their professional judgment, and the character of the workplace context" (McLaughlin, 1993, p. 98). This view focuses on societal demands and argues that external pressure limits teacher ability to demand high achievement (McNeil, 1986; Sedlak et al., 1986).

Another line of work describes instructional excellence as an individual phenomenon that occurs—or fails to occur—despite context. "One could instruct, one could not instruct; it was up to the individual teacher to decide how to conduct himself or herself in the class" (Cusick, 1983, p. 56). As individuals, teachers make "decisions about how to respond to the students in their classrooms" (McLaughlin, 1993, p. 98), and the resulting interplay between teacher and student creates "rising or falling spirals of expectations" (Wilson & Corcoran, 1988, p. 100).

Still another view emphasizes the strength of teachers collectively and the role of school as community in supporting high achievement (Bryk & Driscoll, 1988). "A more communal environment . . . help[s] foster the types of social organization that we now see as critical to helping high school students learn more" (Lee et al., 1995, p. 11), and there is indication that "perhaps the teachers' competence and professional commitments to high intellectual quality for all students push[es] . . . schools to adopt [changed] organizational features" (Newmann & Wehlage, 1995, p. 15). "This collective perspective has to permeate the entire process of organizational development to create schools that can focus on learners" (Darling-Hammond, 1997b, p. 50).

Together these forces—the societal, the individual, and the collective—merge in the act of learning and teaching, as powerful societal demands flow through classrooms, and people respond, both individually and collectively. The act of holding high expectations for student achievement emerges from the confluence, a churning amalgamation of the attraction of engagement and the press of demand. As we follow this ebb and flow of political demand and human response that is the heart of student achievement, an indelible picture emerges: "The shear magnitude of the teaching task is immense" (Little, 1990, p. 189).

In this chapter, we weave a dynamic portrait of the incredible complexity of holding high expectations, creating a picture of engagement and motivation in the secondary classrooms. First, we develop an understanding of teacher engagement in the work of learning and teaching, regardless of context, as the linchpin of high achievement. We then explore student motivation to engage in learning. Finally, we explore the dynamics of teacher engagement and student motivation within the context of two very different goals: preparing students to attend college versus preparing students to earn a diploma. Unpacking this rocky terrain of press for differentiated achievement, we first view understanding of extrinsically motivating goals as an essential context for secondary learning. We then view the emerging role of clear standards and authentic assessment as a force that alters context. Throughout, we focus on (a) the dynamics that spin off from different societal demands in the classroom; (b) the tension and interplay between individual, school, and external locus of control; (c) the strength of the individual versus the strength of the collective; (d) the power of goal alignment; and (e) the synergy of engagement and demand.

Teachers Engage in Teaching

*Teachers must typically withstand two countervailing features of life in
secondary schools. They must find sources of engagement and motivation in
the face of (1) multiplicity of goals, with a corresponding ambiguity regarding valued directions and outcomes and (2) a relative devaluing of
academic achievement in competition with other priorities.*

—Little (1990, p. 190)

In the face of daunting external forces, how can teachers and schools expect high
achievement for all? Within the context of external pressure, teachers respond by—
either throwing themselves into the challenging work it takes to engage all students
in the hard work of meeting high achievement expectations or "progressively
disengag[ing] themselves from their academic roles and responsibilities" (Sedlak
et al., 1986, p. 123). According to Louis and Smith (1992), teacher engagement
focuses either on "general qualities of human relationships in the school" (p. 120) or
on engaging in learning and teaching (see also Rosenholtz, 1989). In this section, we
focus on teacher motivation to engage in core technology. We look first at teachers'
sense of meaning and importance in their work as critical foundations for their willingness to give persistent effort. We look next at teachers' sense of possibility, including self-efficacy and accepting responsibility as critical links to teacher action.

Teachers Hold a Sense of Importance About Teaching

Teachers are motivated to engage in teaching because they see it as important.
Researchers have found that "teachers' attitudes, beliefs, and feelings about their
work play a important role in supporting or undermining effective practice"
(McLaughlin & Talbert, 1990, p. 3) and that "teachers' belief that they are making a
positive difference in their students' growth and capacity" (p. 3) is important to
teacher engagement. Sense of meaning is linked to teacher persistence (Louis & Miles,
1990) and to teacher discretionary effort (Metz, 1990a; Wilson & Corcoran, 1988)
that " go[es] well beyond the minimums defined by work rules" (Corcoran, 1990,
p. 161). If teachers are to invest large amounts of time and energy in the work of
teaching, they need to have "a sense that effective teaching is important and valuable" (Metz, 1993, p. 130).

In some ways, sense of importance is an individual attribute (Larson, 1992)
linked to the intrinsic reward system that teachers find both "most satisfying" (Metz,
1990a, p. 41) and "probably indispensable" (Metz, 1993, p. 130). Because extrinsic
rewards are often beyond the teacher's scope of control, focus on an internal sense of
"deep meaning" (Louis & Miles, 1990, p. 212) adds a form of control and empowerment to the teacher's reward structure (Lortie, 1975).

In other ways, however, teachers' sense of importance is an externally created
phenomenon affected by the value that "individuals, groups, and institutions attach
to the work at hand" (Little, 1990, p. 189). "Authority is socially conferred" (Grant,

1988, p. 144), and community values "have the most obvious impacts on the respect and status accorded to teachers and hence on teachers' sense of efficacy and relevance" (Louis, 1990, p. 30). "Over and over again, teachers told site visitors that respect for teaching was important to school success" (Wilson & Corcoran, 1988, p. 88). Yet many teachers have a strong sense that they hold relatively low prestige professionally in the public eye (Grant, 1988; Perrone, 1985; Sedlak et al., 1986) and that because the public is so diverse, "there is no way in which teachers can obtain community respect and support from all sectors" (Louis, 1990, p. 32).

Individually, many teachers have difficulty engaging within this complicated social context:

> Teachers often feel isolated and lonely. They frequently feel victimized by students, parents, and administrators. They often are held in low esteem by and receive little respect from these important groups. These attitudes about teaching are sources of stress for teachers and obstacles to their productivity. (Wilson & Corcoran, 1988, p. 17)

Collectively, however, teachers can "create a particular ethos, or set of values, attitudes and behaviors which will become characteristic of the school as a whole" (Rutter et al., 1979, p. 179) and "independently affect the belief system of the entire school" (Bryk & Driscoll, 1988, p. 6).

Thus teachers, banding together, can create a school context that mediates the impact of externally imposed values and supports their individual work, "enhanc[ing] their sense that they [are] doing important, effective work" (Metz, 1990a, p. 54). Even so, there is evidence that indicates that schools vary in their ability to support teacher engagement according to the social class of the school (Bryk & Driscoll, 1988; Metz, 1990a) as well as other factors; thus the effects of external forces are not tempered evenly.

Teachers Hold a Sense of Possibility About Learning

> I don't care what anybody tells you, it's the family structure that's causing the schools to fail. I can teach a kid and give him the material, but I can't make the kid learn. (Datnow, 1997, p. 216)

> In a positive teacher culture, individual educators believe they are personally accountable for the success of each student. This self-imposed accountability means that teachers accept responsibility for helping each student overcome impediments to success. (Wehlage, Rutter, Smith, Lesko, & Fernandez, 1989, p. 135)

According to many researchers, accepting responsibility for student achievement is an essential ingredient for student and school success (Lee et al., 1995; Murphy, Weil, Hallinger, & Mitman, 1982; Tschannen-Moran, Hoy, & Hoy, 1998; Wehlage et al., 1989). According to Murphy (1992b), this acceptance includes "attacks on the practice of blaming the victim for the shortcomings of school itself [and the] insistence on requiring the school community to take a fair share of the responsibility for what happens to the youth in its care" (p. 95). Teachers who accept responsibility understand that "the creation of a school culture is more dependent on the adults in the school than on the characteristics of students or economic climates of the community in which the school is located" (Louis & Miles, 1990, p. 88). Furthermore, teachers who accept responsibility understand that student academic performance "reflects their own success at helping students find and develop themselves and their talent" (Darling-Hammond, Ancess, & Falk, 1995, p. 62).

When teachers place blame on "parents for the low achievement, bad attitudes, and scholastic gaps of the students" (Romo & Falbo, 1996, p. 218), on "the breakdown of the family structure in American society" (Datnow, 1997, p. 216), on poverty, on the school (Wigfield, Eccles, & Rodriguez, 1998), or on "the student, both as the source of the problem and as the entity which has to change to solve the problem" (Sedlak et al., 1986, p. 89), "these teachers avoid blaming themselves" (Datnow, 1997, p. 216). The tendency to blame others and to complain suggests "a sense of powerlessness" (Louis & Miles, 1990, p. 152) and "a sense of being out of control at all levels" (p. 167). Teachers who feel powerless tend to disengage (McLaughlin, 1993), "baffled about these youths' lack of success and . . . frustrated in their attempts to understand and affect their academic performance" (Phelan, Davidson, & Yu, 1998, p. 193). Rendered helpless through blame, teachers are awash, left without a personal or a collective engine to drive action.

Accepting responsibility for student achievement is closely linked to teachers' sense of efficacy, teachers' belief that they have the capacity to influence how well students learn (Tschannen-Moran et al., 1998). Most teachers in successful schools believe that "all of the students can be motivated to master essential skills and content . . . [and] this conviction is a critical source of the high levels of energy and commitment to tasks by staff and students in these schools" (Wilson & Corcoran, 1988, p. 99). Thus teachers who have a strong sense of efficacy are able to take action (Murphy et al., 1982). On a continuum that ranges from blaming others on the one hand to believing in personal capacity to make a difference, regardless of circumstances (Donmoyer & Kos, 1993), on the other, the sense of efficacy is empowering, giving teachers a source of control and providing them with a foundation for accepting responsibility.

Teacher efficacy is strongly linked to student achievement, motivation, and self-efficacy outcomes as well as to a wide range of positive teacher behaviors (Brophy, 1982; Good, 1981; Good & Brophy, 1986). Teachers who blame students tend to exhibit negative behavior (Sedlak et al., 1986), whereas teachers who believe they can succeed in teaching students are more likely to demonstrate a range of positive teaching behaviors (Fullan, 1988)—effort, goals, level of aspiration, persistence, resilience, openness to new ideas, commitment to teaching, and levels of planning and organization (Tschannen-Moran et al., 1998). In action-oriented schools and classrooms, "teachers are not waiting for curriculum guides, nor are principals reading 'directives.' They are mutually creating and sustaining a world" (Grant, 1988, p. 175).

Students Engage in Learning

> *Teachers must come to terms with what students desire to know, with students' definitions of knowledge.*
>
> —Sedlak et al. (1986, p. 99)

> *Teachers personally engage their students.*
>
> —Bryk and Driscoll (1988, p. 4)

In order to be meaningful, school knowledge must become *real* by connecting to the present reality of students' lives and to their dreams of the future:

> Most of the time, what keeps students going in school is not intrinsic motiva-tion—motivation derived from the process of learning itself—but extrinsic motivation—motivation that comes from real or perceived consequences as-sociated with success or failure, whether these consequences are immediate (in the form of grades, the reactions of parents, or the responses of friends) or delayed (in the form of anticipated impact on other educational settings or in the adult world of work). (Steinberg, 1996, p. 72)

In this section, we look first at students' sense of the importance of their schoolwork as the critical foundation for willingness to give persistent effort. We look next at stu-dents' sense of possibility, including their perception of future value and their belief in the attainability of future goals as critical links to student action.

Students Hold a Sense of Importance About Learning

Students are strongly motivated to learn when school connects to their own lives and concerns (Bryk & Driscoll, 1988; Darling-Hammond et al., 1995; McLaughlin, 1993; Page, 1991). "In order to be emotionally engaged in school, students must be-lieve that what they are learning there is either interesting or valuable—and preferably both" (Steinberg, 1996, p. 72). Sense of importance for students is linked to student interest, relevance, perceptions of friends and parents, and teacher enthusiasm.

Learning Is Interesting

There are two opposing perspectives on motivating students to learn through student interest. According to one view, students are engaged by a focus on serious is-sues related to personal reality: "A lot of teachers just aren't aware of the real world that these kids face. They have their head in the sand" (Louis & Miles, 1990, p. 64). Other "teachers see today's students burdened and distracted as never before by vari-ous family dysfunctions, peer pressures, substance abuse, pregnancies, demands of jobs or other out-of-school responsibilities, and general lack of support from family or the larger community" (McLaughlin, 1993, p. 82). School work that "weav[es] their learning into a chain of utterances emanating from their lives" (Nystrand, Gamoran, Kachur, & Prendergast, 1997, p. 16) results in " 'substantive engagement,' a sustained commitment to and involvement with academic content and issues" (p. 16).

Furthermore, students are engaged by "feel[ing] connected to the wider society" (Miron, 1996, p. 176) as well:

> Kids in this school talk about topics like politics and race and other things that normally kids wouldn't think about. I mean, everyone's still interested in music and clothes and that kind of stuff, but there's also another part where kids are serious. They know the reality of the world. (Darling-Hammond et al., 1995, p. 71)

Others take a different view of the role of student interest, looking at "the broader context in which our children are educated . . . to understand how schools are linked to other forces in students' lives" (Steinberg, 1996, p. 58):

> While schools and teachers differ in how engaging they are, most discussions of contemporary education overemphasize the responsibility of school to be engaging and ignore the obligation of students to be "engageable." Indeed, our exclusive focus on how to make schools more engaging is one of the central problems of the school reform movement. (Steinberg, 1996, p. 63)

Drawing attention to nonacademic attractions that compete for students' attention, such as student employment, extracurricular activities, and time spent with peers (Lamborn, Brown, Mounts, & Steinberg, 1992; Steinberg, 1996; Wilson & Corcoran, 1988), this viewpoint sees "engagement in school [as] a two-way street—schools need to be interesting, but students need to be willing and able to be interested" (Steinberg, 1996, p. 63).

Newmann, Wehlage, and Lamborn (1992) allude to the "importance of fun, play, and humor" (p. 27) in interesting students in schoolwork. "Fun reduces the distress of intense pressure to succeed and the boredom of unchallenging, but perhaps necessary, routines" (pp. 27-28). This area needs further exploration.

Learning Is Relevant to the Real World

In a similar vein, the relevance of school to the outside world is a major determinant of importance, and "the authenticity of schoolwork depends largely on its connections to work beyond instructional settings" (Newmann et al., 1992, p. 26). Authentic tasks are considered "meaningful, valuable, significant, and worthy of one's effort, in contrast to those considered nonsensical, useless, contrived, trivial, and, therefore, unworthy of effort" (p. 23).

For school knowledge to be deemed *real*, it must mesh with student reality. When school knowledge is in disagreement with their own knowledge, students are unwilling to "appropriate school-supplied knowledge, even from a well respected teacher" (McNeil, 1986, p. 198) until they can determine its credibility, and they use their own life experiences and information—whenever it is available—to make that determination. If, "in the classroom, there is deep silencing about the issues of genuine concern to students and teachers as well" (Miron, 1996, p. 178), there is no way for students to resolve differences between school knowledge and their own. Thus some school knowledge will remain suspect at best, "irrelevant to their lives" (Phelan et al., 1998, p. 191) at worst. "Teachers need to make the content of their teaching more relevant to the lives of students" (Romo & Falbo, 1996, p. 239). As a student at Central Park East Secondary School in New York City said, "Habits of mind stay in my mind whether inside of school or outside of school—so we'll continue to use this" (Darling-Hammond et al., 1995, p. 71).

Friends and Parents Perceive Learning as Valuable

Another area of student value is how success or failure influences students' relationships with friends and parents. In recent years, "there has been increasing recognition of the importance of social influences on learning and motivation" (Wigfield et al., 1998, p. 73). Peer influences are particularly important factors in adolescent motivation, and this influence can be either positive or negative (Metz, 1993; Renzulli, Reis, Hebert, & Diaz, 1995; Steinberg, 1996). The discussion of parental influence can be found in other chapters of this book.

Teacher Enthusiasm Adds Value to School Work

Teacher enthusiasm for subject matter and for teaching is tightly linked to student motivation (Metz, 1993; Phelan et al., 1998), and enthusiasm is one way to communicate teacher perception of the importance of schoolwork. "When teachers communicate excitement and enthusiasm, and students see that the teacher is engaged actively (rather than merely attempting to transmit content), they are more likely to become involved themselves" (Phelan et al., 1998, p. 198). High school teacher enthusiasm is linked, in part, to "the success they [teachers] experience in getting to teach the subjects that they know and like, in the schools they want, with students they consider both able and interested, among colleagues they admire" (Little, 1993, p. 144). Thus enthusiasm for teaching is linked to teacher engagement in teaching as well as to student engagement in learning (Metz, 1993).

Students Connect Sense of Possibility With Learning

Students engage in school when they see learning as both personally possible and offering possibilities for personal gain. They are motivated to engage in learning when they connect work in school with their future, and sense of possibility is linked most strongly with perception of future extrinsic reward. We look in particular at the role of relevance to future, aspiration, success, control, and rigor.

School Is Relevant to Students' Future

Students must see school as a means of getting ahead in life (Gallien, 1992; MacLeod, 1995; Natriello, McDill, & Pallas, 1990). According to one view, when school is connected to "a broad constellation of skills and knowledge that [are] essential prerequisites to subsequent enterprises (e.g., college, work, citizenship)" (Brantlinger, 1993, p. 101) that prepares students to be able to manage in life, students are more likely to engage (Darling-Hammond et al., 1995; Miron, 1996). By connecting school to students' futures in a developmentally appropriate way, teachers can better "prepare them to assume adult roles and responsibilities" (Taylor, 1994, p. 120).

In addition, connection to more specific future goals adds power to motivate students (Miron, 1996; Page, 1991). Steinberg (1996) found that "for most high school students, [one of] the main motivators of effort [is] grades (both for what they may bring in immediate rewards and because of their importance to college admission)" (p. 74). Miron (1996) found even students who perceive themselves as poor students "value an education that would prepare them for college" (p. 170) and value earning good grades.

Students Hope for a Better Future

If students are to be motivated to engage, they must have hope—a sense of efficacy (Murphy et al., 1982). They must believe school is the path to a better future. Yet most studies of student aspiration are focused primarily on the negative—lack of hope (MacLeod, 1995; Wilson & Corcoran, 1988). Lack of hope is linked empirically to low income and minority status, where "the spiral of declining expectations may be reinforced by . . . awareness that education does not bring the same benefits to members of their group that it does to members of majority or affluent groups" (Wilson & Corcoran, 1988, p. 100). Through sense of aspiration, students "feel they are headed up the ladder of social mobility and believe that schooling is going to get them there" (MacLeod, 1995, p. 110). More specifically, aspiration is affected by "the perceived accessibility of occupations . . . [, and] for a variety of class-related reasons, low-income students have fewer educational and occupational options" (Brantlinger, 1993, p. 169).

On the other hand, in studying ethnic differences in engagement, Steinberg (1996) found the greatest differences in students who believed "not getting a good education would hurt their chances in the labor force" (p. 90). According to this finding, "it is undue optimism, not excessive pessimism, that may be holding Black and Latino students back in school" (p. 91).

Students Are Successful in School

Students are unlikely to stay in unrewarding environments (Bryk & Driscoll, 1988), and lack of academic success in school is one of the strongest research-determined correlates linked to students' dropping out of school (Natriello et al.,

1990). Although much of the research on student success is targeted toward students who are at risk, "all youth—at risk or not—need to acquire a personal sense of competence and success" (Wehlage et al., 1989, p. 27).

Again, Steinberg (1996) offers a different view:

> It appears that students are motivated much more to avoid the negative consequences of failure than to reap the positive rewards of success. To the extent that this is true, then, students' behavior in school will depend more on how easy or difficult schools make it for students to fail than on how easy or difficult they make it for students to succeed. (p. 76)

Others counter that, psychologically and emotionally, students differ in their ability to persist in the face of failure: "In a fundamental sense, being 'held back' in school is as emotionally wrenching as being 'held back' in life" (Page, 1991, p. 225). Phelan and colleagues (1998), furthermore, point out "concern[s] about the psychosocial costs that may result from students' obsession with high grades and test scores" (p. 186) for particular groups of students focused too stringently on success.

School Success Is Under Student Control

Sense of control is linked with school success.

> In order to succeed, students must also believe that they have some control over how well they do in school, that their performance is somehow related to their effort, and that trying harder will lead to an improvement in their grades and test scores. (Steinberg, 1996, p. 91; see also Knisley, 1993; Newmann et al., 1992)

Students with healthy attributional style—those who believe success in school is a product of personal effort that is under their control—are more successful than students who see success as "the result of innate ability, an easy assignment, favorable treatment by teachers, or just plain good luck" (Steinberg, 1996, p. 92). When students feel a sense of control, they are motivated to engage in the work of school.

Rigorous School Work Prepares Students for Future Success

Finally, students are engaged by demanding, intellectually stimulating work (Perrone, 1985; Sedlak et al., 1986), an essential prerequisite for future success. Although

> . . . some students . . . tune out mainly because they cannot keep up . . . , for many more, disengagement is not a reaction to too much pressure or to classes that are too difficult, but a response to having too little demanded of them and to the absence of any consequences for failing to meet even these minimal demands. (Steinberg, 1996, p. 68)

After looking at engagement and motivation as compelling forces of attraction drawing students and teachers into the world of high expectations, we shift our attention to the power of context in affecting teacher and student engagement.

Engagement Varies With Context

Teaching effectiveness is shaped by the complex interplay of the multiple embedded contexts of the secondary school workplace.
—McLaughlin and Talbert (1990, p. 4)

The overarching intimate tie between schooling and the re-creation of an occupational and economic hierarchy in each new generation has an overwhelming impact on daily school experiences, for teachers and students together.
—Metz (1990a, p. 101)

The "bargain" or "arrangement" or "treaty" is a common theme . . . that provides a number of clues about the formidable task confronting the standards-raising movement.
—Sedlak et al. (1986, p. 8)

In this section, we situate learning and teaching in context of the different demand systems that flow routinely through high school classrooms, following the forked path of "dual aims and differentiated curricula" (Chapter 1) as societal goals land firmly on the teacher's desk. These systems push schools and teachers to hold different expectations for high school students, depending on the students' end goal: (a) entering and succeeding in college or demanding postsecondary training or (b) obtaining a diploma and entering the world of work (Oakes & Lipton, 1996; Page, 1991). As pressure to obtain these distinct demands ripples through classrooms, the impact on teacher capacity to sustain academic press varies. Teachers in precollege-track classrooms hold high expectations with relative ease, whereas teachers in general and lower track classrooms hold high expectations with immense difficulty (Murphy & Hallinger, 1989).

We look first at separation of students into different ability tracks, focusing on issues of assignment, treatment, and differentiated expectations. We then touch briefly on the dynamics that provide the contextual updraft associated with precollege coursework. We next unpack "the specific dynamics that lie behind the much publicized lowered expectations that students and teachers are bringing to the classroom" (McNeil, 1986, p. 158), giving full attention to the uphill battle teachers face in holding high expectations for "the unspecial" (Powell et al., 1985, p. 174). Finally, we look at demands emerging from standards and assessment systems and at attempts to change context for learning.

Collectively, we shed light on the powerful cultural wind shear that buffets teachers working in ordinary schools, illuminating the complex, interactive factors that create strong academic press for some and strong press for low achievement for others, requiring many teachers to "work against the grain" (Metz, 1990a, p. 101). Only then can we understand the extraordinary complexity of the teacher's world and the tremendous heart, courage, and talent required of successful teachers in expecting all students to achieve at high levels.

Expectations Follow a Dual Path

> The most important question in the area of educational reform in general, and educational equity specifically, is what is going to be taught—to whom and by whom. (Murphy & Hallinger, 1989, p. 131)

High school consists of "essentially two distinct educational worlds, one preparing students for college, the other preparing adolescents for the workplace at best, and for nothing in particular at worst" (Sedlak et al., 1986, p. 48). Secondary students are expected to achieve at different levels, depending on their track placement. For schools in general, the evidence is overwhelming that track placement is mediated through achievement differences that go back to grouping practices in the elementary years, but these findings "are clearly not applicable to curricular tracking at the secondary level" (Murphy & Hallinger, 1989, p. 134). At the high school level, some find evidence of bias in track placement (Datnow, 1997; Romo & Falbo, 1996). "Even when white and minority students are comparable in their scores on achievement tests, minorities are more likely than their white peers to be placed in lower tracks" (Oakes & Lipton, 1996, p. 173). Others find little evidence of bias in placement (Alexander & Cook, 1982; Alexander, Cook, & McDill, 1978), concluding that ethnicity is the most important demographic in student achievement because of ethnic differences in engagement (Steinberg, 1996): "A more reasonable reading of the evidence is that Asian students perform better in school because they work harder, try harder, and are more invested in achievement—the very same factors that contribute to success among *all* ethnic groups" (p. 87). Viewed in tandem, these two perspectives might begin to inform the dynamics of mutual impact between teacher and student that create the "rising or falling spirals of expectations" (Wilson & Corcoran, 1988, p. 100) so critical to student achievement.

Although clear understanding of student assignment to separate tracks at the high school level is ever emerging, once students are either assigned to or elect to participate in different tracks, the evidence of differences in "throughputs" (Murphy & Hallinger, 1989, p. 135)—instruction, curriculum, and learning environments—is increasingly strong (Miron, 1996; Oakes & Lipton, 1996; Page, 1991). For the most part, students in different tracks have widely varying access to educational resources:

The available evidence indicates that curriculum assignment, in addition to its sorting function, is an institutional mechanism for the systematic and selective allocation of important learning resources, systematic in that the allocation occurs in regular patterns and selective in that the resources are distributed in a different manner to various curricular groups. (Murphy & Hallinger, 1989, p. 135)

Thus lower track high school students "with records of lower achievement are more likely to find themselves in classrooms that emphasize lower order skills, repetitive drill techniques, and basic knowledge" (Lee et al., 1995, p. 5). High school students in higher-track classes—disproportionately White and Asian (Oakes & Lipton, 1996), disproportionately wealthy (Lee at al., 1995)—access higher quality schooling (Lee at al., 1995; Murphy & Hallinger, 1989).

Beginning in the middle school years, placement differences seem to be mediated through systemic differences in the overall speed and direction of achievement that: (a) increasingly limit program options and (b) influence student choice (Oakes & Lipton, 1996). These differences are linked to students' ultimate purpose in obtaining a high school education:

Rather than being propelled through the same curriculum at different speeds, . . . [middle school] students are pulled intentionally through different curricula toward different "end points": different high schools, different post high school expectations. . . . The differentiated curriculum conforms to larger social purpose—preparing students for different futures—and creates even greater curricular differences than would be expected from differences in pace and consequent losses in coverage. (p. 172)

In the next two sections, we follow this dual path of pressure as it flows through classrooms, looking first at press for high achievement when college is the classroom goal and looking second at the press for low achievement that often occurs when earning a diploma is the classroom goal.

Focus on College as Goal Creates Press for High Achievement

Goal Alignment Provides Strong Support

When classrooms focus on preparing able students both for successful entry into college and for flourishing academic careers once they arrive on campus, press for high achievement is naturally wrapped in context of a clear, desirable goal. Thus when "schooling gets defined as preparation for entry into elite colleges and universities" (Miron, 1996, p. 178), teachers are able to work with certitude. Teachers, parents, and students are focused clearly on the same goal, and the system has the capacity to achieve that goal (Page, 1991).

This alignment of "expectations for students on the part of parents and teachers . . . [is] deeply colored by parents' social class" (Metz, 1990a, p. 99). Parents who went to college themselves "take for granted" (Brantlinger, 1993, p. 169) that their children will attend college, and they press schools to provide a strong preparatory education (Sedlak et al., 1986) that will prepare their adolescents "for entry into elite colleges and universities" (Miron, 1996, p. 178). For privileged students, the parents' status affects "students' own assessment of their life chances and so of the usefulness of school" (Metz, 1990a, p. 99). For precollege students, high school is directly linked to their future goal, and "accruing school credentials enable[s] high-income adolescents' college plans" (Brantlinger, 1993, p. 101).

Through a "successful match of teachers' and students' aims in the high-SES [socioeconomic status]. . . schools" (Metz, 1990a, p. 103), goals of parents, students, and teachers merge—even though the match "isolat[es] the most privileged and ambitious students from the other young people of their generation" (p. 103). When school, teacher, parent, and student goals are aligned in focusing on college, a powerful academic updraft both propels students toward high achievement and supports teachers in holding high expectations.

Academic Achievement Is Essential to Reaching Strong Goals

With college as the goal, demand for high academic performance is naturally embedded in the process of obtaining a high school credential. Academic rigor is demanded both by parents and by the system.

Professional and managerial level parents and their children are

> . . . interested in the substance of education. . . . They also [see] knowledge in a more open-ended light and approach it with a confidence that allow[s] students to question and even expect to participate in creating it. They [are] . . . self-assured, almost patrician, in their approach to education. (Metz, 1990a, p. 94)

Systemically, the precollege curriculum consists overall of a more rigorous collection of courses than does general-track curriculum (Murphy, Hull, & Walker, 1987; Oakes & Lipton, 1996; Sadker & Sadker, 1994; Davenport, Davison, Kuang, Ding, Kim, & Kwak, 1998). Students in higher track courses receive better instruction, have greater opportunity to learn academics, and are immersed in learning environments infused with higher expectations (Murphy & Hallinger, 1989). "More rigorous content coverage accounts for much of the achievement advantage of college-preparatory classes" (Gamoran, Porter, Smithson, & White, 1997, p. 325), and "the pace, complexity, and challenge of classroom instruction [is] higher . . . than elsewhere" (p. 326).

In precollege classes, order is assumed, and it is more likely to be linked with focus on achievement. High-track faculty members perceive "that the 'largely professional . . . parents demand a rigorous academic program' but loose disciplinary standards: 'They want a college campus atmosphere' " (Page, 1991, p. 170). Teachers "expect students to be 'good' and, consequently, emphasize academic progress" (pp. 33-34).

Strong Resources Support High Achievement

Privileged parents are adroit in obtaining resources for their children. Through " 'politicking' by savvy parents who want their children placed in the best classes" (Oakes & Lipton, 1996, p. 175), wealthier parents "can usually find schools or tracks or individual teachers that provide sufficient rigor to enable their children to compete successfully for admission to elite universities" (Sedlak et al., 1986, p. 179). Insistent parental demand from the privileged combines with higher teacher status, among other factors, to make high-track placement very appealing to teachers. The more highly qualified and experienced teachers, perhaps the greatest of resources, teach most frequently in the more rigorous, high-status programs (Murphy & Hallinger, 1989) in which "the social and academic status of students attaches itself to their teachers" (Metz, 1990a, p. 99).

Together, these forces—goal alignment, academic rigor, and resources—press high achievement for students who will attend college, and they support high school faculty who teach precollege courses in their holding of high expectations. Yet there is another reality, a very different secondary landscape. We next turn our gaze to the teaching and learning architecture that supports low teacher expectations, low student achievement, and disengagement—a world crisply focused on awarding sufficient credentials for graduation and maintaining order, a reality in which achievement fades into chalk-dusted shadows.

Focus on Diploma as Goal Creates Press for Low Achievement

That unevenness could not have been resolved by simply hiring "smarter" teachers. Many of the smartest, best educated of these teachers felt that "really to teach" would be going "against" expectations at their school, not fulfilling them. (McNeil, 1986, p. 157)

Secondary schools have been asked to be nearly all things to all students; goal ambiguity and goal overload are facts of life for many secondary teachers and administrators. (Little, 1990, p. 189)

In this section, we look at the negative spin that occurs when weak goal attraction, pressure to graduate, and demand for order reduce, if not extinguish, societal press for high achievement. When earning enough credits to meet requirements for a diploma is more important than achievement, "control and credentialing become the rationale for the educational experience" (McNeil, 1986, p. xiii), and the dynamics of negative press are set in motion. This tragic "downward spiral" (Metz, 1993, p. 113)—a path paved with weak goal attraction, press to earn a diploma, negotiated order, school knowledge, and disengagement—actively pushes for low achievement. Within this context, teachers persevere with great difficulty in holding high expectations for student achievement.

Diploma Is Weak Goal With Limited Power to Motivate Students

I got to come do what I have to do to get out of school. (Miron, 1996, p. 153)

The high school diploma, as a terminal credential, has weak power to compel high achievement. Although "students believe in the benefits associated with getting a diploma or a degree, . . . they are skeptical about the benefits associated with either learning or doing well in class" (Steinberg, 1996, p. 75). For students who are not attending college, "the 'real world' offers no rewards for academic success" (Wehlage et al., 1989, p. 180), and at-risk students who drop out are "often astutely aware of the lack of job market benefits of obtaining a diploma" (Brantlinger, 1993, p. 69).

In addition to a perception of weak future value, the literature speaks of high immediate costs. MacLeod (1987/1995) notes the economic costs of delayed entry into adulthood as factors students weigh in deciding whether or not to remain in school. There are personal costs as well. For some, "school learning is viewed as a subtractive process with few identified benefits, in which individuals must sacrifice something of their collective sense of identity in adopting the behaviors and values favored in school" (Taylor, 1994, p. 123). MacLeod (1987/1995) found that poor students tend to blame personal inadequacy on poor academic performance rather than the system and hold a lower sense of aspiration and hope. Others, however, found that when poor students fail, "they attribute their performance to unfair teachers, bad luck, low innate ability, or having to confront an exceptionally difficult test, all factors over which they have no personal control" (Steinberg, 1996, p. 92). In either case, there are added psychological costs for struggling students to remain in school and graduate.

Pressure to Earn Diploma Is Dissociated From Pressure to Achieve

Parents and the community expected students to earn credentials and to follow the rules. They made few inquiries about curriculum and few efforts to intervene in school practice on behalf of their children. (Metz, 1990a, pp. 73-74)

Even though the diploma is relatively weak, schools are pressed by parents, central office, and school boards to keep students in school, to reduce failure rates, and to increase graduation rates (Powell et al., 1985). Metz (1990a) traces a clear path from external demands to the classroom teacher. "The school board [is] concerned about high failure rates for the student body as a whole" (p. 62) and they "pressur[ed] the principal to lower the failure rates in the classes of teachers with unusually high rates" (p. 62). Principals, then, exert pressure on teachers based on "the community's lack of interest in the substance of the curriculum and . . . adherence to community priorities" (p. 66).

When pressure for earning grades and graduating is the core focus, some students find they "can do well in school even if they give only minimal compliance to the system" (Cusick, 1983, p. 213), and they tend to do only "what survival necessitates" (Page, 1991, p. 228).

> Within a belief system in which all that counts is graduation—in which earning good grades is seen as equivalent to earning mediocre ones, or worse yet, in which learning something from school is seen as unimportant—students choose the path of least resistance. (Steinberg, 1996, p. 75)

Whereas higher SES parents are more likely to demand achievement as well as grades, lower SES parents are "much less concerned about the level of challenge they [students] were exposed to or the content of the curriculum" (Metz, 1990a, p. 62). In response to poor academic performance, lower SES parents are more likely to request that students "be moved to a lower track where the work would be easier" (p. 62). Thus the pressure to earn credits for graduation is further separated from pressure to achieve.

When the grade goes on the report card, the teachers' world and the external world meet, because "teachers retain the ultimate responsibility for determining what is a 'passing' score in a test or in a class" (Wilson & Corcoran, 1988, p. 101). Under pressure to award credit, teachers enter the classroom armed with coveted grades and credits—sole path to the goal of graduating—to face the task of engaging students in the work of earning credits for a relatively weak credential. In addition, they must maintain order.

Pressure to Maintain Order Results in Negotiation for Credential

> We assert the purposes of our schools is to increase learning, but we have organized schools in ways that distort that purpose and even contradict it. (McNeil, 1986, p. xi)

> What administrators wanted were teachers who liked and related to the students, who had few discipline problems, or who at least handled those they had themselves. Beyond that it seemed that they asked little of the teachers, leaving them alone as individuals to work out their own patterns of instruction, patterns that went unscrutinized as long as there was no trouble or rumor of trouble in their classes. (Cusick, 1983, p. 43)

For teachers, students, and administrators, order often supersedes learning as the dominant focus of schools (McNeil, 1986; Page, 1991). "The basic requirement for teachers [is] not that they instruct from some agreed-on course of study. It [is] not even that they instruct. It [is] that they be capable of maintaining some state of moderate order among the students" (Cusick, 1983, p. 56). Students, too, are pressed to maintain order: "A student must understand what he is to do, not do; where he is to go, not go; and when he is supposed to both do and go. If he understands these things and complies with them to a reasonable degree, he will have little trouble with school" (p. 213).

When order receives disproportionate focus in the context of gaining a weak diploma, a well-documented process of negotiation goes on between teacher and student (Powell et al., 1985; Sizer, 1984). "Teachers lessen their demands for academic work, for time on task, or for conformity" (Metz, 1993, p. 112), and "students agree to play the game without making trouble for teacher" (Newmann, 1985, p. 15).

A number of factors contribute to this compromise (Sizer, 1984) or "tacit conspiracy" (Sedlak et al., 1986, p. 5). First, the incentive system rewards teachers "for controlling their classes rather than for ensuring engagement with subject matter" (Sedlak et al., 1986, p. 168). Second, high school students "are older and do not accede as automatically to the wishes of adults as elementary students" (Wilson & Corcoran, 1988, p. 6). Third, administration focuses disproportionately on maintaining order and "processing students through the required credentials" (McNeil, 1986, p. xix) to obtain a diploma. Fourth, teachers are awarded autonomy in exchange for controlling and passing students. "Feeling little support for their professional authority and even less provisions for efficiencies of time and effort, . . . the teachers set about to create their own authority, their own efficiencies" (McNeil, 1986, p. xx). And, fifth, bargaining is *normal*:

> Each teacher and learner approaches the classroom on the basis of a personal assessment of costs and rewards. Bargaining, which lies at the core of the classroom (or any organizational or human relationship) is not an aberration from the norm and cannot be eliminated through more rational administrative processes. (Sedlak et al., 1986, p. 184)

Thus teacher and student quietly barter—order the student's bargaining chip, credentials the prerogative of the teacher—and the cycle of low-level academic demand that results in press for low achievement and low levels of knowledge in the classroom is firmly established.

Negotiation Results in Defensive Teaching

The fact is, "not teaching" was one way to deal with a class, not a good way according to any learning theory, but a way that kept students orderly. No one disobeyed a direction that was never given, no one failed to hand in an assignment that was never assigned, no one flunked a test when there were none, and no student-teacher conflicts, fights, or cases of insubordination showed up in the office. (Cusick, 1983, p. 56)

The dominant response to teaching for order is to significantly lower expectations for effort and achievement (Cusick, 1983; McNeil, 1986; Powell et al., 1985; Sedlak et al., 1986). Teachers create order by teaching " 'defensively,' choosing methods of presentation and evaluation that they hope will make their workload more efficient and create as little student resistance as possible" (McNeil, 1986, p. 158). "Most of the teachers observed used a combination of teaching styles and strategies. Some taught defensively only when they felt threatened by a particular administrative policy (de-tracking), by a certain group of students, or by lack of confidence with the course material or more open instructional methods" (p. 197). Others disengage more fully and "fall into a ritual of teaching and learning that tends toward minimum standards and minimum effort" (p. xi).

When the negotiation dynamic is in place, a strong picture of teaching strategies focused primarily on order emerges from the literature. One strategy is to ignore students who "sit in the back of the room and ignore the lesson so long as they tacitly agree not to disrupt the class too often" (Sedlak et al., 1986, p. 95), thus maintaining "a veneer of harmony" (Page, 1991, p. 104). Some teachers "engage in a poor form of individualized teaching, letting students work in class for the whole term on any project they chose with little guidance and few demands as long as they [keep] quiet" (Grant, 1988, p. 162).

Another strategy is to focus on "build[ing] some decent relations with the students" (Cusick, 1983, p. 71) as "what teachers had to fall back on" (p. 52), and "those good relations, rather than the agreed-on and approved body of knowledge, become the real genesis of curriculum" (p. 71). Some focus on developing a relationship grounded in respect for authority and compliance: "Despite students' negotiation of free time in class, teachers were greatly concerned that all students turn in all work. . . . Some of the teachers spoke explicitly of their desire to teach obedience and responsible work habits" (Metz, 1990a, p. 67).

Adjusting the learning process so that students become passive learners by "transform[ing] the role of the student into client or consumer rather than active learner" (McNeil, 1986, p. 192) is another defensive teaching strategy. Teachers limit the scope of instructional strategies out of fear "that this could be disruptive, might result in a noisy classroom, and establish a possible external view that they had lost control" (Perrone, 1985, p. 651). In return, students "do not disrupt the pace of lectures or question the authority or expertise of the teacher, [and] the teacher will not place many demands on the student working for course credit" (McNeil, 1986, p. 193).

Finally, teachers control knowledge as a way to manage student behavior. Using mystification, they "surround a controversial or complex topic with mystery to close off discussion of it" (McNeil, 1986, p. 169). Through simplification, they address complex topics in a superficial way, in addition to using fragmentation and omission to impose "firm limits on the complexity and topicality of class discussions" (p. 166).

As a result of these negotiated teaching strategies, teachers and students swim in a sea of artificial knowledge.

Defensive Teaching Creates School Knowledge

Defensive, controlling teaching does more than make content boring; it transforms the subject content from "real world" knowledge into "school knowledge," an artificial set of facts and generalizations whose credibility lies no longer in its authenticity as a cultural selection but in its instrumental value in meeting the obligations teachers and students have within the institution of schooling. (McNeil, 1986, p. 191)

School knowledge is "divorced from the lively cultural content of societal experience" (p. 191) and is separated from student—and often teacher—interest:

Consider the position of a teacher faced with a set of students, many of whom have a history of nonachievement. They may be perfectly decent adolescents, quite open to good relations with teachers and peers, but with little interest in literature, history, mathematics, science, world affairs, or auto mechanics. One has to "survive" for the period with these students who give so much evidence of so little interest in the acquisition of positive knowledge. (Cusick, 1983, p. 71)

In addition to being uninteresting, school knowledge consists of "content that neither the teachers nor the students take very seriously. It is frequently distinct from their personal knowledge" (McNeil, 1986, p. 184). As a result, teachers "water down course content and reduce their own teaching efforts [while] the students cooperate patiently in class, while silently negotiating how much course content to believe and remember after they are tested on it" (p. xx).

School Knowledge Is Linked to Disengagement

When teachers use negotiated teaching strategies and create school knowledge, both teachers and students are more likely to disengage rather than to engage in the work of learning and teaching (Powell et al., 1985; Sizer, 1984). "Adults who visit high school classrooms are often struck by the dullness of the lessons. Those who visit systematically note the overwhelming prevalence of boring content, dull presentations and bored but patient students" (Goodlad, 1984, p. 26)—"dull presentations . . . not caused merely by poor teacher preparation or teacher burnout but by deliberate, often articulated, decisions teachers have made to control the students by controlling the content" (McNeil, 1986, p. 191). When this occurs, "students have even less reason to be engaged" (Metz, 1993, p. 113), and pressure to disengage increases.

Standards and Authentic Assessment Alter Context

> The reform literature espouses higher standards. Everyone is for raising expectations. (Wilson & Corcoran, 1988, p. 154)

Two colliding systems swirl through the lives of teachers and students—both individually and collectively—as the traditional system of awarding grades and credits meets the restructured system that holds students, teachers, and schools to demanding standards of academic performance. Using clear expectations held in context of authentic measures of success, the nation attempts to address problems of differentiated expectations, to assist teachers in holding high expectations as well as to demand improved teaching, and to reverse the tides of negative press.

In this final section, we look briefly at the role of standards and assessment in attempting to reverse the downdraft of expectation that floods our secondary schools. We look first at the role of standards in defining what students should know and be able to do. We then examine the strengths of authentic assessment in setting higher levels of performance for both students and teachers. Although the role of the school-to-career movement also affects negative press by providing context for knowledge and attempting to nest high achievement in the context of real goals, that body of literature is beyond the scope of this work.

Clear Standards Set Universal Goals for High Achievement

Standards define "minimum levels of performance and behavior for students. Standards are inexorably intertwined with expectations" (Wilson & Corcoran, 1988, p. xiii). To be useful, standards must be clear (Fullan, 1988), and they must be visible (Darling-Hammond et al., 1995). "Explicit criteria help the whole school focus on its mission" (p. 54).

Scope is a thorny issue in the standards movement. On the one hand, "a narrow curriculum has positive effects on students, especially when it is tied to a strong academic focus and a high level of academic press" (Lee et al., 1995, p. 11). According to the *less-is-more* (Sizer, 1984) Coalition of Essential Schools philosophy, it is more important to know some things well than to know many things superficially. The move to define "common learnings" (Sedlak et al., 1986, p. 54), however, has not necessarily reduced the "curriculum sprawl" (p. 162) so common in high schools (Powell et al., 1985). Further work exploring the inherent tension between depth and breadth of knowledge as affected by standards is necessary.

Authentic Assessment Defines Level of High Achievement

> If tests determine what teachers actually teach and what students will study for—and they do—then the road to reform is a straight but steep one: Test those capacities and habits we think are essential, and test them in context.

Make them replicate, within reason, the challenges at the heart of each academic discipline. Let them be—authentic. (Wiggins, 1989, p. 41)

Expectations are defined explicitly through the assessment system used to measure student achievement. According to Wiggins (1989), authentic assessment is "the central vehicle for clarifying and setting intellectual standards" (p. 42) and gives meaning to the high school diploma. "Until we specify what students must directly demonstrate to earn a diploma, they will continue to pass by meeting the de facto 'standard' of being dutiful and persistent—irrespective of the quality of their work" (p. 42).

Traditional evaluation systems do not "measure the ability to think deeply, to create, or to perform in any field" (Darling-Hammond et al., 1995, p. 6) or "reflect current understandings of how students learn" (p. 6). Authentic assessment attempts to address the "dangers of monolithic evaluation systems" (Newmann, 1985, p. 19) and the "narrowed curriculum" that results from instruction driven by traditional systems, with its "overemphasis on superficial content coverage and rote drill on discrete skills" (Darling-Hammond et al., 1995, p. 7). Authentic assessments are "productive means of not only monitoring but also promoting student learning, including developmental assessments, performance tasks, exhibitions, and portfolio-like processes" (Wolf, Bixby, Glenn, & Gardner, 1989, p. 33).

Authentic Assessment Engages Teachers and Learners

In general, authentic assessment has a number of advantages in engaging students and teachers.

1. Authentic assessment is designed to alter the context for learning:

First, serious thinking, like any performance, is a combination of humility and risk. It takes on noisy, ill-defined problems, alternately collecting data, observing, and hazarding guesses. . . . It involves large projects that combine invention and investigation with craft and insight and embedded accuracy. Second, like other performers, someone engaged in thought sustains a long arc of work over time and across obstacles. Thinking involves rehearsals, revisions, criticisms, and new attempts arranged in nothing like the straightforward orderings we offer in discussions of the scientific method or the directions for writing a term paper. . . . Finally, thought, like performance, involves interpretation. Like an actor or musician, a historian or a scientist has to decide how to make sense of information and beliefs. (Wolf et al., 1989, p. 34)

2. Authentic assessment is designed to connect schoolwork with reality:

Keisha's portfolio also illustrates how students come to understand the uses of mathematics and science in daily life. Not only in her science portfolio but also in her discussion of her internship at a brokerage firm, in her design of a house to scale, and in her discussion of the relative effectiveness of birth control devices, she uses an understanding of accounting principles, measurement, and statistics with competence and ease. (Darling-Hammond et al., 1995, p. 47)

3. Authentic assessment is designed to be interesting:

The "exhibition of mastery," proposed by Ted Sizer in *Horace's Compromise* (1984) and a cornerstone of the "Essential School," . . . was initially proposed as an antidote to boredom, not merely as a more valid form of assessment. (Wiggins, 1989, p. 42)

4. Authentic assessment is designed to improve instruction:

Rather than seeing tests as after-the-fact devices for checking up on what students have learned, we should see them as instructional. The central vehicle for clarifying and setting intellectual standards. (Wiggins, 1989, p. 42)

5. Authentic assessment is designed to set rigorous levels of expectation:

The public nature of many of these assessments holds them up to scrutiny, promoting effort as well as equity and accountability. Students and their parents know the criteria and process for judgement. They are not secret or beyond question. Students know what constitutes excellence and what they must do to attain it. . . . Shared exemplars of student work communicate the nature and the diverse range of high-quality performances to staff and students alike. (Darling-Hammond et al., 1995, p. 260)

6. Authentic assessment is designed to involve teachers and students:

As compared with measurement, assessment is inevitably involved with questions of what is of value rather than simply with correctness. Questions of value require entry and discussion. In this light, assessment is not a matter for outside experts to design; rather, it is an episode in which students and teachers might learn, through reflection and debate, about the standards of good work and the rules of evidence. (Wolf et al., 1989, pp. 51-52)

In short, authentic assessment attempts to alter the context for learning and teaching so that the classroom is more engaging to students and teachers. At the same time, however, strong accountability systems create context for learning based on strong demands for high performance. The impact of this interplay needs further study.

Conclusions

> *Setting goals is easy, implementing them is more difficult.*
> —Wilson and Corcoran (1988, p. 18)

As we have shown, holding high expectations for student achievement is no simple matter. Teacher and student engagement is linked to sense of importance and sense of meaning, and both are contextual. The context for secondary learning and teaching is linked powerfully to a dual system of extrinsically motivating goals. On the one hand, the goal of attending college is both important and meaningful and thus drives high achievement. On the other, the goal of earning a diploma fails to meet these criteria of importance and meaning, has limited power to motivate, and interacts with demand for order to create a dynamic of negative press that drives low achievement. The role of standards and authentic assessment in reversing the tides of negative press and in motivating teachers and students to engage in high achievement is still emerging.

In the next two chapters, we build on the concept of high expectations and explore more directly the teacher's ability to translate high expectations into reality. In Chapter 5, " Personal Support," we explore the ebb and flow of human relationships that supports teachers and students in high performance. In Chapter 6, "Academic Autonomy," we examine the art and science of creating thoughtful classroom environments for learning.

5

Personal Support

For students as well as adults, the communal school offers strong affective ties. To attend such a school is a source of meaning—a chance to be a part of something of value.

—Bryk and Driscoll (1988, p. 5)

Supportive social organization is seen as critical to helping high school students learn more (Lee, Smith, & Croninger, 1995), and "the overall ethos of . . . school seem[s] to provide support and context which facilitate[s] good teaching" (Rutter, Maughan, Mortimore, Ouston, & Smith, 1979, p. 139). As Bryk and Driscoll (1988) discovered, "When the school feels like a community, it is a better place for those who work and study there" (p. 1). This concept of school as community of support for teachers and learners conjures images of the idyllic, a pastoral landscape crystallized in time. "The community metaphor draws attention to norms and beliefs of practice, collegial relations, shared goals, occasions for collaboration, and problems of mutual support and mutual obligation" (McLaughlin, 1993, p. 99). The process of creating these communities, however, is another matter entirely.

Creating school community is a microcosm of the dynamics that create American culture (Page, 1991):

Culture simultaneously differentiates and integrates: It is a process of carving the inchoate world into distinctive domains while also integrating the domains in a system of relationships. . . . More than traditional cultures, America is expressed precisely around categories of membership and difference. . . . Although individualism and community are expressed and experienced as oppositional, paradoxically they form two aspects of a single, defining, internal pattern of alternation. . . . In short, American culture exists in the ongoing play between individualism and community. Selection of one symbol over the other is not possible because both are cherished. (pp. 14-15)

In short, creating community is a distinctly human endeavor and, as such, is a rather messy matter.

Up close, every school community emerges to some extent from a caldron of diversity—an ever evolving amalgamation of people whose ideas, opinions, strengths, and weaknesses vary. This tension between gathering together communally versus separating as individuals and subgroups is an integral part of the empirically defined high school culture despite the apparent contradiction (Little & McLaughlin, 1993; Page, 1991). As a result, the fabric of community in the American high school is as diverse as our country itself, and school cultures made of sturdy denim, silken tapestry, quilted patchwork, and tattered remnants dot the national landscape. As these school communities vary, both learning and teaching differ profoundly (Bryk & Driscoll, 1988; Lee et al., 1995; Wilson & Corcoran, 1988).

In this chapter, we unravel the intricacies of relationships that, collectively and continuously, become the school ethos and create a web of support—or a net gaping with failure—for students and teachers alike. We first define school community as the central source of support for effective teaching and learning. Next, we look at communal dynamics that press social separation, including those of teacher subgroups, teacher competition, and student subgroups. Finally, we unpack the relationship dynamics of creating a unified community that both supports and challenges students and teachers alike, including understanding of teachers as supportive individuals, the dynamics forming supportive teacher-student relationships, and the dynamics teachers use to create a supportive professional community. Undercurrents of unity and separation flow throughout, regardless of the dominant area of focus.

By following this human tide of unity and separation that becomes school and classroom, we (a) inform understanding of the relationship dynamics that create resilient, supportive secondary school communities and (b) identify potential undertow that threatens communal support.

School Community Supports Teachers and Students

Social community provides support for learning and teaching. In this section, we provide sufficient material to ground understanding of community. We first ground this chapter with a brief sketch of the concept of school community. We then discuss limitations of community separated from focus on academic press. Finally, we view problems as providing common ground for building community.

Community for Learning Provides Support

Adults in schools with strong communal identities share "a distinctive pattern of social relations, embodying an ethos of caring that is visibly manifest in collegial relations among the adults of the institution" (Bryk & Driscoll, 1988, p. 1). This staff collegiality and collaboration is fundamental to creating a cohesive, professional culture (Louis & Miles, 1990; Wilson & Corcoran, 1988), where "close collaboration across diverse groups—teachers, students, and parents—[is] the central driving force in the organization" (Oxley, 1997, p. 627). In total, "these relations partly define the school as a unique organization that affects each person in the school" (Frank, 1998, p. 172).

Healthy school communities are grounded in common values (Louis & Miles, 1990; Natriello, McDill, & Pallas, 1990; Newmann, 1997): "As members of a school interact and influence one another, teachers develop shared understandings, educational practices, and mechanisms for decision making" (Frank, 1998, p. 172). When teachers agree to take collective responsibility for student achievement (Lee & Smith, 1996; Ogden & Germinario, 1995), to hold students to common norms and expectations (Grant, 1988), and to share commitment for school success (Brouillette, 1997; Lee & Smith, 1996; Marks & Louis, 1997), both they and their students benefit.

The sense of school community has influence beyond the school itself. "Schools with trusting, caring relationships among the teachers and between the principals and the teachers . . . tend to have such relationships between teachers and pupils in the classroom, between parents and teachers, and between schools and homes" (Goodlad, 1997, pp. 135-136). Furthermore, strong schools reach out to their communities, and "exemplary schools actively recruit the human resources of their communities. Whether they are parents or not, community members are viewed as potential contributors to the school" (Wilson & Corcoran, 1988, p. 113). Thus good high schools become extended communities, engaging the larger society in support of student and school success.

Community Is Not an End in Itself

> Collegiality is not a fully legitimate end in itself unless it can be shown to affect, directly or indirectly, the nature or the degree of pupil development. (Huberman, 1993, p. 13)

In viewing teaching as an essentially communal activity, we find that building *community* is not inherently synonymous with developing strong *learning community,* where focus on high achievement is central (Corcoran & Wilson, 1985; Newmann, 1997). Unchecked and misaligned, focus on collegiality can create a community of adults focused primarily on adult interests, in which peer pressure can subvert focus on student success and actually impede student benefit (Bruckerhoff, 1991). Furthermore, "shared beliefs can support shared delusions about the merit or function of instructional orthodoxies or entrenched routines. This collective agreement can generate rigidity about practice and a 'one best way' mentality that resists change or serious reflection" (McLaughlin, 1993, p. 95). In addition, time is "a precious commodity in public schools" (Wilson & Corcoran, 1988, p. 17), and time for collaboration competes with a wide array of other demands, including time for individual planning and work (Firestone & Rosenblum, 1988; Louis & Miles, 1990; Peronne, 1985). Thus when decoupled from learning and teaching, community building can divert time and attention from students and achievement.

Communal support for students, separated from focus on achievement, creates direct complications for students as well (Newmann & Wehlage, 1994; Page, 1991). When teachers want "more than anything . . . [for] students to know [they] care about them" (Nystrand, 1997, p. 53), they can "kill with kindness" (Sadker & Sadker, 1994, p. 124). When this occurs, "there [does] not seem to be any subject matter other than . . . cordial relations" (Cusick, 1983, p. 53), and caring separated from focus on achievement contributes to student disengagement (Wehlage, Rutter, Smith, Lesko, & Fernandez, 1989).

In summary, creating community that is separate from clear focus on academic press undermines support for both learning and teaching. Ironically, it is struggle with problems of core technology that provides the common ground fundamental to building learning community.

Problems in Learning and Teaching Provide Common Ground for Community Building

> Indeed, the greater the group agreement on crucial issues the greater the tolerance which is possible for individuality and idiosyncrasy on other matters. (Rutter et al., 1979, p. 194)

Depending on how teachers view challenges, problems in core technology offer a gathering place central to community building or become formulae for disaster. A problem-focused orientation "begins by identifying and clarifying the nature of what needs to change—the problem—before deciding what to do" (McQuillan, 1997, pp. 644-645). Used as common ground and communal focus (Louis & Kruse, 1995; Ogden & Germinario, 1995), the struggle to resolve problems that affect teaching and learning—the ordinary, the intractable, and the overwhelming—becomes the nucleus effective schools use to construct powerful secondary learning communities.

Teaching is a "highly underrated act" (Gregory & Smith, 1987, p. 11), and there is no shortage of common problems. Operating in an environment in which turbulence is the norm (Louis & Miles, 1990), "good problem-coping is often needed" (Fullan, 1988, p. 23) if teachers are to persist within the context of this complicated backdrop. Their work environment often includes an array of complications such as poor facilities, limited resources, safety issues, rocky school-district relationships, community tensions, and a history of failed innovations (Boyer, 1983; Louis & Miles, 1990; Metz, 1990a). Yet common "problems that frustrate teachers on a daily basis . . . are . . . neglected as reformers focus on the big issues of restructuring schools and empowering the profession" (Corcoran, 1990, p. 160).

The rhythm of teachers' worklife includes issues of time, pace, volume, and ongoing interruption (Corcoran, 1990; Larson, 1992; Sedlak, Wheeler, Pullin, & Cusick, 1986) as well as the "unexpected, the non-routine" (Louis & Miles, 1990,

p. 271). Changes in instruction present complex challenges to teachers that require them to "think, invent, and reflect on their work[, and] teachers must work hard to sustain reform in their schools" (Lee, Smith, & Croninger, 1995, p. 5). In leading and managing change, teachers must deal with the "uncertainty, complexity, turbulence, and the cussedness of many different people" (Louis & Miles, 1990, p. 288). Capacity is affected by staff turnover, eroding teacher talent, and a wide range of students' skills (Grant, 1988; Louis & Miles, 1990; Sedlak et al., 1986). To complicate matters, teacher work is "rendered uncertain" (Metz, 1993, p. 104) by factors such as "the lack of reliable, clearly effective strategies for accomplishing classroom work; the difficulty of judging long-term effects on students; and the prospect of collegial criticism" (p. 104).

Facing these problems alone is overwhelming. So teachers, like their students, gather as peers—sometimes as viscous community, but most certainly in the fluid, overlapping human layers that make up school society: subgroups.

The Dynamics of Separation Affect Community

The vision of the schoolhouse as a bonded community of adults and children is very much among us. On the face of it, it is an unlikely vision to transport into real life. Think of it: a sort of vastly extended family comprising at least a few hundred people, most of them unrelated to one another, all the children put together simply by virtue of living in the same neighborhood, and most of the adults coming together more by the vagaries of their career paths and the arbitrary assignments of the central office than by affiliation or community of purpose. More like a ship of fools, actually, than a gathering of kindred souls.

—Huberman (1993, p. 11)

The thought of teachers working together as a group to create nurturing intellectual community and to develop a responsive, student-oriented culture is comforting. Teachers working individually and in distinct groups—a jumble of random togetherness with pockets of excellence, flashes of strife, and bone-grinding resistance—is less so. In this section, we first unpack the dynamics of creating high school teacher subgroups, including organizational, social, and individual pressures that affect separation. We then visit the role of conflict in increasing separation, as teachers live and work in hierarchical competition. Finally, we examine the dynamics of separation that predominate among students as peers, further affecting learning and teaching.

Teachers Live and Work in Subgroups

The characteristic concentration on school-level collegiality obscures the multiplicity of salient reference groups both within the school and in the larger occupation. Teachers associate with colleagues in many settings or circumstances: in their departments, groupings associated with instructional or cocurricular assignments, the school, district-level activities, and teachers' organizations. Teachers' affiliations with one another may be circumstantial, a by-product of a common teaching assignment; they may be induced, a result of mandated committee responsibilities, special assignments, or special projects; or they may be elective, an attachment to teachers' organizations, informally organized special-interest groups, and friendship nets. Each of these occasions and locations of teacher interaction provides a microcontext for collegial relations that may operate by quite different rules, focus on different issues, and carry different significance for teachers' lives and careers. (Little & McLaughlin, 1993, pp. 3-4)

School communities are home to a wide range of overlapping subgroups (Hallinger & Murphy, 1986; Lee & Smith, 1994; Wilson & Corcoran, 1988), and these subgroups are naturally and effervescently different: "The 'schools' . . . [teachers see] themselves working in reflect substantively different sites" (Siskin, 1997, p. 610). In this section, we explore the labyrinth of relationships between teachers and their colleagues, looking closely at the interplay—both positive and negative—between collectivism and individualism. Teachers create these subgroups and affiliations by choice and by circumstance in response to formal organizational boundaries, through social dynamics, and as a function of individualism.

Formal Structures Create Division

Subject affiliation and departmental membership powerfully define professional community in these comprehensive high schools. They do not, of course, exhaust the possibilities. (Little, 1993, p. 158)

Doing a good job as a high school teacher means successfully teaching history or art or Spanish. (Johnson, 1990, p. 171)

Courses of study and departments are "critical sites for teachers' sense of identity, practice, and professional community, deeply woven into the social, political, and intellectual workings both of the profession and of individual schools" (Siskin, 1997, p. 605). They "represent organizational subunits within which different educational structures and processes, collegial relations, and organizational cultures can be established" (McLaughlin & Talbert, 1990, p. 7).

Departments vary widely (Little, 1993; McLaughlin & Talbert, 1990), and, "in many ways, working in different departments is like working in different organizations" (Johnson, 1990, p. 174). Departments "exude a certain spirit, one that varies widely both within and between schools" (Little, 1993, p. 157), and adopt their own "intellectual and moral stance" (p. 154). Some offer a "productive intellectual center for teachers' lives" (Little, 1990, p. 216), whereas others offer little support or even create barriers (Johnson, 1990). Despite criticism (Bryk, Lee, & Smith, 1990), "subject matter departments continue to dominate the social and political organization of secondary schools" (Little, 1993, p. 149).

Subject specialties further contribute to differences (Johnson, 1990; Little, 1990; Little, 1993). For example:

> These discipline-based differences show up in the varying ways teachers understand—and sometimes undermine—school reform efforts. The data from separate studies, decades and continents apart, show remarkable consistency: Whether we call it detracking, destreaming, or mixed ability-grouping, English teachers accept reform eagerly, whereas math teachers oppose it intensely—using, in each case, the same rationales and almost the same words. (Siskin, 1997, p. 612)

Other subject specialties differ as well (Grant, 1988; Johnson, 1990), differences that "are intensified by the height and strength of those 'circus rings' within the local arena, the subject departments" (Siskin, 1997, p. 612).

Tracking constitutes "other common ground among teachers; for example, teachers' assignments to classes of high-track, average, or remedial students might constitute a more powerful basis of interdependence or affiliation than departmental membership" (Little, 1990, p. 197). Thus structural elements—subject matter departments, subjects themselves, and tracking—all play a part in subdividing high school teachers, providing support for some and complications for others.

Social Relationships Create Division

> There are couples and cliques, sudden and unexpected allegiances among former adversaries, arrivals and departures that change the social alchemy overnight, flare-ups that give way to emotional reconciliations, hundreds of unintended slights that are never pardoned, and hundreds of small kindnesses that are appreciated far beyond their immediate import. (Huberman, 1993, p. 12)

There are social pressures to divide as well as structural pressures to separate, and "the formal organization is not always most salient for people" (Frank, 1998, p. 187). Friendships affect subgroups, and teachers may choose to spend time with selected colleagues in nonschool activities. Veteran faculty grow up together—"[hanging] on through the bad years, in part because of interpersonal loyalties" (Louis & Miles, 1990, p. 65). In addition, affiliations outside school "can modify the significance of school-level groups or collegial subunits and provide yet another standard of professionalism or colleagueship" (Little & McLaughlin, 1993, p. 4).

Social subgroups are sometimes related to teachers' social class as well as to that of the schools in which they teach (Metz, 1990a). For some, "teachers' ties to the school [do] not overlap their personal lives very much . . . [and they do] not create close ties to one another or to the school's neighborhood" (p. 80). In other instances, "many teachers live in the community and others wish they could. There [is] much more similarity and continuity between the teaching staff and the community" (p. 59). Race and ethnicity also play a part in creating teacher subgroups, as does gender (Datnow, 1997; Metz, 1990a).

Teachers separate themselves philosophically as well. "Teachers align themselves with colleagues whose work they admire and distance themselves from others whose work they disparage" (Little, 1990, p. 199). Some are idealistic and child-centered (Little, 1993). Others "respond to their dilemma with active cynicism" (Metz, 1993, p. 116). Although subgroups of teachers committed to excellence can provide support for some, this same process can form "an in-group of believers and an out-group of resisters. Such polarization can easily slow down or block improvement" (Louis & Miles, 1990, p. 28).

Individualism Creates Division

> The press for teachers to work together as colleagues is strong, but so is the desire or perhaps necessity for teachers to feel that they have the freedom and autonomy as individuals to construct classrooms that make sense to them and their students. (Little & McLaughlin, 1993, p. vii)

There are fundamental differences in viewing teaching as an individual activity. Some see the teacher as an independent artisan working selectively with his or her peers. In this instance, solitary work within a school setting that is less than optimal is seen as a positive choice, in which teachers are "willing to face isolation to pursue their excited and committed approaches to their subjects. Most of these teachers [seek] social support from groups formed around their academic interests, but outside the school" (Metz, 1990a, pp. 95-96). Although separated within the school, these teachers are not truly isolated in the larger context.

Teachers can be isolated as a function of their particular place within the organization. For some, it is a choice: "Teachers may . . . find a satisfying personal niche in the organization . . . that permit[s] [them] to forge idiosyncratic and entrepreneurial attachments to the school program" (Little, 1990, p. 191). Many prefer isolation as the wall that protects their highly valued classroom autonomy, even though it may create uncertainty and anxiety (Cusick, 1983; Huberman, 1993; Lortie, 1975). For others, isolation is simply a function of the work: "You do your thing in your class, and you leave, and you don't talk to anyone about it" (Boyer, 1983, p. 158; see also Goodlad, 1984; Lightfoot, 1983; Sizer, 1984).

In either case, true isolation in teaching "enormously limits their [teachers'] views of themselves as significant professionals" (Perrone, 1985, p. 648). "Lack of contact with others who [hold] different views or struggle with similar problems deprive[s] these teachers of critical feedback about their practices and beliefs, as well as exposure to possible responses or alternative practices for contemporary classrooms" (McLaughlin, 1993, p. 99). Teacher isolation in high schools affects students as well and is associated with lower student achievement (Gregory & Smith, 1987; Rutter et al., 1979).

Hierarchical and Competitive Teacher Culture Presses Separation

> If departments become not only the primary, but also the exclusive, reference group for teachers, it is likely that decisions about curriculum and staffing . . . will result from political struggles rather than from some balanced understanding of schoolwide needs. (Johnson, 1990, p. 182)

> Anything that deals with the curriculum or instructional issues is pretty much essential school ground. Tech prep and voc ed deal with—well, I'm not sure what they deal with but it's not essential school stuff. (Teacher, quoted in Prestine & Bragg, 1998, pp. 20-21)

Secondary teachers are stacked predictably, rank and file. They are distinguished by differences in seniority, by variations in leadership status (Louis & Miles, 1990), as well as by "subject matter expertise . . . [as] the basis of teachers' authority in the classroom and their power in the organization" (Page, 1991, p. 106). In a similar vein, teachers are distinguished, for better or for worse, by the academic and social status of the students they serve (Little, 1993; Page, 1991).

Academic and vocational teachers provide a graphic example of holding different power within the school, institutionally and socially (Little, 1993; Louis & Miles, 1990; Prestine & Bragg, 1998): Although these two groups of teachers "are united or divided by the priorities they express and the views they hold regarding 'what's best for kids', . . . nonetheless, it is the differences rather than the similarities" (Little, 1993, p. 144) that predominate.

There are differences among other disciplines as well, even though the distinctions are often more fine grained. For example:

> Among the academic domains, teachers make fine (if not always well-informed) distinctions regarding one another's teaching demands—observing, for example, that the load is easier in math, where the curriculum is highly standardized and evaluation of student work is straightforward. (Little, 1993, p. 140)

Overall, relative value is affected "not only from the perceived rigor of one's undergraduate education and professional preparation but also from the perceived intellectual demand of course content in the secondary curriculum" (p. 140).

Teacher subgroups actively compete among themselves for scarce resources (Datnow, 1997; Finley, 1984; Powell, Farrar, & Cohen, 1985; Talbert, 1995)—for "space, equipment, up-to-date texts, supplemental materials, professional development monies, and the like" (Little, 1993, p. 153). They compete for the best quality students (Finley, 1984), with elective teachers—"relegated to the marginal realm of an electives department" (Little, 1993, p. 159)—at a distinct disadvantage because "policy orientation . . . favors the academic curriculum" (p. 159). Teachers compete for teaching assignments, and the political dynamics of seniority (Finley, 1984) interact with the politics of leadership (Metz, 1990a), as "teachers jockey among themselves . . . [and] principals use class assignments as rewards and sanctions" (Oakes & Lipton, 1996, p. 176). Once placed, teachers in these differentiated positions have unequal ability to further affect the system (Little, 1993), and the hierarchy tends to become self-perpetuating.

Although separation into subgroups is portrayed empirically as either supporting or inhibiting, depending on the situation, conflict between and among groups in high schools is viewed overwhelmingly as negative. Probing the extent to which struggle and conflict may play a contributing role in community development needs further inquiry.

Student Culture is Grounded in Separation

High school students' perspectives in a particular school are likely to be a blend of those fostered in the community (or subunits within it), those fostered by the school staff, and those developed and fostered by the student body (and its subgroups) as it also socializes newcomers. (Metz, 1990a, p. 44)

During adolescence . . . all friendships are said to increase in intensity and volatility. (Brantlinger, 1993, p. 157)

Maintaining friendships is one of the central reasons students attend school (Romo & Falbo, 1996), and students, like teachers, live and work in subgroups of their own (Steinberg, 1996). And "it turns out [that] knowing where an individual adolescent fits into the peer culture of his or her school tells us a great deal about that student's orientation toward academics" (p. 24). Peers influence "day-to-day matters such as doing homework, concentrating in class, or taking their studies seriously" (p. 25), and they "become powerful competitors to adult authority" (Wilson & Corcoran, 1988, p. 6). Although peer influence is powerful, it can be either positive or negative (Cuellar, 1992; Lee, Bryk, & Smith, 1993; Newmann, 1997; Renzulli, Reis, Hebert, & Diaz, 1995; Rutter et al., 1979; Sedlak et al., 1986): "In other words, although peer pressure in early adolescence is a given, *harmful* peer pressure is not" (Steinberg, 1996, p. 142).

As we noted in Chapter 3, the stratification of tracking results in segregation of peer groups (Newmann, 1997; Oakes, 1985; Page, 1991; Wigfield, Eccles, & Rodriguez, 1998), leaving concerns that "this practice could leave many schools without any high-achieving adolescents worthy of emulation who might encourage academic engagement among their indifferent and apathetic peers" (Sedlak et al., 1986, p. 56). However, according to Brantlinger (1993), "attitudes about tracking reflect adolescents' track status" (p. 83), and many high-track students—unlike their lower track peers—prefer separation. Students have their own social structure, and "fear of speaking up emanate[s] both from their perceptions of classmates' prejudices and their knowledge of differential power relationships in the classroom" (Phelan, Davidson, & Yu, 1998, p. 188). Peer conflict is further linked to differences in social class and race, as well as to categorical differences in student response to social distance between their homes and their school (Brantlinger, 1993; Cusick, 1983; Miron, 1996; Phelan et al., 1998).

Although the literature is replete with issues of separation, it also offers insight into the power of teachers who work in symphony with their students to create high school communities that support learning and teaching.

Teachers Weave Community Through Dynamics of Unity

The patterns of social relations in the school influence virtually every aspect of the institution.
—Bryk and Driscoll (1988, p. 1)

In this final section, we follow the dynamics of unity that promote the creation of learning community, focusing in particular on teacher contributions. We look first at teachers as supportive individuals, the essence of school community. We look next at the dynamics of forming supportive teacher-student relationships. Finally, we look at the dynamics teachers use to create supportive professional relationships with one another.

Effective Secondary Teachers Are Supportive Individuals

For the first time in his life, Frankie really admired and respected his teacher. (MacLeod, 1995, p. 92)

High school teachers . . . are more likely to view themselves as subject matter specialists, and less likely to see themselves as having responsibility for the 'whole child,' a task that is delegated to administrators or guidance specialists. (Louis & Miles, 1990, p. 10)

The relationship between teachers and their students is the lifeblood of learning, and teachers' success in relating to students is a powerful tool indeed (Firestone & Rosenblum, 1988; Murphy & Hallinger, 1985; Page & Valli, 1990). In this section we review empirical insights on the teachers' power of self as a potent tool for student support, looking at teacher personal characteristics and relationship behaviors that students perceive as supportive and that are linked to higher levels of student performance: being open, trustworthy, respectful, caring, and demanding.

Effective Secondary Teachers Are Open and Share Self

> Borders between adults and students are . . . avoided when teachers exhibit
> humor, openness, and consideration, all of which serve to bridge age and sta-
> tus barriers and connect students with adults in school environments.
> (Phelan et al., 1998, p. 197)

"Students across types . . . want to feel connected personally to their teachers"
(Phelan et al., 1998, p. 197), and teachers who can interact honestly as human and
humane adults are strongly situated to engage their students in learning (Ogden &
Germinario, 1995; Oxley, 1997; Page, 1991; Rivera & Poplin, 1997). Students relate
to teachers who let students see them as people and who let them know that they
"have thoughts, feelings, and experiences that both enliven and go beyond the academic content of the classroom" (Phelan et al., 1998, p. 197). At the same time,
invoking "intimacy or appeal to friendship when they [teachers] need student cooperation . . . [and using] self-revelation, pleas, and reminiscences designed to gain sym-
pathy by exposing the teacher's vulnerability" (Grant, 1988, p. 163) is ineffective.
This difference might suggest the importance of teachers remaining in an adult role
rather than a peer-like role.

Effective Secondary Teachers Are Trustworthy

> You know, you tell the teacher something. . . . And you said this is between
> you and me. But then it's really not. (Miron, 1996, p. 161)

Teacher trustworthiness is critical to student respect (Grant, 1988; Miron,
1996). On one front, trustworthiness is measured by teacher ability to maintain con-
fidentiality with information shared in confidence. In a broader sense, it occurs when
students feel that teachers will not gossip about them. Trustworthiness is also related
to teacher fairness in dealing with student differences (Gregory & Smith, 1987;
McQuillan, 1998; Page, 1991).

Effective Secondary Teachers Are Respectful and Courteous

> A teacher who takes advantage of or ridicules a student may earn an immedi-
> ate laugh from some, at the cost of long-term resentment by many. (Grant,
> 1988, p. 143)

Respect and courtesy is also a central student concern. Students "are likely to be
influenced—either for good or ill—by the models of behaviour provided by teachers
both in the classroom and elsewhere" (Rutter et al., 1979, p. 189). Modeling respect
extends beyond student-teacher interactions to the broader community: Students
respond to teacher respect for students (Firestone & Rosenblum, 1988; Nystrand,
1997), to teacher courtesy "in relations between and among adults and students"

(Metz, 1990a, p. 79), and to "norms of civility, which affect the relations among individuals in the institution" (Bryk & Driscoll, 1988, p. 6). McLaughlin (1994) found that students believe "the way teachers treat you as a student—or as a person actually" (p. 9)—is more important that any other factor in determining student commitment and attachment to school.

Effective Secondary Teachers Are Caring and Helpful

> All the students and parents in our study differentiated good teachers from bad ones. They saw good teachers as people who bent over backward to help students learn. Bad teachers were the ones who didn't try to help all students learn. (Romo & Falbo, 1996, p. 221)

Students relate positively to approachable adults who understand and care about adolescents (McLaughlin, 1994; Phelan et al., 1998; Rutter et al., 1979; Wilson & Corcoran, 1988). Student perception of caring is a complex phenomenon, however, and "adolescents' interpretations of events and views of people [are] filtered through subjectivities influenced by social class" (Brantlinger, 1993, p. 107). Phelan and colleagues (1998) found major variation in students' interpretations of teacher behavior depending on differences in student type:

> Some students (often those who are academically high achieving) associate assistance with schoolwork as indicative of teachers who care. . . . For such students, academic assistance demonstrates that teachers are aware of and concerned about helping them meet long-term educational goals. For other students (particularly those having trouble with academic work), teachers' attitudes and personality characteristics (e.g., patience, humor, tolerance, ability to listen) and person-to-person assistance with schoolwork constitute caring. Many of these youths express a preference for direct, personal interaction. For them, caring means the expression of interest and concern that goes beyond assistance with schoolwork. (p. 197)

Regardless of this complexity, student perception of teachers as caring and helpful is a critical factor in student support (Meier, 1995; Miron, 1996; Page, 1991).

Effective Secondary Teachers Are Demanding

> Teachers, not students, are given the responsibility for deciding what students should learn, how they should learn it, and how fast they should assimilate it. . . . Teachers who do not determine what will be done and see that it is done are simply not skilled in the art of teaching. (Metz, 1993, pp. 108-109)

Students want teachers to hold high expectations for student behavior and to demand that they give great effort (Natriello et al., 1990; Ogden & Germinario,

1995; Rivera & Poplin, 1997; Wilson & Corcoran, 1988), to "both provide support and hold them to the sorts of expectations that would lead to growth and maturity" (McQuillan, 1997, p. 645).

Teachers provide positive models by holding high expectations for their own performance, shaping student behavior through feedback, as well as through making explicit demands for student performance (Rutter et al., 1979). There is "a reluctance to accept excuses, an expectation that people would get down to work" (Grant, 1988, p. 175):

> [The teacher] must have the courage to make demands on a student, to insist that he rewrite the same paragraph until it begins to make sense and do work that is often difficult for him—and sometimes boring. The teacher must sustain the student in engagement with a subject that has its own logic and is independent of the student's impulses or subjective will. (p. 143)

Strict without meanness, "good teachers know how to . . . handle kids" (Brantlinger, 1993, p. 99) and to keep the focus on instruction and learning. By "mak[ing] it very clear that what they do really is significant" (Grant, 1988, p. 144) and "taking students seriously, teachers elicit the best from students by expecting the most" (Nystrand, 1997, p. 92).

Altogether, these relationship behaviors offer teachers a powerful tool—the power of self—for creating strong, supportive relationships with their students, the heart of core technology, and for enhancing student performance.

Teachers Form Supportive Relationships With Students

> At this time of continuing pressure to restructure schools, there is unprecedented agreement on the part of policymakers, reformers, and school people alike that the teacher/student relationship is at the heart of any authentic school change. (Little & McLaughlin, 1993, p. vii)

> Classrooms are . . . a unique type of social system; no other profession is structured so that its service is delivered day after day, in a fairly set routine, to groups rather than to individuals, and groups that are often unwilling clients. Yet within this group the needs of individuals must be met. (Larson, 1992, p. 36)

In this section, we examine empirical findings on the dynamics of teachers and students working together in high schools to create supportive relationships, classrooms, schools, and extended communities. We look at three major dynamics that define this relationship: (a) teachers engaging students in supportive relationships, (b) students influencing teachers, and (c) teachers responding positively to student diversity.

Teachers Engage Students in Supportive Relationships

> The teacher/student relationship is perhaps the most profound and conse-
> quential of "working conditions" for teachers, the one that most directly
> affects their commitment to work and their motivation to learn. (Little,
> 1990, p. 192)

> The adults stand unambivalently in loco parentis, and, like good parents, the
> teachers and staff exercise a caring watchfulness, concerned with all aspects
> of a child's development. (Grant, 1988, p. 178)

Nurturing interaction between teachers and their students, both academic and
personal, is essential to providing students with effective student support (Meier,
1995; Nauman, 1985; Phelan et al., 1998) and, as we have just seen, is of extreme
importance to teacher success and satisfaction as well. Teachers support students in
establishing strong connections with adults, harnessing relationship power by establishing bonds with individuals and with whole classes in a role that extends beyond
the classroom (Bryk & Driscoll, 1988; Cusick, 1983; Gregory, 1993; Newmann,
1981; Ogden & Germinario, 1995; Wehlage et al., 1989).

When teachers fail to relate, "students move about bereft of relationships with
anyone but their exact age and grade peers, . . . [and] there is no thick, complex and
powerful counterculture to balance the one that has been developed for adolescents
only" (Meier, 1995, p. 113). When students and teachers relate successfully, on the
other hand, "emotional bonds . . . play a crucial role in engaging and motivating students to learn" (Lee, Smith, & Croninger, 1995, p. 6). In reality, both academic and
personal relationships merge: "Even when teacher interactions with students are socially motivated, these contacts provide opportunities for academic teaching as well as
expressions of concern for students' personal well-being, . . . [and] informal teacher-
student contact can simultaneously promote academic effectiveness" (Bryk &
Driscoll, 1988, p. 7).

Although there is much emphasis on teachers interacting with individual students, teacher-student relationships cannot be divorced from the context in which
they occur, and teachers must relate to the class and to students as a whole as well as
to individuals (Frank, 1998; Nystrand, 1997; Rutter et al., 1979; Wehlage et al.,
1989). Learning and teaching, as a social activity, is both contextual and reciprocal:

> Learning in classrooms is not done in isolation; instead it occurs in the con-
> text of relationships with teachers and peers. . . . These relationships, along
> with the different roles that emerge for students and teachers in various class-
> rooms, strongly influence how students learn. (Wigfield et al., 1998, p. 74)

Rutter and his colleagues (1979) "found that teachers in . . . more successful
schools spent higher proportions of their time interacting with the class as a whole,
rather than with individual pupils" (p. 116).

Teachers Are Affected by Students

> Actually to teach, to make learning happen, and especially to transform or develop the thinking of another person, a teacher must have that person's assent and cooperation. Anyone who has had close contact with a child of 18 months or older knows that although children are socially subordinate to adults, children have sufficient independence of mind to make teachers . . . crucially vulnerable to their decisions about cooperation. (Metz, 1993, p. 105)

Students are powerful partners in school community, although much of the school workplace literature ignores them (McLaughlin, 1993; Miron, 1996; Sedlak et al., 1986). As distinct individuals, students vary widely and give a host of different responses to similar school and life situations (Phelan et al., 1998; Wang & Gordon, 1994; Wang & Reynolds, 1995). They decide whether or not—as well as how—they will engage in school and learning (McLaughlin, 1994; Perrone, 1985). And, as we saw in the previous chapter, they weigh the value of school in relation to their own, personal possibilities, then make decisions on engagement based on their conclusions. Furthermore, as a group, students have volume on their side. In the end, "there are more students than there are adults in a school. Ultimately, the teachers' control depends on winning the students' assent" (Metz, 1993, p. 109).

Students derive additional power from the social context of their relationships with their teachers (Boyer, 1983; Sedlak et al., 1986). Teachers are highly dependent on positive association with their students for job satisfaction and sense of identity (Lortie, 1975; Metz, 1993; Sedlak et al., 1986): "Success in the profession stems mainly from [teachers'] successful relationships with [their] students, not [their] peers. When it comes to considering change, the opinions that matter most to teachers are likely those of their charges, not their peers" (Larson, 1992, p. 34).

Teachers depend on relationships with whole classes as well as with single students:

> From teachers' perspectives, "trouble" is not limited to . . . conflicts. . . . They always expect bland acquiescence to slip to adamantine silence, recalcitrance in answering even the simplest of questions, . . . stoniness in reaction to their jokes, or superciliousness in the face of their enthusiasm: "They're a sea of blank faces—I want to shake them to wake them up." (Page, 1991, p. 155)

Student behavior is so potent that teachers regularly modify their own behavior in response to students (Natriello & Dornbusch, 1983; Oehmen, 1981; Page, 1991). Teacher responses vary from class to class and are "constructed uniquely in terms of the differences in the characteristics of the different classes taught by the same teacher" (McLaughlin, 1993, p. 81).

Teachers Are Responsive to Student Differences

It would seem easier to sustain a communal organizational life when the institution attracts like-minded individuals. This observation raises questions about the role of diversity in the student body and the limitations that diversity may place on school life. How much differentiation among students and faculty is possible within a "community" framework? Can a school create a unified organization even though a diverse array of cultures and groups are represented among its students? Some limitations must exist. (Bryk & Driscoll, 1988, p. 12)

Responsive secondary teachers respond to students as individuals with unique needs (Oxley, 1997; Page & Valli, 1990; Wilson & Corcoran, 1988). Cultural differences present enormous complexity and challenge and "can be paramount in affecting the types of interactions (positive and/or negative) that occur in school" (Phelan et al., 1998, p. 3):

One important key to teachers' success in enabling all students to achieve at high levels was knowledge about these students' families, cultures, and life outside school. Absent this understanding, teachers fail to connect with these students in the ways they did with yesterday's traditional student cohort. (McLaughlin, 1994, p. 9)

The literature abounds with descriptions of teacher preference for working with students with whom they feel most comfortable (Frank, 1998; Metz, 1990a; Metz, 1993; Miron, 1996; Nystrand, 1997; Phelan et al., 1998), and much of that like-mindedness is cultural and social: "Such students are likely to be easier to teach, and as a result, teachers' sense of efficacy and satisfaction should be greater" (Bryk & Driscoll, 1988, p. 13). Students struggle with maintaining cultural identity (Miron, 1996; Phelan et al., 1998; Wang & Gordon, 1994), and this struggle is affected by school differences: "Being African-American in one school setting . . . is a vastly different qualitative experience than that found in a different setting. Students' experience of their own (and others') ethnicity, then, differs" (Miron, 1996, p. 142).

Effective teachers affect this difference by supporting students in transition and in maintaining their cultural identities and by adapting with flexibility to their differences in learning styles and cultural preferences (Brouillette, 1997; Engstrom, 1981; Metz, 1990a; Miron, 1996; Phelan et al., 1998). Exchanges between students and teachers, then, "affect future student relations and characteristics as the cycle is continued" (Frank, 1998, p. 198).

With the complexity of the school environment, the wide range of problems that teachers cope with on a daily basis, and the intensity and challenges of relating successfully to students of all backgrounds, teachers need strong support. So they turn to one another.

Teachers Form Supportive Relationships
With One Another

> During our darkest hours, we gravitated toward collegial networking. We had a hard basis of caring and respect to see us through. (Louis & Miles, 1990, p. 55)

In this section, we explore key dynamics teachers use to create collegial support—"a feeling of sharing and a set of actions for the common good" (Wehlage et al., 1989, p. 142). We look at four main processes that teachers use to foster professional community: (a) using empowerment to build learning community, (b) creating a culture of intellectual vitality, c) weaving a common vision, and (d) developing an environment that supports change. We emphasize the dynamics of creating schoolwide community, although similar dynamics characterize efforts to create strong teacher subgroups.

Teachers Use Empowerment to
Build Teacher Community

> In this building, the teacher is the school executive. (Wilson & Corcoran, 1988, p. 89)

Although teacher empowerment is essential to creating secondary community (Newmann, 1997; Ogden & Germinario, 1995), it is not in itself enough (Louis & Kruse, 1995). Effective teachers use empowerment to accept communal responsibility for student achievement (Bryk & Driscoll, 1988; Lee & Smith, 1996; Lee, Smith, & Croninger, 1995; Ogden & Germinario, 1995) and to create supportive yet demanding learning communities focused on learning (Larson, 1992; Wilson & Corcoran, 1988). Teachers are essential leaders and partners in creating learning communities, and "a gradual shift of control from administrator to department heads and teachers . . . is essential to carry out . . . elements of evolutionary planning such as the action orientation, a focus on reflection, and the collective development of themes and sagas" (Louis & Miles, 1990, pp. 214-215). Leadership opportunities include formal positions such as department head assignments as well as informal positions of leadership such as those secured through membership in dominant teacher groups (Louis & Miles, 1990; Oxley, 1997; Rutter et al., 1979; Siskin, 1997).

Teachers use peer networks both to support and to demand good teaching. Teachers support one another in a variety of ways such as through peer recognition (Bryk & Driscoll, 1988), peer mentorship (Huberman, 1993), and team collaboration (Firestone & Rosenblum, 1988; Lee & Smith, 1996; Meier, 1995). In addition, they create peer pressure to teach well (Louis & Miles, 1990), particularly in indoctrinating new faculty (Brouillette, 1997; Rutter et al., 1979). All the while, they must "defin[e] a workable balance between individual needs and collective responsibilities" (Huberman, 1993, p. 14), because "professional egalitarianism runs deep in school buildings, and noninterference with the core work of others constitutes a sign of professional respect" (p. 29)—an issue that tends to inhibit peer demand among veteran faculty.

Teachers Create a Culture of Intellectual Vitality

Harnessing the energy of esprit de corps created by developing joint solutions to common problems, teachers work "to improve the intellectual climate of the school" (Boyer, 1983, p. 159). When reaching for common goals by working with stimulating people (Wilson & Corcoran, 1988) and by "reflect[ing] on the effectiveness of their own techniques and processes" (Wilson & Daviss, 1994, pp. 147-148), teachers in productive high schools create "spirited, reflective professional community . . . [that] actually generate[s] motivation to roll up one's sleeves and endeavor to meet the unfamiliar and often difficult needs of contemporary students" (McLaughlin, 1993, p. 98).

Teachers struggle with critical issues having "strong substantive emphasis" (Louis & Miles, 1990, p. 81), discussing ideas such as "what they believe should be included in effective secondary education" (Hannay & Ross, 1997, p. 590) and holding "honest dialogue about real problems" (Grant, 1988, p. 253). Teacher competence, both in subject matter (Bodenhausen, 1988; Goldhaber & Brewer, 1996; Monk, 1994) and in teaching talent (Perrone, 1985; Romo & Falbo, 1996), is a priority as teachers "think, invent, and reflect on their work" (Lee, Smith, & Croninger, 1995, p. 5).

Teachers in high schools that promote high levels of student achievement create intellectual community by "building internal resource—and resource-getting—capacity" (Louis & Miles, 1990, p. 261; see also Brouillette, 1997). In these schools, teachers look both inside and outside the school for information (Huberman, 1993; Louis & Miles, 1990), stockpiling tentative solutions to the problems they face or anticipate facing. "Together, teachers' collective experience composes a rich pool from which new practices or changed conceptions can be fashioned" (McLaughlin, 1993, p. 99).

Teachers Weave Common Vision

Schools *can* and *must* move forward without everyone on the train—but there will be more people on the train if it is clear where it is going. (Louis & Miles, 1990, p. 237)

Clear, powerful mission focused on learning and teaching—"a common vision of what the school is about and what kind of people the students should become" (Bryk

& Driscoll, 1988, p. 4)—is a dominant force in effective high schools (Cawelti, 1997; Murphy & Hallinger, 1985; Newmann, 1997; Talbert, 1992; Wilson & Corcoran, 1988). Vision building is born of action (Larson, 1992), and visions evolve as a "complex braid of the evolving themes of the change program. . . . Visions are developed and reinforced from action, although they may have a seed that is based simply on hope" (Louis & Miles, 1990, p. 237).

Common vision propels further action as well and is, therefore, not only a powerful force for unifying community but is also a dynamic force for change: "The vast majority of the . . . [change] facilitators . . . are beginning to develop new images of secondary school education and what that might mean for students, teachers, and the community at large" (Hannay & Ross, 1997, p. 594). "Broad, ennobling, feelingful, *shared* images . . . are an important feature guiding successful improvement" (Louis & Miles, 1990, p. 293), and common vision gives unified direction to teacher work (Powell, Farrar, & Cohen, 1985).

Teachers Create a Culture That Supports Change

In intellectual communities, the work is never done. Revisions in "collaborative norms, skills and practices among educators and between educators and other partners in the community and elsewhere, focussing on new approaches to teaching, learning, assessment, and continuous problems solving" (Fullan, 1997, p. 46), are essential components of thoughtful school environments.

Change cultures define productive high schools. Creating a culture of change requires risk-taking and tolerance for ambiguity (Fullan, 1990; Louis & Miles, 1990) and is dependent on having teachers willing to risk leaving colleagues behind. Change requires jumping in—"support and commitment cannot all be built in advance: They tend to develop *after* people have intensive, successful experience with the change, not before" (Louis & Miles, 1990, p. 29). Thus risk-taking is reinforced by success (Louis & Miles, 1990). At the same time, effective change is grounded in knowledge and in teachers' use of data to make calculated, informed decisions (Hannay & Ross, 1997).

Timeliness is an issue, and "school improvement needs resting phases between those of high energy" (Louis & Miles, 1990, p. 97). Persistence is a critical attribute, because instructional changes take a lot longer than people think they will (Prestine, 1998), and they present "great difficulties in coordinating, orchestrating and sustaining" (Fullan, 1988, p. 20). As Louis and Miles (1990) reported, "Even small scale changes require up to two years for good stabilization, . . . and a five- to ten-year perspective is typical for more substantial reforms" (p. 30).

Thus in productive high schools, the teacher community provides a resilient foundation of social and intellectual support for teacher work, undergirding individual teachers in their efforts to support students in the classroom.

Conclusion

As we have shown, building support for learning is indeed a complex endeavor. The slippery web of relationships that form community is ever evolving, and constant motion is the norm. As teachers and students unify, they tend to create strong subgroups, which inherently create separation. Subgroups are dependent on the health of the whole for strong support and overall success, yet they are naturally positioned to compete for scarce resources. Problems can contribute to separation and dissent, yet they also serve as common ground that unifies a widely diverse collection of individuals. Harnessed for the common good, these seemingly contradictory dynamics weave a fabric of support for teachers and students that becomes the nucleus for enhanced student performance.

Motivated to achieve high expectations and supported by strong community, teachers and students are positioned to go to work. We next explore another central aspect of core technology in the next chapter on Academic Autonomy.

6

Academic Autonomy

The classroom is where it finally all happens. It is here that the major formal efforts to teach youth occur. If there is no success at this level there is, for most students, no other place to go to learn. And it is within the classroom that innovations succeed or fail.

—Larson (1992, p. 36)

We must understand that education rests on the practical wisdom of a teacher working in a particular context with a unique mix of children having complex needs. The teacher must be free to devise appropriate means to broad cultural ends; she is not a drill instructor working from a manual.

—Grant (1988, p. 158)

Classroom instruction is exceptionally difficult, remarkably ambiguous work. A "highly complex, unstable, and furiously interactive task" (Huberman, 1993, p. 16), teaching is "undercut and rendered uncertain by a host of factors [such as] the lack of reliable, clearly effective strategies for accomplishing classroom work [and] the difficulty of judging long-term effects on students" (Metz, 1993, p. 104). To respond successfully in this uncertain context, teachers must have freedom to ply their craft. Yet autonomy is a double-edged sword. As we saw in Chapter 4, teacher autonomy separated from press for high achievement contributes to a firm, downward spiral of expectation linked with negotiating grades and order. Thus teacher "autonomy contributes to irresponsible and disastrous teaching, as much as it is essential to imaginative and effective teaching" (Sedlak, Wheeler, Pullin, & Cusick, 1986, p. 121).

In attempting to compensate for this dynamic, some support the tenet that teaching should be a rational, standardized science (Grant, 1988; McNeil, 1986), viewing teachers "more as lab technicians than principal investigators" (Louis, 1990, p. 28). Many, however, see high-performance teaching as being essentially a unique art form (Kaufman & Aloma, 1997; Lightfoot, 1983; Little, 1993; Sizer, 1984)—a wellspring of "context-sensitive, continuously evolving, interactive responses that many teachers call on to run stimulating, instructionally effective classrooms" (Huberman, 1993, p. 19). Viewed empirically, effective teaching emerges as a masterful, fluid performance that is grounded in a firm content and pedagogical knowledge base.

In this chapter we explore the dynamics of autonomous learning and teaching, focusing in particular on the role of teacher autonomy, nested in the context of press for high achievement and strong academic support, as essential to successful learning and teaching at the high school level. We look, as well, at the role of student autonomy, because effective teachers share their freedom and empower students as learners. The interactive, flowing academic relationship between teachers and students in tandem supports effective learning and teaching.

We look first at the role in high achievement of academically demanding learning environments. Second, we visit the dynamics of academically responsive learning environments that support student learning. Third, we look at the role of student autonomy in learning as effective teachers share their power. Finally, we explore the power of authentic learning and teaching in supporting high levels of student performance.

Effective Teachers Create Academically Demanding Learning Environments

These . . . teachers agreed that all students can learn and that the role of the teacher is to provide opportunities in the classroom for all students to excel.

—Datnow (1997, p. 218)

The underlying epistemology of classroom interaction defines the bottom line for learning: What ultimately counts is the extent to which instruction requires students to think, not just report someone else's thinking.

—Nystrand (1997, p. 72)

Effective teachers harness their autonomy to create classroom environments focused on student achievement, and they do so in a number of ways. First, teachers must be well prepared for the subject they teach to provide learning opportunities for students (Gamoran & Nystrand, 1992; Hannay & Ross, 1997; Sedlak et al., 1986): "The what of instruction—the content and subject matter—is critical to learning" (Nystrand, 1997, p. 73). Students' achievement improves when "teachers already deeply immersed in the what and how of [teaching], who have learned their subject matter once for themselves and once for teaching it to others" (Goodlad, 1997, p. 135) are placed in classrooms. According to Little (1990), "When teachers are poorly prepared at the outset to treat a subject in depth, or when their competence erodes as the field passes them by, academic goals are likely to suffer" (pp. 202-203).

Second, good teachers are both clear and demanding as they convey subject matter, thus making content and expectations comprehensible (Bratlinger, 1993; Phelan et al., 1998). In selecting practices that make students more successful learners, effective teachers emphasize maintaining high intellectual standards and developing deep understanding (McNeil, 1986; Newmann, Marks, & Gamoran, 1996; Sizer, 1984; Page, 1991). They place students in "challenging and serious epistemic roles requiring them to think, interpret, and generate new understandings" (Nystrand, 1997, p. 7). Emphasizing a high order of thinking that "signifies challenge and expanded use of the mind" (Newmann, 1992b, p. 63), effective teachers focus their teaching efforts on developing "good thinking" (Nickerson, 1988, p. 4).

Third, effective teachers create densely packed learning environments in which "more classroom time is allocated to academic learning [and] more allotted time is engaged academic learning time for students" (Wilson & Corcoran, 1988, p. 122). Classroom interruptions are minimized, including disruptions for dealing with negative behavior, and emphasis is greater on engaging students frequently and intensively in learning content (Driscoll, 1987; Gamoran, 1987a; Keith & Cool, 1992; Metz, 1990a; Murphy, Hull, & Walker, 1987; Page, 1991; Rutter, Maughan, Mortimore, Ouston, & Smith, 1979).

Effective Teachers Create Academically Responsive Learning Environments

> *These relationships between teachers, students, and subject matter are the stuff of schooling.*
> —McLaughlin (1993, p. 98)

Learning and teaching occur in a socially interactive context—"between a self and a pedagogical other" (Nystrand, 1997, p. 95)—that supports achievement (Huberman, 1993; McLaughlin, 1994; Page, 1991). Effective teachers develop individualized, context-sensitive teaching styles, and they respond to students both as individual learners and as whole classroom groups.

Effective Teachers Develop Individualized, Contextually Appropriate Teaching Styles

Teachers develop a very personal style as they aim each day to balance affect, control, and cognition. No one "formula" works for all teachers; rather, each instructor undergoes a process of trial and error that often involves considerable pain and distress before he/she begins to find "what works." But what works with one group may not be as successful with another because of a particular mix of personalities and needs. Style is never perfected because each year a new group of students arrives and the process begins again. Considerable energy is diverted from delivering the content per se because of constant pedagogical demands. (Larson, 1992, p. 39)

Autonomous in their classrooms, teachers have "the responsibility and the prerogative to stipulate whether classrooms are businesslike or boisterous, enlightening or merely entertaining" (Page, 1991, p. 82). The balance between analysis and improvisation offers opportunity for individualization of teaching, and successful teachers develop individual teaching preferences and styles that are both subject and context particular (Grant, 1988; Kaufman & Aloma, 1997; Little, 1990; McLaughlin & Talbert, 1990).

Within the varying, complex environment of the classroom, masterful teachers respond to instructional challenges with ill defined "cognitive chunk[s] that trigger automatically a series of chained responses when several, often subtle, indices appear" (Huberman, 1993, p. 17). This phenomenon highly complexifies the sharing of trade knowledge, because effective teachers are often unable to completely explain their responses.

Effective Teachers Analyze Student Understanding and Adapt Practice Accordingly

As part of the process of analysis and adaptation, effective teachers improvise: The teacher has a general goal for the time period. . . . The core materials for these activity formats are prepared and ready at hand, and the teacher begins the sequence as planned. As soon as he or she sees, however, that several children are squirming in their seats or wrinkling their brows in apparent confusion or that the two problems worked at the board entail faulty algorithms, the remainder of the sequence is cast aside, and our teacher begins improvising with a series of ad hoc responses to the new situation. (Huberman, 1993, p. 15)

Effective teachers harness the power of content knowledge by interacting academically with their students, meshing analysis of student understanding with adjustments in instructional processes through adaptive problem solving (Alfassi, 1998; Darling-Hammond, Ancess, & Falk, 1995; Louis & Miles, 1990; Oxley, 1997):

In order to move beyond traditional "transmission" teaching, teachers need knowledge about their students' existing understanding of a subject, as well as knowledge about students' academic (and non-academic) interests. That knowledge helps teachers make relevant connections, and to consider subject matter through the eyes of learners. Without that knowledge, teachers end up teaching to the class as a whole, rather than a roomful of individuals, and they cast students in a passive role. (McLaughlin, 1994, p. 11)

In the face of the ambiguity of successful core technology, teachers

> . . . must try one approach, assess its effect on the students' learning, and if the student still is not learning, then they must try another approach, and on and on, until the student demonstrates understanding and is performing up to specific scholastic standards. (Romo & Falbo, 1996, p. 222)

Effective secondary teachers respond to students as individual learners. According to Louis and Miles (1990), "Whole-person involvement means individualized treatment of students, in and out of the classroom" (p. 25). Successful secondary teachers form nurturing academic relationships with students, providing "specific feedback aimed toward improving individual student's work" (Newmann, 1985, p. 16) as well as "focus[ing] their resources on problem students and attempt[ing] to turn them toward success" (Wilson & Corcoran, 1988, p. 128).

In responding to students as individuals, teachers must attend to diversity. Student achievement is affected by differences in gender (Hamilton, 1998; Larson, 1996; Meece & Jones, 1996; Oakes, 1990; Reap & Cavallo, 1992) as well as by differences in student "histories, and cultural backgrounds, . . . current contexts for learning, and . . . their families" (Darling-Hammond et al., 1995, p. 261). Effective teachers recognize and accommodate learner differences in cognitive styles, achievement levels, preferences for amount of structure and direction, and preferences for academic or personal relationships with teachers (Andrews, 1996; Matthews, 1996; Metz, 1993; Phelan et al., 1998; O'Brien, 1994; Ornstein, 1997).

Effective teachers also attend to classes of students as a whole, responding to the uniqueness of different groups as well as meeting the wide range of needs of individual students (Fullan, 1988; Little, 1990; Oxley, 1997). By attending to both individual and group levels of understanding and responding accordingly, teachers are able to adjust instruction for maximum effectiveness.

Effective Teachers Create Intellectually Fluid Learning Environments

> Speaking and listening are the motor and motivation for learning. (O'Keefe, 1995, p. 3)

Effective secondary teachers deliberately create rich learning environments, blending control and autonomy to construct intellectually open yet academically challenging classrooms for learning. As teachers and students interact with one another, "knowledge constructed in classrooms (and other educational settings) shapes, and is shaped by, the discursive activity and social practices of members" (Gee & Green, 1998, p. 119).

Teachers control the flow of learning in a number of ways. They use discussion as both tool and process for learning (Larson, 1997). Effective teachers foster extensive use of discourse, integrating classroom talk with reading, writing, and a wide range of other topics, and harnessing the power of probing discussion to develop depth of understanding (Gamoran, 1992; Gamoran & Nystrand, 1992; Nystrand, 1997).

Effective teachers attend to pace, alternating order and spontaneity (Page, 1991): "Given the freedom and uncertainties of genuine conversation, learning is often built on surprises" (Nystrand, 1997, p. x). Through authentic conversation, they decentralize the speaking voice and offer their students freedom to contribute, freedom to disagree, freedom to change their minds and to develop understanding over time, and freedom to follow their own interests (Clinchy, 1997; Heipp & Huffman, 1994; Nystrand, 1997; Page, 1991). At the same time, effective teachers "never want to shortchange the technical" (Metz, 1990a, p. 55); they vacillate "between opening up instruction to make demands on students to invite their discussion and controlling the content" (McNeil, 1986, p. 197).

Effective Teachers Empower Students as Learners

Effective teachers create communal environments that support learning by empowering students as individual learners as well as by harnessing the power of cooperative learning. They assist students in taking responsibility for becoming "competent, resourceful learners, rather than dishing out answers in ways that maintain the teacher as powerful and the student as passive" (Darling-Hammond et al., 1995, p. 73).

Effective Teachers Empower Students as Individual Learners

When students are denied a voice, they often make themselves heard through resistance and disruptive behavior (MacLeod, 1995; Miron, 1996; Page, 1991). Although they may have little formal power, "because of their numbers, students simply overwhelm many schools and promote values that serve their perceived interests" (McQuillan, 1997, p. 14). Successful secondary teachers "follow their students voices . . . [and] take their students seriously, finding—sometimes creating—ways to let their students know that what they think counts" (Nystrand, 1997, p. 108). Students value teachers who take students' voices and concerns into account and who place "students and their work at the center of the conversation" (Darling-Hammond et al., 1995, p. 255).

Much of the literature has focused on the school-level perspective of giving students positions of responsibility, and the literature also speaks of student classroom-level responsibility as having a positive impact on student success (Bratlinger, 1993; Darling-Hammond, 1997a; Frank, 1998; Louis & Miles, 1990; McQuillan, 1995; Ogden & Germinario, 1995). Within the classroom, students are empowered primarily as learners: "The good news is that they . . . get more power. The bad news is that they . . . also get more responsibility" (McQuillan, 1998, p. 197). When students are taught to regulate their own learning and are supported in being self-directed, they are more likely to focus on school and to engage fully in academic work (Darling-Hammond et al., 1995; Ornstein, 1995; Williams, 1996). Student empowerment is hardly a simple matter, however, and reactions to empowerment among students in different tracks and from different backgrounds appear to include differences (Bratlinger, 1993; Brouillette, 1997).

Teachers Harness the Power of Cooperative Learning

> Classroom cooperation is often considered cheating. Only recently has re-search produced a conception of 'cooperative learning' that demonstrates effectiveness in promoting learning among a range of students. (Wehlage, Rutter, Smith, Lesko, & Fernandez, 1989, p. 182)

Effective teachers include cooperative learning, not just individualized or competitive structures, as a powerful strategy for supporting secondary student achievement (Johnson, Johnson, & Smith, 1995; McQuillan, 1997; Newmann & Thompson, 1987; Pederson & Digby, 1995). With broad impact across a wide range of diverse students,

> . . . a consistent finding in cooperative learning research has been that in het-erogeneous groups students, whether highly skilled or struggling with the subject, can make gains in achievement and social skills that exceed the gains they would have made in homogeneous groups or classrooms. (Oakes & Lipton, 1996, p. 182)

The literature indicates, however, that differences such as gender, sociability, ability, and ethnicity affect student preferences for cooperative learning. According to McLaughlin (1994), "Students, especially nontraditional students, favor cooperative learning" (p. 11), whereas others prefer competition (Becker & Rosen, 1992; Li & Adamson, 1992). Cooperative learning is further complicated by differences in willingness to seek help, with "students who perhaps need the most help (those with a lower sense of competence) . . . [being] the ones least likely to engage in help seeking" (Wigfield, Eccles, & Rodriguez, 1998, p. 102).

There are many types of cooperative-learning strategies, and strategies are combined with a great range of other instructional options with differing results. Among the positive impacts of effective cooperative-learning experiences are individualizing instruction, increasing motivation, improving sociability across diverse groups, and increasing on-task behavior (Canady & Rettig, 1995; Nystrand, 1997; Okebukola, 1992).

Effective Teachers Create Authentic Learning Environments

Classroom practice should be more authentic, and authenticity should be widespread, not limited to a few good classes.

—Lee, Smith, and Croninger (1995, p. 11)

Intellectual accomplishment that is worthwhile and meaningful can be considered authentic.

—Newmann, Marks, and Gamoran
(1995, p. 282)

Effective teachers create authentic learning environments that are connected to context, support active construction of high-quality knowledge, provide focus through coherence across disciplines, and offer depth and richness. In this section, we explore each of these qualities.

Effective Learning Environments Are Connected to Context

> Having been given the chance to engage in work on the world's terms through internships and college courses makes it easier to go out into the world with expectations—matched with skills—for success. (Darling-Hammond et al., 1995, p. 71)

As we saw in Chapter 4, secondary students are motivated to achieve at high levels when schoolwork is connected to their own personal reality, both present and future. Thus effective learning environments provide relevance in relationship to student motivation systems and, as such, provide effective context for learning (Bratlinger, 1993; Page, 1991; Phelan et al., 1998). Effective learning environments "blur what has been too great a demarcation line between the secondary schools and higher education institutions" (Perrone, 1985, p. 654) and also connect the school to the world of work (Romo & Falbo, 1996; Stevenson, Kochenek, & Schneider, 1998). In effective classrooms, *relevant* learning experiences not only engage students but also maintain high demands for achievement, avoiding the tendency to drop the level of academic expectations that often occurs when teachers "preach the value of 'life skills' " (Page, 1991, p. 191).

Effective Learning Environments Support Active Construction of High-Quality Knowledge

> Students at all achievement levels told us that they prefer classrooms where they can take an active part in their own learning, classrooms where they can

work interactively with their teachers to construct knowledge and understanding. We found these active student roles to be particularly important to the engagement and academic success of non-traditional students, who generally failed to thrive in teacher-dominated classrooms. (McLaughlin, 1994, p. 11)

Effective classrooms are living environments (Cohen & Seaman, 1997; Sizer, 1984) in which "students take an active role in learning by discovering answers and producing knowledge" (Oxley, 1997, p. 628). Perkins (1998) found that active learning follows these broad principles:

1. Learning for understanding occurs principally through reflective engagement in approachable but challenging performances.

2. New understanding performances are built on previous understandings and new information provided by the instructional setting.

3. Learning a body of knowledge and know-how for understanding typically requires a chain of understanding performances of increasing challenge and variety.

4. Learning for understanding often involves conflict with older repertoires of understanding performances and their associated ideas and images. (pp. 52-53)

Activities such as case studies, simulations, student projects, seminars, out-of-school experiences, and connecting with postsecondary programs (Canady & Rettig, 1995; Johnson, Wardlow, & Franklin, 1997; Perrone, 1985; Sweeney, 1992) "engender a sense of school membership through academics" (Wehlage et al., 1989, p. 190) and provide "value beyond school" (Newmann et al., 1995, p. 5). According to O'Keefe (1995),

Evidence is accumulating that students who take an active role in the construction of meaning, whether through inquiry, problem solving, or any number of methods that place them in a position of building knowledge, instead of just storing information, learn more and better. (p. 4)

Furthermore, there is evidence that active learning has a positive impact on achievement for students of all ability levels (Darling-Hammond et al., 1995; Lee et al., 1995).

Yet emphasis on active learning is not, in itself, enough. Newmann and colleagues (1996) found that "reform efforts may increase active learning without enhancing the intellectual quality of students' work" (p. 280) and focus on the necessity for active, constructed learning that sets "standards of intellectual quality rather than teaching techniques or processes as the central target of instruction" (p. 280).

Effective Learning Environments Make Connections Across and Within Disciplines

Fragmentation of learning, common at the secondary level, is a byproduct of "the reduction of any topic to fragments or disjointed pieces of information" (McNeil, 1986, p. 167) as well as of the compartmentalization of knowledge that results from separate subjects taught according to a rigid and unyielding schedule of classes (Cusick, 1983; Sedlak et al., 1986). As we saw in Chapter 4, "high school students in low-achieving classes are far more likely than their higher-achieving counterparts to be involved in such contrived, fragmented learning" (Nystrand, 1997, p. 103).

According to Wehlage and colleagues (1989), reforms "should have their roots in a more comprehensive and adequate conception of learning, and in restructured curriculum that is much less fragmented and superficial" (p. 181). Effective teachers provide focus and coherence by connecting learning across disciplines (Keating & Keating, 1996; Perrone, 1985). Furthermore, they coordinate efforts between classrooms (Lee et al., 1995), connecting course content both by "developing integrated subject matter . . . [and by] channeling students into logical patterns of courses" (Murphy et al., 1987, p. 11).

Effective Learning Environments Offer Deep, Rich Learning Experiences

Combining cooperative groups with a thematic or problem-solving orientation can provide a rich intellectual, yet concrete, context to help students organize knowledge, construct meanings, and sustain interest. It also acknowledges and attends specifically to the social construction of knowledge. (Oakes & Lipton, 1996, p. 183)

Secondary education is traditionally "dominated by an obsession with coverage of vast amounts of information in many different subjects. Coverage is characterized by racing through topic after topic to 'expose' students to the key concepts and facts of a broad school subject" (Wehlage et al., 1989, p. 184). In thoughtful classrooms, however, students and teachers follow a different rhythm for learning, focusing in depth on subjects rather than skimming the surface (Sizer, 1984).

Newmann (1991) found six main dimensions to be most fundamental to learning in depth: (a) There was sustained examination of a few topics rather than superficial coverage of many; (b) the lesson displayed substantive coherence and continuity; (c) students were given an appropriate amount of time to think, that is, to prepare responses to questions; (d) the teacher asked challenging questions and/or structured challenging tasks (geared to the ability level and preparation of the student); (e) the teacher was a model of thoughtfulness; and (f) students offered explanations and reasons for their conclusions (Section headings, pp. 9-10).

Authentic student assessment is "designed explicitly to gauge students' abilities to think, analyze, adapt, and integrate their knowledge and skills" (Wilson & Daviss, 1994, p. 144) and to focus students' attention through "sustained inquiry and coaching" (p. 146). Using portfolios, students prepare collections of work that demonstrate competence in key areas, and they demonstrate their competence publicly through exhibitions and by internalizing external standards of excellence in the process (Darling-Hammond et al., 1995; Wiggins, 1989).

Conclusion

In summary, teacher and student autonomy—buoyed by expectations for high achievement and powerfully supported by school community—is a vital ingredient in secondary student learning. In the next section, we look at the structural supports that nurture this teacher-student relationship for learning.

PART III

Weaving Support for a Personalized, Academic High School

I maintain that the comprehensive high school is an inhumane institution. It is modeled after the turn-of-the-century factory and, true to its design, teachers are treated as unthinking workers whose main responsibility is to batch-process raw material, their students, into a finished product. . . . The comprehensive high school is largely uncaring, undemocratic, and uninspiring. The educational growth of students is but one of many institutional goals. The professional development of teachers and administrators is, at best, a secondary concern. The institution does little to promote learning, trust, or understanding. The structure simply does not allow teachers to understand students as learners nor students to shape the education they receive. The routines promoted by this structure exhaust too many teachers and administrators to the point at which cynicism and lethargy are commonplace.

—McQuillan (1997, p. 645)

There are many themes throughout this work, but if one theme could be extracted that is overarching and paramount, it is a message that the high school of the 21st century must be much more student-centered and above all much more personalized in programs, support services, and intellectual rigor.

—National Association of Secondary School
Principals (NASSP) (1996, p. vi)

The comprehensive public high school is no stranger to controversy and criticism. Reports describing the falling Student Aptitude Test (SAT) scores and decreased achievement of American teenagers compared with students in other industrialized nations (Steinberg, 1996) are commonplace and serve to fuel the fire. Information on the continuing rise in dropout rates, a trend that has continued since the 1970s (Bryk & Thum, 1989; Sedlak, Wheeler, Pullin, & Cusick, 1986), reaching a four-year high of 12% in 1995 (Schools Need Answers, 1997), turns up the heat on those working in schools. Newmann (1997), addressing the current statistics on dropouts, stated that although

> . . . a dropout rate of about 10% may seem low, it still involves over 1 million youngsters per year who according to the Committee on Economic Development are marginally literate, virtually unemployable, and who drain the economy in welfare and social service costs. (pp. 17-18)

In the past, our economy could accommodate a larger number of individuals who could not perform academically or who dropped out of school, but that time is coming to an end. The decreased earning capacity of high school dropouts reflects an increased burden on taxpayers. Natriello, McDill, and Pallas (1990) suggest that "the evolving United States economy will no longer have places for those who are not able to perform well in school and graduate" (p. 159).

Research suggests that several variables have an impact on student achievement levels, one of the most important of which is the school environment and its organization (McLaughlin, 1994; Newmann, 1997; Wilson & Corcoran, 1988; Witte & Walsh, 1990). It is this organizational effect that has prompted researchers to examine schools to understand why some are more successful than others (Chubb & Moe, 1990; Grant, 1988; Kruse, Louis, & Bryk, 1995; Steinberg, 1996; Wehlage, Rutter, Smith, Lesko, & Fernandez, 1989). Newmann (1997) underscores the importance of this perspective:

> Understanding the organizational properties that contribute to achievement should move school improvement efforts beyond the education of teachers to improve classroom practice. Improving the quality of classroom practice remains the most immediate lever for enhancing student achievement, but viewing schools from an organizational perspective shows that improvement

of classroom practice itself will require reform efforts that extend well beyond educating individual teachers to teach their subjects well. (p. 3)

In this section, we explore the environment and organization of successful high schools. Our goal is to discover themes that help explain successes. The spotlight is on those school-level factors that can support or detract from the ability of teacher and students to teach and learn effectively—our focus in the last section of the book. In exploring the literature in this area, we found that the idea of personalization emerged as a critical organizing force. McLaughlin (1994) has argued that "when it comes to encouraging student engagement with school and a willingness to work hard to achieve academic goals, the extent to which a secondary school environment is a personal one matters more than any other single factor" (p. 10). Thus the three chapters in this section highlight the organizational components necessary for a personalized high school environment: (a) a school anchored on a clearly defined learning imperative; (b) a school built upon humanized, intellectual relationships for learning; and (c) a school nested in a dynamic, adaptive culture for change situated in a local context. In reviewing the empirical literature, we find reason to believe that high schools can be successful and provide examples and practices that support our assessment. We also find support for the focus on improving high schools to be a national concern, an idea best summed up in the NASSP report *Breaking Ranks* (1996):

High school lays the foundation for what Americans become, and what Americans become shapes the high school that serves succeeding generations. Now, buffeted by powerful and unsettling winds, both the high school and the country are searching for stability and renewal. As a pivotal institution in the lives of young people, the high school can serve as a linchpin in efforts to improve the American condition, touching the lives of almost every teenager and, consequently, contributing to the betterment of the country. (p. 3)

7

Anchoring Schools on a Clearly Defined Learning Imperative

A picture emerges from our analyses of a distinctive organizational environment that appears particularly effective: smaller high schools where there are substantial opportunities for informal adult-student interactions, where teachers are committed to and interested in working with students, and where students are pursuing similar courses of academic study within an environment that is safe and orderly. These are institutions whose structure and functioning coalesce around a sense of shared purpose. The result is a coherent school life that is apparently able to engage both students and teachers alike.

—Bryk and Thum (1989, p. 377)

Learning is a social as well as an intellectual process. It depends on inter-actions between students and teachers. These interactions are strongly influenced by the perceptions that each group holds of the other. When teachers believe that students are willing and able to learn and students believe that teachers care about them and want them to succeed, the results are astounding in terms of both the students' academic achievements and the teachers' professional growth.

—Texas Education Agency (1992, p. 26)

When we think of school, we imagine a place in which students come to learn and teachers are present to enhance and facilitate learning. We see a high school in which the primary purpose is educating young people well and in which all activities center on teaching and learning. Unfortunately, as we have noted earlier, this is not true in many comprehensive high schools. Indeed, many if not most high schools have lost their educational focus. In contrast, research shows that successful high schools are places that clearly focus on an educational agenda.

This chapter provides a picture of the successful high school as a place centered on learning, with all stakeholders involved in the educational process. Two major concepts define the idea of a school anchored on a clearly defined "learning imperative" (Beck & Murphy, 1996, p. 41): a focus on a clear, powerful educational agenda and a driving force of community commitment to success. The first half of the chapter focuses on learning as a primary goal, emphasizing the importance of a clear vision of learning and teaching goals along with planning for those goals that involves all stakeholders. The second half of the chapter addresses community commitment to success, emphasizing the need for high expectations and standards of success for all students, for a belief that all students can achieve to their potential and for action to be taken on that belief, and for responsibility for the success of each student to be shared by all staff. This combination of academic focus and shared responsibility for success helps create a high school environment that nurtures student success.

Focused on a Clear, Powerful Educational Agenda

> *In comprehensive high schools, well-intentioned efforts lead to a smorgasbord of curricular programs, elective courses, social services, and extracurricular activities. Staff members specialize in different academic subjects or in working with single categories of students (college-bound, vocational, at-risk, limited-English, special need, athletes, musicians and artists). Parents and community groups ask the school to respond to special issues (eating disorders, drunk driving, sex education). Reform initiatives offer funding for diverse projects (site-based decision making, business-school partnerships, performance assessment). External agencies impose mandates for staff development, school evaluation, delivery of particular services.*
>
> *When viewed in isolation, each program, project and service usually seems justified, but their piecemeal incorporation into school destroys organizational coherence. As staff and students participate in all this, their lives become fragmented and incoherent. The school functions more as a shopping mall whose enterprises connect only through their presence in the same physical structure; or as an overdecorated Christmas tree whose ornaments cast countless unique sparkles, but have nothing in common except for their location on the same tree.*
>
> —Newmann (1997)

> *But American school people have been singularly unable to think of an educational purpose that they should not embrace. As a result, they have never made much effort to figure out what high school could do well, what high schools should do and how they could best do it.*
>
> —Powell, Farrar, and Cohen
> (1985, pp. 305-306)

High schools face a plethora of demands (Goodlad, 1984). Students need to be educated for the future while being connected to their past, challenged but not overwhelmed, and nurtured mentally, physically and emotionally, and all this must be accomplished within the constraints of a regular school schedule. Indeed, studies of secondary schools "show repeatedly that most students, like most adults, do not regard academic work as the primary purpose of schools: they give greater importance to social and vocational matters and to personal development" (Powell, Farrar, & Cohen, 1985, p. 303). Yet one of the strongest features found in successful high schools is a clear focus on learning as the primary goal of the institution. For example, Wilson and Corcoran (1988) discovered that "a significant characteristic of these unusually successful schools" was their clarity of educational focus "by articulating a set of goals and using them to make choices and guide actions" (p. 76).

School Has a Clear Vision of Learning and Teaching Goals

> For a school to be educationally successful, it must be a community of professionals working together toward a vision of teaching and learning that transcends individual classrooms, grade levels, and departments. The entire school community must develop a covenant to guide future decisions about goals and operation of the school. (Ogden & Germinario, 1995, p. 23)

Successful high schools have at their core an understanding of and dedication to learning and teaching. It is this vision or mission that allows the school to achieve academic excellence for its students (Murphy & Hallinger, 1985). This focus on learning is evidenced in effective high schools by the presence of a shared purpose, mission, or vision; goal consensus and shared values; well articulated goals; a focus on learning and teaching; instructional and cultural leadership; and a common academic core of courses.

Shared Purpose, Vision, or Mission

> First, an organizationally effective school appears to be one characterized by a very high degree of goal consensus and agreement and communication of the *vision* of what the school ought to be and needs to accomplish. (Ellet & Logan, 1990, p. 13)

High schools that excel are those guided by a clear vision or mission. For a number of years, studies on high schools have provided evidence that "high schools to be effective must have a sense of purpose, with teachers, students, administrators, and parents sharing a vision of what they are trying to accomplish" (Boyer, 1983, p. 66). A number of researchers have concluded that a significant common factor in successful high schools is a clear purpose, mission, or vision that is highly visible in the decision making and planning processes of the school (Bryk, Lee, & Holland, 1993; Ellet & Logan, 1990; Hannay & Ross, 1997; Hill, Foster, & Gendler, 1990; Ogden &

Germinario, 1995). A vision points toward the future; it "relates a school to its place in society and gives larger meaning to the work that is being done by administrators, teachers, and students" (Louis & Miles, 1990, p. 23) and "makes the institution itself an active factor in the educational process rather than merely a neutral physical setting in which education goes on" (Powell et al., 1985, p. 201). In some cases, the mission preceded the action. In other instances, the vision emerged after the initiation of school improvement activities that were centered around particular themes that "as they became linked, gradually reflected an image of what the school could become, and thus served to motivate staff members" (Louis & Miles, 1990, p. 206).

The vision sometimes begins with a single individual, but for it to have a school-wide impact, educators in effective schools operate with "a sense of shared purpose . . . which appear[s] to be a product of shared values" (Merz & Furman, 1997, p. 68). A good leader helps the staff "mold the vision into something they [can] all share" (Wood, 1992, p. 236). In one school with a particularly strong culture built around a guiding vision, the "mission [was] not simply the 'philosophy' statement prepared by some authority to satisfy some regulation or other: It represent[ed] a commitment that suffuse[d] everything the school [did]" (Raywid, 1995, p. 49). In their study of over 200 successful secondary schools, Wilson and Corcoran (1988) found that "a vision, a shared philosophy, form[ed] the basis for decisive action and the creation of a shared moral order. These [were] essential ingredients of successful schools" (p. 80). In another study, the movement from vision to a shared school philosophy ushered in a school culture "characterized in each case by respectful relationships, trust, the centrality of learning, and the on-going discussions and conversations focused on making sense of events and experiences" (Foster, 1998, p. 16).

More effective schools have principals that not only help create strong, clear visions but also encourage others in the school to verbalize their own philosophies, individually and collectively (Louis & Miles, 1990; Wilson & Corcoran, 1988). Chubb and Moe (1990) noted that "the best schools tend to be led by principals who provide a clear vision of where their schools are going and who know how to get teachers moving in one direction" (p. 91). Research on high schools receiving national recognition for excellence also has concluded that leadership involvement in creating and sustaining vision is an essential factor of school success (Murphy & Hallinger, 1985; Wilson & Corcoran, 1988).

Goal Consensus and Shared Values

> If a school is to become an excellent organization, those within it must be guided by core values that grow out of the shared vision. Whereas vision represents the long-term target, values direct the daily effort toward that target. (DuFour & Eaker, 1992, p. 37)

A major problem faced by high schools is that of diversity of goals and purposes: "Yes, we all agree that the goal is to educate students—but in what, and for what?" (Louis & Miles, 1990, p. 7). Anyone studying high schools recognizes the complexity of the organization, which by design is divided and subdivided into semiautonomous specialized units, each with its own goals (Fullan, 1990; Hallinger & Murphy, 1986; Lee & Smith, 1994). The size and structural organization of the typical high school leads to goal diversity (Wilson & Corcoran, 1988), which increases competition for "scarce resources, including teachers' and students' time and attention" (Talbert, 1995, p. 76). Effective high schools not only have a vision but also develop "precise statements of goals and priorities which establish the parameters for school practice" (Ogden & Germinario, 1995, p. 24). Reviews of research on exemplary secondary schools list goal consensus or shared values among all school staff as a primary ingredient of school success (Louis & Miles, 1990; Merz & Furman, 1997; Natriello et al., 1990).

In order for goals to be effective, they must be "about the purposes of the institution . . . reflect[ing] a common destiny for a school's students" (Bryk & Driscoll, 1988, p. 6), implemented by being "kept visible and actually be[ing] used to set priorities and allocate resources" (Wilson & Corcoran, 1988, p. 18). Shared values permeate every aspect of school life—improving instruction for students, enhancing teachers' professional community, and increasing the "likelihood of teachers' success" (Newmann, 1997), and improving relationships between individuals in the school (Kruse et al., 1995; Lee, Bryk, & Smith, 1993; Murphy, Hallinger, & Mesa, 1985). Bryk and Driscoll (1988) have concluded that goal consensus and shared values are "reflected primarily in beliefs about the purposes of the institution, about what students should learn, about how adults and students should behave, and about what kinds of people students are capable of becoming."

Well Articulated and Understood Goals

Having a vision and clear goals is only effective if they are communicated throughout the school (Murphy, Weil, Hallinger, & Mitman, 1985). Statistics show that more than 50% of exemplary high schools regularly communicate goals to staff, students, and parents and that the goals are understood, supported, and followed (Garibaldi, 1993; Wilson & Corcoran, 1988). Discussions among staff members at faculty meetings, inservice or professional development sessions, and departmental meetings serve as a forum in which teachers can understand and internalize the developing school vision (Louis & Miles, 1990; Ogden & Germinario, 1995). Just as the vision drives the discussion, the discussion continues to shape the direction of the high schools, increasing "understanding of the alternative perspective held by staff members . . . [and creating] collaborative opportunities that are breaking down the isolationists' subject-departmental culture" (Hannay & Ross, 1997, p. 590). Beyond discussion, in productive high schools goals are written and distributed to parents and students in handbooks, letters, memos, and manuals (Bobbett & French, 1992). The key is to have goals clearly articulated and communicated to all those participating in the life of the school (Murphy et al., 1985). As an example, in one high school, the mission was so pervasive it was seen everywhere,

> . . . from the bulletin boards to the all-school projects, to trips taken and the particular way the surrounding community [was] used as the object of in-

quiry, to the way each class [was] conducted, to the way teachers address[ed] and quer[ried] students and the way they address[ed] and quer[ried] one another. (Raywid, 1995, p. 70)

Focus on Learning and Teaching

Along with equal access to knowledge and a climate for professional practice, a school's commitment to make the push for achievement manifest in all its activities is a key enabling condition for improved schoolwide learning. (Tewel, 1995, p. 151)

As one might expect, high schools identified as effective have academics at the center of the organizational mission, building toward a goal of academic excellence for all students (Anderson, 1985; Harnisch, 1987; Newmann, 1997; Wilson & Corcoran, 1988). As early as 1979, Rutter, Maughan, Mortimore, Ouston, and Smith reported that students performed better both academically and behaviorally in schools with an academic focus. Subsequent studies consistently reinforce the conclusion that higher achievement scores are reported in schools having a greater emphasis on academics (Harnisch, 1985; Hoy, Tarter, & Bliss, 1990; Lee, Smith, & Croninger, 1996), a finding that is equally valid in urban, suburban, and rural settings (Corcoran & Wilson, 1985). Whereas, a strong academic press is prevalent in excellent high schools, many studies reveal, however, "that such engagement, especially at the high school level, is often conspicuous by its absence" (Murphy, 1991, p. 52) and that "a complex, tacit conspiracy to avoid sustained, rigorous, demanding, academic inquiry" (Sedlak, Wheeler, Pullin, & Cusick, 1986, p. 5) exists in most high schools (Powell et al., 1985; Sizer, 1984).

Schools and teachers "direct student effort to appropriate academic outcomes—through high-quality curriculum, effective pedagogy, and an instructional climate that rewards rigorous academic work by all students" (Newmann, 1997). This not only includes creating a culture that promotes programs and activities supporting academics (Sizer, 1984)—and one in which "distractions that interfere with serious purpose are not tolerated" (NASSP, 1996, p. 8) but also includes framing the school as "a formal organization that seeks to rationally, effectively, and efficiently promote student learning" (Lee et al., 1993, p. 229). By having a focus on student learning, schools are able to increase teachers' professional community by providing a focus for teachers' work and by improving working conditions for teachers (Newmann, 1997; Powell, 1990). In high schools involved in major restructuring efforts, it was found that the key to success was focusing on teaching and learning (Cawelti, 1997), and that those schools that failed to "directly address the troublesome issue of student learning over time . . . miss[ed] their ultimate target" (King & Weiss, 1995, p. 90).

Instructional and Cultural Leadership

Effective leaders exercise a wide range of skills and use a variety of styles. But through diverse approaches, they tend to concentrate on four common challenges: focusing school activity on student learning aimed at high intellectual quality; nurturing among staff a participatory, respectful collaborative work life; promoting innovation, reflection and development consistent with the school mission; and working to secure the social and structural support that teachers need to enhance instructional quality. (Newmann, 1997)

The role of the principal in today's successful school has transcended the traditional notion of functional management, power, behavioral style, and instructional leadership. The best schools have principals who consider their most important task as establishing a school culture. Whether through collaboration, consensus building, personal influence, or modeling, the principal is able to promote a school's vision for success by promoting a culture where staff, students, and community members have school goals that become more important than their own self-interests. In this new role as cultural leader the principal seeks to define, strengthen, and articulate enduring values and beliefs that give the school its unique identity. (Ogden & Germinario, 1995, pp. 27-28)

Schools that have been able to develop and maintain robust academic cultures and develop a strong "academic press" (Murphy, Weil, Hallinger, & Mitman, 1982, p. 22) are most often led by principals who act as instructional leaders working to create a school environment supporting high-level intellectual activity as well as being "good and sensitive managers" (Garibaldi, 1993, p. 8) who support and nurture the people involved in their activities (Anderson, 1985). Reviews of exemplary high schools find that principals in these schools have specific goals and strategies to increase the amount of time school members spend on academic learning (Roueche & Baker, 1986), giving "relatively greater priority to higher-order individual needs: academic excellence, personal growth and fulfillment, and human relations skills" (Chubb & Moe, 1990, p. 81). Practices chosen by individual principals vary, but some include spending time with teachers and evaluating their instructional strengths and weaknesses, meeting with small groups of students or teachers to discuss school problems and suggestions for improvement, increasing academic coursework, and developing professional development to meet specific school needs (Grant, 1988; Hallinger & Murphy, 1985; Hallinger, Murphy, Weil, Mesa, & Mitman, 1983; Murphy, 1990; Murphy, Hallinger, Weil, & Mitman, 1984; Ogden & Germinario, 1995).

Given the nature of high schools and the demands placed on school administrators, being an instructional and cultural leader is quite difficult to accomplish and often remains more of a goal than a reality (Larson, 1992). In looking at the typical high school principal, it is clear that "once appointed, the principal is expected to be all things to all people" (Boyer, 1983, p. 221). Most principals state that they spend a majority of their time on administrative and managerial tasks rather than on those that directly affect curriculum and instruction (Boyer, 1983; Larson, 1992; Murphy, 1990; Murphy, Hallinger, Lotto, & Miller, 1987). It appears that principals must consciously develop strategies to focus on academic and cultural improvement and support. Yet the research shows that the investment is well rewarded in terms of enhanced student learning (Austin & Holowenzak, 1985; Louis & Miles, 1990).

Common Core as a Focus for Academics

> Evidence suggests that "good" schools also have a strong academic struc-
> ture. Rather than a broad range of courses at many different levels, rather
> than many students selecting courses according to their "personal tastes"
> (the universalistic model), our evidence supports the positive values of a nar-
> row and academic curriculum, with a strong organizational push for all stu-
> dents to take (and master) these courses. . . . Results here indicate, quite con-
> sistently, that in such "core curriculum" schools, students learn more, and
> learning is more equitably distributed. (Lee et al., 1996, pp. 17-18, 20)

For much of the current century, as we described in Part I, schools have tried to
meet the increasing diversity of the student body by offering a greater variety of
courses designed to meet individual interests and needs. Some reports released almost a decade ago found that schools with a large curricular offering were successful
as long as all students mastered a "core set of curriculum standards" (Murphy &
Hallinger, 1985, p. 19). One researcher reported that there was no evidence supporting the notion that "the presence of certain courses in the high school curriculum
makes a school either good or bad" (Rogers, 1987, p. 37) but failed to comment on
the effect of the absence of a common academic core. It was concluded that although
high schools known for academic excellence offered a large number of elective
courses to students, they also had an academic core of coursework that all students
were expected to take (Boyer, 1983).

These findings continue to be supported today: Schools offering a strong academic core that all students are required to complete show greater academic achievement than other high schools (Alexander & Cook, 1982; Alexander & Pallas, 1983;
Lee, Smith, & Croninger, 1995; Wilson & Corcoran, 1988). A common core "seems
to induce a higher level of achievement—and one which is distributed in a more socially equitable manner" (Lee, 1995, p. 83; see also Grossman, Kirst, Negosh, &
Schmidt-Posnere, 1985; Murphy, 1989). High schools vary in what they call a common core and in what they determine is necessary for all students to learn. Some
schools choose thematic approaches focusing on the learning process rather than
content, whereas other schools have a minimum required number of courses in each
of the traditional learning domains (Boyer, 1983; Smith & Lee, 1996; Wood, 1992).
The key in both cases is that there is a core body of knowledge focused on high-level
academic activity.

School Takes Action on Goals

The extant research strongly supports the importance of the academic organization of high schools (including course-taking requirements, guidance
functions, and policies affecting the assignment of students and teachers to
schools and classes within schools). In fact academic organization is the pri-

mary mechanism influencing both the average level of student achievement and how that achievement is distributed with regard to such background characteristics as race and class. These statistical relationships are by far the strongest links between any aspect of school organization, either internal or external, and student achievement. (Lee et al., 1993, p. 229)

Research reveals the need to place academic organization high on the list of important variables to spotlight when unpacking the characteristics of productive high schools (Smith & Lee, 1996). Research shows that having a vision or a clearly articulated set of goals and objectives is not enough to make a school effective; the plan must be put into action (Bryk, 1994; Hill et al., 1990; Wilson & Corcoran, 1988). Thus good high schools not only have a vision and develop concrete goals from that vision, they also ensure that the vision and goals are central to the planning process of the school (Murphy & Hallinger, 1985). Goals provide the direction for action, but it is the daily activities of school staff that affect learning, and in good high schools, those goals are "taken seriously and [are] translated into daily actions that affect day-to-day activities" (Wilson & Corcoran, 1988, p. 75). It is this "movement to action" component of vision and planning that separates exemplary schools from the vast majority of high schools that lack a learning and teaching emphasis (Gilchrist, 1989; Larson, 1992; Roueche & Baker, 1986; Wilson, Webb, & Corbett, 1995). High schools that take action on their goals have an academically oriented organizational structure, systems for monitoring student progress, ongoing examination of practices, and collaborative problem solving.

Academically Oriented Organizational Structure

Academic press captures the content of a school's normative environment—one that pushes all students into a specific type of course work and emphasizes the importance of academic learning. It has been argued that pressing all students toward this end may disadvantage less able students, who may not be able to succeed in such courses. Our results suggest that this is not the case. High schools, which have this agenda, show a more equitable distribution in learning. (Smith & Lee, 1996, p. 16)

Research has shown, to no great surprise, that course work is a key to student achievement. Students who take more academic courses and more courses that are academically rigorous tend to achieve more than students who do not. (Chubb & Moe, 1990, p. 92)

Statements like the ones above highlight an essential finding of productive schools: High schools that emphasize academics for their students will have more successful students. Yet even with overwhelming evidence, many high schools still operate as if they knew nothing about or were indifferent to knowledge about what is needed for learning to occur (Goodlad, 1984; Powell et al., 1985; Sizer, 1984). Curricula are created, schedules are configured, and time is allocated to meet a multitude of goals, many of which have little to do with academic achievement. This is not true of exemplary high schools, which "pay attention to the task at hand. Student achievement in the classroom commands the attention of teachers and administrators" (Wilson & Corcoran, 1988, p. 122).

In good schools, time is valued as a scarce resource (Murphy et al., 1985), and it is used to provide "appropriate opportunity for student learning" (Ogden & Germinario, 1995, p. 38) by spending more class time on "academic learning" (Wilson & Corcoran, 1988, p. 122). Teachers assign homework on a regular basis and hold high expectations for its completion (Rutter et al., 1979). Although time spent in learning activities and homework policies is important to the success of a school (Keith, 1982; Paschal, Weinstein, & Walberg, 1984), the strongest factor affecting student achievement is the number of academic courses students take and the focus on academics in those courses (Cooley & Leinhardt, 1980; Murphy & Hallinger, 1989; see also Alexander & Pallas, 1983; Pallas & Alexander, 1983; Shanahan & Walberg, 1985; Smith & Lee, 1996; Walberg, Fraser, & Welch, 1986; Welch, Anderson, & Harris, 1982). Indeed, Lee and colleagues (1995) concluded that high schools are more successful for students if they have a "well-defined curricular focus, based on a strong academic component experienced by all students" (p. 4). Findings supporting the connection between increased academic achievement and students' academic course-taking are especially robust for minority and low-ability students (Bryk et al., 1993; Chaney, Burgdorf, & Atash, 1997; Spade, Columba, & Vanfossen, 1985; Wilson & Corcoran, 1988).

Systems for Monitoring Student Progress

Two ways that high schools create academic focus are through the development of standards and the use of assessments for monitoring student progress. Studies of successful high schools report that many effective schools have developed common standards for students (Newmann, 1997; Ogden & Germinario, 1995). Curriculum standards lay out what the school expects students to know and to be able to do when finishing a course or a course of study. In most states, standards are developed at the state level in the department of education, but in a few states, that task is left to the district or to individual schools (Cawelti, 1997). An example at the state level is the North Carolina Lead Teacher Project, which guides faculties through the process of setting their own standards for accountability (Natriello et al., 1990). In one case, teachers modified previously set standards to meet the needs of their students, "in essence adapting their standards for performance within a framework of equal opportunity" (Newmann, 1997). Standards also appear in the form of competency or graduation requirements, which have an effect on student achievement. Schools that have graduation or competency requirements have students who take more academic classes and thus increase academic performance (Chaney et al., 1997; Harnisch, 1985).

The second part of the student monitoring system is assessment of how well the standards are being met. The goals of quality assessments are to measure individual student progress in particular skills or knowledge of particular content, to determine student readiness to progress to the next grade level, to motivate those in schools by connecting performance and consequences, and to evaluate the educational performance of schools and their students (Consortium on Renewing Education, 1998). Educational research supports assessment systems that closely align with the school and curriculum standards as a characteristic of good schools (Murphy et al., 1985) and as a key to improving student achievement (Murnane & Levy, 1998). Gilchrist (1989) underscored this by saying, "As important as goal setting is, however, it is a waste of time and energy if performance is not continuously assessed in terms of the goals" (p. 140). Assessment systems allow schools to monitor student progress, which is usually done by using standardized tests, portfolios, and other performance-based assessments (Fine, 1992; Wilson & Corcoran, 1988). Guidelines for assessment in one large school system state that "students should be evaluated on the basis of their performance, not hours spent in the classroom" (Christman & Macpherson, 1996, p. 5). By frequently monitoring student progress and providing feedback, schools can head off potential academic problems before they become serious (Wehlage et al., 1989). Assessment instruments and procedures are sometimes established at the state level and then sent to schools to implement, as is the Kentucky Instructional Results Information System (KIRIS) in Kentucky (Lindle, Petrosko, & Pankratz, 1997). On a broader scale, curriculum review serves as a type of assessment for the overall school program. Curriculum reviews are conducted regularly by a majority of exemplary high schools (Wilson & Corcoran, 1988).

Ongoing Examination and Evaluation of Practices

> Best schools see the value of evaluation as a tool for self and school renewal. In addition, evaluation is looked on as a collegial activity by which both the teacher and the principal develop a greater understanding of their roles and performance as it relates to the mission of the school. In best schools, evaluation is an ongoing process—something that is systematized and purposeful, something that does not happen just once or twice a year, but, in a very real sense, takes place every day. (Ogden & Germinario, 1995, p. 44)

The first step taken by many productive high schools is evaluating the school's programs in light of their vision and goals, examining what it is they are trying to accomplish (Tewel, 1995). As Ogden and Germinario (1995) discovered, "the best schools are constantly asking questions about what their students should be learning, how they can best teach and support student learning, and how well their students are doing" (p. 14). This self-assessment can occur in various ways, including principal evaluations, surveys, open-forum discussions, or committee meetings. Often the process involves staff, students, and parents (Wilson & Corcoran, 1988). In good schools, feedback from the assessment is used to modify and reshape goals and action plans. This idea of ongoing evaluation is described by Louis and Miles (1990) as

> . . . evolutionary planning, . . . evolutionary in the sense that, although the mission and image of the organization's ideal future may be based on a top-level analysis of the environment and its demands, strategies for achieving the mission are frequently reviewed and refined based on internal scanning for opportunities and successes. (p. 193)

Collaborative Problem Solving

Although it is often a difficult thing to accomplish in a comprehensive high school, studies show that schools in which all stakeholders have a voice in decision making are associated with higher student achievement (Clark, Lotto, & McCarthy, 1980; Fullan, 1990; Rutter et al., 1979). By providing opportunities for input from all school members concerning problems the school is dealing with or policies that need to be implemented, commitment to goals is increased and shared vision is enhanced (Foster, 1998; Wilson & Corcoran, 1988). In some studies we reviewed, this began with a small group of interested individuals developing a core of people able to influence the larger school population (Louis & Miles, 1990). In productive high schools, the mindset is that "the people who implement policies should have maximum decision-making power and flexibility" (Christman & Macpherson, 1996, p. 8).

School members of more effective secondary schools are involved in solving a variety of problems, both academic and nonacademic. In these schools, the school climate and structure is designed to enhance collective problem solving and planning (Little & McLaughlin, 1993; Purkey & Smith, 1983). Using faculty meetings to discuss instructional issues increases collegiality among staff members (Wilson & Corcoran, 1988), and when schoolwide effort is directed toward student learning, "the strength of professional community boosts the instructional capacity of the school" (Newmann, 1997). For this boost to occur, the school must become a place in which "instruction is viewed as problematic and is often discussed" (Louis & Kruse, 1995, p. 215).

One important element in schools successful at problem solving is a focus on the needs of the students in their particular school. Discussions concerning problems faced by specific students and potential solutions to those problems occurred more frequently in schools identified as more effective (Hill et al., 1990; McLaughlin, 1994). Some schools had groups of staff, students, and parents that met regularly with administrators to discuss problems and suggest ideas for school improvement (Ogden & Germinario, 1995). One school created a *hot list* of students at risk for failure and met weekly to discuss strategies for helping those students and to report on the progress of targeted students (Shore, 1995). Although schools handled the process differently, collective problem-solving was a recurring theme in the literature on productive high schools that we reviewed. Wilson and Corcoran (1988) sum this up: "These unusually successful secondary schools face up to their problems. They are truly 'can do' organizations that refuse to succumb to ready rationalization for performances that are below expectations" (p. 129).

A key factor in schools being able to implement a schoolwide approach to problem solving is the support and encouragement of the administration. If the principal is not willing to move from the more traditional leadership role and allow others to be involved in decision making, faculty discussion about school problems have little impact. In all the schools in which collective problem solving has been successful, the principal has been able to "give up some typically visible leader behaviors" (Newmann, 1997) and allow staff members to be responsible for running meetings and programs, to have input in policy decisions, and to develop solutions to school problems (Grant, 1988; Louis & Kruse, 1995; Ogden & Germinario, 1995; Tewel, 1995).

Motivated by a Community Commitment to Success

Good schools and school systems are populated by confident people who expect others to perform to their personal level of quality. Teachers expect students to achieve. Students know they are expected to achieve, and they expect, in turn, to have involved, competent teachers. Principals are surprised by teachers who fail. Teachers are surprised by administrators who ask little of themselves and others.

—Wilson and Corcoran (1988, p. 121)

In productive high schools, all members of the school staff are committed to student success (Wilson & Corcoran, 1988). This commitment is expressed by an expectation that all students can and will learn, which translates into an increased probability of student achievement (Hallinger & Murphy, 1987). Research consistently supports the notion that "schools with high levels of collective responsibility for learning are those where students learn more in all subjects" (Lee & Smith, 1996, p. 127). This attitude of collective responsibility produces a community committed to success for students in their school (Bryk & Driscoll, 1988), as is expressed in the goals of one effective high school:

> The school is a democratic learning community in which everyone is a learner, everyone is a teacher, and everyone willingly accepts responsibility for supporting, encouraging, and assuring learning by their peers. Students and staff participate in decisions about learning and the learning environment. They share in the responsibility for maintaining the school community. (McQuillan, 1995, p. 6)

The presence of community and commitment to the community go hand in hand in effective high schools (Bryk et al., 1993). High schools characterized by higher levels of professional community also had higher levels of student achievement (Merz &

Furman, 1997). Schools motivated by community commitment to success have high expectations for all students, believe all students can achieve and can act accordingly, and feel that the staff is collectively responsible for student success.

School Has High Expectations for All Students

> The literature on effective schools consistently stresses the need for high expectations in school. Teachers and principals in successful schools believe students (all students) can learn. In some ways, it is a paradoxical situation. Does the staff believe the students can learn and, therefore, do learn? Or do the students learn, and, therefore, the staff believes they can learn? It is probably more of the former. Staff's positive beliefs come first. However, success takes more than a belief that students can learn. It takes a commitment that all students *will* learn. (Ogden & Germinario, 1995, p. 69)

> One of the unspoken problems in American education today is that teachers and administrators have reached a comfort level with a certain rate of student failure. The fact is, teachers often gauge the appropriate rigor of their instruction by the amount of student failure. If all students do well, teachers are more likely to conclude "It must have been too easy" than "The kids and I did a good job." Most teachers would be horrified if 50% of their students failed. They would agonize over those failures and attempt to develop ways to reduce the rate of failure. However, if the failure rate is 10% or 5%, teachers often suffer no disquiet. They are comfortable with this rate of student failure. (DuFour & Eaker, 1992, p. 124)

Studies of effective teachers and successful schools have consistently emphasized the connection between teachers' expectations and students' performance (Brophy & Good, 1985; Lee et al., 1993; Lezotte, Hathaway, Miller, Passalacqua, & Brookover, 1980; Murphy et al., 1985; Purkey & Smith, 1983). This holds true in successful high schools in which research shows that higher academic achievement and increased levels of student learning occur in schools that have "high levels of academic expectations and environmental press" (Bryk et al., 1993, p. 133), in which all students are expected to learn and achieve academically (Firestone & Rosenblum, 1988; Lee et al., 1995; Murphy & Hallinger, 1985; Rutter et al., 1979; Wilson & Corcoran, 1988). This translates into "a conviction held by both the student and teachers that classrooms are an environment where success is inevitable" (Roueche & Baker, 1986, p. 29) for all students regardless of race, ethnicity, gender (Garibaldi, 1993; Newmann, 1997; Wilson & Corcoran, 1988), or placement in a primarily academic or vocational program (American Federation of Teachers, 1997).

Reports have shown that students in exemplary high schools recognized that high expectations meant greater effort was expected on their part in schoolwork and academics (Lee et al., 1995; Ogden & Germinario, 1995) as well as in all other aspects of school life (Duke, 1995; Murphy & Hallinger, 1985; Wilson & Corcoran, 1988). Rather than students shrinking away, rebelling, or dropping out, which is what educators often fear (Newmann & Wehlage, 1994), students in schools with high expectations for learning responded favorably to academic press, not only in increased achievement but also in praise for "their teachers for making them work harder than they might have if left up to their devices" (Wilson & Corcoran, 1988, p. 103). Students who were poorly prepared or were previously low achieving were pushed by school staff to catch up through extra time and effort directed toward bridging the deficiency gap (Hill et al., 1990; Powell et al., 1985).

However, this is not the case in many high schools today. Studies show that although some students leave school because of the rigor of the academic program, many others depart because "they find it insufficiently challenging . . . [and] encounter teachers whose expectations for them are too low" (Natriello et al., 1990, p. 100). Research shows that "students fulfill their teachers' prophecies, performing up to or down to the projections and standards held for them" (Lee & Smith, 1996, p. 109). In an attempt to meet the personal and emotional needs of students or because of concerns about alienating students or increasing dropout rates, many high schools have lowered academic expectations (Newmann & Wehlage, 1994). Also, placing students of varying ability levels on different tracks still occurs in many high schools, despite research findings that seriously question the overall soundness of this strategy and that reveal negative effects on students' sense of efficacy, especially for those in the lower tracks (Brouillette, 1997; Coleman & Hoffer, 1987; Murphy & Hallinger, 1989; Oakes, 1985; Page & Valli, 1990). Although it is not "legitimized" and appears in different forms, tracking is "highly institutionalized in American education" (Talbert, 1995, p. 78). Studies consistently have shown that there are higher expectations placed on students in high-track classrooms than in low-track classrooms, and therefore, high-track students experience school differently from, and are often more successful than, students in the lower track (Lee & Smith, 1996; Murphy & Hallinger, 1989; Oakes, 1985). On the other hand, studies of productive high schools show that they had "nearly eliminated tracking, ability grouping, and general remedial classes" (Newmann, 1997) and had heterogeneously grouped students into classes in which all were expected to achieve (Mitchell, Russell, & Benson, 1990; Wilson & Corcoran, 1988). The implications of tracking and unequal expectations for students are poignantly expressed in the NASSP (1996) report as follows.

> One of the most important ways that a high school respects its students is by having high academic expectations for all of them. When a school assigns some students to courses with watered-down content, it transmits an unmistakable message to them: The school does not view them as capable of performing higher level work. Little is expected of these students as they are consigned to a dead-end journey, pursuing courses that are pale imitations of the more meaningful courses available to others. (p. 50)

A key element in the high-expectation equation is a principal who has high expectations for his or her staff. Research reveals that principals of successful high schools have high expectation for themselves (Murphy & Hallinger, 1985) and set high standards for their staff as well as the students in the school (Murphy, 1990;

Wilson & Corcoran, 1988). Good principals not only expect a great deal from their staff but also support them in meeting their expectations (Hallinger & Murphy, 1985; Kruse et al., 1995; Murphy, 1990).

School Believes All Students Can Achieve to Potential and Acts Accordingly

It is not enough for schools to have high expectations for their students. They must also act on those expectations to help all students meet school goals (Christman & Macpherson, 1996; Corcoran & Wilson, 1985; Meier, 1995). Effective high schools combine "stress in the form of high expectations" (Fullan, 1990, p. 233) with other school factors such as "strong management and incentives for students with an extensive program of teacher training and inservice" (p. 233) to improve student performance. Actions taken by staff in exemplary high schools reflect these expectations of increased learning for all students regardless of previous ability grouping or tracking level (Oakes, 1985; Wilson & Corcoran, 1988). One successful high school expressed this dynamic of belief-driven action in stating that expectations are derived from "the staff, together with students and parents, identify[ing] skills, conceptual understandings, habits of mind, and knowledge that all students demonstrate" (McQuillan, 1995, p. 6) and then in describing how the school provided support for all students to successfully achieve those expectations. Effective high schools translate academic press into actions by providing attention to at-risk students, establishing rewards for academic and personal achievement, and individualizing achievement goals.

Attention to At-Risk Students

At the core . . . is a renewed concern for the education of all students, especially those who have been ineffectively served in the past—the so-called at-risk students. This interest has arisen for two major reasons. The first is economic. For the first time in our history we are facing the economic imperative to educate all students to relatively high levels of performance. The surplus of workers is shrinking while levels of competence required in the workplace are increasing. A good education for all seems to be economically desirable. At the same time, the deeply ingrained belief that the role of schooling is to sort students into two groups—those who will work with their heads and those who will toil with their hands—is being challenged. (Murphy, 1991, p. 60)

As noted earlier, the number of students who drop out of high school each year is alarming. Students from low socioeconomic backgrounds and from minority groups are often considered as students at risk for dropping out of school. Research reveals that nearly one in four students who begins high school will drop out before completion (Boyer, 1983), a statistic that is considerably higher in urban districts (Consortium on Renewing Education, 1998) and among minority populations (Bryk et al., 1993; Natriello et al., 1990). Studies have shown that one of the reasons students give for dropping out is "lack of academic success in school" (Natriello et al., 1990, p. 99). Discouragement and disinterest cause many students to leave school, both mentally and physically (Boyer, 1983).

Looking at effective high schools, we found that particular attention was paid to keeping students in school and interested in academic pursuits (Bryk & Driscoll, 1988; Ogden & Germinario, 1995). Bryk and Thum (1989) found that "students are more likely to persist to graduation in schools where there is an emphasis on academic pursuits, an orderly environment and less internal differentiation" (p. 375). Some schools work on reducing student alienation and increasing commitment to the school by targeting extracurricular programs to involve at-risk students (Wehlage et al., 1989), with the most successful programs being "comprehensive and intensive" (Ogden & Germinario, 1995, p. 85). High schools most effective at retaining students have clear methods for identification of at-risk students. They also engage those students in small group instruction and counseling programs to help deal with academic, personal, and emotional barriers to the students' success (Ogden & Germinario, 1995; Raywid, 1995). Not only does this affect the potential dropouts who remain in school but research has also shown that "there is a general tendency for higher achievement growth in those schools which hold more students through to the final year of secondary school" (Ainley, 1994, p. 13).

Rewards for Academic and Personal Achievement

Higher expectations and standards are also frequently coupled with strong reward systems. It is not enough to simply increase demands on students. There is also a need to recognize their accomplishments. (Wilson & Corcoran, 1988, p. 105)

Past successes are used to build new ones. The old adage that success breeds success takes on concrete meaning in these [successful high] schools. . . . Positive accomplishments are not just treated as useful public relations gimmicks but are actively integrated with the school's culture. Success becomes the expected and predictable outcome of commitment to the school's values. (Corcoran & Wilson, 1985, p. 39)

One way that exemplary high schools have increased student achievement is by rewarding students for effort and achievement of school goals (Roueche & Baker, 1986; Rutter et al., 1979; Wynne, 1980). Higher levels of academic achievement have been reported in high schools that "recognize student achievement and provide rewards for good grades or behavior" (Anderson, 1985, p. 109). These productive high schools hold award assemblies, institute honor societies, and create academic halls of fame and student-of-the-month awards to honor students for academic accomplishments (Ohiwerei, 1996; Roueche & Baker,1986; Shore, 1995; Wilson & Corcoran, 1988), with the purpose of fostering a climate that recognizes and encourages academic excellence. One school went as far as awarding to students discount coupons for merchandise, movie passes, T-shirts, and other prizes for excellence in achievement and attendance (King & Weiss, 1995).

Rewards were not limited to academics but included recognition of student success in sportsmanship, leadership, behavior, the arts, and community service (Duke, 1995; Ogden & Germinario, 1995). Along with expanding the areas for rewards, productive high schools also use various forms of reward. Recognition does not have to be limited to formal awards and ceremonies (Austin & Holowenzak, 1985). Rutter and colleagues (1979) found that "all forms of reward, praise or appreciation tended to be associated with better outcomes" (p. 123).

Individualization of Achievement Goals

> We understand that every student cannot be brilliant. Each student, however, can enjoy a measure of success on his or her own terms that represents solid achievement and genuine accomplishment in completing substantial and meaningful academic work. (NASSP, 1996, p. 5)

> Finally, [in successful high schools] there was a sense of optimism about students' potential for learning. Throughout our discussions, teachers repeatedly expressed their conviction that, despite many students' discouraging record of failure, the right kind of environment and opportunities could stimulate the innate potential buried within each individual. Act[ion] on this belief . . . was best facilitated by the strategy of building on students' strengths rather than focusing too often on their deficits and weaknesses. (Wehlage et al., 1989, pp. 137-138)

Students enter schools and individual classrooms at varying levels of ability. High schools noted for excellence take students at their individual entry level and do what is necessary to help them achieve the standards set for all students (Kleinfeld, McDiarmid, & Hagstrom, 1989; Newmann, 1997). These schools recognize the needs of individual students and provide the necessary resources, time, and energy on the part of the staff to bring students to high levels of achievement (Austin & Holowenzak, 1985; Bryk et al., 1993; Larson, 1992). Research has shown that low-ability students had greater success in math when "schools did not accentuate their weakness, but instead provide[d] a favorable academic environment—supportive teachers and guidance counselors who expect[ed] them to go to college" (Spade et al., 1985, p. 13). Students previously identified as having low academic potential were pushed toward more academic coursework, as were all other students in the school (Bryk et al., 1993; Raywid, 1995; Wilson & Corcoran, 1988).

All Staff Share Responsibility for Student Success

> In schools where most teachers feel they can make a real difference in the academic performance of students—instead of blaming low performance on students' attitudes, background and other factors beyond teachers' control—students learn more and learning is more equitably distributed. (Lee et al., 1995, p. 8)

> In a positive teacher culture, individual educators believe they are personally accountable for the success of each student. This self-imposed accountability means that teachers accept responsibility for helping each student overcome impediments to success. This belief inheres a broad obligation to promote academic success along with personal and social competence. (Wehlage et al., 1989, p. 135)

No one person in a school is solely responsible for the success or failure of a student. Exemplary high schools have recognized that fact and work to build a shared sense of responsibility among all staff members for helping students to achieve academic goals (Ogden & Germinario, 1995). It is through this shared responsibility and by an evenly balanced commitment to the school, to the students, and to learning that student achievement is enhanced (Firestone & Rosenblum, 1988). Productive high schools manifest shared responsibility for student success through a staff collectively responsible for student learning and through leadership that is active in building collective responsibility.

Staff Collectively Responsible for Student Learning

> In [high] schools with high levels of collective responsibility, where these attitudes are also consistent among the faculty, students learn more in all subjects. Equally important, collective responsibility is associated with less internal stratification in these outcomes by social class. We conclude that schools where most teachers take responsibility for learning are environments that are both more effective and more equitable. (Lee & Smith, 1996, p. 130)

> Collective responsibility for student learning captures the shared conviction among a school's teachers that all students—despite disadvantage and past failure—can and will learn if given opportunity and support. Where collective responsibility for student learning is strong, teachers respond to the challenge of instructing all students as a mutual endeavor marshaling their shared professional knowledge, wisdom, and commitment. (Marks & Louis, 1997, p. 251)

Numerous studies on factors that affect success in high schools have shown that when teachers have high expectations for student learning and take personal responsibility for making that happen, students learn more (Firestone & Rosenblum, 1988;

Lee & Smith, 1996; Kruse et al., 1995; Roueche & Baker, 1986). It has usually fallen to the individual teacher to "shoulder most of the burden for student motivation and success" (Ogden & Germinario, 1995, p. 68). Research suggests, however, that a greater impact is made when school members collectively take responsibility to promote high standards for academics and behavior for all students (Lee & Smith, 1996; Ogden & Germinario, 1995; Wilson & Corcoran, 1988). Collective responsibility creates a culture that "permits staff to take an active, responsible role for the well-being of the whole school, as well as the students" (Taylor-Dunlop & Norton, 1995, p. 5), a culture which has been correlated with success in secondary schools (Lee et al., 1996; Wehlage et al., 1989).

One major difference in schools with high levels of collective responsibility is their refusal to place blame for low achievement on the individual students, their background or family, or on other school members (Lee et al., 1996; Smith & Lee, 1996; Tewel, 1995). As we have reported elsewhere, one of the major

> . . . contributions of the effective schools movement . . . is its attack on the practice of blaming the victim . . . and its insistence on requiring the school community to take a fair share of the responsibility for what happens to the youth in its care. (Murphy, 1992b, p. 95)

In less effective high schools, blame shifting often occurs as a way for teachers to "preserve their professional self-respect" (Firestone & Rosenblum, 1988, p. 289; see also Raywid, 1995). Austin and Holowenzak (1985) point out that

> . . . the major "no-no" in exceptional schools is to assume that it's the child's fault. . . . It is a challenge to the administration and to the faculty to find out how to succeed with the child rather than saying that it's the child's fault, that he or she cannot succeed. (p. 71)

Teachers in highly effective secondary schools put out extra effort, beyond the regular class session, to help low-ability students or students from economically disadvantaged backgrounds to achieve academic success (Corcoran & Wilson, 1985; Hill et al., 1990; Newmann & Wehlage, 1994). Reports on effective secondary schools have concluded that they did whatever was necessary "to ensure that no students fell through the cracks because of academic or adjustment problems; and to ensure that students with special needs received programs consistent with mainstream, core curriculum standards" (Murphy & Hallinger, 1985, p. 20).

High schools in which collective responsibility is the norm also exhibit a proclivity toward teamwork and a strong professional community (Gaziel, 1997; Kruse et al., 1995). In productive high schools, it is important not only that all teachers share responsibility for student learning but also that the "pedagogical growth and development of all teachers [is] considered a community-wide responsibility" (Kruse et al., 1995, p. 27). Teachers in these successful secondary schools work together in planning, evaluating, and revising programs and curricula as well as in being involved in peer assessment, coaching, and sharing ideas to improve teaching ability (Corcoran & Wilson, 1985; Louis & Miles, 1990).

Leadership Active in Building Collective Responsibility

As is true with any climate or culture variable within a school, the leader plays a significant role in the development of collective responsibility for student success (Murphy, 1990). Studies have reported that effective principals are a key factor in "the creation and maintenance of quality programs and practices in successful secondary schools" (Wilson & Corcoran, 1988, p. 148; see also Austin & Holowenzak, 1985; Louis & Miles, 1990). Effective principals modeled the behavior they expected to see in their staff (Gilchrist, 1989), working collaboratively with teachers to help develop school programs and solve school problems. They regularly went into classrooms to be involved in learning (Larson, 1992).

Summary

Public declarations about the need to improve education are echoed from the street corner to the senate floor. Demands are placed on high schools to prepare students for the future—academically, as well as personally, socially, politically, and morally. The problem is that in many cases, plans for improvement have not been well grounded or have been incomplete and implemented in a piecemeal fashion. Until we look at the high school holistically and deal not with individual courses or teachers but with the organization as a whole, success for all students will remain an American dream. We must begin with the core of learning and teaching, organizing it in ways that are effective for all those in the schools, then move on to the people who make up the school community, nurturing, supporting, and developing the students, teachers, and staff of the high school. We have looked at the organization of high schools that have been effective in educating their students and found that a personalized learning environment is the common theme.

In this chapter we addressed the importance of personalized high schools being organized around a clearly defined learning imperative. The first part of the chapter dealt with having a focus on learning and with actions directed toward that focus. The second part dealt with motivation, commitment, and community as they lead to success for all students. These ideas were supported through examples and practices found in exemplary high schools across the country. Clearly, the evidence supports the need for high schools to organize around learning and teaching. In the following chapter, we focus on the next key to successful high schools—a personalized school built on humanized, intellectual relationships for learning.

8

Building Schools on Humanized, Intellectual Relationships for Learning

> *Educators need attend not only to the technical core of instruction but also to the nature of the human environments in which this instruction occurs. The social processes of school shape the meaning of school events for students and teachers alike. They can help to make schools engaging environments for students and productive workplaces for adults, or they can impede these ends.*
>
> —Lee & Bryk (1989, p. 190)

High schools must not only attend to the technology of learning but also to the people involved in the process—the students, teachers, administrators, and staff who make up the school community. Beginning with some of the earliest studies of high schools, strong relationships and a supportive environment have been identified as key factors leading to student success (Rutter, Maughan, Mortimore, Ouston, & Smith, 1979). Over the years, research has confirmed the importance of dealing with human conditions, such as relationships, when looking at factors leading to success in high schools (Austin & Holowenzak, 1985; McQuillan, 1997; Newmann, 1997).

This chapter describes the successful high school as a place that is actively concerned with the human aspects of learning. The focus of personalization here is the importance of students developing supportive relationships with adults involved in the school community. Importance is placed on supporting the individual students and teachers as well as on providing opportunities for healthy, supportive relationships to be formed between students and adults in the school. Three main elements of personalization surround the idea of student-adult relationships: engagement of students in a cohesive, nurturing culture; teachers operating in a positive, professionally oriented community; and a community of commitment driven by strong student-adult relationships. The first section of this chapter focuses on the needs of students—having activities designed for inclusion, being viewed as individuals and having their needs recognized, and knowing that they are cared for by the adults in the school. The second part of the chapter examines the needs of teachers, primarily the needs for support of professionalism and for an increased capacity for growth and success in teaching. The final section focuses on the student-adult relationship as the primary motivating factor, exploring programs and structures the school adopts to facilitate relationships. It is this attention to supporting both students and teachers, along with creating and nurturing opportunities for student-adult relationships, that dominate the landscape of exemplary high schools.

Students Engaged in a Cohesive, Nurturing Culture

The information we collected on the emotional side of engagement presents a disturbing picture. More than one third of the students we surveyed showed signs of being emotionally disengaged from school, as indexed by measures of mind wandering, lack of interest, or inattentiveness. Half of the students we surveyed say their classes are boring. A third say they have lost interest in school, they are not learning very much, and that they get through the school day by fooling around with their classmates. And remember, ours was a sample of "average" students in "average" American schools—not a sample of "high-risk" school settings.

—Steinberg (1996, p. 71)

Schools exist to serve students; yet often they are the very people who feel alienated, or at least disengaged, from what is going on in the school. Researchers use the degree to which students are engaged in school as a measure of student fit and involvement in high schools. According to Newmann (1981), "Many efforts at school improvement . . . can be viewed as efforts to reduce student alienation: that is, to increase students' involvement, engagement, and integration in school" (p. 546). Student engagement involves everything from concrete measures, such as participation in extracurricular activities, class attendance, and homework completion, to more nuanced measures, such as a sense of belonging within the school community, an appreciation of individual differences, and a culture of caring exhibited by school staff (Newmann, 1981; Ogden & Germinario, 1995; Steinberg, 1996). No matter how it is defined, the conclusion remains the same—students who are engaged in high schools show greater academic achievement than those who are not engaged (Coleman, Hoffer, & Kilgore, 1982; National Association of Secondary School Principals (NASSP), 1996; Ogden & Germinario, 1995; Rutter et al., 1979). High schools that want to be successful must understand how to create a nurturing, cohesive environment for their students. One highly successful high school expresses its underlying belief in this type of environment by stating that:

A humane, caring, and personalized school—a place where all students [are] welcomed, [are] known well, and [are] heard and, consequently, a place where all students [feel] a stake in the institution, not simply in their own success—[is] central to fostering essential academic goals. Students learn to think best, to use their minds well, to try out ideas, to express their views, to interact in teams, and to absorb themselves in a dynamic learning process in an environment where they feel trusted, respected, and encouraged. (Mackin, 1996, p. 11)

School Designs Activities for Inclusion

Best schools actively seek ways to enrich the school environment for students. The students' perceptions of the school environment tend to have a direct impact on the functioning of students within the school. Moreover, evidence exists that the learning environment is a critical element that can be either conducive or detrimental to student success. In a real way, "unfriendly schools" tend to promote student disengagement by establishing real or perceived obstacles for student success. These obstacles lead to student feelings of isolation, alienation, and ultimately, feelings of failure. "Friendly" schools provide students with a climate that values involvement in school decisions, systematically develops students' interest in learning, and creates opportunities for students to build sustained relationships with teachers and other adults. (Ogden & Germinario, 1995, pp. 67-68)

In successful high schools, the climate is welcoming and inclusive of its students. It is this inclusive climate that allows students to feel membership in the school and encourages participation in the life of the school. Adults in the school care for and nurture students when they have the opportunity to be involved in the students' academic and personal growth. In effective high schools, this inclusive environment is denoted by student involvement in extracurricular activities, increased peer interaction through shared experiences, schoolwork relevant to students' life, students' feeling of belonging, transitional programs for new students, and appreciation for multicultural perspectives.

Presence of and Involvement in Cocurricular and Extracurricular Activities

A high school properly provides for social and personal needs, as well as for those that are strictly academic. Given the benefits that students can obtain, high schools should promote cocurricular activities for all students. Cocurricular pursuits, after all, can undergird the goal of teaching students to be responsible and fulfilled human beings, providing them with opportunities that develop character, critical thinking, sociability, and specific skills. (NASSP, 1996, p. 18)

A great deal of research is available on the effects of student involvement in school activities and its impact on student achievement. Although some reports point to negative results, for example, that time spent in activities is time spent away from academics, in general, the findings show a positive correlation between student involvement in activities and enhanced academic performance (Bryk, Lee, & Holland, 1993; NASSP, 1996; Oxley, 1990; Steinberg, 1996). One study concluded that the greatest predictor of adult success was involvement in school activities (Rogers, 1987). Wilson and Corcoran (1988) also found higher rates of extracurricular participation in successful secondary schools, noting that "almost 65% of the schools reported unusual or exceptionally active student governments" (p. 61). By participating in clubs, student government, music, or sports, students have opportunities to exhibit leadership and deepen connections to the school community, opportunities which in turn have a positive effect on learning and achievement (Bryk et al., 1993; Roueche & Baker, 1986).

It is important to note that exemplary schools maintain their focus on academics "keeping academic learning primary and cocurricular events secondary" (Roueche & Baker, 1986, p. 29). Schools organize their schedules to support and encourage involvement by all students in extracurricular or cocurricular programs. Some extend the lunch period to allow a special club meeting time (Meier, 1995) or schedule a special club period into the calendar once a month (Ogden & Germinario, 1995), allowing all students to participate, not just those who are able to stay after school. Some schools arrange for school buses to run later than their regular schedule on certain days to increase student involvement in extracurricular events, especially by youngsters who are typically underrepresented in school activities (Gilchrist, 1989). Research shows that participation in extracurricular activities has a greater impact on achievement for students in minority groups and for academically below-average, low-achieving, and female students (Oakes, 1985; Steinberg, 1996; Tye, 1985).

Common Activities That Increase Peer Interactions

> Membership in a communal school is also characterized by a common agenda of activities. The activities, which may range from required academic courses to such schoolwide events as assemblies or football games, serve a pragmatic function. They provide school participants with face-to-face encounters in which they get to know one another. They afford a common ground that facilitates personal ties and socializes members to school norms. (Bryk et al., 1993, p. 277)

As we see in news reports about increased school violence, the isolated, individual context most high school students find themselves in leads to increased absenteeism, dropping out, and delinquency (Bryk & Thum, 1989; Rutter et al., 1979). Schools that decrease emphasis on individual competition and increase attention to group success show increased academic achievement and improved school climate (Anderson, 1985). School discipline improved in high schools in which students worked effectively in teams (Furtwengler, 1991).

Exemplary high schools have a common core of activities, both academic and nonacademic, around which school members have meaningful interaction (Bryk &

Driscoll, 1988; Bryk et al., 1993). These activities provide students with a sense of school membership and belonging (Newmann, 1997). For students to be engaged in high school, they must feel a sense of attachment to the school and to the people in that school, a task that is accomplished in successful schools through a common academic core and increased involvement in shared extracurricular and cocurricular activities (Natriello, McDill, & Pallas, 1990; Wehlage, Rutter, Smith, Lesko, & Fernandez, 1989).

Peer influence is strong in the high school setting, and that influence can positively or negatively affect academic achievement "depending on the student's position in the peer group, whether the group approves or disapproves of academic effort, and the amount of time devoted to peer social activities that detract from academic outcomes" (Lee, Bryk, & Smith, 1993, p. 223). Research shows that peer influence on achievement is much higher than parental influence, particularly in the daily activities that lead to success in school (Steinberg, 1996). Student engagement, which as we have shown has a significant affect on student achievement, is largely affected by support from peers (Newmann, 1997). Effective high schools find ways to use peer influence as a positive force to improve academic achievement.

One important issue that research strongly supports is that the traditional approach of homogenous grouping of students does not increase achievement, in fact it tends to have an overall negative effect (Oakes, 1985). Students learn more and are more successful in diverse settings, in which grouping is done to increase heterogeneity (NASSP, 1996), mixing students of various abilities, races, and socioeconomic backgrounds. This is especially true for students who are low achieving or would traditionally end up in the *lower-track* (Oakes, 1985), but it is true for average students as well. Traditional curricular arrangements and tracking often make it difficult for students of varying ability levels to interact or experience shared activities (Newmann, 1997; Oakes, 1985). Successful high schools often institute structural conditions that increase peer interaction.

One way schools increase positive peer interaction is through peer mentoring, peer mediation, and peer tutoring, all of which are linked to enhanced academic performance (McQuillan, 1997). Mentoring has shown positive results for both parties involved, in both improved achievement and improved attitudes toward school (Natriello et al., 1990). One report highlights the importance of peer interaction by stating "a student-to-student tutoring program can sidestep personal or psychological issues that grow out of a school's usual structures and power relationships and that thwart learning" (Wilson & Daviss, 1994, p. 186). Another way schools work to increase peer interaction is to reduce the overall number of students that any one individual interacts with on a daily basis. Reduced school size is explored more fully later in this chapter.

Schoolwork Is Relevant to Present and Future Life

In order to be emotionally engaged in school, students must believe that what they are learning there is either interesting or valuable—and preferably, both. This does not mean that they must find every lesson, every assignment, and every bit of information communicated in class absolutely riveting. But to become and remain engaged in school, students must have some sense that what they are doing on a daily basis holds some value—that as a result of being engaged and exerting effort, they will acquire some bit of useful knowledge, learn an important skill, or grow in some way that is fulfilling, satisfying, or personally meaningful. (Steinberg, 1997, pp. 72-73)

Successful high schools make sense to their students. Studies of high-achieving schools conclude that students see the curriculum as relevant (Goodlad, 1984), and that they "identify what they do in school as necessary and meaningful for their present and future" (Christman & Macpherson, 1996, p. 90). A major complaint students have about school is not that it is "too difficult, but rather that it is irrelevant and boring" (Rivera & Poplin, 1997, p. 105). When work is relevant, students find purpose in schoolwork and are more likely to take it seriously and complete assignments, something that doesn't often happen in high schools without a clear purpose or focus (Firestone & Rosenblum, 1988).

Effective high schools find ways to connect what goes on in school to the daily life of students. Highly effective programs are those that include experiential learning, out-of-class connections, and real-life activities, allowing students to apply what they learn in school toward solving real-world problems (Firestone & Rosenblum, 1988; Ogden & Germinario, 1995; Pearce, 1992). For learning to make sense, it must be tied to prior learning and grounded in students' personal experience (NASSP, 1996; Texas Education Agency, 1992).

Successful high schools also find ways to connect activities to life after high school (Ogden & Germinario, 1995). Traditionally, students who understand the connection between achievement in high school and access to further education are highly motivated (Steinberg, 1996). Students profiled in the studies of effective high schools that we reviewed agreed that going to school was necessary for their future employment (Ainley, 1994; Tye, 1985). One method that schools have employed to make curriculum relevant is to "align curriculum with career paths and aim directly at developing those skills and attitudes that will help students be proficient problem solvers and responsible citizens" (Ogden & Germinario, 1995, p. 80; see also American Federation of Teachers (AFT), 1997). Career groups in which students explore career options is one method used to "bridge the gap between the capabilities of high school graduates, especially those who are not college-bound, and the skills, knowledge, and work habits needed to be successful in the workplace" (Ogden & Germinario, 1995, p. 113). Some schools have attached an incentive to achievement, paying students for earning high grades (Natriello et al., 1990), and other schools focus on working collaboratively with local businesses, allowing students to make connections with people in the work force (Ogden & Germinario, 1995).

Career-oriented programs that students self-select are particularly successful in making school relevant to students who don't do well in traditional curricular programs (Firestone & Rosenblum, 1988; Pearce, 1992). Minority students, in particular, often find it difficult to see the meaning of schoolwork because it is rarely culturally relevant to them (Natriello et al., 1990), and, therefore, they often fail to see the connection between success in school and success in future life (Fordham, 1986). Research shows that for these minority students and for low-achieving students, it is all the more important to increase the relevancy of academic work and the high school diploma.

Feeling of Belonging and Membership in School

Affiliation occurs when individuals feel connected to others in their surroundings. Isolation in schools often goes beyond a passive disconnection to an active exclusion of students. (Firestone & Rosenblum, 1988, p. 291)

Much support is given to the importance of social bonds that connect the student to the school. These bonds become an essential element in promoting a sense of belonging for the student. (Ogden & Germinario, 1995, p. 78)

As we have noted throughout this volume, high schools tend to be impersonal places in which students often feel they don't belong. In effective high schools, however, students feel connected to the school and to the people in the school community, and creation of this environment is a priority at those schools (Firestone & Rosenblum, 1988; Fullan, 1990; Ogden & Germinario, 1995; Raywid, 1993). Wilson and Corcoran (1988) found that a student's "feeling of being a part of a supportive community contributes to reduced alienation and increased achievement" (p. 3). Research supports the connection between student affiliation with the school and their increased academic achievement (Bryk & Driscoll, 1988; Lee & Bryk, 1989) as well as their attitudes and behaviors in personal and academic areas (Merz & Furman, 1997; Oxley, 1990). Teachers in these more productive schools make an effort to know the students and include them in classroom and school activities (Bobbett & French, 1992).

One report describes this concept as "school membership in which the student and school exchange commitments" (Wehlage et al., 1989, p. 120). The commitments are centered on behaviors that show respect, support, and concern for one another. Belonging and membership are important because they provide opportunities for students to feel special (Wilson & Corcoran, 1988). Excellent schools discover ways to help students develop their talents and abilities as a way of discovering themselves as individuals who are unique (Fordham, 1986; Ogden & Germinario, 1995). Studies support the need for students to feel that they are "not anonymous . . . [and] "someone consider[s] them important" (Powell, Farrar, & Cohen, 1985, p. 193).

Organization and structure play a vital role in the way school climate develops, whether it is inclusive or isolating, which directly affects school effectiveness (Gaziel, 1997; Lee et al., 1993). Thus, some larger schools are restructuring school organization to create smaller, more personal environments in which students experience a greater sense of belonging (Cawelti, 1997). In addition, membership and belonging have a greater impact on achievement for traditionally underserved students, especially minority youngsters and low-achieving students (Coleman & Hoffer, 1987;

Gaziel, 1997; Wehlage et al., 1989). Effective high schools work toward a sense of belonging for all students, not just for the small percentage that typically feel they connect with and belong in the community (Gregory & Smith, 1987).

Transition Programs for New Students

> In large high schools, parents and faculty members have become concerned that the institutions overwhelm younger students as they enter high school. Many schools are responding to this problem by establishing student advisory programs, providing smaller classes and more interdisciplinary work with smaller units, and separating the entering class from the rest of the school as much as possible. (Tewel, 1995, p. 81)

Transitions are always difficult, but few are so difficult in the life of teenagers as that of starting at a new high school (Wehlage et al., 1989). To ease the transition, exemplary high schools provide programs for freshman and other new students to help orient them to the school and its culture (Ogden & Germinario, 1995). These programs include pairing new students with peer helpers or buddies, extended time with guidance counselors, school tours, parent orientation nights, and initiation into school activities. By providing transition programs, schools lessen the shock and disruption caused by entering a new school. One such program for freshman has shown remarkable success:

> The Learning Resource Lab (LRL) is a combination of study hall, homeroom and advisory group. Activities to assist with the transition to high school are built into the LRL. The activities include a study hall with adult tutoring, a conflict resolution workshop, career exploration, technology exploration, an introduction to the library media center, a learning styles inventory, free reading every day, a study skills and note-taking workshop, an introduction to various clubs and organizations, a student/handbook policy review, and a harassment prevention workshop.
>
> In the three years since we began implementing this program, we have documented that freshman have fewer failing grades, fewer discipline referrals to the assistant principals, fewer suspensions, fewer absences, and a more positive attitude toward school. (Pierson, 1996, pp. 25-26)

Some schools try to meet the needs of the students by assigning advisors for students and having the student and advisor together develop the students' individual education plan.

Multicultural Sensitivity and Perspective Appreciated

> It scarcely needs saying that a more inclusive curriculum is not necessarily a better one. Yet, in a society in the process of changing color, can courses in African philosophy be considered frivolous? In a nation with a history of

slavery and a continuing record of racial division and inequality, are the study of Black history and literature, and the inclusion of slave narrative on the reading lists of American history and literature courses, the irrelevancies they are described as?

If school is to make all American children feel at home in both school and society, curriculum space must be reserved for the works, experiences, and societal practices of women as well as men, poor people as well as the middle classes, and ethnic, racial, and other minorities. (Martin, 1997, p. 21)

In order for students, particularly minority students, to feel that they belong and share membership in the school, the school must recognize and value the diversity of these students. Ogden and Germinario (1995) found that "successful schools have conscientiously infused a more multicultural perspective into educational programming" (p. 107), and by developing this multicultural perspective, "students learn to value, respect, and understand their own and other's identities" (McQuillan, 1995, p. 6). Often schools create this rich environment by relating what is learned in school to the students' cultural background (Natriello et al., 1990; Roueche & Baker, 1986), allowing students to learn about various cultures that exist within their school (Taylor-Dunlop & Norton, 1995). In these exemplary high schools, students learn that "individuals can be different and yet still get along and appreciate the uniqueness of others" (Gregory & Smith, 1987, p. 26).

School Views Students as Individuals and Recognizes Their Needs

The school must serve all students, and the mix is becoming increasingly diverse with more special education and at-risk youth in regular classrooms, along with an influx of immigrants from non-English speaking and non-Western cultures. How do educators capture audiences whose motivation ranges the spectrum from cooperation to passivity to often-vigorous resistance? By accepting all comers, education in a democratic society holds great promise. On the other hand, by doing so in a time of limited resources, the risk of not being able to serve all groups well increases. (Larson, 1992, p. 31)

Anyone who has been inside high schools recently realizes the diversity of the students—diversity based on a wide range of characteristics. To be effective with all students, schools must consciously deal with this diversity (NASSP, 1996). Wilson and Corcoran (1988) highlight this by stating that "failure to understand the social and economic realities facing different groups of students, and their influence on student attitudes, can lead to misplaced effort, frustration, and failure" (p. 100).

Exemplary high schools work toward viewing their students as individuals and understanding their unique characteristics (Roueche & Baker, 1986). These high schools know their students; work to identify the emotional, social, and academic needs of the students; and develop programs to help meet those needs (Foley & McConnaughy, 1982; Oxley, 1997; Wilson & Corcoran, 1988). One area that some high schools have begun to address is that of teenage parents and the growing need students have for childcare. By providing childcare centers on the school site, high schools can greatly reduce absenteeism, and students can take classes to learn proper parenting skills (Page & Valli, 1990). Successful high schools recognize students as individuals with personal, social, moral, and intellectual needs. These schools attempt to design programs that are "useful for all students and provide enough variety to address a more diverse set of needs" (Fullan, 1990, p. 230; see also Hill, Foster, & Gendler, 1990). One study found that the personalization of the high school environment was shown to have a greater effect on student engagement than any other variable (McLaughlin, 1994). Schools in which student individuality is not taken into account prove to be especially ineffective for many minority students (Fordham, 1986). We found that successful high schools recognize student needs and view their students as individuals; they support the students in having a voice in their education, in taking on more responsibility at school, in engaging in learning activities that are flexible and diverse, and in programs that support the whole child.

Students Have a Voice in Their Education

A third and final feature involved with humanizing the comprehensive high school is to accord students both more power and more responsibility. . . . Everyone involved with schools—students, teachers, and administrators— will need to view students differently. The student voice will have to be acknowledged in new and different institutional contexts. . . . Students should be involved in their education, rather than be passive bystanders. Such a conception of schooling implies a need to bring students into the process of not only defining what educational opportunity should mean but also of clarifying for them the potential value of this opportunity as well as the consequences of wasting this opportunity. (McQuillan, 1997, pp. 668-669)

Students who have a voice in their education are more likely to be engaged in school and to participate actively in academics and activities. Newmann (1997) informs us that "academic achievement depends on students' commitment to and participation in learning" (p. 4). When students find educational material or approaches unacceptable, they often choose not to be involved in school, showing that ultimately "students hold veto power over all educational policies" (Page & Valli, 1990, p. 110). Effective high schools find ways to give students legitimate voice in academic areas, policy decisions, school organization, discipline, and activities (Bobbett & French, 1992; Mackin, 1996; Meier, 1995; Ogden & Germinario, 1995). Using advisory groups, tutorial settings, honor councils, one-on-one meetings with staff, and student forums, schools gain input on how things are going at the school and what suggestions for change the students might have, including changes in the curriculum (Duke, 1995; McQuillan, 1995; Raywid, 1995; Shore, 1995). In some cases, students are given opportunities to debate issues with faculty members and to be involved in staff hiring (Gregory & Smith, 1987). Because this empowerment is relatively new to students in the school setting, they need assistance in how to use the power they are given. Good high schools "did not assume that they could delegate power to students and that students would unproblematically understand how to use it effectively," but instead, the adults in the school "helped students think about how they might effectively enact their power" (McQuillan, 1995, p. 8).

A traditional method, advocated for over 40 years, for giving students voice is through student government organizations and student councils (Conant, 1959). These representative groups often take recommendations or concerns to the administration and faculty. Successful high schools find ways to increase student input through student government groups and rely on that information when making decisions affecting the whole school community (Oxley, 1990). Effective high schools generally have more active student governments, provide more opportunities for student leadership in the school (Louis & Miles, 1990; Wilson & Corcoran, 1988), and work harder to gain input from students who usually would remain unheard— minority, disadvantaged, and at-risk students in particular (Gilchrist, 1989; Grant, 1988; Ogden & Germinario, 1995; Taylor-Dunlop & Norton, 1995). Students in effective high schools know they have been heard because their opinion directly affects decisions that are made, providing evidence that the faculty and staff value their voice. One of the benefits found in schools that afford greater input from students is that students begin to recognize that other people have voices that deserve to be heard (Furtwengler, 1991; McQuillan, 1995).

Students Have More Responsibility in School

> Evidently our society values obedience and passivity very highly at this point in its development. For regardless of what we say about the importance of originality, independence, and responsible self-direction, we do not provide our young people with a schooling environment which allows them to develop such behaviors. (Tye, 1985, p. 335)

High schools have long been viewed as the site of transition from childhood to adulthood, as the place in which children are trained to be productive, adult members of society. For this to happen, students must be given more responsibility for their schooling experience. Studies show that students want to take on more responsibility and become active in their own learning (McLaughlin, 1994; Perrone, 1983). Research also shows that academic performance is positively related to individuals' belief that they are responsible for their own success or failure (Harnisch, 1987). Increased opportunities for student responsibility and involvement have a positive effect on both academic achievement and student behavior (Furtwengler, 1991; Murphy & Hallinger, 1985; Rutter et al., 1979). Effective high schools give students more responsibility in their learning process (Gregory & Smith, 1987), viewing instruction as a "shared responsibility, directed at times by the teacher but at other times by expert community members and by other students" (Haas, 1993, p. 236). Schools in which students are active learners show increased engagement and achievement, especially for traditionally disadvantaged students (McLaughlin, 1994).

As was pointed out, in the area of student voice, increased responsibility is often new to students and successful high schools find ways to help students take responsibility when given the chance (Wood, 1992). Through discussions in council meetings or in other student group gatherings, students are given guidelines, suggestions, and examples that focus on ways to become active participants and to take more responsibility for their schooling (McQuillan, 1995; Wood, 1992). The key to the process seems to be increasing open dialogue between students and teachers about what goes on inside the classroom (Wilson & Daviss, 1994). Some fear that giving students increased responsibility in school will create a climate in which students are in charge and order is impossible to maintain. The reverse is true in the literature on effective high schools that we reviewed. Teachers still have authority and control of school climate, but students become participants in maintaining a positive climate and in following basic guidelines built on mutual respect and individual responsibility (Gilchrist, 1989; Mackin, 1996; Wilson & Corcoran, 1988). In some effective high schools, students are primarily responsible for creating and enforcing school rules and regulations (Duke, 1995).

Flexible, Diverse Programs for Students in Various Situations

> The second view of teaching and learning, the view that underpins the new paradigm for school reform, starts from the assumptions that students are not standardized and teaching is not routine. . . . Far from following standardized instructional packages, teachers must base their judgements on knowledge of learning theory and pedagogy, of child development and cognition and of curriculum and assessment. They must then connect this knowledge to the understandings, dispositions, and conceptions that individual students bring with them to the classroom. (Darling-Hammond, 1997a, p. 46-47)

As noted earlier, high schools do not contain homogeneous groups of students but rather a highly diverse set of individuals occupying the same classrooms and buildings. These high levels of diversity present a challenge to those in high schools when trying to personalize the learning process, and some research shows that "the individualization of instruction has never really taken root at the high school level" (Tye, 1985, p. 288). Experts report that the number one reason students give for dropping out of high school, particularly students of lower socioeconomic status (Wehlage et al., 1989), is the incongruity between the school's academic program and the skills and interests of the students (Natriello et al., 1990). Exemplary high schools find paths to personalize education and individualize instruction for their students in ways that enhance academic performance (Foley & McConnaughy, 1982;

Kleinfeld, McDiarmid, & Hagstrom, 1989; Murphy, 1991; Roueche & Baker, 1986).

Schools use a variety of techniques to accommodate student diversity, one being intensive mentoring or tutoring programs that occur during the regular school day or after school hours to bring remedial students up to par with their peers (Natriello et al., 1990). Schools also alter their traditional time schedule to meet the demands of students who work during the day, offering flexible afternoon or evening programs (Brouillette, 1997). A theme that continually emerges from research is the importance of flexible and varied instructional strategies in reaching the variety of students present in any classroom (Powell et al., 1985; Taylor-Dunlop & Norton, 1995). Effective high schools find ways to incorporate flexibility into instruction by incorporating a variety of instructional strategies and encouraging teachers to diversify practices (Darling-Hammond, 1997a; Gamoran, Nystrand, Berends, & LePore, 1995; Haas, 1993). Research also points to the need for teachers to patiently explain and reexplain information students don't quickly comprehend (Firestone & Rosenblum, 1988). Instructional diversity is often obtained through use of an interdisciplinary team-approach to teaching (Haas, 1993; Oxley, 1990) or of instruction centered on a curricular theme (Pearce, 1992).

Flexibility also shows up in the organizational arrangements of exemplary high schools. Some schools open before the regular school day begins and stay open long after the school day ends, providing students with facilities in which to work, hold club or group meetings, or study in an academically conducive environment (Brouillette, 1997; Natriello et al., 1990; Wood, 1992). Another structural change involves having learning take place outside the school building in real-life work situations. Productive high schools have been successful using apprenticeships, community outreach programs, and Job Corps placements as ways to diversify learning opportunities (Gilchrist, 1989; Natriello et al., 1990).

Programs Support the Whole Youngster, Physically and Mentally

In education, we are beginning to realize that specialized intervention by isolated counselors, reading teachers, disciplinary vice-principals, and so on, cannot prevent at-risk students from slipping through the cracks. And, as educators are beginning to understand, most students are at risk at some point in their educational career. Whole-person involvement means individualized treatment of students, in and out of the classroom. (Louis & Miles, 1990, p. 25)

Productive high schools view students as whole people, complete with academic, personal, emotional, and social needs that must be addressed (Bryk, Lee, & Holland, 1993). These schools recognize that if students have physiological problems, such as illness or hunger, or emotional problems, such as isolation or alienation, those issues must be met along with academic needs in order for students to maximize their learning (Foley & McConnaughy, 1982; Murphy, 1991; Wood, 1992). Research shows that having adults who listen and talk with students on a personal or emotional level affects students attachment to school and their decision to stay in school or drop out (Page & Valli, 1990; Taylor-Dunlop & Norton, 1995; Wehlage et al., 1989). Successful high schools set up programs to deal with specific emotional problems faced by students, such as adjustment to a new school environment, family issues, peer conflicts, and personal problems (Christman & Macpherson, 1996; Rutter et al., 1979; Wehlage et al., 1989). High schools have also begun working with health services and social agencies that provide services to adolescents in ways that coordinate services through the school and support the core academic mission (Merz & Furman, 1997; NASSP, 1996).

An especially productive area of student support is the integration of students' needs into the curriculum, allowing students to deal, in the context of learning, with issues that confront them (Tewel, 1995). Exemplary high schools are "committed to education in its broadest sense, the development of whole students. They induce values, influence attitudes, and integrate diverse sources of knowledge" (Hill et al., 1990, p. 56). Successful high schools find that working in teams, teachers can bring the personal life and problems of students into the curriculum, where personal issues are addressed in ways that enhance learning (Ohiwerei, 1996). In some schools, citizenship, character, values, ethics, thoughtfulness, motivation, and commitment are integrated into the curriculum, either in courses or through schoolwide campaigns, assemblies, and advisory-group discussions (Hill et al., 1990; Ogden & Germinario, 1995).

School Staff Knows and Cares for Students

> We need to give up the notion of an ideal of the educated person and replace it with a multiplicity of models designed to accommodate the multiple capacities and interests of students. We need to recognize multiple identities. For example, an eleventh grader may be a Black, a woman, a teenager, a Smith, an American, a New Yorker, a Methodist, a person who loves math, and so on. As she exercises these identities, she may use different languages, adopt different postures, and relate differently to those around her. But whoever she is at a given moment, whatever she is engaged in, she needs—as we all do—to be cared for. Her need for care may require formal respect, informal interaction, expert advice, just a flicker of recognition, or sustained affection. To give the care she needs requires a set of capacities in each of us to which the schools give too little attention. (Noddings, 1997, p. 35)

Personalization has a human and professional dimension. The human side involves knowing students from the point of view of concerned adult friend, whereas the professional side adds the element of specialized knowledge about particular strengths and weaknesses in learning. . . . All teachers and indeed all school-based professionals should advise students on a regular basis. Therapeutic skills are not what most students need from advisers. What they need are adults who know them as unique learners, complex and distinctive. (Powell et al., 1985, p. 318)

The key to creating a cohesive, nurturing environment for students lies in having a school populated by caring adults. Research strongly supports the idea that high school students want and need—and perform better for—adults who care about them (Bryk, Lee, & Holland, 1993; Corcoran & Wilson, 1985; Noddings, 1997; Perrone, 1983; Wood, 1992). Put another way, "high school must be an institution that unabashedly advocates on behalf of young people" (NASSP, 1996, p. 2). Effective high schools exhibit harmonious relationships among students and staff, which positively affect student achievement (Ogden & Germinario, 1995). Caring in high schools can be defined along two dimensions: caring for students academically and caring for students personally.

Students are Known and Cared for Academically

Students told us "the way teachers treat you as a student or a person actually," counted more than any other factor in the school setting in determining their attachment to the school, their commitment to the school's goals and, by extension, the academic future they imagined for themselves. (McLaughlin, 1994, p. 9)

In effective high schools, students have adults they can talk to about academics and these schools develop, encourage, and support programs and opportunities in which these interactions occur (Boyer, 1983; Foley & McConnaughy, 1982). Students show increased academic achievement in high school environments populated by adults who assist and encourage youngsters (Coburn & Nelson, 1989; Firestone & Rosenblum, 1988; Murphy & Hallinger, 1985; Newmann, 1997; Page & Valli, 1990). Students also value consistency and fairness in the ways adults interact with them, viewing this as respect for the student as an individual and a scholar (Dyer, 1996; Fullan, 1990). Although many people view teenagers as adults who need less adult involvement in their lives, the truth is that students want and need adult concern and attention (Firestone & Rosenblum, 1988; Fullan, 1990; King & Weiss, 1995; Powell et al., 1985). One researcher found that when adults inquired about how a student was doing academically or personally, the students interpreted this as support, and it "contributed to a more general belief that all individuals are important and worthy of adult attention" (Wehlage et al., 1989, p. 131; See also Mackin, 1996). Studies of students who drop out of high school point to student isolation and a feeling that no one at school cares or pays attention to them as significant factors in their decision not to remain in school (Firestone & Rosenblum, 1988; Natriello et al., 1990). Some schools assign each student a personal adult advisor who meets with him or her individually to discuss academic status, progress, and problems (Texas Education Agency, 1992).

Students Are Known and Cared for Personally

> At the very least, children need to love and be loved. They need to feel safe and secure and at ease with themselves and others. They need to experience intimacy and affection. They need to be perceived as unique individuals and to be treated as such. The factory model of schooling presupposes that such conditions have already been met when children arrive at school; that school's raw materials—the children—have, so to speak, been "pre-processed." Resting on the unspoken assumption that home is the school's partner in the educational process, the model takes for granted that it is home's job to fulfill these basic needs. Thus the production-line picture derives its plausibility from the premise that school does not have to be a loving place, the classroom does not have to have an affectionate atmosphere, and teachers do not have to treasure the individuality of students because the school's silent partner will take care of all this. (Martin, 1997)

The statement above expresses a problem seen in many high schools today. Students come to school needing more than adults who are interested in them academically; they need adults who care about them personally. When asked what matters to them about school, what makes a difference, an overwhelming number of high school students respond that having teachers who care about them is the most important thing to them (Coburn & Nelson, 1989; NASSP, 1996; Newmann, 1997; Powell, 1990; Wehlage et al., 1989). Good relationships between students and teachers have been linked to enhanced academic achievement and improved student success (Ainley, 1994; Bryk, Lee, & Holland, 1993). Yet the conditions found in many high schools today do not facilitate the development of student-teacher relationships that enhance student learning (Louis & Miles, 1990; Sizer, 1984). Whether it is large size, curricular differentiation, overextended staff, or lack of support for adults themselves, high schools often reflect a noncaring, impersonal attitude toward their students (Meier, 1995; Oakes, 1985; Sizer, 1984; Wehlage et al., 1989). Effective high schools, by comparison, clearly communicate to students that "the staff in these schools care about students and are doing everything possible to maintain programs to meet their diverse needs" (Wilson & Corcoran, 1988, p. 54; see also Lambeth, 1981; Meier, 1995; Raywid, 1993). Caring is communicated in several ways, such as respect for students as individuals and fair, equitable treatment of all students (Firestone & Rosenblum, 1988; Raywid, 1993; Wood, 1992).

High-achieving high schools are student centered, with a focus on the staff's knowing students by name and knowing where they come from and what their life is like outside of school (Bobbett & French, 1992; McLaughlin, 1994; Newmann, 1997; Oxley, 1997; Roueche & Baker, 1986). Students in these high schools find that when they have problems or need assistance, "someone is always there" (Wood, 1992, p. 45; see also Gregory & Smith, 1987). Teachers have extended roles and responsibility in caring for students outside the regular classroom setting (Bryk & Driscoll, 1988; Foley & McConnaughy, 1982). The understanding that teachers gain about the personal side of students, about students' lives outside the classroom, is used to enhance academic activities and can improve classroom instruction (Lee et al., 1993). Students value honest, authentic communication and interaction from adults, allowing students to see them as real people (Rivera & Poplin, 1997). Students are more open to learning from teachers who know them and are involved in their lives (NASSP, 1996; Oxley, 1997; Powell et al., 1985; Rivera & Poplin, 1997). The result of this strong ethic of caring by school staff creates an overall school climate that increases student commitment to the school and its members (Bryk et al., 1993; Lee et al., 1993; Mitchell, Russell, & Benson, 1990; Ogden & Germinario, 1995; Wilson & Corcoran, 1988).

Teachers Operate in a Positive, Professionally Oriented Community

> The success of a high school depends on its being more than a collection of unconnected individuals. The word "community" implies a commonality of interests and so it should be in any high school. The building of community very much involves the members of the staff. And, on a practical level, the synergy of cooperation ought to end up enabling the educators in a high school to accomplish more for the students than they could by acting on their own. School improvement more readily succeeds in situations in which teachers work in a collegial manner.
>
> —NASSP (1996, p. 90)

Community in high school involves support for both students and faculty. Teachers cannot be expected to care for and support students if they are not supported and cared for themselves. Effective high schools provide opportunities for personal and professional growth, not only for students but also for staff members. These good high schools find ways to support all staff members, knowing that support for professional community will be transferred to students and will ultimately affect achievement (Newmann, 1997). High schools that operate professionally oriented communities for teachers are grounded by two main premises: support for the professionalization of teachers and increased capacity for teacher success and growth.

School Supports the Professionalization of Teachers

> All three of these traits—influence, efficacy, and absenteeism—are likely to represent a force of some independent importance in the educational process. Together they describe what is usually meant by teacher professionalism. Truly professional teachers are ones who are sufficiently knowledgeable, wise, and dedicated that they can be trusted to work effectively without ex-

tensive direction and supervision and to contribute constructively to the overall operation of an effective school. (Chubb & Moe, 1990, p. 90)

In productive high schools, the professionalization of teachers is seen in support from school leaders and esteem and respect from community members and peers, collegial working relationships, teacher involvement in decision making; teacher input into daily work processes, and a more expansive role for teachers.

School Encourages Community to Support Teachers

Teachers often feel isolated and lonely. They frequently feel victimized by students, parents, and administrators. They often are held in low esteem by and receive little respect from these important groups. These attitudes about teaching are sources of stress for teachers and obstacles to their productivity. In successful schools, the reverse appears to be true. Teachers are respected, relationships are supportive and reciprocal, and there is a strong sense of community. (Wilson & Corcoran, 1988, p. 17)

Community is a concept that resonates within most people involved in schools. It brings to mind images of groups of caring adults, gathering around one another and students to support the important mission of educating children. All too often, this sense of community is not found in the comprehensive high school (Sizer, 1984). When schools are unable to develop community among staff members, isolation, distrust, and resistance are pervasive in the culture, and "it becomes difficult for even the most competent individuals to make a positive difference for students" (Newmann, 1997). Wilson and Corcoran (1988) contrast this lack of community with what is found in successful high schools by pointing out that "one of the hallmarks of these schools is a strong sense of communal identity, a sense of belonging to a professional community and an institution whose goals and values are shared" (p. 87). Communal school environments are more likely to promote collective responsibility for students and increased commitment to the school organization on the part of high school faculty, both of which have been shown to increase school success (Bryk & Driscoll, 1988; Lee & Smith, 1996; Marks & Louis, 1997; Newmann, 1997; Wilson & Corcoran, 1988). Research shows that schools that support professional communities for teachers also support learning environments for students in which authentic pedagogy is more likely to occur and be evaluated, resulting in increased achievement (Kruse, Louis, & Bryk, 1995; Murphy, 1991; Newmann, 1997).

Teachers working in these effective, highly communal schools have better attitudes about their schools, their work, and education in general (Bryk & Driscoll, 1988; Lee et al., 1993), a state described by some as "professional satisfaction" (Powell, 1990, p. 117). In successful high schools, teachers report a school culture that respects teaching, providing them "a sense of dignity that comes with being regarded with esteem by colleagues, students, and community members" (Wilson & Corcoran, 1988, p. 88; see also Chubb & Moe, 1990; Fine, 1992; Kruse et al., 1995; Lee, 1995). Schools express this esteem by respecting the work of teachers and supporting their efforts (Corcoran, 1990; Firestone & Rosenblum, 1988; Fullan, 1990; Tye, 1985) and by recognizing good teachers for the outstanding work they do in the school (Gaziel, 1997; Ogden & Germinario, 1995; Ohiwerei, 1996; Wilson & Corcoran, 1988).

Teachers Work and Plan Together

> Highly collegial environments are settings in which teachers report a high level of innovativeness, high levels of energy and enthusiasm, and support for personal growth and learning. Teachers who belong to communities of this sort also report a high level of commitment to teaching and to all of the students with whom they work. (Little & McLaughlin, 1993, p. 94)

One way high schools support the professionalization of teachers is to increase opportunities for the development of collegial working relationships. Research identifies lack of collegiality as having a negative effect on achievement (Anderson, 1985), whereas collegiality and collaboration among high school faculty have a positive impact on student learning (King & Weiss, 1995; Lee & Smith, 1996; Lightfoot, 1983; Ogden & Germinario, 1995; Rutter et al., 1979; Wilson & Corcoran, 1988). Collegiality has been defined in some effective high schools as "both a feeling of sharing and a set of actions for the common good" that improve relationships among school staff in support of professional efforts of individual teachers (Wehlage et al., 1989, p. 142). Positive collegial relationships are particularly important when schools are involved in change activities such as implementing innovations (Larson, 1992; Lee et al., 1993). Collegiality in these schools develops as teachers work together to solve school-level problems (Kruse et al., 1995; Little & McLaughlin, 1993), plan professional development activities (Cawelti, 1997; Tewel, 1995), analyze instructional strategies and classroom practices (Fullan, 1990; Lee & Smith, 1996; Marks & Louis, 1997; Wilson & Daviss, 1994), and discuss how to handle problems and needs of individual students (Hill et al., 1990; King & Weiss, 1995).

Collegial activities take time to plan and implement, time not often found in the daily schedule of comprehensive high schools (Firestone & Rosenblum, 1988; Louis & Miles, 1990). Effective high schools find ways to alter traditional schedules to allow staff members to work together on shared activities, both during school hours and during blocks of time set aside for professional development and improvement (Chubb & Moe, 1990; Meier, 1995; Miles & Darling-Hammond, 1998). Some schools also encourage and support collegial networks outside the school building as a way of improving practice and gaining new information about instruction (Little & McLaughlin, 1993; Pearce, 1992).

Teachers Involved in Decision Making

> This common theme of teacher participation and empowerment is central in current research on successful schools. Although the vehicles for involvement may vary from school to school, the results are most often related to

positive student outcomes and productive teaching environments. Best schools actively create opportunities for the involvement of teachers in most every aspect of school decision making. They have capitalized on the skills and experiences of those who are closest and know most about the teaching-learning process. (Ogden & Germinario, 1995, p. 39)

Participatory management in high schools takes the form of site-based councils, teacher-leaders, advisory councils, school-improvement teams, faculty committees, and student advisory boards and teams, all of which allow members of the community to have a voice in decisions that affect the school as a whole (Newmann, 1997). However it occurs, effective high schools operate using participatory management to encourage commitment, empowerment, engagement, and ownership by students, parents, community members, and staff in support of the school and its educational goals (Foster, 1998; Meier, 1995; NASSP, 1996; Ogden & Germinario, 1995; Wilson & Corcoran, 1988). This is particularly important for teachers who are usually the ones asked to implement decisions made in the school. Research on effective high schools supports the connection between shared decision making and increased academic achievement for the students in those schools (Anderson, 1985; Fine, 1992; Larson, 1992; Ogden & Germinario, 1995; Oxley, 1990), an increase that is even more dramatic for disadvantaged students (Natriello et al., 1990). Studies have also shown that learning is more equitable in schools with higher levels of teacher input into school-level decisions (Lee & Smith, 1996).

Although teacher involvement in decision making does not guarantee school improvement, it is often identified as *a necessary condition* for instructional improvement (Louis & Miles, 1990; Marks & Louis, 1997; Newmann, 1997). For shared decision making to be successful, principals must encourage teachers to become involved in planning and must support teachers as they take on new leadership positions (Chubb & Moe, 1990; Firestone & Rosenblum, 1988). In the literature on successful high schools we reviewed, democratic decision making occurred at the departmental, team, or disciplinary level, thereby creating structures to increase teacher input (Cawelti, 1997; Hill, 1995; King & Weiss, 1995; Little & McLaughlin, 1993). In addition, changes in traditional hierarchy structures in some effective high schools has helped to disperse leadership throughout the staff, providing additional opportunities for teachers to be active in decision making (Foster, 1998; Newmann, 1997; Ogden & Germinario, 1995; Wilson & Corcoran, 1988).

Teachers Have Input Into Their Daily Work Processes

One high school principal expressed views held by many of his peers when he told a site visitor that it was not salaries or reputation that most attracted teachers to his school but the professional environment and the better working conditions. The opportunity to work with talented professionals, to exercise greater discretion over both course content and methods of teaching, and to have more time to work with students and develop curricula were critical factors in his view. (Wilson & Corcoran, 1988, p. 87)

Although teachers might enjoy greater voice in school-level decision making, studies show that what teachers desire most is more control over decisions that affect their daily work (DuFour & Eaker, 1992; Fullan, 1990; Grant, 1988; Wilson & Corcoran, 1988). High schools in which teachers have influence over day-to-day decisions are identified as more enjoyable work environments or "more satisfying workplaces" (Goodlad, 1984, p. 259; see also Corcoran, 1990; Raywid, 1995; Wehlage et al., 1989), conditions that affect teacher performance, commitment, and student success (Louis & Miles, 1990; Wilson & Corcoran, 1988). Teachers particularly desire input on decisions about the planning of curriculum, the academic programs, and the introduction of instructional practices (Canady & Rettig, 1995; Corcoran, 1990; Firestone & Rosenblum, 1988; Garibaldi, 1993; Meier, 1995). In many effective high schools, "teachers actually develop the courses and the programs, adhering to district guidelines, and subject to the approval by the lead teachers" (Wilson & Corcoran, 1988, p. 82). Control over what goes on in their classroom is important to teachers (Lee et al., 1993), and effective high schools capitalize on this, using it as a way to increase teacher input into decision making and to strengthen professionalization (Bobbett & French, 1992; Larson, 1992; Meier, 1995; Tye, 1985; Wilson & Corcoran, 1988).

Changing Roles for Teachers as Generalists, Not Specialists

Teachers who act on their belief in personal accountability often must go beyond the standard set of required teacher activities. In doing so, they practice what we call "extended role." They are willing to do more than impart the subject matter they officially have been hired to teach. (Wehlage et al., 1989, p. 136)

The same is true of another current reform theme that emphasizes the importance of diffused roles for teachers. Such role expansion has been argued as a needed antidote to bureaucracy's fragmentation and the ensuing anonymity imposed on students, with the alienation that, in turn, that can bring (Newmann, 1981). Others have argued that narrow roles have comparable negative effects on staff—resulting in estrangement or minimal commitment as well as in a general lowering of teachers' skills (Raywid, 1995).

In order for teachers to be involved in decision making, move toward collegiality, and increase professionalism, they must adopt new roles that go beyond the classroom walls (Lee et al., 1993; Powell, 1990). In contrast with less successful high schools, which view teachers as subject-area specialists (Louis & Miles, 1990), exemplary high schools encourage and support teachers in their taking on diffuse roles to meet students' needs (Corcoran & Wilson, 1985; Foley & McConnaughy, 1982; Gregory & Smith, 1987; Hill et al., 1990). Teachers take on roles traditionally performed by administrators, specialists, and counselors (Louis & Miles, 1990; Ogden & Germinario, 1995). To prepare teachers to move into these new roles, training and preparation are needed to increase both confidence and skill levels (Little, 1995). Although teachers find that expanding their roles increases complexity, time spent at work, and energy expended, the results can be very rewarding in terms of teacher satisfaction and student success (Gregory & Smith, 1987; Ogden & Germinario, 1995).

School Structure Increases Capacity for Teacher Success and Growth

> Teachers must see themselves as part of a learning community in which their own professional improvement connects itself to the growth of their students. Attempts by teachers to improve should not be viewed, however, solely in terms of individual prescriptions dispensed without considering the well being of the entire faculty. (NASSP, 1996, p. 64)

Steps taken by high schools to develop structures that have increased capacity for teacher success and growth are decreased teacher load, a team or interdisciplinary approach to learning, professional development focused on staff needs, provision of adequate resources, emphasis placed on reflection, and dealing with departments effectively.

Decreased Teacher Load

> Despite research disagreement over how class size and student learning are related, there is very little disagreement (and none in the minds of parents) that personal attention is directly related to how many students a teacher is responsible for. (Powell, 1990, p. 125)

Research strongly supports reducing overall student load as a way of helping teachers improve classroom success (Murphy, 1991). The message is clear that "exemplary [high] schools are committed to establishing favorable teacher-student ratios" (Wilson & Corcoran, 1988, p. 50), which they know will have an impact on achievement (Chubb & Moe, 1990). In most comprehensive high schools, teachers work with between 125 and 150 students each day. However, it is not unusual for a teacher to carry a load of over 150, not including the students they are responsible for in extracurricular activities (Little, 1990; Powell, 1990). Not only does this make it more difficult for teachers to get to know their students, but it also creates mountains of papers for teachers to grade, which means feedback to students cannot occur quickly (Boyer, 1983; NASSP, 1996). Reduced teacher load allows for greater individualization of instruction and for more time for the teacher to address individual student needs (Gregory & Smith, 1987; NASSP, 1996; Powell et al., 1985). Due to more personal attention and a setting that allows teachers to know their students better, relationships between teachers and students are enhanced when student load is reduced (NASSP, 1996; Powell et al., 1985).

High schools in the studies we examined used a variety of structural arrangements to successfully reduce student load. Some reduced the number of classes a teacher taught in a given year or semester (Perrone, 1985). Others created teams that shared responsibility for students, at times having one teacher in charge of large groups of students so other teachers could work with smaller groups (Newmann, 1997). Rearranging staff positions and bringing administrators and support staff into the classroom were also used as a method to reduce teaching loads (Newmann, 1997).

Team and Interdisciplinary Teaching is Encouraged and Supported With Common Planning Time

The goal here is to have schools organized in such a way that teachers can work in teams (within and between school departments) to improve the quality of education. That can't happen, though, unless school systems are decentralized, with individual schools enjoying some freedom to chart their own course. Given that freedom, individual school teams can and should be held responsible for clarifying graduation standards, developing performance assessments, and finding ways to help all students attain high levels of achievement. (Cawelti, 1994, p. 21)

Arranging teachers into instructional teams does not guarantee student learning will improve, but research suggests that teams create the type of supportive, reflective environment that improves practice and ultimately increases achievement (Kruse et al., 1995; Lee & Smith, 1996; McLaughlin, 1994; Newmann, 1997). Working in teams, teachers are able to avoid the problems of isolation faced by most high school teachers (Firestone & Rosenblum, 1988; Lee & Smith, 1996; Perrone, 1985). Effective secondary schools use teams to improve community, provide support, and create a strong climate that influences expectations and student performance (Foster, 1998; Lee, Smith, & Croninger, 1995; Meier, 1995; Wilson & Corcoran, 1988). One format used to create teams is subject integration or interdisciplinary team arrangements (Hargreaves & Macmillan, 1995; Little, 1995; Murphy, 1991; Ogden & Germinario, 1995). Some high schools use their departments as sites for teams to organize and plan courses, allowing different teachers to take the leadership role from team to team (Hill, 1995). Teaming does require extra time on the part of the participants for planning and development, which is a problem in some schools. However, successful high schools rearrange the schedule to provide time for teams to meet during the school day (Canady & Rettig, 1995; Newmann, 1997).

Professional Development Focused on Needs of Staff

A synthesis has been developed focusing on the relationship between staff development and effective secondary schools. The critical importance of ongoing staff development is one of the most consistent and significant findings in the effective-schools research. (Fullan, 1990, p. 230)

Although high schools are concerned with learning, that learning does not always extend to teachers. Perrone (1985) reminds us that in the typical high school

> . . . with the present organizational patterns and expectations, there is little, if any, opportunity for teachers to reflect significantly on the practice; little if any, encouragement or support for teachers to be the "students of learning" Dewey suggested they had to be to remain vital in any professional sense. (p. 656)

Teachers need to be provided with opportunities to engage in ongoing, high-quality learning activities. Secondary school teachers regularly state that they are committed to professional development and a majority indicate that they would like more professional development opportunities (Fullan, 1990; Little, 1990). Key factors in professional development have been identified as the "frequency and quality of the opportunities for social interaction and dialogue about teaching" (Wilson & Corcoran, 1988, p. 14).

Unlike typical high schools, the schools in the literature we studied provided a number of opportunities for teachers' personal and professional growth (Gilchrist, 1989; Wilson & Corcoran, 1988). Effective secondary schools provide time and space for teachers to talk about instructional techniques, classroom management issues, and curriculum and to engage in peer observations and feedback, all of which affect teacher efficacy and classroom performance (King & Weiss, 1995; Kruse et al., 1995; Tewel, 1995; Wilson, & Corcoran, 1988). Research identifies several conditions necessary for staff development to have a positive impact on student achievement: learning opportunities should be ongoing, involve school leaders, include peer observation and feedback, provide follow-up evaluations, and be aligned with needs of individual teachers and overall school goals (Ogden & Germinario, 1995; Stringfield, Ross, & Smith, 1996; Tewel, 1995). Reports on the effective high schools that we reviewed showed that these institutions built their professional development programs around these core ideas.

Successful high schools employ a variety of professional development strategies, such as continuing education at colleges or universities, professional conferences, internships and sabbaticals, workshops, serving on committees, and inservice programs (Hill, 1995; Ohiwerei, 1996; Powell, 1990; Wilson & Corcoran, 1988). In many high-achieving high schools, professional development is designed to meet the needs of teachers at that particular site, often having been decided on and planned by the school staff themselves and often using experts from inside the school district to conduct programs (Austin & Holowenzak, 1985; King & Weiss, 1995; Newmann, 1997; Ogden & Germinario, 1995). Some activities involve the entire school staff, and others are programs that individuals engage in for personal growth (Wilson & Corcoran, 1988). For professional development activities to be successful, adequate funding and necessary time must be available, and school administrators must support and encourage teacher involvement in the activities. Effective high schools are especially adept at finding ways of producing funding, time, and administrative support for the professional development activities they undertake (Cawelti, 1997; NASSP, 1996; Newmann, 1997; Wilson & Corcoran, 1988).

Necessary Resources Provided for Effective Teaching

> Schools may have competent teachers and still lack the capacity to boost student achievement significantly. Individual staff competence must be complemented by adequate technical resources. High quality curriculum, instructional materials, laboratory equipment, computer technology, and physical space for students to work and concentrate all enhance a school's instructional capacity. (Newmann, 1997)

As the above statement implies, teachers cannot be maximally effective without adequate resources for instruction. Resources are one part of a school's instructional capacity, and instructional capacity "affects student engagement in academic work to produce student achievement" (Newmann, 1997). Effective high schools provide higher levels of funding for instruction than less effective schools (Chubb & Moe, 1990; Miles & Darling-Hammond, 1998). Successful high schools also work to ensure that resources are equitably distributed to students as needs are identified and prioritized (Lee et al., 1993). Money is not the only resource needed to increase instructional capacity; adequate time is also needed to plan and carry out effective instruction (Natriello et al., 1990). Teachers need to have the time and energy necessary to meet the variety of demands facing them in high schools (Louis & Miles, 1990):

> If schools are to be systematic about change, there must be time for teachers to do their job well; time to plan and time to reflect on their work. The logic behind this proposal is compelling: improve education by directly improving the quality of classroom teaching. Students change; society changes; technology changes; our understandings about teaching and learning change. So students get the best we can offer and so teachers maintain a sense of professional efficacy, these professionals need time to learn, reflect, and grow. American society must recognize that teaching is a difficult, challenging, draining, and demanding profession, if you do it right. (McQuillan, 1998, p. 199)

Statistics show that even though teachers have preparation periods during the school day, with teachers usually having "only 13 minutes of time for each hour of instruction" (Little, 1990, p. 212), these do not provide sufficient time to allow for proper instructional preparation. High school teachers need more time for planning and reflection on instructional issues (McQuillan, 1997; Perrone, 1985). For teachers to create effective learning environments for students, high schools must provide teachers with productive environments as well (McQuillan, 1997; Natriello et al., 1990; Powell et al., 1985). Time for reflection allows teachers opportunities to work with one another on issues of instructional techniques and practice, curriculum, and student development, which leads in turn to improved teacher performance and enhanced student achievement (Firestone & Rosenblum, 1988; Kruse et al., 1995; Lee & Smith, 1996; Newmann, 1997; Wilson & Corcoran, 1988). Reflection is more than just sharing resources:

[Reflective practice] demands that people consistently set aside time to consider carefully the work of colleagues, criticize it candidly and specifically, and then offer suggestions. In essence, reflective practice means helping others recraft lessons, questions, assignments, visuals, and projects. (Hill, 1995, p. 133)

In effective high schools, reflective dialogue not only improves practice but helps to create community as teachers work with one another, observing and evaluating all aspects of the learning process (Kruse et al., 1995; Ogden & Germinario, 1995). Reflection is extremely useful in helping new faculty members, providing them with opportunities to interact with colleagues and receive feedback from more experienced faculty members serving as mentors and evaluators (Ogden & Germinario, 1995).

Successful high schools have employed several strategies to create adequate time and space for teachers to engage in reflective dialogue. The school-master schedule is readjusted to make time for teams or other groups focused on curriculum to have common planning-periods on a regular basis (American Federation of Teachers, 1997; Little, 1990; Newmann, 1997). Common workspaces convenient to team members are created by changing how school facilities are used (Kruse et al., 1995; Wilson & Corcoran, 1988). Some high schools use support staff, volunteers, aids, and interns to cover teachers' classes and create release time for teachers to be involved in reflection and growth activities (Natriello et al., 1990). By giving attention to these issues, effective high schools encourage reflection among faculty members.

Effective high schools have also found ways to use existing structures and groupings as sources of growth, development, and reflective dialogue (Gregory & Smith, 1987; Kruse et al., 1995; Little & McLaughlin, 1993). By capitalizing on teacher affinity within subject areas, these high schools provide space and time for departments to engage in reflective work. Success of this departmental approach varies both between and within schools, depending on the strength of the department and the support given by administration (Hill, 1995; Talbert, 1995).

Student-Adult Relationships Drive the Community of Commitment

A primary indicator of a student's sense of belonging in a school is the quality of interactions and relationships he/she has with the adults in that school. It is those adults who help model the world for the child. It is those adults on whom the child relies for security, support, and recognition. Through the development of trust between students and those adults around them, fear and apprehension are managed. Thus, students are far more likely to take intellectual risks in classrooms, to feel free to engage in activities throughout the school and to seek adult assistance when confronted with a school or life problem.

—Ogden and Germinario (1995, p. 78)

The social interactions of schooling are not simply a mechanism for accomplishing some other aim, but rather are education itself. In the distinctive workplace of a school, social relations among adults and students are much more than just a factor to be manipulated in the pursuit of academic production.

—Lee et al. (1993, p. 228)

The heart of a high school is the student-adult relationship. One researcher found that "the teacher/student relationship is perhaps the most profound and consequential of "working conditions" for teachers, the one that most directly affects their commitment to work and their motivation to learn" (Little, 1990, p. 192). For students to feel connected to school, they must have "frequent and high-quality interaction with adults" (Wehlage et al., 1989, p. 130). Teachers and students must know one another for teachers to be able to engage students in the academic life of a high school (NASSP, 1996). Christman and Macpherson (1996) sum it up by saying that "for students, good teaching involves good relationships dedicated to meaningful work. Changing student-teacher interactions is at the heart of reforming schools" (p. 90). Highly effective high schools do two things to promote student-adult interactions in schools: organize programs that facilitate relationships and adopt structures that facilitate relationships.

School Organizes Programs That Facilitate Relationships

Rather significant alterations in the structures used to deliver educational services constitute the final component of a restructured core technology for schools. Changes are designed to underscore the centrality of human relationships in schools, to replace program isolation with connectedness, and to promote personal engagement in the teaching-learning process. They represent a fundamental reconceptualization of school climate—a shift from an emphasis on its physical factors and toward a focus on its human elements. (Murphy, 1991, p. 63)

Most secondary schools are designed and organized to process large batches of students. They also are highly differentiated, in the sense that a student may have a different teacher for every period of the school day. Conversely, a given student may be one of 150 or more taught by a particular math or English teacher. The end result is that teachers rarely have sustained and in-depth social contact with their students. . . . Under these circumstances, students may well come to the conclusion that no one at the school cares about their welfare. To counteract this trend and its likely consequences, the school must reorganize the daily schedule to allow students to have more close contact with adults in the school and to ensure that this contact has a positive valance. (Natriello et al., 1990, p. 113)

A common thread that runs through all programs in effective high schools is the emphasis on nurturing, warm, and supportive relationships between students and adults in the school (Merz & Furman, 1997). Research overwhelmingly supports the importance of good relationships between students and teachers as a key factor affecting not only student attitude, but also student achievement (Bryk & Driscoll, 1988; Lee et al., 1993; Lee et al., 1995; Miles & Darling-Hammond, 1998). These connections or bonds between students and teachers serve to motivate and engage students in learning (Lee et al., 1993; McQuillan, 1997). Good relationships also lead to a positive school climate that makes high schools a more enjoyable place to be, work, and learn for everyone (Garibaldi, 1993; Gilchrist, 1989; Merz & Furman, 1997; Wilson & Corcoran, 1988). Teachers in effective high schools are deeply involved in the lives of their students because they genuinely like and understand adolescents (Wilson & Corcoran, 1988). Teachers' interest in students doesn't stop at the schoolhouse door but extends into their personal lives. Time and energy put into developing these personal relationships with students can be draining and exhausting for teachers (McQuillan, 1997; Powell, 1990), but effective high schools find ways to organize programs to facilitate these relationships and support teachers in this important work. As one report reminds us, "The people in schools that work don't sit back and hope that a child connects with a caring adult; they make sure it happens" (Texas Education Agency, 1992, p. 26).

Advisory Groups That Meet Regularly

> One antidote to the impersonal atmosphere of so many high schools is a teacher-advisory program, in which a teacher meets regularly with and advises a small group of students. Such programs are not new; they are widely used in middle school but are less common at the high school level. Generally, in fact, advisories are one component—an important one—of numerous efforts to make schools more student centered and personal. (Witmer, 1992, p. 41)

A strategy many effective high schools have employed to personalize their school is the advisory program (Miles & Darling-Hammond, 1998; Ogden & Germinario, 1995). Every student and every staff member are part of an advisory group. One teacher or staff member gets to know a small group of students by meeting with them on a regular basis. Advisory programs set up structures in which students and adults can develop close, trusting relationships (Newmann, 1997) that not only personalize education but also "complement the curriculum" (Brouillette, 1997, p. 554). High schools that have implemented advisory programs report fewer absences, fewer dropouts, fewer discipline problems, reduced alienation, and a more positive school climate (Gilchrist, 1989; Ogden & Germinario, 1995; Witmer, 1992). As one report stated, "The teacher-advisor system is the best way I know of to ensure that no more of our teenagers slip through the cracks of the system and are lost to us" (Tye, 1985, p. 387; see also NASSP, 1996). As we have already noted, teenagers need personal attention, and advisory programs are able to provide that attention from an adult friend who listens and cares (Gilchrist, 1989; Powell, 1990; Raywid, 1993; Wood, 1992). Advisors serve as advocates for students whenever the need arises, so that a student knows someone is on his or her side (NASSP, 1996; Wood, 1992). When necessary, advisors also serve to coordinate activities between the school, special services, and a students' home (Meier, 1995; Wood, 1992).

Some schools use advisory groups as learning centers. Students learn communication skills, conflict management, decision-making skills, and other important life skills in a setting that is comfortable and safe, and an adult they know and trust guides them (Mackin, 1996; Ohiwerei, 1996; Ogden & Germinario, 1995; Tewel, 1995). In these smaller discussion groups, students have opportunities to offer insight and suggestions about the school, which is used as feedback on school programs and practices (Gregory & Smith, 1987; McQuillan, 1997; Raywid, 1995). Schools often gain valuable information from student comments made in advisory groups. Advisory groups are important to all students but are particularly important to disadvantaged or at-risk students who normally experience higher levels of isolation and alienation in high school (Powell et al., 1985; Witmer, 1992). Students report that the advisory program is one of the best things about their high school (Tewel, 1995).

Mentoring or Tutoring Programs

At the heart of every effort that appeared to be succeeding, we noticed that there was a close relationship between a student and a counselor or teacher— there was a mentor with high standards and clear goals, one who had gained the student's confidence and trust. (Boyer, 1983, p. 246)

Effective high schools implement mentoring or tutoring programs to personalize learning for many students who struggle academically. Mentoring involves connecting a student with an adult who can help them work through academic and personal problems that are affecting their performance in school (Page & Valli, 1990). Mentors often help students see themselves as having the ability to succeed in high school (Taylor-Dunlop & Norton, 1995). Mentors also help students "set academic goals and individualized learning agendas" (Foster, 1998, p. 19). Often, the pairing of students and adult mentors is based on similarity in personality or learning styles (Shore, 1995). Effective high schools also use tutoring programs to help academically troubled students. Tutoring is directed at coaching students through particular courses and is aimed directly at improving academic performance (Powell et al., 1985; Wilson & Corcoran, 1988).

Involvement Together in Extracurricular Activities

Exemplary schools actually plan for such interactions, by scheduling both academic and nonacademic events that will promote student-teacher interaction. The end result is a warm, open climate where teachers know the students personally, and where students have the opportunity to interact frequently and closely with their teachers. (Roueche & Baker, 1986, p. 29)

Given the organization of most high school schedules, teacher-student interactions limited to classroom settings do not allow teachers to really get to know their students. It takes involvement in activities outside the regular classroom setting for teachers to see students as whole persons, and vice versa. Effective high schools organize extracurricular activities so that student-teacher interactions and relationship development are primary foci of the activity (Bryk, Lee, & Holland, 1993; Gregory & Smith, 1987). Participation in school activities helps participants to develop common ground and build social ties. It also provides connections that enhance what goes on in the classroom (Bryk & Driscoll, 1988; Rutter et al., 1979; Wilson & Corcoran, 1988). These connections benefit teachers as well, providing them with "intrinsic rewards that teachers find important in their work" (Lee et al., 1993, p. 216). Shared activities bind students and teachers to each other and the institution, increasing connection, commitment, and engagement in the work of the school (Lee et al., 1993). Although involvement in extracurricular activities is time consuming for teachers and takes time out of their personal lives, teachers often find that the rewards greatly outweigh the costs. Exemplary high schools find ways to support and reward teachers for going the extra mile (Powell, 1990; Wilson & Corcoran, 1988).

Flexible Learning Contexts and Extended Classroom Time

Trusting relationships are more likely to develop if students spend sustained time with teachers on an individual basis or in small groups, and they engage together in a variety of activities. . . . Extension of the student-teacher relationship beyond the typical meeting in a large group for fifty minutes a day to learn a single subject will give students and teachers a more complete understanding of one another. Extended contact generates a greater sense of communality, mutual caring and responsibility, than conventional transient and fragmented roles. (Newmann, 1981, p. 553)

Extended contact between students and adults, as we have said, is important in developing good relationships and has a positive impact on student achievement (Anderson, 1985; Corcoran & Wilson, 1985). Some effective high schools use alternative scheduling as a way of creating more opportunities for student-adult interactions. Block scheduling, seminar courses, independent studies, cooperative learning, and team teaching are all used to allow students and teachers to spend more time together in a learning context (Brouillette, 1997; Lynn, 1994b; McQuillan, 1997; Murphy, 1991; Wehlage et al., 1989). Some high schools in the literature we analyzed used *home-base guidance* groups or homerooms that stay together over multiple years as a tool to facilitate the student-adult relationship (Conant, 1959; McLaughlin, 1994). Multiple-year interactions provide consistency for students and a feeling that someone knows them and their history (McLaughlin, 1994; McQuillan, 1997). A relatively new strategy employed in a few successful high schools is an apprenticeship program, pairing students with adults in the community who help the student learn practical vocational skills as part of the school curriculum (Wood, 1992). The success of these alternative scheduling programs depends on the support of school leaders, both in their ability to marshal resources and their willingness to promote flexible time arrangements (Coleman & Hoffer, 1987).

School Adopts Structures That Facilitate Relationships

The way we keep school—in other words, its culture—must change significantly. We have chosen to deal with students in groups so large that the resentment and cynicism they spawn overwhelm the attempt that teachers make to personalize the high school experience. Should it surprise us that youths, in growing numbers, are not "buying" high school anymore? Should it surprise us that so many reject it and whatever opportunity for learning it does offer? (Gregory & Smith, 1987, pp. 10-11)

As was discussed in Chapter 1, public high schools originally were small, community schools in which students and teachers knew each other in multiple contexts. Comprehensive high schools were created to increase curricular offerings, but that came at the price of increased size (Conant, 1959). Now that a number of generations have passed through these large, impersonal, comprehensive high schools, some researchers have begun to suggest that the current school structure might not deliver all it promised. Studies show that linkages between economies of scale, expanded curricular offerings, and increased academic achievement are much less robust than originally thought (Lee et al., 1993; Lee & Smith, 1997). With all the evidence presented on student-teacher relationships as the key to effective learning, the idea that large comprehensive high schools cannot promote or support these relationships leads to the conclusion that something must be done about the structure of these schools (Raywid, 1995): "The control pressures and scheduling constraints in large high schools make this sort of individual attention impractical. . . . Even caring teachers must dole out individual attention in one- or two-minute packets at the beginning and end of classes" (Gregory & Smith, 1987, p. 74). This leaves us with a problem: What is to be done about the large, comprehensive high school? Studies of effective high schools uncover two solutions: form smaller, separate schools or organize the larger school into smaller units, houses, or teams.

Smaller School Size

Large size and fragmented human contact complicate the management of such schools, which elevates the importance of formal rules to regulate behavior. The environment in comprehensive high schools is therefore less human. (Lee & Smith, 1994, p. 2)

Currently high schools average 1,200 or more students (Siskin, 1995). Yet research strongly supports the fact that large, comprehensive high schools don't work. They don't work for students, they don't work for teachers, and they don't seem to increase academic achievement (Cawelti, 1994; Gregory & Smith, 1987; Lee &

Smith, 1994; McQuillan, 1998; Rogers, 1987; Siskin, 1995). Although actual numbers vary from report to report, most people studying high schools today suggest that they should be no larger than 500 or 600 students (Foley & McConnaughy, 1982; Lee et al., 1993; Lee & Smith, 1997), with some arguing for schools of no more than 200 (Meier, 1995; Wood, 1992). Looking at teachers, analysts often suggest no more than 12 teachers per school (Gregory & Smith, 1987).

Small high schools report higher levels of academic achievement for their students (Goodlad, 1984; Lee & Smith, 1997; Lee et al., 1995; McQuillan, 1998; Ohiwerei, 1996). Smaller school size also has a positive impact on reducing dropout rates, increasing student engagement, and enhancing teacher efficacy (Bryk, 1994; Lynn, 1994b; Raywid, 1995). Learning and achievement are more equitably distributed in smaller high schools (Bryk & Thum, 1989; Foley & McConnaughy, 1982; Lee & Smith, 1997; Raywid, 1995; Louis, Kruse, & Bryk, 1995). This more equitable distribution of achievement is most efficacious for "slower or marginal students" (Rogers, 1987, p. 37; see also Boyer, 1983), "low-income, low-achieving" students (Fine, 1992, p. 8), and students of color (Lee & Smith, 1997).

As was previously stated, the student-teacher relationship is one of the most important factors leading to student success in high schools. And research shows that small school size leads to more frequent and consistent student-teacher interactions, which in turn, help build better relationships between students and teachers (Bryk, 1994; Lee & Smith, 1997; McQuillan, 1997; Powell et al., 1985; Wilson & Corcoran, 1988; Wood, 1992). Small high schools also facilitate better relationships among teachers (Wehlage et al., 1989). Faculty and staff report that it is easier to develop an ethic of caring in a small school (Meier, 1995; Wood, 1992). Small schools also report fewer numbers of discipline problems than larger high schools (Foster, 1998; McQuillan, 1997; Pallas, 1988; Tye, 1985), higher levels of student participation in school activities (Boyer, 1983; Newmann, 1981; Rogers, 1987; Tye, 1985), and a more pleasant school climate in which it is easier for people to confront and deal with school problems (Gregory & Smith, 1987; Lee et al., 1993). None of the benefits happen automatically because a high school is small. To accrue these effects, small high schools have to capitalize on their small size "in ways that give students a sense of belonging" (NASSP, 1996, p. 46), which is key in personalizing high schools.

House Plans and School-Within-a-School Programs

This analysis by Lee and Smith gives critical caution and direction to reformers. Their findings suggest that what matters most about so-called restructuring efforts are the opportunities they provide for creating personalized school environments, settings where teachers and students can come to know one another, and where students feel acknowledged and respected as individuals. (McLaughlin, 1994, p. 11)

Several models have been identified that create smaller, more intimate groups for students with unique needs. However, there is some evidence to suggest that more personalized groupings, such as those offered in smaller schools, would be beneficial for all students. Smaller groupings provide students with the connectedness and interpersonal relationships that enhance learning. Models that provide small schools for all students include the house plan, . . . career path plan, and . . . schools-within-a-school structure. (Pearce, 1992, p. E-10)

As was pointed out in the last few pages, research supports the linkages between small school size and school effectiveness. The problem facing educators is that many high schools are large, imposing structures. They were costly to build, and school districts don't have money to build new, small ones. Using various grouping arrangements, such as house plans, schools-within-a-school, resource schools, and teaming provides viable alternatives for large high schools trying to achieve personalization in size and structure (Christman & Macpherson, 1996; NASSP, 1996).

House plans are organizational arrangements that usually deal with assigning students and teachers to learning units called *houses,* which deal to varying degrees with the curriculum or instruction going on in the house (Raywid, 1995). Houses can be multiage or contain only students from one grade and usually exist for multiple years (Pearce, 1992). Having students and teachers interact in a smaller group over several years allows individuals to know each other well and to develop strong relationships (Little, 1995; Oxley, 1990). House plans have been identified as one way in which large high schools have successfully personalized the school environment and improved student academic achievement (Murphy, 1991; Oxley, 1990, 1997).

A school-within-a-school is a "separate and autonomous unit formally authorized by the board of education and/or the superintendent" that "plans and runs its own program, has its own staff and students, and receives its own separate budget" (Raywid, 1995, p.21). School-within-a-school programs allow large schools to meet diverse student needs in a way that facilitates better relationships between students and staff (NASSP, 1996). These smaller subgroups provide the structure necessary for students to have a sense of belonging (Boyer, 1983; Ogden & Germinario, 1995). In many of these schools, students select programs based on their career interests, which encourages engagement and involvement by the student in their education (Pearce, 1992; Raywid, 1995). Research on school-within-a-school arrangements states that achievement is greater in these types of personalized school groupings (Newmann, 1997; Newmann & Wehlage, 1994; Smith & Lee, 1996).

Other subgroup arrangements include teaming and resource schools. Teaming has been discussed previously and is described as a way to cluster students into small groups in which students and teachers can interact on a more personal basis (Newmann, 1997; Wood, 1992), helping improve the attitude, attendance, and "academic productivity" (Raywid, 1995, p. 44) of students. Resource schools incorporate extra programs into the academic structure of the school to meet the needs of the whole child, providing tutoring, before and after school programs, healthcare, and cultural activities (Haas, 1993).

Summary

In this chapter we pointed to the relationship between students and adults as the key to personalization in high schools. The first part of the chapter dealt with the importance of supporting students by providing a nurturing, inclusive environment that recognizes individual student needs. The next section highlighted the need for creating a professional environment for teachers that enhances their success and growth. The final topic addressed in this chapter is the need for schools to organize programs and facilities in ways that encourage the development of healthy student-adult relationships. It is these relationships that provide the foundation on which good learning takes place. Students and adults working together in schools operating as learning organizations create the optimum environment for academic success.

But learning organizations require individuals to monitor and assess the current situation, making changes as needed to stay on course toward the predetermined goals. In the following chapter, we focus on the need for high schools to recognize the uniqueness of their community and the need to develop the capacity to change in directions leading to improvement.

9

Nesting Schools in a Dynamic, Adaptive Local Culture for Change

A lot of what we do in schools is done more or less out of habit stemming from traditions in the school's culture. These traditions dictate, for the most part, the ways in which schooling is organized and conducted. Many school practices seem to be the natural way to conduct schooling, an integral part of the way schools are. As a result we don't tend to think critically about much of what goes on. I don't mean to imply that these ways of schooling are not taken seriously. To the contrary, I think they are taken so seriously that we can hardly conceive of any alternatives to them. We have deep-seated beliefs and long-held assumptions about the appropriateness of what we do in school. These beliefs are so ingrained in our thinking and behavior—so much a part of the school culture—that we rarely submit them to careful scrutiny. We seldom think very much about where practices came from originally and to what problems in schools they were first seen as solutions. We rarely question the view of the world on which practices are based—what humans are like, what society is like, or even what schools are for. We almost never reflect critically about the beliefs we hold about them or about the manifest and latent consequences that result from them.

—Oakes (1985, p. 5)

Many high schools today look very much as they did 30 years ago both in structure and curriculum. High schools are notoriously slow to change, clinging to the motto, *We have always done it like this so why change now?* The problem is that high schools of the past aren't working well in the present and have little hope of meeting the needs of the future. Effective high schools understand change as a natural part of the evolution of schooling and work to move in the direction necessary to help students achieve academically, while also meeting the human needs of those in the school community (Duke, 1995; Lee & Smith, 1994).

This chapter describes the successful high school as a place in which change is a part of the normal routine and is accepted rather than avoided. For change to be viewed positively in schools, two main elements must be active: schools must be engaged in change-oriented behavior, and ideas must be generated from an adaptive, evolutionary mindset. The first section of the chapter focuses on change in school organization and structure in effective high schools and how those schools are responsive to the local community and the students they serve. The second part of the chapter focuses on the mental and emotional aspects necessary for a culture of change and inquiry to exist in high schools, looking at how schools affect the capacity and will of individuals in the school to change. It is this ability to accept change that allows effective high schools to design and implement programs that meet the needs of their students.

Engaged in Change-Oriented Behavior

People in good schools do things. They have a bias for action, a proclivity for success, and a sense of opportunism. They plan for now, seize decision options when they arise, try new ideas, drop bad trials, and play within their strengths. Good school systems and schools have learned how to avoid talking new ideas to death. Good schools invent a structure and improve their practice.

—Wilson and Corcoran (1988, pp. 121-122)

It is not enough for high schools to understand the need for improvement; it is necessary that they take action, changing the way they conduct school. They must actively seek out ways to improve and increase student achievement through changes in organization, programs, and/or instruction. Effective high schools are involved in evolutionary planning, collaborative improvement procedures, continuous monitoring, and problem solving, all the while recognizing the need to be responsive to the uniqueness of their local communities (Fullan, 1990; Wilson & Corcoran, 1988). In their study of effective high schools, Louis and Miles (1990) describe these schools as having:

> A strong evolutionary characteristic. Both the change program and the school develop steadily, driven by the change themes and the shared vision. New opportunities are sought or appear fortuitously; data on the progress of the improvement effort suggest detours or new avenues; new capacities develop and permit more ambitious efforts than anyone had ever though of. Evolutionary planning is not a hand-to-mouth approach, but coherent, intelligent adaptation based on direct experience with what is working toward the vision and what isn't. (p. 32)

School Removes Ineffective Structures and
Adds Achievement-Focused Innovation

To appreciate the inconsistency between this sensible concept [organizing schools on the basis of student outcomes] and the way we actually organize and operate schools, we need to look closely at the prevalent practice paradigm: the fundamental character and operating relationships of our system of education. That paradigm is both defined by and organized around the calendar. School decision making, curriculum planning, instructional and administrative operations, institutional arrangements, student certification and graduation systems, and student opportunity and eligibility conditions—all are defined by and tied directly to the calendar. The calendar and its adjuncts, the clock and the schedule, exert a pervasive influence on both the organization of schools and the thinking of those who work and study in them. Consider these universally accepted terms: school years, semesters, Carnegie units, seat time, credit hours, class periods, grade levels, programs of study, and student eligibility criteria. They all reflect our time-based way of doing business. Even courses, which we commonly refer to as "bodies of knowledge," are actually time blocks that uniformly last nine months, no matter what the content to be mastered or the success of students in mastering it. . . . In short, we behave as if the entire educational system would collapse if teaching, testing, grading, awarding of credit, and promotion did not follow the calendar-driven two semester schedule. (Spady, 1988, pp. 4-5)

A crucial step in this area is the recognition of the need for change. Of the high schools we reviewed in the literature, the most effective were those that acknowledged the need to change structures, curriculum, and culture to improve the school environment and to enhance academic achievement (Hannay & Ross, 1997; Wilson & Corcoran, 1988). These high schools use self-evaluation as a way to measure effectiveness and to identify areas that need to be examined (Larson, 1992). High schools that have successfully restructured structure and curriculum show considerable gains in student academic achievement (Cawelti, 1997; Lee, Smith, & Croninger, 1995; Lynn, 1994b). Rather than struggle against the process, successful high schools have learned to use change effectively for school improvement. To capitalize on change, high schools recognize the need for self-evaluation and they implement modifications in the organization of the school day and year, student grouping, departmental structure, curricular organization, credit options, and the learning venue.

Change in Daily Schedule

High schools should create more flexible schedules—compatible with learning objectives—to make it easier for each student to meet the requirements of the curriculum. What we have in mind is the kind of flexibility that serves learning by organizing instruction in ways more friendly to teaching and learning. Right now, in most high schools, the schedule is frozen, glacier-like, into 50-minute segments that dictate the amount of instructional time devoted to each course, regardless of what would be most appropriate on a particular day. (National Association of Secondary School Principals (NASSP), 1996, p. 47)

Questions and answers on the topic of school schedules have been raised by educators for 50 years (Conant, 1959). Many high schools determine their schedules not by what is most appropriate for learning but by what is easiest to schedule within the given physical restraints. Research documents that the school clock governs decisions made about school, including those involving the learning opportunities available to students (Canady & Rettig, 1995). The National Education Commission on Time and Learning argued in 1994 that "learning in America is a prisoner of time. . . . The rule, only rarely voiced, is simple: learn what you can in the time we make available" (cited in Canady & Rettig, 1995). Effective high schools are reexamining use of time and developing flexible schedules to meet the needs of their students (Hannay & Ross, 1997). Some schools employ alternative schedules to allow students individual time with teachers, teachers time to have common planning periods, and students time to engage in community service projects outside school (Natriello, McDill, & Pallas, 1990; Raywid, 1995). Many successful high schools have broken away from the traditional 50-minute period. They organize class time into large chunks of time that vary depending on what is needed for specific subjects (Boyer, 1983; Pearce, 1992; Tewel, 1995). In a few cases, high schools have reorganized into teams or clusters that have total control of time and have the ability to individualize schedules, so single classes or units can last all day (Pearce, 1992; Wood, 1992).

One common approach found in a large number of schools is block scheduling. Having courses arranged in 80-90 minute blocks allows teachers time to connect with students for longer periods of time and can be used to lower teacher load and to increase flexibility (NASSP, 1996; Shore, 1995). Block scheduling, when properly organized and implemented, has shown some positive results in increasing achievement and "facilitating variety and depth in classroom learning activities" (Cawelti, 1997, p. 20; see also Miles & Darling-Hammond, 1998; Newmann, 1997). Another method highlights the scheduling of instructional time before and after regular school hours for students who need additional help or attention or who want to use school facilities such as the library for academic work (Shore, 1995; Wood, 1992). Some effective high schools have created structures to allow teachers to be flexible with their time, for example, by adding in slack time for staff in extra planning periods or creating *time banks* for teachers to draw from when needed for professional development or common planning time (Hannay & Ross, 1997; Wilson & Corcoran, 1988). Although it is true that increased instructional time positively affects student learning (Harnisch, 1987; Oakes, 1985; Sedlak, Wheeler, Pullin, & Cusick, 1986), most research suggests that reorganization and better use of current school time is a more productive strategy (Boyer, 1983; Canady & Rettig, 1995; Oakes, 1985).

Change in Organization and Length of School Year

Typically, high schools operate for nine months of the year, an average of 180 days a year, leaving three months of summer when school buildings are unoccupied and most students aren't engaged in formal learning experiences (Canady & Rettig, 1995). Research suggests that increasing the length of the school year provides additional academic time needed to improve student achievement (Boyer, 1983; Bradford, 1987; Rutter, Maughan, Mortimore, Ouston, & Smith, 1979). One source of support for longer school days comes from studies that reveal that students in other advanced countries spend considerably more time at school than do students in America (Brown, 1984). Eliminating summer vacation provides greater continuity for students, lessens concerns for coverage, helps prevent students from forgetting what was learned the previous year, and reduces the need for teachers to spend the first few weeks of the year in review (McQuillan, 1997; Ogden & Germinario, 1995). The flexibility produced by a longer school year can help high schools meet higher academic standards and personalize the learning process (Murphy, 1991; NASSP, 1996).

Change in Learning Contexts and Assessment

The traditional classroom and the typical 45-minute class period are fine for certain activities. Unfortunately, the way schools are presently structured, this is by far the most common learning context students encounter. But why should this be the only setting in which students are expected to learn? How many meaningful experiences are so bound by time and space? What does this suggest about the likelihood of students transferring lessons from their classrooms to the real world? (McQuillan, 1997, p. 659)

Outcome-based learning focuses on the axiom that learning should be the constant and time the variable. This represents a departure from the current educational structure based on Carnegie units, hours per day, and days per year. (Pearce, 1992, p. E-31)

One area of high school organization that is least open to change is the Carnegie unit (a course lasting five periods a week during an academic year) as the single measure that indicates learning and knowledge accumulation. The question that must continually be raised is, "How can we be sure that students are really learning?" (Haas, 1993, p. 230). Exemplary high schools find ways to award credit for actual learning rather than accumulated seat time by assessing students on whether or not they meet predetermined mastery criteria or standards (Pearce, 1992; Wehlage, Rutter, Smith, Lesko, & Fernandez, 1989; Wilson & Daviss, 1994). Successful high schools develop programs that allow learning and the earning of credits to occur both inside and outside the school building. This type of flexible program allows students to move along at their own pace with some progressing quickly through high school, while some students spend a longer time mastering the criteria (Boyer, 1983; McQuillan, 1997; Meier, 1995; Ohiwerei, 1996).

Schools use alternative courses such as independent studies, fast-paced cycles, seminars, or learning labs as ways to provide the flexibility needed to break away from typical credit-for-seat-time arrangements (Boyer, 1983; Foley & McConnaughy, 1982; Raywid, 1995). These types of innovative courses have been found to contribute to higher levels of academic achievement for students and to increase motivation and participation of both higher and lower achieving students (Boyer, 1983; McLaughlin, 1994). Some of these schools use career-focused, technical-based, or experiential programs as the context of curriculum, building standards and assessments into the tasks and skills required to perform the designated job (Brown, 1984; Haas, 1993; Larson, 1992; Pearce, 1992). Effective high schools often use the community as a school itself, involving students in service learning, apprenticeships, and cooperative work experiences as ways to earn credit toward course completion and graduation (Pearce, 1992). Programs such as leadership wilderness-courses, ecology or environmental courses, and cultural-enrichment courses can only be taught outside the physical constraints of the school building. The success of alternative courses depends on the authenticity of the tasks required, the richness of the embedded curriculum, and the alignment of the assessment with the requirements students are asked to meet (Haas, 1993; Louis & Miles, 1990; McQuillan, 1997; Wood, 1992).

Change in Structure for Grouping Students and Teachers

Effective high schools respond to the local context by grouping students and teachers and organizing curriculum in ways that meet the needs of their school community. These high schools are able to reduce student isolation and disengagement, teacher isolation, and departmental balkanization by increasing flexibility in student and teacher grouping structures (Miles & Darling-Hammond, 1998). Due to the large physical structure of current comprehensive high schools and the large number of students served, academic departments serve as functional subdivisions for grouping individuals within the school community (Siskin, 1995). Because the high school curriculum is oriented toward individual subjects within academic disciplines, the departmental structure with subject-matter emphasis usually serves as the professional community for staff—a structure that is often impossible to penetrate (Hargreaves & Macmillan, 1995; Johnson, 1990; Little, 1995; Talbert, 1995). Adding flexibility does not necessarily mean doing away with the current departmental structure, although some schools have chosen that route, but it does mean using departments or any structural arrangement more effectively. One report supporting variety in groupings cautions:

> If departments become not only the primary, but also the exclusive, reference group for teachers, it is likely that decisions about curriculum and staffing will be driven solely by departmental interests and will result from political struggles rather than from some balanced understanding of schoolwide

needs. . . . A second reason for caution is that any department attends to only part of a student's academic and social experience, so strengthening departments might further fragment students' total schooling experience. By contrast, successful interdisciplinary teams in middle schools and experimental high schools put the student rather than the subject at the center of their efforts. (Johnson, 1990, pp. 182-183)

Departments that are too strong and too self-focused prevent schoolwide interaction and can divide faculty in ways that do not promote school goals but serve to divide interests and reduce personalization in high schools (Siskin, 1995; Talbert, 1995). To break down the departmental stronghold, some effective high schools create alternative structures such as teams, clusters, cohort groups, or houses organized around the needs of students rather than subject disciplines (Hargreaves & Macmillan, 1995; Little, 1995; Natriello et al., 1990; Siskin, 1995). Some of these new organizations have proven to be more successful in supporting students and teachers and in affecting achievement (Little, 1995; Siskin, 1995).

Although not all departments are equally successful at developing a strong professional community, with high degrees of variation seen within and between high schools (Talbert, 1995), departments in effective high schools are used as sites of professional development and teacher support in ways that enhance the overall curriculum and school emphasis on high expectations for all students. Strong departments in successful high schools provide opportunities for teachers to improve practice, deepen professional interaction, and have input into instructional decisions (Johnson, 1990; Lee, Bryk, & Smith, 1993; Talbert, 1995). Teachers in these schools also often find collegial support and friendship within the departmental unit (Johnson, 1990; Siskin, 1995).

Change in Delivery Structures and Curricular Organization

Effective high schools have introduced new and different delivery structures and curricular organization. Cooperative learning strategies "in which students work together in teams are stressed by almost everyone connected with restructuring teaching and learning" (Murphy, 1991, p. 58). Teams are organized around instructional or organizational themes, or are task- or product-oriented (King & Weiss, 1995; Martin, 1997; Wilson & Daviss, 1994). Because group members are responsible for each other, cooperative learning arrangements often provide support for students who need extra assistance or information (McLaughlin, 1994). Integrating curriculum combines subject matter "to form a coherent, connected design for learning" (Pearce, 1992, p. E-20), which can be done thematically or topically. Research shows that integrating curriculum often improves student academic achievement (Pearce, 1992).

School Recognizes Its Responsibility to Respond to the Local Community

> I have visited more than two hundred schools. Many were admirable schools, but they differed significantly from one another. True, they shared much: safe and orderly environments, agreements about purpose, engagement in learning, fairness and decency, and a sense of shared norms and ownership— the sense that "this is our school and we're responsible for it." But they differed in organization, academic and moral emphasis, local traditions, and forms of teaching. If school faculties are doing their job, they must shape their responses to accomplishing broad goals. They must take account of particular constituencies and pupil intakes, of strengths and weaknesses of their colleagues, of opportunities within their particular communities, of needs of faculty to experiment and try new approaches to old problems. . . . Such differences should not only be tolerated, they should be encouraged. (Grant, 1988, pp. 222-223)

All communities are not alike, yet those designing high schools treat them all the same, putting identical structures and programs into schools that are quite different. We must realize that "schools are not alike; they are as diverse as the groups of people they serve" (Page & Valli, 1990, p. 109; see also Fullan, 1990; Taylor-Dunlop & Norton, 1995). Curriculum, instructional techniques, and other elements of the core technology cannot successfully be implemented in high schools without first tailoring the program for the specific school (Wilson & Corcoran, 1988). Schools must be responsive in content and learning to the communities they serve. Effective high schools in the literature we reviewed use the community as a source of information to facilitate the learning process in the school as well as a site of learning opportunities (Newmann, 1997; Spade, Columba, & Vanfossen, 1985). Wilson and Corcoran (1988) sum this up by saying:

> Each school and school district represents a unique situation presenting different dilemmas to those that seek to design and implement solutions to school problems. Even schools facing similar problems may require different approaches to their resolution. There don't seem to be any quick and easy paths to school improvement. (p. 120)

School Seeks to Know The Larger Community

In order to know students well, high school staff members must know the students' neighborhoods and communities. This is especially important to minority and at-risk students (Rivera & Poplin, 1997). Exemplary high schools learn about the community in which their students live and incorporate strengths of the local culture into the classrooms (Page & Valli, 1990; Corcoran & Wilson, 1985). Effective high schools have the ability to adapt and respond to the environment in ways that lead to increased understanding of students and their communities (Louis & Miles, 1990). Boundaries between the schools and the community are penetrated and the environmental pressures found in the community are exerted on the school culture and personnel (Hallinger & Murphy, 1987). These schools also take seriously the need to teach moral or character education that reflects values held by the school community (Ogden & Germinario, 1995). High schools learn about the community through focus groups, surveys, and formal and informal meetings (Shore, 1995; Tewel, 1995; Wilson & Corcoran, 1988). Institutions that involve community members in the school, and places in which staff are involved in the community, help create a culture that shows students someone cares about them as individuals (Wilson & Corcoran, 1988). Climate and student academic achievement both improve in schools having good relationships with the community (Anderson, 1985; Roueche & Baker, 1986).

Parents and Community Members Are Involved in School Activities and Planning

> These exemplary schools actively recruit the human resources of their communities. Whether they are parents or not, community members are viewed as potential contributors to the school in a variety of ways. . . . Extensive opportunities are made available for volunteers to give of their time, experiences and good will. (Wilson & Corcoran, 1988, p. 113)

Higher achievement has been associated with parental involvement in high schools (Lee et al., 1993; Taylor-Dunlop & Norton, 1995; Wilson & Corcoran, 1988), and successful high schools find ways to bring the community into the school through involvement in classroom and extracurricular activities (Lee et al., 1993; McLaughlin, 1994; Murphy & Hallinger, 1985). Increasing community and parent involvement in school leads to increased interaction between parents and staff, which in turn positively affects student achievement (Brown, 1984; Goodlad, 1984). Some schools are allowing the parents and other members of the neighborhood to use school facilities before and after school hours to increase the presence of community members in the school building (Cawelti, 1994; Wilson & Corcoran, 1988). School staff also connect to the community through involvement in organizations, clubs, and volunteer groups, establishing a presence and an interest in what is going on in the world of their students (Wilson & Corcoran, 1988). Some staff members use connections to obtain financial resources to support school improvement efforts (Wilson & Corcoran, 1988).

Exemplary high schools also often involve community members in school-level decision making (Larson, 1992; Wilson & Corcoran, 1988). This focus on shared decision making increased achievement in some of the high schools that we examined, (Gaziel, 1997; Lee et al., 1993) but in others had little impact on student learning (Lee et al., 1993; Murphy & Beck, 1995).

Generated From an Adaptive, Evolutionary Mindset

The factors associated with effective schools are clearly those characteristics of "Blue Ribbon professional/collegial/student outcome-based" schools. These schools have the organizational vitality to self-assess, to set and revise student-centered objectives, to plan, to act in unity, and to reassess. . . . They believe that "seeking improvement enlivens the organization for adults and students alike and that improvement is possible regardless of the current state of the organization."

—Joyce, 1993, cited in Ogden and
Germinario (1995, pp. 8-9)

In order for schools to engage in evaluation, assessment, and improvement activities, there must first be a pervasive culture that sees change as normal, useful, and necessary. Students, staff, and teachers must feel that the school recognizes that learning is a process requiring experimentation and ambiguity and resulting in a fair share of missteps and mistakes. Those involved in improvement efforts, particularly schools involved in improvement-oriented self-assessment, need help with the process of change as well as assistance in adjusting to the mental and emotional side effects of change. Research suggests that effective high schools trying to personalize education "put [their] goals in concrete and [their] plans in sand" (Cresswell & Rasmussen, 1996, p. 30). High schools that operate from an evolutionary mindset possess a culture that enhances the capacity for change and creates the will to change.

School Culture Enhances the Capacity for Change

Schools should be nurturing and respectful centers of inquiry. The tone of the school should explicitly and self-consciously stress values of unanxious expectation, mutual trust, and decency—fairness, generosity and tolerance. Students must—in collaboration with their teachers and families—also be active citizens in creating the tone, standards and quality of life of the school. (Christman & Macpherson, 1996, p. 5)

Traditionally, high schools have been seen as places in which students went to collect knowledge from teachers—to learn the right answers for their questions. Many of the high schools we analyzed, however, were reported to be places in which students and teachers worked together to discover information through a process of experimentation. Effective high schools nurture a culture of inquiry that is described by one researcher as having "a commitment to maximal openness and receptivity to student responses, with a willingness to pursue hypotheses even when they seem wrongheaded, . . . and a commitment to casting the student in as intellectually an active and demanding a role as possible" (Raywid, 1995, p. 65). For a culture of inquiry to exist, the school must nurture an environment in which risk taking and open communication are encouraged and individuals feel they can trust one another (Tewel, 1995). Successful high schools are learning organizations in which students and teachers are learners together (Fine, 1992; Louis, Kruse, & Bryk, 1995). Leadership in these schools supports, encourages, and nurtures professional community among teachers, centered on mutual discovery and learning (Louis & Kruse, 1995). Staff members collectively look at school objectives, programs, and practices, continuously evaluating progress toward their goals as a method of self-assessment and as a strategy for collective learning (Hill, Foster, & Gendler, 1990; Newmann, 1997; Ogden & Germinario, 1995; Wilson & Corcoran, 1988).

Successful high schools also recognize change as a distinct pattern in the mosaic of high school activity (Louis & Miles, 1990; Raywid, 1995). One aspect of understanding change is increasing "the staff's ability to become psychologically comfortable with uncertainty—an important ingredient in minimizing its negative impact on the change process" (Tewel, 1995, p. 209). This is not to imply that nothing ever stabilizes at these schools. Successful change also involves establishing some routines and norms "to preserve and ensure the changes made will not be diluted or lost in the swirling morass of contingencies and context" (Prestine, 1998, p. 21). Schools must walk a fine line between institutionalizing change, thereby immobilizing innovation, and maintaining a culture of experimentation (Little, 1995).

Tolerance for Failure in Trying New Things

> Rewards for innovation and tolerance of small failures support intellectual vitality in teachers. But departing from established instructional patterns entails uncertainty and the risk of failure. Yet teachers' and administrators' willingness to take the risks of innovation stood out in all the most successful schools. These faculties had the capacity to learn from small losses. As with most other successful and vital organizations in other sectors, they acquired knowledge useful for future planning by critically examining small failures as well as successes. (Newmann, 1997, pp. 192-193)

Operating a school on the basis of experimentation and inquiry requires an acceptance of a certain number of failed or derailed projects and programs. A school leader in one effective, innovative high school stated that "you have to be prepared for people to make mistakes. That's how we learn. The only people who don't make mistakes are those who don't do anything" (Foster, 1998, p. 16). Tolerance for failure is a foreign concept in many comprehensive high schools. A common element in the reports of successful high schools we examined was the pervasive support and encouragement from staff and administration for trying new things, risking failure, and adapting and learning in response to mistakes (Newmann, 1997; Wilson & Corcoran, 1988). This promotion of experimentation was encouraged for staff (Lee et al., 1993; Wilson & Corcoran, 1988) and also for students (Gregory & Smith, 1987; Haas, 1993).

Leadership Supports and Facilitates Change

> A change facilitator is an administrator who sees him/herself as more of a colleague than a boss, and hence supports and assists teachers in their work. Each was far more an initiator and manager than a reactor to events. They engaged in countless interventions with their staffs—actions or events that influenced the use of an innovation. (Larson, 1992, p. 61)

A culture of inquiry cannot exist in a high school unless the leader is supportive and encouraging of the community members as they engage in experimentation and improvement efforts. Leaders in effective high schools work with their staff to "stimulate intellectual inquiry in the school" (Newmann, 1997), acting as change agents rather than passive observers of the process (Hannay & Ross, 1997). Research advises that the role of school leaders is key to effective change implementation and creates a learning organization in high schools (Gaziel, 1997; Hannay & Ross, 1997; Larson, 1992). A good school leader is seen as "constantly asking 'What is working, and how do we know?' and expects that staff over time will do likewise" (King & Weiss, 1995, p. 94).

School Is Resilient in Times of Crisis

Effective high schools have a unique ability to persevere through hardships and crises. Murphy and Hallinger (1985) describe this as a "sense of resiliency" that allows these schools to bounce back from problems, "not allow[ing] these difficulties to become excuses for failure but, rather, treat[ing] them as problem-solving opportunities" (p. 21). Very little literature can be found on resiliency in successful high schools, not because resiliency is not there but because it has not been a focus of study. However, available research points to the ability to cope with and rebound from crisis as an important element of effective high schools (Boyer, 1983; Louis & Miles, 1990).

Use of Research as a Basis for Change

> [Continuous school improvement] occurs when analysis, evaluation, and experimentation are treated as tools of the profession and are designed to improve the teachers' work in class, foster staff development, help provoke questions, organize analysis, and generate evidence of progress. (Gaziel, 1997, p. 312)

Studies of school improvement show that change initiatives prove to have little affect on student achievement unless they address the barriers to learning experienced by students in that school. Staff in effective high schools use research and research techniques to gather data about their school, which is then used in planning and decision making. Research shows that effective high schools engage in a review process in which teachers "research, formulate, and collect data that will help them to think about action" (Louis & Miles, 1990, p. 204). Because educational research is a low-consensus field, practitioners in schools get scattered, conflicting information and tend to distrust formal research (Larson, 1992). By having school staff, students, and community members involved in the process of gathering, examining, and analyzing data, the results are more trustworthy and more likely to affect what goes on in the planning, decision-making, and goal-setting processes (Hannay & Ross, 1997; Louis & Miles, 1990; Natriello et al., 1990).

School Culture Creates the Will to Change

Openness to improvement within the school is important to ensure teachers' sense of professional community. Teachers also report that a key to successful school restructuring is support for the faculty risk taking, and we would argue that this means that school policies for change should reflect the needs of those willing to carry out innovations. (Kruse, Louis, & Bryk, 1995, p. 37)

Curriculum change calls for changes in people, not just in schedules and instructional materials. And changing people means one must deal with those things that are the psychiatrist's stock in trade—people's fears, apprehensions, personal and philosophical conflicts, and uncertainties about their abilities. These are the things that must be dealt with—although without the services of a licensed psychiatrist. We need principals who can foster a climate that honors experimentation and provides abundant opportunities for faculty members to dialogue, reflect, express their concerns and apprehensions, and otherwise adjust their views so they can embrace newer ways of conducting the educational enterprise. (Lounsbury, 1996, pp. 20-21)

In order for change to take place in a school, the individuals in the school must have both the willingness to change and a commitment to the organization and its people. Change requires a commitment of time, energy, and emotion that cannot be forced but can be encouraged, supported, and developed (Firestone & Rosenblum, 1988; Wilson & Corcoran, 1988). If any one factor can make or break the successful implementation of a program in a school, it is certainly the commitment of those having to do the work. Among high school staff, commitment and caring are closely related, both serving as motivation for what gets done or remains undone as schools approach the difficult work of change (Lee et al., 1995). A school culture that promotes caring also promotes commitment, and this is the climate seen in the reports of effective high schools we examined (Gilchrist, 1989). Individuals in the school do make a difference in the school culture and in how change, innovation, and improvement unfold (Larson, 1992; Prestine, 1998). Commitment and caring on the part of the school leadership is crucial in creating a climate open to change (Chubb & Moe, 1990).

Change also requires a willingness on the part of school staff to do things differently: to take on new roles, to communicate openly, and to share leadership responsibilities, all of which are time-consuming and strenuous (Prestine, 1998). Teachers in effective high schools become more flexible in the roles they assume and work toward changing practices that do not lead to improvement and personalization (Miles & Darling-Hammond, 1998; Wilson & Corcoran, 1988). To learn from one another, teachers must work collaboratively, communicating openly about successes, failures, and concerns (Larson, 1992). Leaders in the stories of the successful high schools that we analyzed involved staff members in decision making and problem solving, sharing leadership, accountability, and responsibility (Louis & Miles, 1990; Ogden & Germinario, 1995).

Summary

This chapter exposed the strategies employed by productive high schools to create environments in which people learn through experimentation, evaluation, and innovation. We looked at the importance of a high school developing a culture of inquiry, with a focus on achievement-oriented improvement and innovation. By understanding the individuals within the school community and addressing changes toward meeting their needs, high schools become more personalized environments.

Overall, in this section—Chapters 7, 8, and 9—we have focused on the importance of a web of support for the personalized high school. Personalization is the key to making high schools more successful for the students, teachers, and administrators who work and learn in them. By organizing around learning and teaching, having high goals and expectations for all students, supporting and nurturing students and teachers, developing structures and programs that facilitate student-adult relationships, and encouraging a culture of inquiry, high schools can affect areas that are directly and indirectly linked to enhanced student success, making the school a place in which people can and want to learn.

10

Linking Schools With the Home and Family

Parents and families are an important yet often overlooked resource in any high school environment. The expanding body of research in this area documents the significant role parental involvement plays in affecting student outcomes. Henderson and Berla (1997), in their work *A New Generation of Evidence: The Family Is Critical to Student Achievement,* offer a detailed summary of 66 studies that documents the significant positive influence of family involvement in education. Henderson and Berla conclude:

> The evidence is now beyond dispute. When schools work together with families to support learning, children tend to succeed not just in school, but throughout life. In fact, the most accurate predictor of a student's achievement in school is not income or social status, but the extent to which the student's family is able to:
>
> 1. Create a home environment that encourages learning.
>
> 2. Express high (but not unrealistic) expectations for their children's achievement and future careers.
>
> 3. Become involved in their children's education at school and in the community. (p. 1)

Looking specifically at high schools in their landmark study *Sources of Educational Climates in High Schools,* McDill, Meyers, and Rigsby (1966) found that "the one contextual variable of any significance is the social commitment that parents and the community served by the school have to quality education" (p. XIII-11). This finding—that family involvement is the one contextual variable that has been linked to student achievement—is highly promising. Of all the contextual variables (such as socioeconomic status, neighborhood resources, school financial support), parental involvement is the one most easily influenced by schools. Unfortunately, although the research strongly supports the positive benefits of family involvement, the literature does not offer much evidence about the most effective types and approaches.

Before turning to a lengthier analysis of the research related to parental involvement in high schools, a definition of the term should be provided. *Parental involvement* is a broad term encompassing everything from what happens between the student and parent in the home to the parents' participation in school governance. Fehrmann, Keith, and Reimers (1987) offer this definition:

> Parental involvement is by no means a unitary construct. . . . Variables that might be included under the general term parental involvement include parents' expectations of school performance (Hess, Holloway, Dischson, & Price, 1984; Parsons, Adler, & Kaczala, 1982; Seginer, 1983); verbal encouragement or interactions regarding school work (Epstein, 1984; Watson, Brown, & Swich, 1983); direct reinforcement of improved academic performance (Karraker, 1972); general academic guidance and support (Bloom, 1984); and student perceptions of the degree to which their parents influenced their plans for after high school and monitored their daily activities and school progress (Keith, Reimers, Fehrmann, Pottebaum, & Aubrey, 1986). (pp. 330-331)

The most recognized categories of family involvement were developed by Joyce L. Epstein (1992). Her model includes six types of involvement "to help families and schools fulfill their shared responsibilities for students' learning and development" (p. 1145):

1. *Basic Obligations of Families.* Families are responsible for building positive home conditions that support learning and behavior throughout the school years.

2. *Basic Obligations of Schools.* Schools are responsible for communicating with families about school programs and children's progress.

3. *Involvement at School.* Parents and volunteers who assist teachers, administrators, and children are involved in classrooms or in other areas of the school, as are families who come to school to support student performances, sports, or other events.

4. *Involvement in Learning Activities at Home.* Teachers offer guidance as they request that parents monitor and assist their own children at home.

5. *Involvement in Decision Making, Governance, and Advocacy.* Parents and others in the community serve in participatory roles in the PTA/PTO, advisory councils, Chapter-1 programs, school-site management teams, or other committees or school groups.

6. *Collaboration with Community Organizations.* Collaboration includes school programs that provide or coordinate children's and families' access to community and support services, such as before- and after-school care, health services, cultural events, and other programs. (pp. 1145-1146)

The word *parental,* when used in this discussion of schools, is not limited to the traditional definition of two, married, biological parents. As Lynn Balster Liontos (1991) explains, "With changing demographics, different cultures and the many forms of family life today, a child is often under the care of the extended family. Sometimes stepparents, noncustodial parents, and grandparents have primary care for a child" (p. 5). The term *parental involvement* is, therefore, used synonymously with *family involvement,* referring to a wide spectrum of nontraditional family-unit structures. This distinction is particularly important to our discussion, because schools need to be sensitive to the diverse needs of families to implement an effective parental involvement program.

Core Research Findings

Three major findings have emerged from the research on family involvement. The first is that parental involvement positively affects student outcomes at all grade levels (Astone & McLanahan, 1991; Baker & Stevenson, 1986; Bryk & Driscoll, 1988; Connors & Epstein, 1994; Dornbusch, Ritter, Leiderman, Roberts, & Fraleigh, 1987; Fehrmann, Keith, & Reimers, 1987; Ginsburg & Hanson, 1986; Henderson & Berla, 1997; McDill, Meyers, & Rigsby, 1966; McKinney and Others, 1986; Nord, Brimhall, & West, 1997; Palmer, Dakof, & Liddle, 1993; Roderick & Stone, 1998; Russell, Mazzarella, White, & Maurer, 1985; Steinberg, 1997). Connors and Epstein (1994), in *Taking Stock: Views of Teachers, Parents, and Students on School, Family, and Community Partnerships in High Schools,* offer a synopsis of research that indicates the benefits that secondary school students receive from their parents' engagement:

- High Expectations: High school students are more likely to graduate or go on to college if their parents expect them to (Conklin & Dailey, 1981).

- Homework Assistance: Top-performing high school students are more likely to have parents who monitor their homework and talk with their teens about their school experiences (Ginsburg & Hanson, 1986).

- Attending School Events: Top-performing high school students report that their parents' attendance at school events demonstrates to them that their parents value education (Dornbusch & Ritter, 1988).

■ Comanaging: Top-performing high school students have parents who offer their teens many opportunities for adult guidance (Clark, 1988), keep close track of how their teens are doing in school, and assist their teens with plans for after high school (Fehrmann et al., 1987).

■ Balancing Activities: Top-performing high school students have parents who help their teens achieve higher grades by monitoring daily activities and ensuring that their teens are engaged in a balanced schedule of learning and leisure activities after school (Fehrmann et al., 1987).

The second major finding is the noticeable decline in the involvement of parents as their children grow older. Steinberg (1997) describes the phenomenon:

Several national studies of American parents' involvement in their children's education have found a steep drop-off in involvement as children get older. In one national study, for example, the proportion of parents of elementary school students who were involved in their children's education was 50 percent higher than among parents of junior and senior high school students, with the most dramatic decline in parents' involvement occurring around the transition from elementary into secondary school. (p. 129)

Other researchers have attempted to explain this decline. McCaleb (1994) summarizes the main reasons for the lack of parental involvement into four main categories: transience, alienation between home and school, school-generated problems, and disintegration (reinterpretation) of the family. The following is a sampling from the literature on parental involvement that expands on this decline:

Efforts to explain declines in involvement often associated with child age usually point to changes in the level of academic work required across the span of school years, changes in parents' beliefs about their ability to help when their children are having problems, and specific developmental changes in children (for example, younger children generally express more interest than older children in parental involvement; adolescents' emergent focus on independence and autonomy usually depresses active interest in overt parental involvement). (Hoover-Dempsey & Sandler, 1997, p. 28)

There are reasons why parent involvement drops off drastically in high schools. . . . These include the needs that adolescents have for more autonomy and responsibility, more working parents who live further from the high schools, the more complex organization of the high school, and high school teachers who have greater numbers of students to teach, more specialized training, and more families to involve. (Hollifield, 1994, p. 4)

As students grow older, they face much more complex social pressures and begin asserting their independence from their parents. Many actually discourage their parents from coming to school. Secondary schools also tend to be larger and more compartmentalized, so that no single person is primarily responsible for a particular student. This can leave parents unsure who to contact. Larger attendance areas at the secondary level can also add to transportation problems that keep some parents away. As a result of these and other factors, studies show that parent involvement drops off sharply once students reach middle school, and by the time they reach high school it can be difficult to see at all. (Lynn, 1994a, p. 3)

Why are so many parents uninvolved in their youngsters' schooling? There are at least three different accounts—one that blames work, one that blames schools, and one that blames parents themselves. All are likely to be true. First, many parents who wish to be involved are unable to do so, because of demands on their time from work. . . . A second explanation for the widespread disengagement of parents from their children's education has to do with parents' beliefs about their role in their children's education during adolescence . . . far too many parents believe that once their child leaves elementary school responsibility for managing the child's education is transferred entirely to the school. . . . Finally, the general lack of involvement by parents in school is reflective of widespread parental disengagement in general. Remember, based on our study and the results of several other national surveys, an estimated one third of all parents are not really involved in their children's lives. (Steinberg, 1997, pp. 128-130)

This finding of decreased family involvement, in light of the previously cited literature on the connection between family involvement in high schools and student success, is disheartening:

Given the importance of parental involvement to student success, it is discouraging to report that very few American parents are as involved in their child's education as they should be. Nearly one third of the students we studied say their parents have no idea how they are doing in school. . . . More than half of all students say they could bring home grades of C or worse without their parents getting upset, and one quarter say they could bring home grades of D or worse without upsetting their parents. Even if students are wrong in their assessment of their parents' concern, the fact that so may *think* their parents have little interest in their schooling is evidence of a problem of tremendous significance. (Steinberg, 1997, p. 128)

Whereas the research is quite consistent on both the importance of family involvement and the forces that mitigate against it, that is where the clarity ends. The last major finding is that "research has not yet shown which specific aspects of parental involvement are most important for students' achievement" (Fehrmann et al., 1987, p. 336).

Synthetic Themes

The research literature provides significant individual findings that coalesce around five main themes: (a) trust, (b) shared values and goals, (c) efficacy and positive role construction, (d) parenting style, and (e) demonstrable commitment. In the remainder of the chapter, we elaborate on each of these themes. Collectively, the themes provide a useful framework for educators who hope to promote thoughtful, family-involvement initiatives at the high school level.

Trust

Trust is the fundamental basis for any successful family-involvement initiative. Students need to trust their parents and teachers to help them make appropriate academic decisions. Parents need to trust that educators are working toward the shared goal of helping their children succeed. Teachers and school administrators need to trust that students' families want to be involved in the education of their children and that they have valuable information about and insights into their youngsters' needs and interests. A central problem with traditional parental involvement is that it is so narrowly focused and school-driven that it does not promote trust. Crowson (1992) explains:

> All too often, claim the critics, parental involvement is *guided* (even shaped) toward modes of interaction, patterns of behavior, and topics of discussion that are acceptable to the school. In addition, the involvement of parents is typically *constrained* by separate role expectations for professionals and nonprofessionals, including some strains between them. Third, much of the involvement of parents in the local school, even that legally mandated in the special education staffing, tends to be viewed by school authorities as a *representational* rather than fully participatory activity. Finally parental involvement has tended to mean a *passive* and recipient role for parents rather than an active relationship with the school. (p. 188)

When schools rely on traditional forms of parental involvement, building trust with families is difficult because of the lack of consideration of the wants and needs of the families. Crowson (1992) concludes his discussion by presenting a newly emerging pattern of parental involvement that needs to replace the traditional forms, a pattern that is *responsive, open, participative,* and *active.* Epstein (1992) fills out the contours of this pattern in her discussion of two critical research findings: (a) that "effective practices of partnership are *developmental* and (b) that they

> . . . are *responsive to the common and different needs of families,* so that all families feel equally welcome at school and included in their children's education and so that schools find ways to inform and involve families with unique histories, strengths, and needs. (p. 1145)

Only when families believe that schools are genuinely trying to assist them in meeting their unique needs to rear successful children will parents begin to become engaged with schools.

Overcoming traditionally held school beliefs toward family involvement is a formidable undertaking. As Steinberg (1997) describes:

> Although schools pay lip service to the benefits of parental involvement, their actual behavior reflects mixed feelings about how much and in what ways they actually want parents to be engaged. That is, although schools insist they want parental participation—and complain loudly about the lack of involvement of parents—in actuality, schools only want parents to be involved on the school's own terms. (p. 129)

Not only do educators often dominate the family-involvement agenda, they often grossly misread the desire of families to participate. In Connors and Epstein's (1994) survey of six high schools, the researchers found that:

> Over 90% of the parents and teachers agreed that parent involvement was necessary at the high school level. These teachers also said that involvement was important for a good high school, teacher effectiveness, and student success. . . . Most parents (80%) reported that they wanted to be more involved than they currently were, and many students (50%) wanted their parents to be more involved. But just 32% of the teachers felt it was their responsibility to involve families. (p. 8)

> Eighty-one percent of the high school teachers say that family involvement is important, and 33% say they personally strongly support it—but only 3% of them think that parents strongly support it. A major task of high school partnerships will be to convince these teachers that parents really do want to be involved and that the teachers can effectively involve most families. (Connors & Epstein, cited in Hollifield, 1994, p. 4)

This divergence between teachers' perceptions and parents' desires poses a strong challenge to the development of the trust necessary to create productive parental involvement programs. Teachers' beliefs that families do not want to participate in the education of their children and that it is not the teachers' role to nurture such involvement hamper the quality and effectiveness of any program initiatives. As Hoover-Dempsey and Sandler (1997) describe:

> Particularly given findings that many parents criticize home-school contacts as being empty (characterizing them, for example, as contrived, insubstantial, or awkward, mainly offering opportunities for teachers to talk and parents to listen; e.g., Harry, 1992; Lareau, 1987; Lightfoot, 1978, 1981) and want more meaningful contacts with the schools (e.g., Eccles & Harold, 1994; Connors & Epstein, 1994; Leitch & Tangri, 1988; Moles, 1993), the general invitations and demands presented by schools seem potentially very

influential in parents' decisions about involvement in their children's education. (p. 30)

Research shows that parents are dissatisfied with both the quality and the quantity of home-school contacts. As a matter of fact, one of the major lessons Epstein (1988) draws from her comprehensive study of parental involvement research is that "family requests for involvement are constant. Parents in all types of schools and at all grade levels express the need for clear communications about their children's attendance, behavior, academic progress, the curriculum, and how to help their children at home" (p. 59).

The bottom line is that until high school educators begin to trust families enough to believe that additional efforts in the family-involvement arena will not be wasted, nothing will change. Also, families need to be able to trust that the activities will be substantive and not a waste of their valuable time. Research suggests that students, parents, and teachers need to form partnerships to determine what works best in each community. These decisions should be based on what is known about each of the respective groups and their appropriate role in the family-involvement algorithm. Programs of school-family-community partnerships in high schools need to consider:

- ■ The unique needs of adolescents, such as the need for greater autonomy and responsibility, and the need to develop individual skills and talents

- ■ The unique needs of families, such as more working parents, living greater distances from high schools, and the need to learn about a more complex school organization

- ■ The unique needs of high school teachers, such as having greater numbers of students to teach, more specialized training, and more families to involve (Connors & Epstein, 1994, p. 15)

By beginning to understand everyone's perspective and by opening genuine dialogues addressing the needs and concerns of all parties involved, the seeds of trust will begin to take root. As one high school parent wrote, "Everyone needs to work together. Stop blaming each other about why the kids are the way they are" (Connors & Epstein, 1994, p. 20).

Shared Values and Goals

In addition to a foundation of trust, the literature shows that shared values and goals are an important part of productive relationships between home and school: "The primary goal of school and family partnerships—the bottom line for many educators—is to increase student motivation, achievement, and success in school" (Epstein, 1992, p. 1141). By demonstrating a clear commitment to these goals, trust is deepened, and demonstrating a clear commitment to these goals strengthens family involvement.

In creating a system of shared goals, the challenge is to foster the core values related to the promotion of the academic press of the high school (Cotton & Savard, 1981; Murphy, Hallinger, & Mesa, 1985; Roderick & Stone, 1998). Driscoll (1995) emphasizes that:

> The real challenge is to think of ways in which parents can become involved in the *key* element of the educational organization, its academic program. If the animus of the communitarian school is the support and sustenance of teaching and learning, then accepting parents as full members of the community means finding ways to enable their participation in this core mission of the organization. (p. 224)

In support of the core value of the primacy of academics, research suggests the importance of the following three major goals of parental involvement:

- The improvement of school programs, classroom management, and teacher effectiveness

- The improvement of student learning and development

- The improvement of parents' awareness of their continuing responsibilities and contributions to their children's education and social and personal development across the school years (Epstein, 1988, p. 59)

Most important, students need to be the focal point of the values and goals. Values need to be shared with the students and translated into helping them define and obtain their own individual goals. As Epstein (1992) points out,

> Across the grades, but particularly in the middle and high school grades, students need encouragement to take challenges, persist in difficult work, deal with failure as well as success, and understand the importance of hard work in school (Bempechat & Ginsburg, 1990). Families who receive information in useful forms can help schools help students reach these goals (Epstein & Herrick, 1991). (p. 1144)

As we noted in earlier chapters, the more students observe others advancing the value and goals of academics, the more likely they will be to internalize them. The research tells us that it is highly beneficial for parents to be part of this process.

Schools must partner with families and students to develop the common agenda of activities promoting shared values and goals. Topics that parents or students identify as a need should drive the family-involvement process. For example, in a survey of six high schools, Connors and Epstein (1994) found that parents were most interested in learning about the following topics:

- Planning for the future—college or work, 83%

- Improving report card grades, 68%

- How to help my teen develop his/her talents, 67%

- Peer pressure in adolescence, 64%

- How to deal with stress, 64%

- Doing better on homework, 63%

- Helping teens take tests, 63% (p. 14)

Activities that schools alone determine are important should influence the agenda only to the extent that schools are successful in convincing parents of their necessity. O. Heleen asserts that family involvement can become a reality even with the hardest-to-reach families, if "school systems develop a broad range of participatory opportunities that work cooperatively with parents and the community, allow parents to determine their own needs, provide initially low-investment opportunities, and work with other community structures" (cited in Liontos, 1991, p. 17). Research reveals that when developing a common agenda for family involvement, schools should not only respond to parents' and students' requests but also consider the developmental level of the activity: "Schools must be responsive to family and school concerns that become more important in the upper grades—dropout prevention, family planning and pregnancy prevention, and mastery of basic skills and competencies needed for graduation" (Epstein, 1988, p. 58).

No one, cookie-cutter model of an agenda for family involvement would work for all schools. In their study of 571 exemplary secondary schools, McKinney et al. (1986) offer this description of what parental involvement looks like:

> Educators often remark that it is hard to get parents involved, particularly in junior high and high schools. However, quite the opposite is true in good schools because they don't wait for the community to come to them—they go to the community.
>
>   Many exemplary schools recruit volunteers—parents as well as non-parents—to be clerks or nurses' assistants, to teach, to tutor, or to help plan special school activities. . . . Good schools also work with parents to develop aggressive public relations campaigns. . . . Instead of hiding crises from the community, good schools turn to it for help. . . . Model schools don't just "take" from the community; they give in return. Students visit local nursing homes or help raise money for charity through bike-a-thons and other activities. . . . These activities may not differ from those in other secondary schools. What is different is that they occur more often, involve more people, and are valued more by school leaders. (pp. 15-16)

Secondary schools need to work closely with the community to design their common agenda to meet the unique needs of their students and families.

In productive high schools, shared values are often buttressed by an ethos of caring in all social relations. Bryk and Driscoll (1988) illustrate this point:

On a daily basis, adults transmit appropriate values through their words and
actions, and most students come to adopt these values. . . . When this caring
ethic is commonplace, a social cohesion among staff and students results that
can enhance the schools' academic mission and norms for instruction (see
Murphy, Weil, Hallinger, & Mitman, 1985). (p. 7)

When people demonstrate that they care about one another, working on challenging
tasks, such as improving educational outcomes within a school community, becomes
easier. Promulgation of this ethos of caring "may help students to see that there are
several adults in their lives who care about them, will listen to their concerns and suggestions, and are available to assist them if needed" (Connors & Epstein, 1994,
p. 18). Developing close and caring relationships helps create what Coleman and
Hoffer (1987) term *social capital*. Bryk and Driscoll (1988) describe the benefits of
social capital:

The positive relationship between parents and school staff provides important support for school aims. The social capital expands the human resources
of the school by increasing the information and support available to students. This in turn encourages student engagement in school life and higher
levels of academic achievement. (p. 13)

Care and concern translate into involvement, which evolves into increased social capital and increased student achievement. Underlying successful family-involvement initiatives are powerful, shared values and goals built on the pillars of genuine caring and
commitment to helping all students succeed.

Efficacy and Positive Role Construction

In addition to trust and shared goals, quality linkages between home and school
are characterized by a sense of efficacy among participants. Unless people believe they
can effect change, then the status quo will be difficult to alter. When adults feel unsure about their abilities to help adolescents, it has significant impact on teenagers.
McCaleb (1994) describes this dynamic:

When parents believe that they are "ignorant," that they have no knowledge
of value to teach or share, this self-image is communicated to the children.
Low self-esteem on the part of parents has a profound impact on children.
Children who believe they are ignorant, having been told this all their lives,
also feel less capable of learning anything new. (p. 4)

Hoover-Dempsey and Sandler (1997) offer this theoretical explanation for the importance of a sense of efficacy:

Parents with a strong positive sense of efficacy for helping children succeed
in school are also likely to believe both that effort is preeminent in explaining

success (attributions to effort) and that intelligence is malleable (an incremental theory of intelligence); we also suggest that parents holding this belief set will, further, tend to develop and implement proactive strategies designed to help children succeed in school. Conversely, parents with a weak sense of efficacy for helping children succeed in school are likely to believe *both* that intelligence or ability is fixed (an entity theory of intelligence) and that ability and luck are the preeminent sources of school success (attributions to ability and luck); parents holding this belief set will tend to be relatively passive, rather than planful or proactive, in responding to children's school problems. (p. 27)

Having a strong sense of efficacy makes parents and students become more proactive and effective managers of their education.

Being proactive about a child's education is an important factor in long-term educational success. "The institutional organization of schooling in the United States," Baker and Stevenson (1986) argue, "encompasses a lengthy set of specific academic contests around which parents must organize their management strategies. Parents must do a long series of small things to assist their child toward maximum educational attainment" (p. 165). In the literature, findings on efficacy have important implications for communities with weak family-involvement initiatives. Dornbusch and Ritter (1988) warn that:

> The present organization of schools does not encourage a high level of parent-school relations. . . . If nothing is done, who will be harmed? Our data indicate that the lowest level of family involvement in school programs and processes is among the parents of average students, minority parents, and in stepfamilies and single-parent families. Given these findings, failure to change parent-school relations will perpetuate inequality. (p. 77)

Secondary schools need to work with families to help build a strong sense of efficacy and to collaborate with parents and students to take a proactive approach as they navigate their educational careers. Ultimately, this sense of efficacy needs to be instilled in the youth. For only when they believe that they can succeed academically will academic achievement begin to increase (Murphy, Weil, Hallinger, & Mitman, 1982).

The literature on effective home-school relations also highlights the importance of positive role constructions. Parental role constructions are defined as: (a) the expectations (explicit and implicit) that parents and those in their significant groups hold for their behaviors in relation to children's schooling and (b) the behaviors they enact in relation to their children's schooling (Hoover-Dempsey & Sandler, 1997, pp. 8-9). What kind of parents do adults want to be? What do they expect from their children? How do they interact with their children? These are some of the important questions that must be answered in developing positive role constructions for parents, and the answers are critical to how a child develops. Indeed, parents' aspirations and expectations have a tremendous impact on student outcomes. Palmer et al. (1993) offer this excellent summary of the research related to parental aspirations:

> Parental aspirations exert great influence on children's self-concept of ability and subsequent academic performance (Entwisle, Alexander, Pallas, & Cadigan, 1987; Entwisle & Hayduk, 1988). Parents' expectations for achievement (e.g., parents' achievement orientations about the children's schoolwork, parental aspirations for the children's educational or occupational attainment, and pressure for improvement on interaction tasks) (Hess & Holloway, 1984) and parents' expectations of their children's ability levels (Seigner, 1983) seem to have significant impact on children's own self-perceptions and aspirations, motivation, and subsequent achievement. Furthermore, parents' expectations are more directly related to adolescents' self-concepts and expectancies than are the teens' own past records of academic performance (Parsons, Adler, & Kaczala, 1982).
>
> It seems clear, then, that parents' aspirations and expectations influence achievement over and above adolescents' abilities. (p. 8)

The importance of establishing positive role constructions among parents cannot be overstated because "positive role construction, at strong or moderate levels, seems essential for high likelihood of involvement; parents must feel that they should be involved in their children's education if the basic involvement decision is to be affirmative" (Hoover-Dempsey & Sandler, 1997, pp. 8-9).

Both efficacy and role construction are related to the overall decision a parent makes to become involved. Hoover-Dempsey and Sandler (1997) maintain that this decision to become involved is a function primarily of three constructs:

1. The parent's construction of his or her role in the child's life

2. The parent's sense of efficacy for helping her or his child succeed in school

3. The general invitations, demands and opportunities for parental involvement presented by both the child and the child's school (pp. 8-9)

Hoover-Dempsey, Sandler, and other researchers also reveal how schools can influence parental role-construction and efficacy. High schools play an important role in promoting family involvement. High schools can assist families in building the confidence, sense of efficacy, and skills necessary to help the students succeed. Clark (1988) elaborates on the ways schools can be helpful:

> Very often, parents don't know to which standards, methods, and content their school-age child should be exposed. Their sense of uncertainty, anxiety and fear increases because they begin to perceive themselves as inadequate. . . . When schools fail to provide these parents with factual, empowering information and strategies for supporting their child's learning, the parents are even more likely to feel ambivalence as educators. One consequence is that

the parents lower their standards of excellence at home. . . . To optimize their effectiveness, schools will need to include ways for teachers to share information that empowers parents to function as effective mentors in the family. (p. 95)

Building the beliefs that parents can be effectively involved in their teenagers' education and that students can succeed in school is a team effort. It is promising that "while elementary and secondary schools cannot realistically hope to alter a student's family status, schools *may* hope to influence selected parental process variables in the direction of increased parental involvement" (Hoover-Dempsey & Sandler, 1997, p. 8). With increased parental involvement, not only will student academic outcomes begin to improve but also benefits will accrue to parents and society as a whole. As Urie Bronfenbrenner explains,

Not only do parents become more effective as parents, but they become more effective as people. It's a matter of higher self-esteem. Once they saw they could do something about their child's education, they saw they could do something about their housing, their community and their jobs. (cited in Liontos, 1991, p. 12)

Parenting Style

One specific component of the concept of parental role construction that warrants special consideration is parenting style. A considerable body of literature examining the significance of parenting style in rearing children has emerged over the last 30 years. Baumrind, in the late 1960s and 1970s, conducted studies of young children and their families and developed the three classic categories of parenting styles still referred to today:

1. *Authoritarian:* highly demanding but low in responsiveness to the child

2. *Permissive:* tolerant and accepting toward the child's impulses, as little use of punishment as possible, few demands for mature behavior, and acceptance of considerable self-regulation by the child

3. *Authoritative:* an expectation of mature behavior from the child and of clear setting of standards by the parents; firm enforcement of rules and standards, with commands and sanctions when deemed necessary; encouragement of the child's independence and individuality; open communication between parents and children, with encouragement of verbal give-and-take; and recognition of the rights of both parents and children (Dornbusch et al., 1987, p. 1245)

Research in this area has shown that authoritative parenting is most effective in terms of successful student outcomes.

Dornbusch and colleagues (1987) confirm the link between authoritative parenting and positive student outcomes, in their study of high school students in the San Francisco area; in the process, they provide "evidence that Baumrind's typology of parenting styles, originally formulated to explain social and cognitive development among young children, can successfully be applied to adolescents and related to their academic performance in high school" (p. 1255). More specifically:

> Using a large and diverse sample of San Francisco Bay Area high school students (N= 7,836), we found that both authoritarian and permissive parenting styles were negatively associated with grades and authoritative parenting was positively associated with grades. Parenting styles generally showed the expected relation to grades across gender, age, parental education, ethnic, and family structure categories. . . . Pure authoritative families (high on authoritative but not high on the other 2 indices) had the highest mean grades, whereas inconsistent families that combine authoritarian parenting with other parenting styles had the lowest grades. (p. 1244)

The fact that authoritative parenting increases student achievement at the high school level was corroborated by Steinberg (1997). He discovered that "in every ethnic group, authoritative parenting is associated with better outcomes, and disengaged parenting with worse ones," and that "poor adolescents benefit just as much from authoritative parenting as do wealthy ones, and authoritative parenting works just as well in single-parent homes and in stepfamilies as it does in intact households" (p. 133). Steinberg explains why:

> Simply put, authoritative parenting contributes to the development of the motives, values, beliefs, and behaviors that make students interested in school, and this commitment permits children to achieve more academically. Nonauthoritative parenting, in contrast, undermines these attributes and promotes the development of an orientation toward learning that interferes with school success. (p. 123)

Not only does parenting style affect student achievement, but:

> Parenting style, or variation in family processes, is a more powerful predictor of student achievement than parent education, ethnicity, or family structure. Students whose parents are authoritative do better than similar students whose parents are permissive or authoritarian. (Henderson & Berla, 1997, p. 58)

Recognizing the importance of parenting styles and understanding the components of authoritative parenting are important for high schools. Three characteristics of authoritative parenting distinguish it from other parenting styles:

1. *Acceptance and involvement:* the extent to which the adolescent sees his parents as loving and responsive

2. *Firm control:* the degree of parent monitoring and setting of limits

3. *Psychological autonomy:* the use of noncoercive, democratic discipline, and encouragement to express individuality within the family (Henderson & Berla, 1997, p. 127)

In addition, effective parenting initiatives clarify that:

Parents' beliefs in the importance of developing conformity, obedience, and good behavior in children, for example, have been related to poorer school outcomes, whereas beliefs in the importance of developing personal responsibility and self-respect have been associated with better school performance. (Hoover-Dempsey & Sandler, 1997, p. 12)

High schools need to be aware, however, that developing parenting-skills initiatives is a delicate process. Parents often are not receptive to interventions that are perceived as intrusive or contrary to their cultural traditions. One promising family-involvement approach that is sensitive to families is termed "an additive model of parent acculturation." This model, evaluated by Carmen Simich-Dudgeon, "recognizes and appreciates the family's culture, then seeks to add new roles for the parents to play at home and in the school" (cited in Henderson & Berla, 1997, p. 121). The evaluation of this model, used in two high schools and involving the families of 350 students, showed that limited-English high school students made significant gains in English-language proficiency and writing. The unilateral imposition of parenting classes on parents sends a message that the school feels the parents are bad parents. By using an approach that works with and respects family strengths, parenting-skill initiatives will enhance their appeal and effectiveness.

Overall, assisting parents with their parenting skills can become a central component in any plan to strengthen home-school relations. A review by Palmer and colleagues (1993) of parent training models concludes:

Parent training models, though not always aimed at treating school problems per se, may affect school achievement or adjustment by increasing authoritative parenting (Small, 1990). As documented in the family process literature, the parental competencies indicative of authoritative parenting have been linked to adolescent school performance. (Dornbusch et al., 1987; Steinberg, Elmen, & Mounts, 1989). Thus to the extent that a parent training program increases parents' skills in establishing appropriate behavioral limits and granting psychological autonomy to adolescents in a context of warmth and democracy, school performance may be affected. (p. 13)

Demonstrable Commitment

The final theme emerging from the literature on family involvement is demonstrable commitment. Not only do values and goals need to be fixed, but the commitment to translate beliefs and aims into concrete actions is the key to any successful initiative. As Astone and McLanahan (1991) note, "Helpful participation in a child's school career requires not only that parents *hold* high aspirations, but that they *transmit* their aspirations to their children" (p. 311).

The importance of active engagement is seen clearly in studies examining difference in parental activities in low and high socioeconomic status (SES) schools. Baker and Stevenson (1986), in their study of 41 families with eighth graders managing the transition to high school, found "little evidence that mothers with more education know of more strategies to improve their child's school performance" (p. 160). The difference is that high-SES mothers *used* more of these strategies than low-SES mothers. In general, the higher-SES mothers:

- Had more knowledge about their child's schooling— were more likely to be able to name their child's teachers and identify their child's best and worst subjects

- Had more contact with the school—were more likely to have met their child's teachers and to have attended school events

- Steered their children toward higher education—were more likely to select college-preparatory courses, regardless of their children's performance (Henderson & Berla, 1997, p. 26)

Finally, "high-SES mothers whose children [were] not performing well [were] roughly 11 times more likely to actively manage their children's critical transition to high school" (Henderson & Berla, 1997, p. 26). These findings offer a summons to high schools to help families, particularly low-SES families, in learning how to become active managers of their children's education. For parents who might not have had positive academic experiences themselves, knowledge of how to successfully navigate high school is especially important.

Family involvement promotes personal and academic development if the families stress education; "let the children know they do, and do so continually over the school years" (Liontos, 1991, p. 9). Responsibilities for students have been found to be an important element in school and family partnerships. Teens are striving for greater independence and want to be involved in the decision-making processes concerning their lives. Teens need to be able to engage parents and teachers in discussions about their school performance and future career plans:

In order to support and reinforce students' roles in family-school connections and in their own learning, students need to hear and see evidence that their parents and teachers are working with them to support their education and future goals. And, high school students need ample opportunities to participate in school decisions that affect them. (Connors & Epstein, 1994, p. 16)

The more genuine, obvious, and ongoing the commitment of the school and family toward working with the student is, the more likely the efforts are to be fruitful. For example, in a longitudinal study of over 2,700 high school students in New York, Conklin and Dailey (1981) conclude: "We have shown that consistency of parental support does have an impact on educational activity: the longer postsecondary education has been taken for granted in the home, the more likely students are to enter college" (p. 261).

Nurturing commitment among parents to participate in their youngsters' education is a tremendous challenge. Indeed, the lack of commitment by some parents is startling. One is reminded of the Carnegie urban-schools study that tells of a high school in New Orleans, "which, like others in the city, requires parents to pick up their children's report cards. At one particular school, located in a low income area, 70 percent of the cards remained unclaimed two months after the marking period" (Liontos, 1991, p. 1).

Effective high schools promote commitment by designing activities that are appealing to parents and are substantive in helping families interact with their children. They also help school staff understand the necessity for participating in such activities. High school administrators play an especially important role in establishing successful family-involvement initiatives. In their study of the behaviors of effective and ineffective secondary school principals, Russell et al. (1985) found that developing commitment and support for parental involvement is one of the major characteristics of effective principals. They list five general classes of effective and ineffective behaviors of principals in this domain:

Classes of Effective Behavior:
1. Obtaining active involvement in school activities
2. Communicating personally with the parents of individual students
3. Informing all parents of special programs and activities
4. Interacting directly with parents (and other citizens) to promote the school
5. Establishing direct personal contact between parents and teachers

Classes of Ineffective Behavior:
1. Avoiding interpersonal communication with parents
2. Communicating in a manner that will make parents angry or feel negative toward the school
3. Discouraging parental involvement
4. Succumbing to nonacademic special interest groups
5. Avoiding meeting parents at social or civic functions (pp. 16-17)

One interesting recent finding for high schools to consider in developing family-involvement initiatives is the importance of commitment on the part of the father in student success. Nord et al. (1997) obtained information from the parents of 16,910 kindergartners through 12th graders nationwide about the role of fathers in children's lives. Their findings should be of interest to all schools:

Children do better in school when their fathers are involved in their schools, regardless of whether their fathers live with them. (p. 77)

This report shows that it is not contact, per se, that is associated with student outcomes, but rather active participation in their children's lives through involvement in their schools that makes a difference in school outcomes. (p. xi)

One of their central conclusions is that "by targeting fathers, schools may be able to make greater gains in parental involvement than by targeting mothers or parents in general" (p. 78).

Successful involvement programs also focus on appeals to the strengths of the parents—assuming that most parents do want to be involved in their children's lives and do want their children to succeed academically. Successful schools also build commitment by informing parents of the benefits of parental involvement:

Parental attendance at school events designed for parents was shown to be associated with higher grades. Children whose parents attended Open School Night or College Night, for example earned higher grades compared with children whose parents did not attend. . . . But, there is a simple way to increase parental attendance at school programs, even if no special meetings are called. One high school merely informed parents in a newsletter that parental attendance was associated with higher student grades. That was enough to produce a very large increase in attendance at school events. (Dornbusch & Ritter, 1988, p. 76)

Finally, effective schools ground their initiatives on the foundational goal noted earlier—the centrality of increasing student achievement in school. Only then can the mistrust and misperceptions among families, school personnel, and students begin to be corrected and the school community begin to implement appropriate, meaningful, and effective activities.

Conclusion

The major findings emerging from the literature concerning family involvement in high schools are threefold:

1. Increased parental involvement is associated with higher student achievement.

2. Parental involvement decreases as the child grows older.

3. Research does not offer a definitive answer about which specific approaches or strategies are most effective in promoting parental involvement or in linking parental involvement with student achievement.

On the third finding, a review of four comprehensive studies addressing effective types of parental involvement demonstrates this lack of a definitive answer. Fehrmann and colleagues (1987), in their study of 28,051 high school seniors, found that parental involvement did have an important, direct effect on grades, and their findings suggest that

> . . . parents might well help their high school children achieve higher grades through monitoring the children's daily activities, by keeping close track of how they are doing in school, and by working closely with the students concerning planning for post high school pursuits. (p. 335)

Also, Ginsburg and Hanson (1986), in a study of over 30,000 sophomores nationwide, found evidence that:

> Parents in low-SES white and minority families can contribute significantly to the academic success of their children. For each disadvantaged group, parents of superior students were more likely to monitor their homework, think their children should attend college, and converse with them about the children's experiences. (p. 9)

On the other hand, Steinberg (1997) found a different set of parenting activities to be most effective:

> The type of parental involvement that matters most is not the type of involvement that parents practice most often—checking over homework, encouraging children to do better, and overseeing the child's academic program from home. Our research shows that the type of involvement that makes a real difference is the type that actually draws the parent into the school physically—attending school programs, extracurricular activities, teacher conferences, and "back to school" nights. (p. 125)

Finally, Dornbusch and colleagues (1987) offer a different perspective discovered in their study of high school students in the San Francisco Bay Area. Instead of focusing on specific, school-related activities, they found that:

> Parenting style, or variation in family processes, is a more powerful predictor of student achievement than parent education, ethnicity, or family structure. Students whose parents are authoritative do better than similar students whose parents are permissive or authoritarian. (Cited in Henderson & Berla, 1997, p. 58)

Additional research is needed to further clarify which specific approaches and activities family-involvement initiatives should pursue.

In summary, several related topics need further research to better inform parents, educators, and community members about parental involvement. The following list by Epstein (1988) is particularly appropriate:

- We do not know very much about the effects of particular practices of parent involvement on students and parents at each grade level.

- We need to move parent involvement from rhetoric to practice. This involves state, district, and school policies that are supported by adequate budgets.

- We need to know how teachers and administrators can be educated in pre-service and inservice programs to obtain and update their understanding of school and family connections.

- We need to improve research efforts on the interactions and simultaneous influence of school and family environments.

- And most important, we need to be realistic in our expectations for parent involvement as part of effective school programs. Parent involvement can help, not cure, the problems of weak school programs, of children who miss opportunities, and of families who feel confused about their children and the schools. (p. 59)

The last item in Epstein's list is an appropriate note on which to conclude. Family involvement is not a panacea for increasing student achievement. The research does reveal, however, that particularly at the high school level, it should not be overlooked or considered only as an afterthought.

PART IV

Conclusion

11

Explanation and Integration

Exploring the Theoretical Underpinnings of Research on the Productive High School

We doubted that secondary schools could be improved simply by identifying a list of variables related to student achievement and persuading schools to work on each item in the list. Instead, we felt that educational interventions would be powerful only to the extent that they were grounded in coherent theory that explained how and why certain approaches to instruction, curriculum, and school outcomes were more likely than others to produce favorable student outcomes.

—Newmann (1992c, p. 2)

In the preceding chapters, our focus has been on characteristics of productive high schools—and the evolution of high schools that mitigated against these characteristics being present. We have reported on research exploring a range of factors that correlate with high levels of student achievement. In the course of this work, we have alluded to theories offered by scholars to explain the links between a host of structural, curricular, social, cultural, and pedagogical features and powerful learning by young men and women. In this chapter, we concentrate on these theories in an effort to highlight likely and possible connections between the development of adolescents' academic and life skills and factors such as small-size, heterogeneous classes, a limited and focused curriculum, caring relationships, and teacher collegiality.

Two goals guide us as we undertake this exploration of the theoretical links between correlates of achievement and actual student learning. The first goal is an explanatory one. Throughout this book, we have reported on a large body of research identifying variables linked to positive academic and developmental outcomes for adolescent learners. Embedded in each of the investigations we consider are certain assumptions or expectations about how learning occurs and the conditions likely to foster it. At times, these assumptions are articulated explicitly; often, they are not. Regardless, they are there and, interestingly, tend to vary greatly in emphasis and focus. Some scholars, for instance, believe that some high schools are more productive than others because they are responsive to adolescents' unique developmental needs. Others concentrate, instead, on teachers and assert that teachers whose needs for professionalism and autonomy are met are more likely to create effective, productive high schools. Still others suggest that the engine of productive schools is sensitivity to students' cultures and the ability to develop programs and activities that honor and connect with the surrounding communities. Some assert that certain kinds of curricula are more likely to evoke engagement in teens. Here we make an effort to create a framework within which we review both explicit and implicit theories that attempt to explain links between certain correlates of student achievement and actual learning.

A second goal in this chapter grows out of, and builds on, the successful accomplishment of our first objective. After creating a framework within which we situate explanations of the power of certain features of secondary schools, we attempt to synthesize or integrate these explanations. That is, we look for themes and patterns that cut across and link the various theories. Before we embark on an exploration of theories attempting to explain the why and how of productive high schools, however, we briefly turn our attention to the reasons that we believe such an undertaking is important.

Exploring Theories: A Central Part of Our Quest for Understanding

> Nothing is more helpful than a good theory, even a complicated theory, if it helps managers to understand what is happening and what they can do about it.
>
> —Bolman and Deal (1984, p. 241)

In a discussion of the challenges of studying school effectiveness, Lee, Bryk, and Smith (1993) make an observation that underscores the importance of the search for theories to explain the connections between "organizational characteristics" (p. 177) of productivity and academic achievement. They note that the goal of schooling, and of efforts to improve it, is the enhancement of learning—something that "occurs in individuals" (p. 177). However, because "such learning occurs in formal organizations" (p. 177), we have tended to focus on characteristics of school organizations rather than on "the process[es] through which schools actually affect student learning" (p. 177). Lee and her colleagues are actually making this point to underscore the need for better research on school outcomes. Their contention also highlights the need for a serious and ongoing search for the "assumptions or premises about the relationships among the various elements" (Murphy & Beck, 1995, p. 20) of productive schools and the outcomes that define productivity or effectiveness in the first place. If we do not attempt to surface these theories, we run the risk of conceptually doing the very thing that Lee and her colleagues condemn for methodological reasons. We run the risk of "fail[ing] to make a critical distinction between the school as an organization and the instructional process of schooling" (Lee et al., 1993, p. 177). If we do this and presume that power lies in certain inert characteristics rather than in the processes these characteristics encourage, we face the danger of focusing our research efforts and our practical resources on things that ultimately cannot live up to their promise to effect change (Murphy, 1991).

Having made an argument for the importance of considering theory in our effort to understand productive high schools, we now must admit that any theory—as important as it may be—is inherently limited. This is the case for at least two reasons. First, theories, by their very nature, are best guesses or, to borrow from John Dewey, warranted assertions. Thus they are always tentative—always "in the making" (James, 1948, p. 203). Although they can and should be refined and improved by high-quality research, theories always lack certainty. Theories are limited in another way too. Because they seek to explain relationships between two or more variables, theories inevitably concentrate on some dimensions of a situation and ignore or minimize others. Thus theories depend on oversimplifications of complex reality. Richard Rorty (1979), reflecting on both the contributions and limitations of research and the theories that frame it and emerge from it, suggests that robust knowledge is built as a certain consensus emerges around key ideas. As we reflected on empirical investigations of productive high schools and on the theories that attempt to make sense of findings that emerge from them, we discovered a consensus around several themes.

There are many different ways we might organize our discussion, and, indeed, there are many different fields from which we might draw theories that could assist us in the effort to understand how overt, observable dimensions of successful high schools influence inner and private processes, such as motivation and learning. To narrow the scope of our discussion, we concentrate on theories explicitly and implicitly expounded by scholars that link the characteristics of productive schools that we have discussed in earlier chapters with student achievement. As we considered these various ideas offered to explain links between learning and factors such as staff collegiality and collaboration (Chapters 5, 6, & 7), a clear powerful mission focused on learning and teaching (Chapters 5, 6, & 7), a limited and relevant curriculum (Chapter 7), small size (Chapter 7), social processes in schools (Chapter 8), and connections with parents and others in outside communities (Chapters 9 & 10), it seemed to us that the theories tended to fall into certain broad categories. A number of them are structural in as much as they posit that variables, such as "an academic core for all [students]" (Bryk, Lee, & Holland, 1993, p. 132), small school or class size and heterogeneous classes, affect achievement by enhancing access to learning opportunities. Others are more psychological in nature, linking distinct characteristics of good secondary schools with human needs—both the teachers' needs and the students' developmental needs. Still other theories tend to concentrate on the ways that features of certain schools contribute to a social ecology that promotes learning. We organize our discussion around these three broad categories.

Explaining Connections Between Characteristics of Productivity and Student Learning

> *An understanding of how schools contribute to academic success can be used to guide efforts in secondary school improvement.*
>
> —Newmann (1998, p. 104)

Structural Theories

In Chapters 1, 2, and 3, we examine, in some detail, the development of the large, comprehensive high school. We point out that this institution was built, in part, on certain assumptions or theories, many of which are nicely articulated in the work of James Bryant Conant (1959, 1967). Essentially, Conant (1967) argued that good high schools will offer a broad curriculum to "do justice to the desires and potentialities of all its students" (p. 13). This, in Conant's (1959) view, would require a core of courses "in English and American literature and composition [and] social studies . . . [with] ability grouping" (p. 19) in these courses. It would also necessitate a number of "nonacademic programs" for average and poor students and "special arrangements for the academically talented students" (p. 19). In Conant's view, to offer such a broad and diverse set of programs and courses, good high schools would need to have a fairly large staff and an enrollment large enough to support a range of courses.

Conant's ideas, it seems, were built on a set of assumptions about the purposes and values that should govern secondary education and the structures most able to accomplish these purposes and honor these values. Essentially, Conant (1959) embraced the idea that "equality of opportunity and equality of status" (p. 8) require that schools offer each student educational opportunities to equip him or her for a place in society that matched individual aptitudes, interests, and abilities. He also articulated a commitment to the values of "efficiency, rationality, continuity, precision, [and] impartiality" (Tyack, 1978, p. 28). Like so many of his contemporaries, Conant presumed that high schools could fulfill their purposes in an efficient and economical manner only if they were designed according to bureaucratic principles. Lee and her colleagues (1993) describe such schools:

> From the bureaucratic perspective, schools are seen as "formal organizations" characterized by a functional division of adult labor into specialized tasks: teaching roles defined by subject matter and types of students; an emphasis on social interactions that are rule governed, are affectively neutral, and have limited individual discretion; a form of authority that is attached to the role within the organization rather than to the person occupying the role. (p. 173)

These authors underscore a point we make throughout this book. Many of the bureaucratic features of high schools have fallen far short of the hopes Conant and others pinned on them. Indeed, a diffuse mission that leads to differentiated curricula; allowing, and indeed depending on, large size (in terms of student enrollment and staffing); and the promotion of ability grouping or tracking—all aspects of the comprehensive secondary school—has been linked to a host of problems including student and teacher disengagement and low levels of achievement (Garet & Delaney, 1988; Lee & Bryk, 1988; Newmann, 1998; Powell, Farrar, & Cohen, 1985; Oakes, 1985; Sizer, 1984). In contrast, a coherent and focused mission leading to a delimited curriculum with an academic core for all students, allowing for small size, and enabling heterogeneous classes has been associated with "authentic learning, . . . depth of understanding[, and] success for all students" (Newmann, 1992a, pp. 206-207).

When scholars seek to explain the power of "a common core of academic experience[s]" (Bryk et al., 1993, p. 125), "small size" (Gregory & Smith, 1987, p. 132), and "heterogeneous grouping" (Newmann, 1992a, p. 205), they frequently offer fairly straightforward structural theories. That is, they argue that these features focus educational resources on activities most likely to lead to high achievement, to increase students' opportunities to learn (primarily by extending the time within a typical day that is devoted to learning), and to enhance access to high quality instruction for all students.

Lee, Bryk, and Smith (1993) are among those suggesting that links between student achievement and a focused mission manifested in a common set of core academic courses may be due to the fact that such a curriculum directs teachers and teaching to those activities most likely to promote student achievement. They acknowledge that this contention runs counter to the claims of school reformers, throughout most of the 20th century, who embraced the idea that increasing the size of schools increases quality by promoting "specialization of personnel and more effective use of particular kinds of capital equipment" (Chambers, 1981, p. 31; see also Conant, 1959, 1967; Daft & Becker, 1980; Fox, 1981; Morgan & Alwin, 1980; Riew, 1986). Drawing on research of Powell and colleagues (1985), Oakes (1985), and others, Lee and her colleagues (1993) suggest that in most schools, specialization actually results in a diffusion of effort, energy, and resources and that in contrast, "constrained curricular offerings coupled with a proactive stance by adults encouraging academic pursuits for all students" (p. 156) actually focuses energy and efforts in productive ways.

At least some of the theories proffered for the efficacy of small high schools in fostering student achievement are structural in nature. Several authors (e.g., Bryk et al., 1993; Gregory & Smith, 1987; Sizer, 1984) allude to a simple and straightforward explanation of the power of *smallness* when small size is also a feature of classes. This is the idea that in these settings, students enjoy a personalized environment and more individual attention, and teachers, in turn, are more able to customize instruction. Lee and her colleagues (1993) also assert that the small size has a focusing effect that is similar to that of a core curriculum, and they note that in many instances, the two occur simultaneously and complement one another:

> Smaller schools must focus their resources on core programs, with the consequence that marginal students are either excluded or absorbed into more general programs that may not meet their needs. The latter "constraint" against meeting specialized needs may in practice actually benefit students, especially those at the lower end of the ability distribution. (p. 187)

Lee and her coauthors suggest that the combined effects of small size and a limited curriculum may be especially powerful for *lower end* students because they are the ones often relegated to low-level classes when such classes are offered. The lack of such courses, by default, pushes these students into achievement-oriented courses and attenuates the negative impact of placement in nonacademic classes.

The description of the results of small size and focused academics offered by Lee, Bryk, and Smith (1993) actually features de facto "detracking." Other scholars (e.g., Gamoran, 1987b; Murphy & Hallinger, 1989; Newmann, 1992a, 1992c; Oakes, 1985; Rosenbaum, 1976, 1980; Sedlak, Wheeler, Pullin, & Cusick, 1986) write more directly about the ways heterogeneous class structures influence student achievement. These authors assert that, structurally, the tracking of some students into low-ability classes results in "diminished access to what increasingly are being recognized as the more satisfactory conditions of learning" (Goodlad, 1984, p. 156). They also insist that tracking is more than a structural impediment to learning. The authors cited above, basing their claims on empirical investigations that uncovered a connection between track placement, socioeconomic status, and race, argue that ability grouping of students can also become an insidious political mechanism that "tend[s] to reinforce prevailing economic, social, language, and educational inequalities" (Sedlak et al., 1986, p. 51). They, in turn, suggest that heterogeneous grouping of students in high school classes has a redistributive effect that is especially advantageous for poor students of color. These students gain access not only to improved educational opportunities but also to relationships and experiences with persons who possess higher levels of status and political power.

Psychological Theories

The theories discussed in the preceding section highlight three characteristics of productive high schools: a focused academic curriculum, small size, and heterogeneous grouping of students. The scholars proffering these features stress that working independently and together, they influence learning because they create structural conditions that afford students greater access and higher quality opportunities to learn. Another set of theories, and those articulating them, suggests that some of the variables associated with productivity have a positive impact on learning because of their alignment with teacher and student needs. In this section, we consider some of these. We begin with a consideration of theories that posit connections between conditions that address teachers' needs and their students' learning. We then examine those that join curricular, extracurricular, and social features of good high schools with adolescents' need to develop a sense of identity. Next, we turn our attention to theories linking pedagogical and curricular dimensions of many effective schools with the needs most teens have for the sense of efficacy, mastery, or control. Finally, we discuss a set of theories that focus on ways peer influence shapes teens' thinking and behaviors.

Much of the research discussed in earlier chapters focuses on relationships between teachers and their colleagues (Little & McLaughlin, 1993; Metz, 1990b;

Siskin, 1997) in productive high schools. Essentially, a fairly robust set of studies links the presence of a sense of "professional community" (Siskin, 1997, p. 605) among teachers involved with enhanced student performance. One set of theories explaining the links between supportive professional relationships among teachers and student achievement seems to be built on Maslow's (1970) notion of a hierarchy of human needs. Essentially, Maslow posited that persons cannot and will not act in ways that address higher order needs (such as the need for efficacy or achievement) until more basic needs (including the need for supportive relationships) has been met. Roland Barth (1990) is one analyst whose ideas seem to be built, at least in part, on a Maslow-like framework. Arguing that the creation of "collegiality and relatedness among adults who work in schools" (p. 32) is a necessary precursor to the development of effective instructional programs, he writes,

> The relationships among adults in schools are the basis, the precondition, the sine qua non that allow, energize, and sustain all other attempts at school improvement. Unless adults talk with one another, observe one another, and help one another, very little will change. (p. 32)

Other scholars whose ideas parallel those of Barth attend to the ways participation in some sort of a professional community meets teachers' needs for "autonomy of the most fundamental and meaningful variety: control posited in the up-close workplace and collegial context and in attitudes of 'we can do it' and collective expertise" (McLaughlin, 1993, p. 97). Linda McNeil (1986) is one who offers an intriguing way of thinking about the link between teachers' sense of participation in a community that honors their autonomy and high quality instruction and student learning. She does this, however, by exploring what happens when these conditions do not exist. McNeil argues that certain things happen in schools in which the work and roles of teachers are prescribed and limited by administrators and policymakers who presume we can "reform pedagogy by strengthening the controlling functions of management" (p. xxii). McNeil maintains that an obsession with control leads to the valuing and pursuit of "classroom order and efficiency" (p. 160), the simplification, standardization, and division of curricular knowledge, and a type of pedagogy she labels "defensive teaching" (p. 157). She notes that defensive teaching affects the content students receive.

> The original classroom study of social studies content (McNeil, 1977) found content tightly controlled by teachers, reduced to simplistic fragments, and treated with little regard for a reference to resources in the students' experiences. (p. 159)

McNeil's later research has confirmed these findings and revealed that defensive teaching affects far more than curricular content. She notes that when schools and classrooms are organized around the bureaucratic ideal of control, access to learning is managed and limited. Describing economics teachers in control-oriented high school classes, she writes, "The economics information they made available to their students . . . reflected not their level of training or interest in the subject, nor their particular political position on a topic, but their skill at maintaining classroom control" (p. 160).

Implicit in McNeil's (1986) notion that bureaucracy and a focus on control inhibits both the quality of teaching and students' opportunities to learn is the idea that school communities that afford teachers a sense of professional autonomy encourage excellent teaching and enhance the likelihood that students will learn. Authors (Little & McLaughlin, 1993; McLaughlin, Talbert, & Bascia, 1990) frame this theoretical perspective in various ways. For example, McLaughlin, 1993, writes,

> Strong professional communities establish a locus of control in the profession. . . . To this point, almost every teacher who felt excited about the workplace, challenged and engaged in issues of practice and pedagogy, and who expressed energy and continued enthusiasm for the profession was a member of a strong collegial community, a community of learners. And every teacher we encountered who was engaged in the active, demanding form of pedagogy called "teaching for understanding," in which students and teachers construct knowledge together, belonged to such a community. (p. 97)

McNeil, McLaughlin, and others who share their perspective assert that high schools that foster teachers' sense that they are members of professional communities, ones in which they have autonomy to work individually and collectively to make decisions about, and to implement, curriculum and pedagogy, meet basic needs of adult educators. Barth (1990) argues that the satisfaction of such needs removes barriers to improvement. Furthermore, he and McLaughlin argue that collegial relationships with others provide an important motivation for the pursuit of excellent teaching and that such relationships also create conditions in which teachers can grow through professional conversations about problems of practice.

In the preceding paragraphs, we focused on theories suggesting that participation in a professional community meets a teachers' needs for collegiality and that this, in turn, fosters a sense of autonomy. The theory continues by positing that teachers who feel some sense of professional control and who work with others who share this sense are more likely to teach effectively.

Another set of theories that underlies some of the research we cited in earlier chapters, instead of focusing on teachers, concentrates on the ways certain features of productive high schools address adolescent developmental needs. A number of scholars who fall into this camp implicitly or explicitly accept Erik Erikson's (1968) notion that the primary task of adolescence is the development of a strong sense of identity (Csikszentmihalyi & Schmidt, 1998; Elkind, 1984; Newmann, 1981; Swanson, Spencer, & Peterson, 1998). Many of these analysts assert that aspects of schooling that assist students in developing a solid sense of self also contribute to the ability of these students to process and integrate academic and nonacademic events into powerful and lasting learning experiences.

David Elkind (1984) is among those who accept the idea that a central task of adolescence is the development of a coherent sense of self. Indeed, he argues that a strong and integrated identity provides a foundation—perhaps the only secure foundation—for meeting the academic and social challenges of young adulthood. In *All Grown Up and No Place to Go,* he considers a focused curriculum and small size, two of the features of productive schools we discussed in the previous section. Unlike the structural theorists, Elkind believes that a delimited course of study and smallness promote learning because they create environments that promote integrated learning. This, in turn, contributes to the development of an integrated, coherent sense of self for adolescent learners. He begins his discussion of the former by decrying the development of the department store style of curriculum we described in Chapter 3. Elkind claims that a "smorgasbord curriculum" (p. 147) has many negative effects on "the self-differentiation and identity formation" (p. 150). He writes,

> A healthy sense of self and identity is acquired by differentiation and higher-order integration. An integrated curriculum fosters such growth at both the personal and intellectual level. . . . A smorgasbord curriculum, in contrast, has obvious disadvantages from the standpoint of defining a personal identity. . . . Knowledge is kept in separate categories that cannot be related or brought together. This gives rise to a kind of compartmentalization of thinking about the self as well. (p. 150)

In contrast, Elkind claims that

> An integrated curriculum fosters . . . growth at both the personal and intellectual level. This is why it has been advocated by educators . . . who are concerned with the whole student rather than with one particular skill or bit of knowledge. When a student learns something in one class that sheds light on another, when he or she realizes what a scientific discovery, for instance, did to the political thinking of an era, there is growth and integration. Such learning adds not only to young people's sense of intellectual integration but also to their sense of personal integration. (p. 150)

In a similar vein, Elkind (1984), drawing insights from his own practice and research, maintains that "school size affects teenagers' efforts to define themselves" (p. 143) and that largeness hinders and smallness helps pursuit of an integrated identity. Elkind offers several hypotheses to explain the links between "large school size and large class size . . . [and] teenagers' efforts at self-definition" (p. 143). One is that large numbers of students make it difficult for adults to establish close "mentoring" (p. 143) with adolescents who may need assistance as they navigate through the stormy teenager years. He also writes,

> Self-definition . . . is facilitated by being with people who know us well and who give us useful information about ourselves. The more people who know

us well, the more likely we are to get a balanced view of ourselves. . . . In large schools teenagers know and are known by fewer people than would be the case in small schools. (pp. 143-144)

Fred Newmann (1981) concurs with Elkind's contention that sustained and supportive relationships help to provide a context in which teens develop a coherent sense of self. And, like Elkind, he asserts that the fragmented nature of life in most modern high schools has a deleterious effect on the quest for a identity because "it typically fosters transient interactions between teachers and students and creates barriers to generalized affiliative adult-student relationships" (Newmann, 1981, cited in Lee et al., 1993, p. 216). For Newmann and, indeed, for many other scholars (e.g., Bryk et al., 1993; Csikszentmihalyi & Schmidt, 1998; Noddings, 1988), a central problem with a compartmentalized curriculum and the structures that support it is its negative effect on relationships between teachers and students. Csikszentmihalyi and Schmidt (1998) claim that "isolation from adult role models" (p. 11) means that teenagers must navigate their journey toward their mature identity without guides. Noddings (1988) and Bryk and colleagues (1993) assert that transient, impersonal relationships between students and teachers deprive them of the opportunity to work in an "environment [in which] people know, trust, and care about one another" (p. 142). This, in turn, hinders the fulfillment of basic human needs and has an especially harmful effect on teens who, in addition to facing the "everyday stresses" of modern life, are in the midst of the complex process of "intellectual as well as social maturation" (Csikszentmihalyi & Schmidt, 1998). In contrast, they argue that when adults "accept responsibility to shape adolescents' lives through personal interaction and individual example" (Bryk et al., 1993, p. 144), students develop socially, personally, and academically. These authors stress that the cultivation of healthy adult-adolescent relationships requires a commitment on the part of both parties. They also point out that such relationships flourish more readily in schools in which the structure and curriculum support them.

Concurring with the authors cited above that "the social dynamics and developmental dynamics of adolescence" (Newmann, Wehlage, & Lamborn, 1992, p. 15) pose a unique set of educational challenges, Newmann (1992c) asserts that "the most immediate persisting issue for students and teachers is . . . student disengagement" (p. 2). Building on this idea, these authors believe that productive high schools manage to elicit high levels of performance because they have found ways to engage adolescents in learning. In the view of Newmann and his colleagues (1992), engagement is intimately linked to a sense of competence, something that for "most people, especially children . . . [is] one of the most powerful bases for human action and motivation" (p. 19). They further claim that this sense of competence is nurtured when students "establish affective, cognitive, and behavioral connections to the institution" (p. 20); experience a "sense of membership" (p. 18); and are engaged in "tasks that are considered . . . valuable, significant, and worthy of one's effort" (p. 23). These authors highlight a variety of factors that contribute either to students' feelings of connection to their school and its inhabitants or to their belief that the work they are doing is valuable and important. On the former issue, they assert that a productive sense of membership is encouraged when "students' organizational affiliation is grounded in clear educational purposes" (p. 21). It is further supported by "a sense of fair treatment" (p. 21), "personal support from teachers and peers" (p. 22), a "sense of success" (p. 22) and accomplishment, and caring, "nonacademic contact between staff and students" (p. 23). In turn, Newmann and his coauthors praise an academic program that offers "extrinsic rewards" (p. 24) and builds on the "intrinsic interest" (p. 25) of students. They further posit that "engagement with and internalization of knowledge depend to a large degree on the opportunities students have to 'own the work' " (p. 25). And they contend that students will perceive work as authentic if they can see its "connection to the 'real' world" (p. 26). Thus, for these scholars, the efficacy of features such as a relevant curriculum and a focused cocurricular program lies in their ability to encourage either a feeling of connection to school or a sense that academic work is worth doing. They maintain that these experiences lead to a sense of competence and that this, in turn, encourages intensive and productive engagement with learning.

Newmann (1998) believes that many conditions work together to promote student engagement. Among these factors are positive relationships with "student peers" (p. 93). Other scholars agree with this notion but emphasize to a much greater extent the power of peers to influence how well adolescents do in school (Brown & Theobald, 1998; Csikszentmihalyi & Larson, 1986; Lee et al., 1993; Ogbu, 1985, 1986, 1988). Several important themes emerge from research that examines the ways peer relations "support or undermine serious academic work" (Newmann, 1998, p. 93). Several of these are clearly articulated by Brown and Theobald (1998). Reporting on research that asked adolescents, "What's the best thing about school?" (p. 112), these authors write, "Teenagers offer up a variety of answers to this question, but the most common reply routinely refers to peer relations" (p. 112). They remind us that peer relationships tend to be built outside of classrooms and show that "adolescents are profoundly affected by their experiences outside the classroom as well as within it" (p. 109). Furthermore, Brown and Theobald echo a conclusion reached by other researchers (Coleman, 1961; Csikszentmihalyi & Larson, 1986; Epstein, 1983; Ogbu, 1985, 1986, 1988) that all too often "adolescent peer interactions, outside and inside the school, . . . foster a student culture that is nonacademic or even antiacademic" (Lee et al., 1993, p. 222). For Brown and Theobald and, indeed, for others of the scholars we have just cited, the power of peers to influence teens' engagement with school is linked, at least in part, to the ways friendships address certain developmental needs. One of these, discussed earlier in some detail, is the quest for a sense of self. In the view of some analysts (e.g., Clasen & Brown, 1985; Eckert, 1989), peer group identity supplies individual teens with some sense of their individual or private identity. Another need felt acutely by many adolescents is for help "as they negotiate transitions among home, school, and peer contexts" (Phelan, Davidson, & Cao, 1990, cited in Brown & Theobald, 1998, p. 113). Although they emphasize different needs, the authors noted in this paragraph are united in their acceptance of the idea that certain aspects of productive schools influence student learning because they encourage the kinds of peer relations that support academic work.

Social Ecological Theories

We elected to discuss in the preceding section the theory that certain features of effective high schools elicit or promote student achievement by encouraging an academically oriented peer culture. And many of the scholars who proffer this theory focus on the important role peers play in adolescent development. We could just have easily presented this concept in this section, because in the paragraphs that follow, we explore the idea that the power of productive secondary schools lies in their ability to create a particular kind of social ecology. Lee and colleagues (1993) suggest that what we are calling social-ecological theories are driven by a "communitarian perspective [that] views schools as 'small societies,' organizations that emphasize informal and enduring relationships and are driven by a common ethos" (p. 173). Scholars holding this perspective tend to presume that high schools that foster student achievement do so because they are places in which the *informal and enduring relationships* among students and teachers and the *common ethos* they share focus on learning and on behaviors that promote it.

James Coleman and Thomas Hoffer (1987) express the seminal theory that fits within the social-ecological category. They write about "structural consistency and functional communities" (p. 6) and about "value consistency and value communities" (p. 8). After extensive research on the impact, or lack thereof, of schools on student achievement, these scholars turned their attention to understanding the mechanisms by which institutions exerted influence. Essentially, they hypothesized that in stable, nonmobile environments, connections between family members, friends, and neighbors extend across generations, leading to a kind of "structural consistency between generations." This "creates what can be described as a functional community, a community in which social norms and sanctions, including those that cross generations arise out of the social structure itself, and both reinforce and perpetuate that structure." (p. 70) Coleman and Hoffer note that functional communities have both negative and positive effects on their members. Of relevance to schools is the concept that:

> Functional community augments the resources available to parents in their interactions with school, in their supervision of their children's behavior, and in their supervision of their children's associations, both with others their own age and with adults. . . . Parents at all social and educational levels need these resources as an aid in raising their children and monitoring their schooling, but the parents in most desperate need of them are the parents with least personal resources: parents with little education, few organizational skills, little self-confidence, and little money. (pp. 7-8)

After discussing functional communities, Coleman and Hoffer turn their attention to the idea of "value consistency and value communities" (p. 8). Noting that the two types of communities "have some affinity" (p. 8) but are not necessarily coterminous, they suggest that value communities augment the impact of personal or private values. They further suggest that schools that resemble functional or value communities amplify educational energy and resources and provide environments conducive to learning.

Embedded in Coleman and Hoffer's (1987) concept of functional or value communities is the idea that much of the power of these social collectives is derived from their ability to communicate values and "social norms and sanctions" (p. 7) across generational and geographical boundaries. Other scholars, although they do not disagree with this idea, focus on other aspects of communitarian schools that, in their view, help to explain the ways in which such institutions influence their members. Lee and colleagues (1993) point to "substantial research [that] documents that when parents volunteer in their children's schools and classrooms, positive consequences accrue for both students and teachers" (p. 191) that provide support for the efficacy of communitarian schools. Implicit in this statement and in some of the research to which they refer (Epstein, 1985; McKey, Condelli, Ganson, Barrett, McConkey, & Plantz, 1985) is the notion that schools with greater connections to their surrounding communities are more likely to tap into the instrumental value of parental involvement in schools. Lee and her colleagues also refer to other studies (Comer, 1980; Ogbu, 1985, 1986, 1988) that focus on the power of alignment between a school's values and those of students' outside communities and on problems that result when such an alignment does not occur.

Lee, Bryk, and Smith (1993; see also Bryk et al., 1993) explore a number of other aspects of communitarian schools that in their view, help to explain how and why such schools exercise power over students' lives. Their research on Catholic schools led them to propose that in schools that resemble communities, the role of teacher is likely to be diffuse and open rather than bureaucratically defined.

> This broadly defined role creates many opportunities for faculty and student encounters. Through these social interactions, teachers convey an "intrusive interest" in students' personal lives that extends beyond the classroom door into virtually every facet of school life. (p. 141)

These authors suggest that the personal relationships that occur within communities contribute to teachers' sense of satisfaction with work and that this, in turn, energizes their teaching. The authors also assert that the students' sense that they are known and cared for is a powerful motivation for engagement with school.

Integrating the Theories: Lessons for Productive High Schools

Each frame provides a different way of interpreting events, and each implies a very different approach to effective management. Together, they offer a comprehensive view.

—Bolman and Deal, 1984 (pp. 240-241)

These schools achieved success, not primarily as a result of systemic policy pressure from external sources, but through a process of reflective dialogue within the schools.

—Newmann (1992a, p. 213)

As we noted in the introductory section, two goals guided us as we developed this chapter. The first was an explanatory one. We wanted to identify and explore theories, attempting to explain how and why correlates of productivity—the characteristics and qualities of good high schools—influence learning. The second goal was an integrative one. After identifying various theories, we hoped, essentially, to look across them to see if we could pull together important ideas about the underlying mechanisms that operate in productive secondary schools to influence student development and academic achievement. In this section, we present key lessons that emerged for us as we sought to understand how good high schools work. We examine two themes that seem to permeate the various theories we have discussed and conclude with lessons these themes offer for the reform of secondary schools.

The Importance of Relationships in the Promotion of Student Learning

A central theme cutting across many of the theories discussed above is that high schools are sites of supportive relationships between and among teachers and students and are places likely to foster high levels of powerful learning. From a structural perspective, close relationships between students and school personnel create opportunities for teachers to work more closely with each student, to monitor academic progress, and to construct programs of study that address individual needs, interests, and learning styles. Psychologically, such relationships also meet a number of needs.

For teachers, the establishment of "collegial relationships" (Barth, 1990, p. 30) and participation in a "spirited, reflective professional community" (McLaughlin, 1993, p. 98) encourages a sense of autonomy and agency. This, in turn, promotes a number of productive dynamics:

> [Such a community is] a workplace setting that allows examination of assumptions about practice, focuses collective expertise on solutions based on classroom realities, and supports efforts to change and grow professionally. Strong professional communities allow the expression of new ideas and innovations in terms of specific curricula and student characteristics. Energetic professional communities at the school or department level actually generate motivation to role up one's sleeves and endeavor to meet the unfamiliar and often difficult needs of contemporary students. (p. 98)

When students are the recipients of care and support from teachers, they are offered adult mentors who can serve as both models and guides as teens seek to navigate the developmental task of acquiring a strong sense of self. Such teens are also more likely to be motivated to engage with their schoolwork and to seek help if they encounter problems inhibiting their learning. And when adolescents have strong relationships with peers who value school and learning, the chances of their developing an identity that values and pursues academic achievement are greatly enhanced.

From a social-ecological perspective, caring relationships between and among adults and young people who inhabit schools—especially if they extend beyond the school walls to students' families—help to create trans-generational and transcultural communities. In these communities, the impact of educational resources is amplified because messages and values from both home and school regarding the importance of learning are supported by a host of individuals. Furthermore, the establishment of such communities creates what we referred to earlier as a web of supportive relationships. Such a web links parents and educators in ways that enable them to support one another and support young people, too. It also creates pathways to enable teachers to understand, respect, and use students' cultures to create meaningful and effective learning experiences.

The Importance of a Learning Imperative in the Promotion of Student Learning

Personalized relationships are important in high schools. However, they seem to create the conditions for academic achievement only when they are linked with what we call a "learning imperative" (Beck & Murphy, 1996, p. 41). Such an imperative has the dual effect of focusing policies and activities—and those who create and enact them—on the promotion of learning as the primary purpose of schooling and of driving teachers and administrators to excellence in the development of curriculum and the delivery of instruction. The structural theories discussed earlier share an assumption that certain features of productive schools, such as a focused and limited curriculum, small size, and heterogeneous groupings positively influence learning because they increase access to learning opportunities for all students. The psychological theorists, in turn, even as they locate the power of certain variables for meeting certain needs (e.g., the presence of strong professional communities for teachers and of relationships and conditions that foster a well-defined sense of self and identity for teens), assume that this occurs within an academic context. Social-ecological theories posit that schools functioning as cross-generational and cross-cultural communities create environments that support and encourage learning because they amplify and focus educational resources and because they help to establish connections between teachers, parents, and others in the students' lives that enable all to better support academic efforts.

Scholars who write at length about the importance of teachers' professional communities (Barth, 1990; Little, 1982; McLaughlin, 1993; Rosenholtz, 1989) stress the distinction between *collegiality* and *congeniality*:

Congeniality suggests people getting along with one another. Friendly, cordial associations. . . . People enjoying each other's company and getting along. . . . Collegiality is the presence of four specific behaviors, as follows:

> Adults in schools *talk about practice*. These conversations about teaching and learning are frequent, continuous, concrete, and precise. Adults in schools *observe each other* engaged in the practice of teaching and administration. These observations become the practice to reflect on and talk about. Adults engage together in *work on curriculum* by planning, designing, researching, and evaluating curriculum. Finally adults in schools *teach each other* what they know about teaching, learning, and leading. Craft knowledge is revealed, articulated, and shared. (Barth, 1990, pp. 30-31)

The theories we reviewed, without exception, emphasized the importance of collegial relationships—of participation in professional communities—for teachers.

In a similar vein, when scholars suggest that supportive relationships help create communities that draw educators, teens, parents, and others into a caring communities that amplify educational efforts—and when they write of the ways supportive student-teacher relations foster a sense of adolescent identity that includes a view that teens are capable learners—the very fact that key players in these relationships are educators begins to underscore the importance of linking support with attention to the academic arena. And the reality that many scholars (e.g., Lee et al., 1993; Newmann, 1998) believe that supportive relationships between teachers and their students provide a mechanism that enables both to communicate with one another about curricular issues underscores at least one way in which personal relationships support achievement. A strong argument for the importance of linking relationships with a learning imperative is also found in the research and supporting theories pointing out that interactions with peers who do not value schooling has a strong and negative impact on teens' engagement with learning.

The Need for Learning-Driven Community Models for Secondary Schools

> To accomplish major improvements on a systemic basis will require far more than teachers' understanding of what currently seems to "work," or the introduction of new tests, new curricula, or new organizational structures for schools and districts. Significant advances in student engagement will depend on communities and the nation as a whole confronting a number of controversial issues dealing with educational aims for children, the content of teacher education and professional development, redistribution of power and authority in the conduct of schooling, and public willingness to invest not only in innovative schooling, but in the building of more basic social support for children. (Newmann, 1992c, p. 9)

An overwhelming conclusion, based on research we reviewed and the theories that attempt to explain the connections between learning and certain features of productive high schools, is that there is a prominence of mechanisms that encourage powerful, rich, deep, and personal connections between persons involved in the educational enterprise and between these individuals and the acts of learning and teaching. These relationships cannot flourish widely and consistently in bureaucratic schools. Indeed, if a bureaucracy is *doing its job,* it will, in effect, create roles, rules, and structures that make the development of a personalized, academic learning culture difficult if not impossible.

If we wish to have productive high schools, researchers, practicing educators, parents, policymakers, and citizens must have the courage to create institutions very different from most that inhabit our communities. We must strive to create models of learning-driven school communities that allow for and encourage excellence and support and then devote ourselves to implementing these models. Such efforts will challenge us intellectually, emotionally, and interpersonally. They will require resources, energy, and patience. Our perspective is that we must undertake these efforts, drawing strength and encouragement from the reality that an impressive body of empirical evidence and a robust set of theories support this work.

References

Ainley, J. (1994, April). *Multiple indicators of high school effectiveness.* Paper presented at the annual meeting of the American Educational Research Association, New Orleans, Louisiana.

Alexander, K. L., & Cook, M. A. (1982, October). Curricula and coursework: A surprise ending to a familiar story. *American Sociological Review, 47*(5), 626-640.

Alexander, K. L., Cook, M. A., & McDill, E. L. (1978, February). Curriculum tracking and educational stratification: Some further evidence. *American Sociological Review, 43*(9), 47-66.

Alexander, K. L., & Pallas, A. M. (1983). *Curriculum reform and school performance: An evaluation of the "new basics."* Baltimore: Johns Hopkins University, Center for Social Organization of Schools.

Alexander, W. M., Saylor, J. G., & Williams, E. L. (1971). *The high school: Today and tomorrow.* New York: Holt, Rinehart & Winston.

Alfassi, M. (1998, Summer). Reading for meaning: The efficacy of reciprocal teaching in fostering reading comprehension in high school students in remedial reading classes. *American Educational Research Journal, 35*(2), 309-332.

American Federation of Teachers. (1997). *Quest '97: Building on the best: Learning from what works: Four promising programs.* Author.

Anderson, C. S. (1985). The investigation of school climate. In G. R. Austin & H. Garber (Eds.), *Research on exemplary schools* (pp. 97-126). Orlando, FL: Academic Press.

Anderson, V. E., & Gruhn, W. T. (1962). *Principles and practices of secondary education* (2nd ed.). New York: Ronald.

Andrews, W. E. (1996, February). *Practicing what we preach: New roles for professional educators.* Paper presented at the annual meeting of the American Association of Colleges for Teacher Education, Chicago, IL.

Angus, D., & Mirel, J. (1995). Rhetoric and reality: The high school curriculum. In D. Ravitch & M. Vinovskis (Eds.), *Learning from the past: What history teaches us about school reform* (pp. 295-328). Baltimore: Johns Hopkins University Press.

Astone, N. M., & McLanahan, S. S. (1991, June). Family structure, parental practices, and high school completion. *American Sociological Review, 56*(3), 309-320.

Austin, G. R., & Holowenzak, S. P. (1985). An examination of 10 years of research on exemplary schools. In G. R. Austin & H. Garber (Eds.), *Research on exemplary schools* (pp. 65-82). Orlando, FL: Academic Press.

Baker, D. P., & Stevenson, D. L. (1986, July). Mothers' strategies for children's school achievement: Managing the transition to high school. *Sociology of Education, 59,* 156-166.

Banathy, B. H. (1988). An outside-in approach to design inquiry in education. In *The re-design of education: A collection of papers concerned with comprehensive educational reform: Vol. 1* (pp. 51-71). San Francisco: Far West Laboratory for Educational Research & Development.

Barth, R. S. (1990). *Improving schools from within: Teachers, parents, and principals can make the difference.* San Francisco: Jossey-Bass.

Beck, L. G., & Murphy, J. (1996). *The four imperatives of a successful school.* Newbury Park, CA: Corwin.

Becker, W. E., & Rosen, S. (1992, June). The learning effect of assessment and evaluation in high school. *The Economics of Education Review, 11*(2), 107-118.

Beers, D., & Ellig, J. (1994). An economic view of the effectiveness of public and private schools. In S. Hakim, P. Seidenstat, & G. W. Bowman (Eds.), *Privatizing education and educational choice: Concepts, plans, and experiences* (pp. 19-38). Westport, CT: Praeger.

Bobbett, G. C., & French, R. L. (1992, November). *Evaluating climate in nine "good" high schools in Tennessee, Kentucky, and North Carolina.* Paper presented at the annual meeting of the American Educational Research Association, Atlanta, Georgia.

Bodenhausen, J. (1988, April). *Does the academic background of teachers affect the performance of their students?* Paper presented at the annual meeting of the American Educational Research Association, New Orleans, Louisiana.

Bolman, L., & Deal, T. (1984). *Modern approaches to understanding and managing organizations.* San Francisco: Jossey-Bass.

Boyer, E. L. (1983). *High school: A report on secondary education in America.* New York: Harper & Row.

Bradford, J. C., Jr. (1987). *Ten-year follow-up study of the development and implementation of a quarter plan to provide year-round schools in grades 9-12 in the city of Buena Vista.* Buena Vista, CA: Buena Vista City Public Schools.

Bratlinger, E. A. (1993). *The politics of social class in secondary school: Views of affluent and impoverished youth.* New York: Teachers College Press.

Brophy, J. E. (1982, April). Successful teaching strategies for the inner-city child. *Phi Delta Kapan, 63*(8), 527-530.

Brophy, J., & Good, T. L. (1985). Teacher behavior and student achievement. In M. Wittlock (Ed.), *Third handbook of research on teaching* (pp. 328-375). New York: Macmillan.

Brouillette, L. (1997, December). Revisiting an innovative high school: What happens when the principal leaves? [Special Issue]. *Educational Administration Quarterly, 33,* 546-575.

Brown, B. F. (1984). *Crisis in secondary education: Rebuilding America's high schools.* Englewood Cliffs, NJ: Prentice Hall.

Brown, B., & Theobald, W. (1998). Learning contexts beyond the classroom: Extra-curricular activities, community organizations, and peer groups. In K. Borman & B. Schneider (Eds.), *The adolescent years: Social influences and educational challenges* (Ninety-seventh yearbook of the National Society for the Study of Education, pp. 109-141). Chicago: University of Chicago Press.

Bruckerhoff, C. (1991). *Between classes: Faculty life at Truman High.* New York: Teachers College Press.

Bryk, A. S. (1994). More good news that school organization matters. In *Issues in restructuring schools* (Issue Report No. 7, pp. 7-9). Madison, WI: University of Wisconsin-Madison, School of Education, Center on Organization and Restructuring of Schools. (ERIC Document Reproduction Service No. ED 376 565)

Bryk, A. S., & Driscoll, M. E. (1988). *The high school as community: Contextual influences and consequences for students and teachers.* Madison, WI: University of Wisconsin-Madison, National Center on Effective Secondary Schools.

Bryk, A. S., Lee, V. E., & Holland, P. B. (1993). *Catholic schools and the common good.* Cambridge, MA: Harvard University Press.

Bryk, A., Lee, V., & Smith, J. B. (1990). High school organization and its effects on teachers and students: An interpretation summary of the research. In W. Clune & J. Witte (Eds.), *Choice and control in American education* (pp. 135-226). Newbury Park, CA: Falmer.

Bryk, A. S., & Thum, Y. M. (1989, Fall). The effects of high school organization on dropping out: An exploratory investigation. *American Educational Research Journal, 26* (3), 353-383.

Burke, C. (1992). Devolution of responsibility to Queensland schools: Clarifying the rhetoric critiquing the reality. *Journal of Educational Administration, 30*(4), 33-52.

Callahan, R. E. (1962). *Education and the cult of efficiency.* Chicago: University of Chicago Press.

Campbell, R. F., Fleming, T., Newell, L., & Bennion, J. W. (1987). *A history of thought and practice in educational administration.* New York: Teachers College Press.

Canady, R. L., & Rettig, M. D. (1995). *Block scheduling: A catalyst for change in high schools.* Princeton, NJ: Eye on Education.

Carnegie Council on Adolescent Development. (1989). *Turning points.* Washington, DC: Author.

Cawelti, G. (1994, July). Let's reinvent high school. *The American School Board Journal, 181*(7), 19-22.

Cawelti, G. (1997). *Effects of high school restructuring: Ten schools at work.* Arlington, VA: Educational Research Service.

Chambers, J. G. (1981). An analysis of school size under a voucher system. *Educational Evaluation and Policy Analysis, 3,* 29-40.

Chaney, B., Burgdorf, K., & Atash, N. (1997, Fall). Influencing achievement through high school graduation requirements. *Educational Evaluation and Policy Analysis, 19* (3), 229-244.

Christman, J. B., & Macpherson, P. (1996). *The five-school study: Restructuring Philadelphia's comprehensive high schools* (Report prepared for the Philadelphia Education Fund by Research for Action). Philadelphia, PA: Pew Charitable Trusts.

Chubb, J. E., & Moe, T. M. (1990). *Politics, markets, and America's schools.* Washington, DC: Brookings Institution.

Clark, D. L., Lotto, L. S., & McCarthy, M. M. (1980, March). Factors associated with success in urban elementary school. *Phi Delta Kappan, 61*(7), 467-470.

Clark, R. M. (1988, Winter). Parents as providers of linguistic and social capital. *Educational Horizons,* 93-95.

Clasen, D. R., & Brown, B. B. (1985). The multidimensionality of peer pressure in adolescence. *Journal of Youth and Adolescence, 16,* 451-468.

Clinchy, E. (Ed.). (1997). *Transforming public education: A new course for America's future.* New York: Teachers College Press.

Coburn, J., & Nelson, S. (1989, January). *Teachers do make a difference: What Indian graduates say about their school experience.* Portland, OR: Northwest Regional Education Laboratory.

Cohen, D. K. (1988). *Teaching practice: Plus ça change. . .* (Issue Paper 88-3). East Lansing, MI: Michigan State University, National Center for Research on Teacher Education.

Cohen, D. K., & Neufeld, B. (1981, Summer). The failure of high schools and the progress of education. *Daedalus,* 69-89.

Cohen, F., & Seaman, L. (1997, March). Research versus 'real-search'. *Phi Delta Kappan, 78*(7), 564-567.

Coleman, J. S. (1961). *The adolescent society.* New York: Cromwell-Collier.

Coleman, J. S., & Hoffer, T. (1987). *Public and private high school: The impact of communities.* New York: Basic Books.

Coleman, J. S., Hoffer, T., & Kilgore, S. (1982). *High school achievement: Public, catholic, & private schools compared.* New York: Basic Books.

Comer, J. (1980). *School power: Implications for an intervention project.* New York: Free Press.

Conant, J. B. (1959). *The American high school today: A first report to interested citizens.* New York: McGraw-Hill.

Conant, J. B. (1967). *The American high school revisited.* New York: McGraw-Hill.

Conklin, M. E., & Dailey, A. R. (1981, October). Does consistency of parental educational encouragement matter for secondary school students? *Sociology of Education, 54,* 254-262.

Connors, L. J., & Epstein, J. L. (1994, August). *Taking stock: Views of teachers, parents, and students on school, family, and community partnerships in high schools* (Report No. 25). Baltimore: Johns Hopkins University, Center on Families, Communities, Schools & Children's Learning.

Consortium on Productivity in the Schools. (1995). *Using what we have to get the schools we need, a productivity focus for American education.* Washington, DC: Economic Policy Institute.

Consortium on Renewing Education. (1998, November). *20/20 vision: A strategy for doubling America's academic achievement by the year 2020.* Nashville, TN: Vanderbilt University, Peabody Center for Education Policy.

Cooley, W. W., & Leinhardt, G. (1980, January/February). The instructional dimensions study. *Educational Evaluation and Policy Analysis, 2*(1), 7-25.

Corcoran, T. B. (1990). Schoolwork: Perspectives on workplace reform in public schools. In M. W. McLaughlin, J. E. Talbert, & N. Bascia (Eds.), *The contexts of teaching in secondary schools: Teachers' realities* (pp. 142-166). New York: Teachers College Press.

Corcoran, T. B., & Wilson, B. L. (1985, July). *The secondary school recognition program: A first report on 202 high schools.* Philadelphia: Research for Better Schools.

Cotton, K., & Savard, W. G. (1981). *Parent participation.* Portland, OR: Northwest Regional Educational Laboratory.

Cremin, L. A. (1955, March). The revolution in American secondary education, 1893-1918. *Teachers College Record, 56*(6), 295-308.

Cremin, L. A. (1961). *The transformation of the school: Progressivism in American education 1876-1957.* New York: Vintage.

Cresswell, R. A., & Rasmussen, P. (1996, December). Developing a structure for personalization in the high school. *NASSP Bulletin, 80*(584), 27-30.

Crowson, R. L. (1992). *School-community relations, under reform.* Berkeley, CA: McCutchan.

Csikszentmihalyi, M., & Larson, R. (1986). *Being adolescent.* New York: Basic Books.

Csikszentmihalyi, M., & Schmidt, J. (1998). Stress and resilience in adolescence: An evolutionary perspective. In K. Borman & B. Schneider (Eds.), *The adolescent years: Social influences and educational challenges* (Ninety-seventh yearbook of the National Society for the Study of Education, pp. 1-17). Chicago: University of Chicago Press.

Cuban, L. (1984). *How teachers taught: Constancy and change in American classrooms 1890-1980.* New York: Longman.

Cuellar, A. (1992). *From dropout to high achiever: An understanding of academic excellence through the ethnography of high and low achieving secondary school students.*

San Diego, CA: San Diego State University, Imperial Valley Campus Institute of Borders Studies.

Cusick, P. A. (1983). *The egalitarian ideal and the American high school: Studies of three schools.* New York: Longman.

Daft, R. L., & Becker, S. W. (1980). Managerial, institutional, and technical influences on administration: A longitudinal analysis. *Social Forces, 59,* 392-413.

Dahrendorf, R. (1995, Summer). A precarious balance: Economic opportunity, civil society, and political liberty. *The Responsive Community,* 13-39.

Darling-Hammond, L. (1997a). Reframing the school reform agenda: Developing capacity for school transformation. In E. Clinchy (Ed.), *Transforming public education: A new course for America's future* (pp. 38-55). New York: Teachers College Press.

Darling-Hammond, L. (1997b). *The right to learn: A blueprint for creating schools that work.* San Francisco: Jossey-Bass.

Darling-Hammond, L., Ancess, J., & Falk, B. (1995). *Authentic assessment in action: Studies of schools and students at work.* New York: Teachers College Press.

Datnow, A. (1997). Using gender to preserve tracking's status hierarchy: The defensive strategy of entrenched teachers. *Anthropology & Education Quarterly, 28*(2), 204-228.

Davenport, E. C., Jr., Davison, M. L., Kuang, H., Ding, S., Kim, S., & Kwak, N. (1998, Fall). High school mathematics course-taking by gender and ethnicity. *American Educational Research Journal, 35*(3), 497-514.

Donmoyer, E. R., & Kos, R. (1993). At-risk students: Insights from/about research. In E. R. Donmoyer & R. Kos (Eds.), *At-risk students: Portraits, policies, programs, and practices* (pp. 265-290). Albany, NY: State University of New York Press.

Dorn, S. (1996). *Creating the dropout: An institutional and social history of school failure.* Westport, CT: Praeger.

Dornbusch, S. M., & Ritter, P. L. (1988, Winter). Parents of high school students: A neglected resource. *Educational Horizons,* 75-77.

Dornbusch, S. M., Ritter, P. L., Leiderman, P. H., Roberts, D. F., & Fraleigh, M. J. (1987, May). The relation of parenting style to adolescent school performance. *Child Development, 58*(5), 1244-1257.

Driscoll, M. (1987). *Stories of excellence: Ten case studies from a study of exemplary mathematics programs.* Reston, VA: National Council of Teachers of Mathematics.

Driscoll, M. E. (1995). Thinking like a fish: The implications of the image of school community for connections between parents and schools. In B. Schneider & P. Cookson, (Eds.), *Creating school policy* (pp. 209-236). Westport, CT: Greenwood.

DuFour, R., & Eaker, R. (1992). *Creating the new American school: A principal's guide to school improvement.* Bloomington, IN: National Educational Service.

Duke, D. L. (1995). *The school that refused to die: Continuity and change at Thomas Jefferson high school.* Albany, NY: State University of New York Press.

Dyer, T. J. (1996, December). Personalization: If schools don't implement this one, there will be no reform. *NASSP Bulletin, 80*(584), 1-8.

Eckert, P. (1989). *Jocks and burnouts: Social categories and identity in the high school.* New York: Teachers College Press.

Elkind, D. (1984). *All grown up and no place to go.* Reading, MA: Addison.

Ellet, C. D., & Logan, C. (1990, April). *Analyses of school level learning environment: Organizational coupling, robustness and effectiveness.* Paper presented at the annual meeting of the American Educational Research Association, Boston, MA.

Engstrom, G. A. (1981). *Mexican-American and Anglo-American student perceptions of the learning environment of the classroom: A study of schooling in the United States* (Technical Report Series, No. 22). Los Angeles: University of California, Graduate School of Education.

Epstein, J. (1983). The influence of friends on achievement and affective outcomes. In J. L. Epstein & N. Karweit (Eds.), *Friends in school: Patterns of selection and influence in secondary schools* (pp. 129-160). New York: Academic Press.

Epstein, J. (1985). Home and school connections in schools for the future: Implications of research on parental involvement. *Peabody Journal of Education, 78,* 373-380.

Epstein, J. L. (1988, Winter). How do we improve programs for parent involvement? *Educational Horizons,* 58-59.

Epstein, J. L. (1992). School and family partnerships. In M. Alkin (Ed.), *Encyclopedia of Educational Research* (6th ed., pp. 1139-1151). New York: Macmillan.

Erickson, E. (1968). *Identity, youth, and crisis.* New York: Norton.

Fehrmann, P. G., Keith, T. Z., & Reimers, T. M. (1987). Home influence on school learning: Direct and indirect effects of parental involvement on high school grades. *Journal of Educational Research, 80* (6), 330-337.

Fine, M. (1992, July). *Chart[er]ing urban school reform: Philadelphia style.* Unpublished manuscript.

Finley, M. K. (1984, October). Teachers and tracking in a comprehensive high school. *Sociology of Education, 57*(4), 233-243.

Firestone, W. A., & Rosenblum, S. (1988, Winter). Building commitment in urban high schools. *Educational Evaluation and Policy Analysis, 10* (4), 285-299.

Fisher, C. W. (1990, January). The Research Agenda Project as prologue. *Journal of Research in Mathematics Education, 21*(1), 81-89.

Foley, E. M., & McConnaughy, S. B. (1982). *Towards school improvement: Lessons from alternative high schools.* New York: Public Education Association.

Fordham, S. (1986). *Black student school success: An ethnographic study in a large urban public school system* (Preliminary report submitted to the Spencer Foundation). Chicago: Spencer Foundation.

Foster, R. (1998, April). *Leadership in two secondary schools with a reputation for success.* Paper presented at the annual meeting of the American Educational Research Association, San Diego, CA.

Fox, W. F. (1981). Reviewing economics of size in education. *Journal of Education Finance, 6,* 273-296.

Frank, K. A. (1998). Quantitative methods for studying social context in multilevels and through interpersonal relations. In P. D. Pearson & I. Ashgar (Vol. Eds.), *Review of Research in Education: Vol. 23* (pp. 171-216). Washington, DC: American Educational Research Association.

Fullan, M. (1997). Broadening the concept of teacher leadership. In S. Caldwell (Ed.), *Provisional development in learning-centered schools* (pp. 34-48). Oxford, OH: National Staff Development Council.

Fullan, M. G. (1988, September). *Change processes in secondary schools: Toward a more fundamental agenda* (CRC No. P88-111). Stanford, CA: Stanford University, Center for Research on the Context of Secondary Teaching.

Fullan, M. G. (1990). Change processes in secondary schools: Toward a more fundamental agenda. In M. W. McLaughlin, J. E. Talbert, & N. Bascia (Eds.), *The contexts of teaching in secondary schools: Teachers' realities* (pp. 224-255). New York: Teachers College Press.

Furtwengler, W. J. (1991, April). *Reducing student misbehavior through student involvement in school restructuring processes.* Paper presented at the annual meeting of the American Educational Research Association, Chicago, IL.

Gallien, L. B., Jr. (1992). *Lost voices: Reflections on education from an imperiled generation.* Report of an examination of attitudes of black males towards education at five secondary schools with distinct sagas, ERIC Document Reproduction Service No. ED 346 092)

Gamoran, A. (1987a). *Instruction and the effects of schooling*. Madison, WI: University of Wisconsin, National Center on Effective Secondary Schools.

Gamoran, A. (1987b). The stratification of high school learning opportunities. *Sociology of Education, 60*, 135-155.

Gamoran, A. (1992). *Alternative uses of ability grouping: Can we bring high quality instruction to low-ability classes?* Madison, WI: University of Wisconsin, Center on Organization and Restructuring of Schools.

Gamoran, A., & Nystrand, M. (1992). Taking students seriously. In F. M. Newmann (Ed.), *Student engagement and achievement in American secondary schools* (pp. 40-61). New York: Teachers College Press.

Gamoran, A., Nystrand, M., Berends, M., & LePore, P. C. (1995, Winter). An organizational analysis of the effects of ability grouping. *American Educational Research Journal, 32*(4), 687-715.

Gamoran, A., Porter, A. C., Smithson, J., & White, P. A. (1997). Upgrading high school mathematics instruction: Improving learning opportunities for low-achieving, low-income youth. *Educational Evaluation and Policy Analysis, 19* (4), 325-338.

Garet, M. S., & Delaney, B. (1988). Students' courses and stratification. *Sociology of Education, 61*, 61-77.

Garibaldi, A. M. (1993). *Improving urban schools in inner-city communities* (Occasional Paper No. 3). Cleveland, OH: Cleveland State University, Levine College of Urban Affairs, Urban Child Research Center.

Gaziel, H. H. (1997, May/June). Impact of school culture on effectiveness of secondary school with disadvantaged students. *Journal of Educational Research, 90* (5), 310-318.

Gee, J. P., & Green, J. L. (1998). Discourse analysis, learning, and social practice: A methodological study. In P. D. Pearson & A. Iran-Nejad (Eds.), *Review of Research in Education: Vol. 23* (pp. 119-170). Washington, DC: American Educational Research Association.

Gilchrist, R. S. (1989). *Effective schools: Three case studies of excellence*. Bloomington, IN: National Educational Service.

Ginsburg, A. L., & Hanson, S. L. (1986). *Values and educational success among disadvantaged students*. Washington, DC: U.S. Department of Education and Decision Resources Corporation.

Goldhaber, D. D., & Brewer, D. J. (1996, January). *Why don't schools and teachers seem to matter? Assessing the impact of unobservables on educational productivity*. Revision of paper presented at meetings of the Econometric Society, San Francisco, California.

Good, T. L. (1981, February). Teacher expectations and student perceptions: A decade of research. *Educational Leadership, 38* (5), 415-422.

Good, T. L., & Brophy, J. E. (1986). School effects. In M. Wittrock (Ed.), *Third handbook of research on teaching* (pp. 570-602). New York: Macmillan.

Goodlad, J. I. (1984). *A place called school: Prospects for the future*. New York: McGraw-Hill.

Goodlad, J. I. (1997). *In praise of education*. New York: Teachers College Press.

Grant, G. (1988). *The world we created at Hamilton High*. Cambridge, MA: Harvard University Press.

Gregory, T. (1993). *Making high school work: Lessons from the open school*. New York: Teachers College Press.

Gregory, T. B., & Smith, G. R. (1987). *High schools as communities: The small school reconsidered*. Bloomington, IN: Phi Delta Kappa Educational Foundation.

Grossman, P., Kirst, M. W., Negosh, W., & Schmidt-Posnere, J. (1985, July). *Curricular change in California comprehensive high schools 1982-83 to 1984-85*. Stanford, CA: Policy Analysis for California Education.

Haas, T. (1993). Schools in communities: New ways to work together. In G. A. Smith (Ed.), *Public schools that work: Creating community* (pp. 215-245). New York: Routledge.

Hallinger, P., & Murphy, J. (1985, November). Assessing the instructional management behavior of principals. *Elementary School Journal, 86* (2), 217-247.

Hallinger, P., & Murphy, J. (1986, May). The social context of effective schools. *American Journal of Education, 94* (3), 328-355.

Hallinger, P., & Murphy, J. (1987, April). *Social context effects on school effects.* Paper presented at the annual meeting of the American Educational Research Association, Washington, DC.

Hallinger, P., Murphy, J., Weil, M., Mesa, R. P., & Mitman, A. (1983, May). School effectiveness: Identifying the specific practices and behaviors for principals. *NASSP Bulletin, 67*(463), 83-91.

Hamilton, L. S. (1998, Fall). Gender differences on high school science achievement tests: Do format and content matter? *Educational Evaluation and Policy Analysis, 20* (3), 179-189.

Hampel, R. L. (1986). *The last little citadel: American high schools since 1940.* Boston: Houghton Mifflin.

Hannay, L. M., & Ross, J. A. (1997, December). Initiating secondary school reform: The dynamic relationship between restructuring, reculturing, and retiming [Special Issue]. *Educational Administration Quarterly, 33,* 576-603.

Hargreaves, A., & Macmillan, R. (1995). The balkanization of secondary school teaching. In L. S. Siskin & J. W. Little, (Eds.), *The subjects in question: Departmental organization and the high school* (pp. 23-47). New York: Teachers College Press.

Harnisch, D. L. (1985, October). *An investigation of the factors associated with effective public high schools.* Paper presented at the annual meeting of the American Educational Research Association, Chicago, IL.

Harnisch, D. L. (1987, March/April). Characteristics associated with effective public high schools. *Journal of Educational Research, 80* (4), 233-241.

Hawley, W. D. (1989). Looking backward at education reform. *Education Week, 9* (9), 23, 35.

Heipp, R. T., & Huffman, L. E. (1994, February/March). High school students' perceptions of the Paideia Program. *The High School Journal,* 206-215.

Henderson, A. T., & Berla, N. (Eds.). (1997). *A new generation of evidence: The family is critical to student achievement.* Washington, DC: Center for Law and Education.

Herbst, J. (1996). *The once and future school: Three hundred and fifty years of American secondary education.* New York: Routledge.

Hill, D. (1995). The strong department: Building the department as a learning community. In L. S. Siskin, & J. W. Little, (Eds.), *The subjects in question: Departmental organization and the high school* (pp. 123-140). New York: Teachers College Press.

Hill, P. T., Foster, G. E., & Gendler, T. (1990). *High schools with character.* Santa Monica, CA: RAND.

Hoffer, T. (1987). *Educational outcomes in public and private schools.* Unpublished doctoral dissertation, University of Chicago, Chicago, IL.

Hollifield, J. H. (1994). High schools gear up to create effective school and family partnerships. In J. H. Hollifield (Ed.), *Research and Development Report: Vol. 5* (pp. 1-6). Baltimore: Johns Hopkins University, Center on Families, Communities, Schools & Children's Learning. (ERIC Document Reproduction Service No. ED 380 229)

Hoover-Dempsey, K. V., & Sandler, H. M. (1997). Why do parents become involved in their children's education? *Review of Educational Research, 67* (1), 3-42.

Hoy, W. K., Tarter, C. J., & Bliss, J. R. (1990, August). Organizational climate, school health, and effectiveness: A comparative analysis. *Educational Administration Quarterly, 26*(3), 260-279.

Huberman, M. (1993). The model of the independent artisan in teachers' professional relations. In J. W. Little & M. W. McLaughlin (Eds.), *Teachers' work: Individuals, colleagues, and contexts* (pp. 11-50). New York: Teachers College Press.

Hutchins, C. L. (1988). Design as the missing piece in education. In *The redesign of education: A collection of papers concerned with comprehensive educational reform: Vol 1* (pp. 47-49). San Francisco: Far West Laboratory for Educational Research and Development.

James, T., & Tyack, D. (1983, February). Learning from past efforts to reform the high school. *Phi Delta Kappan, 64*(6), 400-406.

James, W. (1948). Pragmatism's conception of truth. In *Essays in Pragmatism.* New York: Hafner.

Johnson, D. M., Wardlow, G. W., & Franklin, T. D. (1997). Hands-on activities versus worksheets in reinforcing physical science principles: Effects on student achievement and attitude. *Journal of Agricultural Education, 38*(3), 9-17.

Johnson, D. W., Johnson, R. T., & Smith, K. A. (1995). Cooperative learning and individual student achievement in secondary schools. In J. E. Pederson & A. D. Digby (Eds.), *Secondary schools and cooperative learning: Theories, models, and strategies* (pp. 3-54). New York: Garland.

Johnson, S. M. (1990). The primacy and potential of high school departments. In M. W. McLaughlin, J. E. Talbert, & N. Bascia (Eds.), *The contexts of teaching in secondary schools: Teachers' realities* (pp. 167-183). New York: Teachers College Press.

Kaufman, K., & Aloma, R. (1997, April/May). Orchestrating classroom complexity: Interviews with inner city educators. *The High School Journal,* 218-226.

Keating, J., & Keating, J. M. (1996, December). *Preliminary results, implications, and applications from a study comparing a traditional vs. an integrated high school science program.* Paper presented at the first annual Global Summit on Science and Science Education, San Francisco, CA.

Keith, T. Z. (1982, April). Time spent on homework and high school grades: A large-sample path analysis. *Journal of Educational Psychology, 74*(2), 248-253.

Keith, T. Z., & Cool, V. A. (1992, Fall). Testing models of school learning: Effects of quality of instruction, motivation, academic coursework, and homework on academic achievement. *School Psychology Quarterly, 7*(3), 207-226.

King, J. A., & Weiss, D. A. (1995). Thomas Paine High School: Professional community in an unlikely setting. In K. S. Louis & S. D. Kruse (Eds.), *Professionalism and community: Perspectives on reforming urban schools* (pp. 76-104). Thousand Oaks, CA: Corwin.

Kleinfeld, J., McDiarmid, G. W., & Hagstrom, D. (1989, May). Small local high school decreases Alaska native dropout rates. *Journal of American Indian Education, 28*(3), 24-30.

Kliebard, H. M. (1995). *The struggle for the American curriculum 1893-1958* (2nd ed.). New York: Routledge.

Knisley, C. C. (1993, October). *Factors influencing rural Vermont public high school seniors to aspire or not to aspire to a four year college education: A research study.* Paper presented at the annual conference of the National Rural Education Association, Burlington, Vermont.

Koos, L. (1927). *The American secondary school.* Boston: Ginn.

Krug, E. A. (1964). *The shaping of the American high school.* New York: Harper & Row.

Krug, E. A. (1972). *The shaping of the American high school, 1920-1941.* Madison, WI: University of Wisconsin Press.

Kruse, S. D., Louis, K. S., & Bryk, A. S. (1995). An emerging framework for analyzing school-based professional community. In K. S. Louis & S. D. Kruse (Eds.), *Professionalism and community: Perspectives on reforming urban schools* (pp. 23-44). Thousand Oaks, CA: Corwin.

Lambeth, C. R. (1981, April). *Teacher invitations and effectiveness.* Paper presented at the annual meeting of the American Educational Research Association, Los Angeles, CA.

Lamborn, S. D., Brown, B. B., Mounts, N. S., & Steinberg, L. (1992). Putting school in perspective: The influence of family, peers, extracurricular participation, and part-time work on academic engagement. In F. M. Newmann (Ed.), *Student engagement and achievement in American secondary schools* (pp. 153-181). New York: Teachers College Press.

Larson, B. E. (1997, March). *Teachers' conceptions of discussion as method and outcome.* Paper presented at the annual meeting of the American Educational Research Association, Chicago, Illinois.

Larson, J. O. (1996, April). *"I'm not just interested": Gender-related responses in a high school chemistry curriculum.* Paper presented at the annual meeting of the National Association for Research in Science Teaching, St. Louis, MO.

Larson, R. L. (1992). *Changing schools from the inside out.* Lancaster, PA: Technomic.

Latimer, J. F. (1958). *What's happened to our high schools?* Washington, DC: Public Affairs Press.

Lee, V. E. (1995). Two views of high school organization: Bureaucracies and communities. In W. T. Pink & G. W. Noblit, (Eds.), *Continuity and contradiction: The futures of the sociology of education* (pp. 67-100). Cresskill, NJ: Hampton.

Lee, V., & Bryk, A. S. (1988). Curriculum tracking as mediating the social distribution of high school achievement. *Sociology of Education, 61,* 78-94.

Lee, V. E., & Bryk, A. S. (1989, July). A multilevel model of the social distribution of high school achievement. *Sociology of Education, (62),* 171-192.

Lee, V. E., Bryk, A. S., & Smith, J. B. (1993). The organization of effective secondary schools. In L. Darling-Hammond (Ed.), *Review of research in education: Vol. 19* (pp. 171-267). Washington, DC: American Educational Research Association.

Lee, V. E., & Smith, J. B. (1994). High school restructuring and student achievement: A new study finds strong links. In *Issues in restructuring schools* (Issue Report No. 7, pp. 2-6, 17). Madison, WI: University of Wisconsin-Madison, School of Education, Center on Organization and Restructuring of Schools. (ERIC Document Reproduction Service No. ED 376 565)

Lee, V. E., & Smith, J. B. (1996, February). Collective responsibility for learning and its effects on gains in achievement for early secondary school students. *American Journal of Education, 104,* 103-147.

Lee, V. E., & Smith, J. B. (1997, Fall). High school size: Which works best and for whom? *Educational Evaluation and Policy Analysis, 19* (3), 205-227.

Lee, V. E., Smith, J. B., & Croninger, R. G. (1995). *Another look at high school restructuring. More evidence that it improves student achievement and more insight into why.* Madison, WI: Center on Organization and Restructuring of Schools.

Lee, V. E., Smith, J. B., & Croninger, R. G. (1996, January). *Understanding high school restructuring effects on the equitable distribution of learning in mathematics and science* (Rev. Ed.). Madison, WI: University of Wisconsin, Center on Organization and Restructuring of Schools.

Lezotte, L., Hathaway, D. V., Miller, S. K., Passalacqua, J., & Brookover, W. B. (1980). *School learning climate and student achievement: A social systems approach to increase student learning.* Tallahassee, FL: Florida State University, Site Specific Technical Assistance Center.

Li, A. K., & Adamson, G. (1992, Fall). Gifted students' preferred learning style: Cooperative, competitive, or individualistic? *Journal for the Education of the Gifted, 16* (1), 46-54.

Lightfoot, S. L. (1983). *The good high school: Portraits of character and culture.* New York: Basic Books.

Lindle, J. C., Petrosko, J. M., & Pankratz, R. S. (1997, May). *1996 review of research on the Kentucky Education Reform Act* (Report prepared by the University of Kentucky/University of Louisville Joint Center for the Study of Educational Policy). Frankfort, KY: Kentucky Institute for Educational Research.

Liontos, L. B. (1991). *Involving the families of at-risk youth in the educational process.* Eugene, OR: ERIC Clearinghouse on Educational Management.

Little, J. W. (1982). Norms of collegiality and experimentation: Workplace conditions of school sources. *American Educational Research Journal, 19* (1), 325-340.

Little, J. W. (1990). Conditions of professional development in secondary schools. In M. W. McLaughlin, J. E. Talbert, & N. Bascia (Eds.), *The contexts of teaching in secondary schools: Teachers' realities* (pp. 187-223). New York: Teachers College Press.

Little, J. W. (1993). Professional community in comprehensive high schools: The two worlds of academic and vocational teachers. In J. W. Little & M. W. McLaughlin (Eds.), *Teachers work: Individuals, colleagues, and contexts* (pp. 137-163). New York: Teachers College Press.

Little, J. W. (1995). Subject affiliation in high schools that restructure. In L. S. Siskin & J. W. Little, (Eds.), *The subjects in question: Departmental organization and the high school* (pp. 172-200). New York: Teachers College Press.

Little, J. W., & McLaughlin, M. W. (Eds.). (1993). *Teachers work: Individuals, colleagues, and contexts.* New York: Teachers College Press.

Lortie, D. C. (1975). *Schoolteacher: A sociological study.* Chicago: University of Chicago Press.

Louis, K. S. (1990). Social and community values and the quality of teachers' work life. In M. W. McLaughlin, J. E. Talbert, & N. Bascia (Eds.), *The contexts of teaching in secondary schools: Teachers' realities* (pp. 17-39). New York: Teachers College Press.

Louis, K. S., & Kruse, S. D. (1995). *Professionalism and community: Perspectives on reforming urban schools.* Thousand Oaks, CA: Corwin.

Louis, K. S., Kruse, S. D., & Bryk, A. S. (1995). Professionalism and community: What is it and why is it important? In K. S. Louis & S. D. Kruse (Eds.), *Professionalism and community: Perspectives on reforming urban schools* (pp. 3-22). Thousand Oaks, CA: Corwin.

Louis, K. S., & Miles, M. B. (1990). *Improving the urban high school: What works and why.* New York: Teachers College Press.

Louis, K. S., & Smith, B. (1992). Cultivating teacher engagement: Breaking the iron law of social class. In F. M. Newmann (Ed.), *Student engagement and achievement in American secondary schools* (pp. 119-152). New York: Teachers College Press.

Lounsbury, J. H. (1996, December). Personalizing the high school: Lessons learned in the middle. *NASSP Bulletin, 80* (584), 17-24.

Lynn, L. (1994a). Building parent involvement. In *Brief to Principals* (Brief No. 8). Madison, WI: University of Wisconsin-Madison, Center on Organization and Restructuring of Schools.

Lynn, L. (1994b). Views from the front line: Three experienced high school principals interpret the Lee and Smith study. In *Issues in restructuring schools* (Issue Report No. 7, pp. 13-14). Madison, WI: University of Wisconsin-Madison, School of Education, Center on Organization and Restructuring of Schools. (ERIC Document Reproduction Service No. ED 376 565)

Mackenzie, G. N. (1942). Emerging curriculums show new conceptions of secondary education. In P. B. Jacobson, R. Lindquist, G. N. Mackenzie, H. Spears, & B. L. Johnson (Eds.), *General education in the American high school* (pp. 82-104). Chicago: Scott, Foresman.

Mackin, R. A. (1996, December). "Hey Dr. Bob, can we talk?": Toward the creation of a personalized high school. *NASSP Bulletin, 80* (584), 9-16.

MacLeod, J. (1995). *Ain't no makin' it: Aspirations and attainment in a low-income neighborhood.* Boulder, CO: Westview. (Original work published 1987)

Marks, H. M., & Louis, K. S. (1997, Fall). Does teacher empowerment affect the classroom: The implications of teacher empowerment for instructional practice and student achievement performance. *Educational Evaluation and Policy Analysis, 19* (3), 245-275.

Martin, J. R. (1997). A philosophy of education for the year 2000. In E. Clinchy (Ed.), *Transforming public education: A new course for America's future* (pp. 15-26). New York: Teachers College Press.

Maslow, A. H. (1970). *Motivation and personality.* New York: Harper & Row.

Matthews, D. B. (1996, March/April). An investigation of learning styles and perceived academic achievement for high school students. *Clearing House, 69* (4), 249-254.

McCaleb, S. P. (1994). *Building communities of learners: A collaboration among teachers, students, families & community.* New York: St. Martin's.

McDill, E. L., Meyers, E. D., & Rigsby, L. C. (1966). *Sources of educational climates in high schools.* Baltimore: Johns Hopkins University.

McKey, R. H., Condelli, L., Ganson, H., Barrett, B. J., McConkey, C., & Plantz, M. C. (1985). *The impact of Head Start on children, families, and communities* (Final report of the Head Start Evaluation, Synthesis and Utilization Project). Washington, DC: Government Printing Office.

McKinney, K., & Others (1986). *Good secondary schools: What makes them tick?* Washington, DC: Office of Education Research and Improvement.

McLaughlin, M. W. (1993). What matters most in teachers' workplace context? In J. W. Little & M. W. McLaughlin (Eds.), *Teachers' work: Individuals, colleagues, and contexts* (pp. 79-103). New York: Teachers College Press.

McLaughlin, M. W. (1994). Somebody knows my name. In *Issues in restructuring schools* (Issue Report No. 7, pp. 9-12). Madison, WI: University of Wisconsin-Madison, School of Education, Center on Organization and Restructuring of Schools. (ERIC Document Reproduction Service No. ED 376 565)

McLaughlin, M. W., & Talbert, J. E. (1990). The contexts in question: The secondary school workplace. In M. W. McLaughlin, J. E. Talbert, & N. Bascia (Eds.), *The contexts of teaching in secondary schools: Teachers' realities* (pp. 1-14). New York: Teachers College Press.

McLaughlin, M. W., Talbert, J. E., & Bascia, N. (Eds.). (1990). *The contexts of teaching in secondary schools: Teachers' realities.* New York: Teachers College Press.

McNeil, L. M. (1977). *Economic dimensions of social studies curriculum: Curriculum as institutionalized knowledge.* Unpublished doctoral dissertation, University of Wisconsin-Madison, Madison, WI.

McNeil, L. M. (1986). *Contradictions of control: School structure and school knowledge.* New York: Routledge.

McQuillan, P. J. (1995, April). *Knowing and empowerment: Or, student empowerment gone good.* Paper presented at the American Educational Research Association, San Francisco, CA.

McQuillan, P. J. (1997, December). Humanizing the comprehensive high school: A proposal for reform [Special Issue]. *Educational Administration Quarterly, 33,* 644-682.

McQuillan, P. J. (1998). *Educational opportunity in an urban, American high school.* Albany, NY: State University of New York Press.

Meece, J., & Jones, G. (1996, February/March). Girls in mathematics and science: Constructivism as a feminist perspective. *The High School Journal,* 242-248.

Meier, D. (1995). *The power of their ideas: Lessons for America from a small school in Harlem.* Boston: Beacon.

Merz, C., & Furman, G. C. (1997). *Communities & schools: Promise & paradox.* New York: Teachers College Press.

Metz, M. H. (1990a). How social class differences shape teachers' work. In M. W. McLaughlin, J. E. Talbert, & N. Bascia (Eds.), *The contexts of teaching in secondary schools: Teachers' realities* (pp. 40-107). New York: Teachers College Press.

Metz, M. H. (1990b). Real school: A universal drama amid disparate experience. In D. Mitchell & M. Foertz (Eds.), *Political educational association yearbook, 1989: Educational politics for a new century* (pp. 75-91). Philadelphia: Falmer.

Metz, M. H. (1993). Teachers' ultimate dependence on their students. In J. W. Little & M. W. McLaughlin (Eds.), *Teacher's work: Individuals, colleagues and context* (pp. 104-136). New York: Teachers College Press.

Meyer, J. W., & Rowan, B. (1975). *Notes on the structure of educational organizations: Revised version.* Paper presented at the annual meeting of the American Sociological Association, San Francisco, CA.

Miles, L. H., & Darling-Hammond, L. (1998, Spring). Rethinking the allocation of teaching resources: Some lessons from high-performing schools. *Educational Evaluation and Policy Analysis, 20* (1), 9-29.

Miron, L. F. (1996). *The social construction of urban schooling: Situating the crisis.* Cresskill, NJ: Hampton.

Mitchell, V., Russell, E. S., & Benson, C. S. (1990, September). *Exemplary urban career-oriented secondary school programs.* Berkeley, CA: National Center for Research in Vocational Education.

Mojkowski. C., & Fleming, D. (1988). *School-site management: Concepts and approaches.* Andover, MA: Regional Laboratory for the Educational Improvement of the Northeast and the Islands.

Monk, D. H. (1994). Subject area preparation of secondary mathematics and science teachers and student achievement. *Economics of Education Review, 13* (2), 125-145.

Morgan, D. L., & Alwin, D. F. (1980). When less is more: School size and student social participation. *Social Psychology Quarterly, 43,* 241-252.

Murnane, R. J., & Levy, F. (1996). *Teaching the new basic skills: Principles for educating children to thrive in a changing economy.* New York: The Free Press.

Murnane, R. J., & Levy, F. (1998, March). Standards, information, and the demand for student achievement. *Economic Policy Review, 4* (1), 117-124.

Murphy, J. (1989, Fall). Educational reform and equity: A reexamination of prevailing thought. *Planning and Changing, 20* (3), 172-179.

Murphy, J. (1990). Principal instructional leadership. In L. S. Lotto & P. W. Thurston (Eds.), *Advances in educational administration: Changing perspectives on the school: Vol. 1, Part B* (pp. 163-200). Greenwich, CT: JAI.

Murphy, J. (1991). *Restructuring schools: Capturing and assessing the phenomena.* New York: Teachers College Press.

Murphy, J. (1992a). *The landscape of leadership preparation: Reframing the education of school administrators.* Newbury Park, CA: Corwin.

Murphy, J. (1992b). School effectiveness and school restructuring: Contributions to educational improvement. *School Effectiveness and School Improvement, 3* (2), 90-109.

Murphy, J. (1996). *The privatization of schooling: Problems and possibilities.* Newbury Park, CA: Corwin.

Murphy, J. (1998). *The privatization of schooling: Problems and possibilities.* Newbury Park, CA: Corwin.

Murphy, J. (1999). New consumerism: Evolving market dynamics in the institutional dimension of schooling. In J. Murphy & K. S. Louis (Eds.), *Handbook of research on educational administration* (2nd ed., pp. 405-419). San Francisco: Jossey-Bass.

Murphy, J. (2000, February). Governing America's schools: The shifting playing field. *Teachers College Record, 102*(1), 57-84.

Murphy, J., & Beck, L. G. (1995). *School-based management as school reform: Taking stock.* Newbury Park, CA: Corwin.

Murphy, J., & Hallinger, P. (1985, January). Effective high schools: What are the common characteristics? *NASSP Bulletin, 69*(477), 18-22.

Murphy, J., & Hallinger, P. (1989, March-April). Equity as access to learning: Curricular and instructional treatment differentials. *Journal of Curricular Studies, 21*(2), 129-149.

Murphy, J., Hallinger, P., Lotto, L. S., & Miller, S. K. (1987, December). Barriers to implementing the instructional leadership role. *Canadian Administrator, 27*(3), 1-9.

Murphy, J., Hallinger, P., & Mesa, R.P. (1985). School effectiveness: Checking progress and assumptions and developing a role for state and federal government. *Teachers College Record, 86*(4), 616-641.

Murphy, J., Hallinger, P., Weil, M., & Mitman, A. (1984, September). Instructional leadership: A conceptual framework. In *The Education Digest, 50*(1), 28-31. (Reprinted from *Planning and Changing, 14*(3), 137-149. 1983, Fall.)

Murphy, J., Hull, T., & Walker, A. (1987, July-August). Academic drift and curricular debris: An analysis of high school course-taking patterns with implications for local policy makers. *Journal of Curriculum Studies, 19*(4), 341-360.

Murphy, J., Weil, M., Hallinger, P., & Mitman, A. (1982, December). Academic press: Translating high expectations into school policies and classroom practices. *Educational Leadership, 40*(3), 22-26.

Murphy, J., Weil, M., Hallinger, P., & Mitman, A. (1985, Spring). School effectiveness: A conceptual framework. *The Educational Forum, 49*(3), 361-374.

National Association of Secondary School Principals. (1996). *Breaking ranks: Changing an American institution.* Reston, VA: Author.

Natriello, G., & Dornbusch, S. M. (1983, Spring). Bringing behavior back in: The effects of student characteristics and behavior on the classroom behavior of teachers. *American Educational Research Journal, 20*(1), 29-43.

Natriello, G., McDill, E. L., & Pallas, A. M. (1990). *Schooling disadvantaged children: Racing against catastrophe.* New York: Teachers College Press.

Nauman, C. (1985). *Teacher culture in successful programs for marginal students.* Paper presented at the annual meeting of the American Educational Research Association, Chicago, IL.

Newlon, J. H. (1934). *Educational administration as social policy.* New York: Scribner.

Newmann, F. M. (1981, November). Reducing student alienation in high schools: Implications of theory. *Harvard Educational Review, 51*(4), 546-564.

Newmann, F. M. (1985). *Educational reform and social studies: Implications of six reports.* Boulder, CO: Social Science Education Consortium.

Newmann, F. M. (1991). *Classroom thoughtfulness and students' higher order thinking: Common indicators and diverse social studies courses.* Madison, WI: University of Wisconsin, National Center on Effective Secondary Schools.

Newmann, F. M. (1992a). Conclusion. In F. M. Newmann (Ed.), *Student engagement and achievement in American secondary schools* (pp. 182-218). New York: Teachers College Press.

Newmann, F. M. (1992b). Higher-order thinking and prospects for classroom thought-fulness. In F. M. Newmann (Ed.), *Student engagement and achievement in American secondary schools* (pp. 62-91). New York: Teachers College Press.

Newmann, F. M. (1992c). Introduction. In F. M. Newmann (Ed.), *Student engagement and achievement in American secondary schools* (pp. 1-10). New York: Teachers College Press.

Newmann, F. M. (1996). Introduction: The school restructuring study. In F. M. Newmann (Ed.), *Authentic achievement: Restructuring school intellectual quality* (pp. 1-16). San Francisco: Jossey-Bass.

Newmann, F. M. (1997). How secondary schools contribute to academic success. In K. Borman & B. Schneider (Eds.), *Youth experiences and development: Social influences and educational challenges.* Berkeley, CA: McCutchan.

Newmann, F. M. (1998). In K. Borman & B. Schneider (Eds.), *The adolescent years: Social influences and educational challenges* (Ninety-seventh yearbook of the National Society for the Study of Education, pp. 88-108). Chicago: University of Chicago Press.

Newmann, F. M., Marks, H. M., & Gamoran, A. (1995, April). *Authentic pedagogy and student performance.* Paper presented at the annual meeting of the American Educational Research Association, San Francisco, CA.

Newmann, F. M., Marks, H. M., & Gamoran, A. (1996, August). Authentic pedagogy and student performance. *American Journal of Education, 104,* 280-312.

Newmann, F. M., & Thompson, J. A. (1987). *Effects of cooperative learning on achievement in secondary schools: A summary of research.* Madison, WI: University of Wisconsin, National Center on Effective Secondary Schools.

Newmann, F. M., & Wehlage, G. G. (1994). From knowledge to understanding. In *Issues in restructuring schools* (Issue Report No. 7, pp. 15-16). Madison, WI: University of Wisconsin-Madison, School of Education, Center on Organization and Restructuring of Schools. (ERIC Document Reproduction Service No. ED 376 565)

Newmann, F. M., & Wehlage, G. G. (1995). *Successful school restructuring: A report to the public and educators.* Madison, WI: University of Wisconsin-Madison, Center on Organization and Restructuring of Schools.

Newmann, F. M., Wehlage, G. G., & Lamborn, S. D. (1992). The significance and sources of student engagement. In F. M. Newmann (Ed.), *Student engagement and achievement in American secondary schools* (pp. 11-39). New York: Teachers College Press.

Nickerson, R. S. (1988). On improving thinking through instruction. In E. Rothkopf (Ed.), *Review of Research in Education: Vol. 15* (pp. 3-57). Washington, DC: American Educational Research Association.

Noddings, N. (1988). An ethic of caring and its implications for instructional arrangements. *American Journal of Education, 96,* 215-231.

Noddings, N. (1997). A morally defensible mission for schools in the 21st century. In E. Clinchy (Ed.), *Transforming public education: A new course for America's future* (pp. 27-37). New York: Teachers College Press.

Nord, C. W., Brimhall, D., & West, J. (1997). *Fathers' involvement in their children's schools.* Washington, DC: National Center for Education Statistics.

Nystrand, M. (with Gamoran, A., Kachur, R., & Prendergast, C.) (1997). *Opening dialogue: Understanding the dynamics of language and learning in the English classroom.* New York: Teachers College Press.

Oakes, J. (1985). *Keeping track: How schools structure inequality.* New Haven, CT: Yale University Press.

Oakes, J. (1990). Opportunities, achievement, and choice: Women and minority students in science and mathematics. In C. B. Cazden (Ed.), *Review of Research in Education: Vol. 16* (pp. 153-222). Washington, DC: American Educational Research Association.

Oakes, J., & Lipton, M. (1996). Developing alternatives to tracking and grading. In L. I. Rendon, R. O. Hope, & Associates (Eds.), *Educating a new majority: Transforming America's educational system for diversity* (pp. 168-200). San Francisco: Jossey-Bass.

O'Brien, T. P. (1994, Fall). Cognitive learning styles and academic achievement in secondary education. *Journal of Research and Development in Education, 28*(1), 11-21.

Odell, C. W. (1939). *The secondary school.* Champaign, IL: Garland.

Oehmen, S. J. (1981). *Some effects of training students as managers of a program to indirectly modify academic and behavioral teacher ratings of students.* Unpublished doctoral dissertation, Memphis State University, Memphis, Tennessee.

Ogbu, J. U. (1985). A cultural ecology of competence among inner-city Blacks. In M. B. Spencer, G. K. Brookins, & W. R. Allen (Eds.), *Beginning: The social and affective development of black children* (pp. 49-56). Hillsdale, NJ: Erlbaum.

Ogbu, J. U. (1986). The consequences of the American caste systems. In U. Neisser (Ed.), *The school achievement of minority children: New perspectives* (pp. 19-56). Hillsdale, NJ: Erlbaum.

Ogbu, J. U. (1988). Class stratification, racial stratification, and schooling. In L. Weiss (Ed.), *Class, race, and gender in American education* (pp. 163-182). Albany, NY: State University of New York Press.

Ogden, E. H., & Germinario, V. (1995). *The nation's best schools: Blueprints for excellence.* Lancaster, PA: Technomic.

Ohiwerei, G. O. (1996). *Developing strategies for excellence in urban education.* Commack, NY: Nova Science.

Okebukola, P. A. (1992). Concept mapping with a cooperative learning flavor. *American Biology Teacher, 54* (4), 218-221.

O'Keefe, V. (1995). *Speaking to think thinking to speak: The importance of talk in the learning process.* Portsmith, NH: Boynton/Cook.

Ornstein, A. C. (1995, December/January). Motivation and learning. *The High School Journal,* 105-110.

Ornstein, A. C. (1997, April/May). How teachers plan lessons. *The High School Journal,* 227-237.

Oxley, D. (1990, June). *An analysis of house systems in New York City neighborhood high schools.* Philadelphia: Temple University, Center for Research in Human Development & Education.

Oxley, D. (1997, December). Theory and practice of school communities [Special Issue]. *Educational Administration Quarterly, 33,* 624-643.

Page, R. N. (1991). *Lower track classrooms: A curricular and cultural perspective.* New York: Teachers College Press.

Page, R., & Valli, L. (1990). *Curriculum differentiation: Interpretive studies in US secondary schools.* Albany: State University of New York Press.

Pallas, A. M. (1988, Summer). School climate in American high schools. *Teachers College Record, 89*(4), 541-554.

Pallas, A. M., & Alexander, K. L. (1983, Summer). Sex differences in quantitative SAT performance: New evidence on the differential coursework hypothesis. *American Educational Research Journal, 20*(2), 165-182.

Palmer, R. B., Dakof, G. A., & Liddle, H. A. (1993). *Family processes, family interventions, and adolescent school problems: A critical review and analysis.* Philadelphia: Temple University, National Center on Education in the Inner Cities.

Parsons, T. (1960). *Structure and process in modern societies.* Glencoe IL: Free Press.

Paschal, R. A., Weinstein, T., & Walberg, H. J. (1984, November-December). The effects of homework on learning: A quantitative synthesis. *Journal of Educational Research, 78* (2), 97-104.

Pearce, K. (1992, December). Learning organization: Reorganizing learners, learning process, setting, time, and staff in the comprehensive high school. In *New Designs for the Comprehensive High School. Volume II—Working Papers.* Berkeley, CA: National Center for Research in Vocational Education.

Pederson, J. E., & Digby, A. D. (1995). *Secondary schools and cooperative learning: Theories, models, and strategies.* New York: Garland.

Perkins, D. (1998). What is understanding? In M. S. Wiske (Ed.), *Teaching for understanding: Linking research with practice* (pp. 39-57). San Francisco: Jossey-Bass.

Perrone, V. (Ed.). (1983). Portraits of high schools. A supplement to Carnegie Foundation for the Advancement of Teaching, *High school: A report on secondary education in America.* Princeton, NJ: Princeton University Press.

Perrone, V., & Associates (1985). *Portraits of high schools: A supplement to high school: A report on secondary education in America.* Princeton, NJ: Princeton University Press.

Petrie, H. G. (1990). Reflecting on the second wave of reform: Restructuring the teaching profession. In S. L. Jacobson & J. A. Conway (Eds.), *Educational leadership in an age of reform* (pp. 14-29). New York: Longman.

Phelan, P., Davidson, A. L., & Yu, H. C. (1998). *Adolescents' worlds: Negotiating family, peers, and school.* New York: Teachers College Press.

Pierson, G. N. (1996, December). Learning resource lab: Academic coaching for freshmen. *NASSP Bulletin, 80* (584), 25-26.

Powell, A. G. (1990). The conditions of teachers' work in independent schools. In M. W. McLaughlin, J. E. Talbert, & N. Bascia (Eds.), *The contexts of teaching in secondary schools: Teachers' realities* (pp. 111-141). New York: Teachers College Press.

Powell, A. G., Farrar, E., & Cohen, D. K. (1985). *The shopping mall high school: Winners and losers in the educational marketplace.* Boston: Houghton Mifflin.

President's Commission on Privatization. (1988). *Privatization: Toward more effective government.* Washington, DC: Government Printing Office.

Prestine, N. A. (1998, April). *Disposable reform? Assessing the durability of secondary school reform.* Paper presented at the annual meeting of the American Educational Research Association, San Diego, CA.

Prestine, N. A., & Bragg, D. (1998, April). *Never the twain shall meet? Looking for linkages in secondary school reform.* Paper presented at the annual meeting of the American Educational Research Association, San Diego, CA.

Purkey, S. O., & Smith, M. S. (1983, March). Effective schools: A review. *Elementary School Journal, 83*(4), 427- 452.

Ravitch, D. (1983). *The troubled crusade: American education, 1945-1980.* New York: Basic Books.

Raywid, M. A. (1993). Community: An alternative school accomplishment. In G. A. Smith (Ed.), *Public schools that work: Creating community* (pp. 23-44). New York: Routledge.

Raywid, M. A. (1995, December). *The subschools/small schools movement—taking stock.* Madison, WI: University of Wisconsin-Madison, Center on Organization and Restructuring of Schools.

Reap, M. A., & Cavallo, A. L. (1992, March). *Students' meaningful understanding of science concepts: Gender differences.* Paper presented at the annual conference of the National Association for Research in Science Teaching, Boston, MA.

Reese, W. J. (1995). *The origins of the American high school.* New Haven, CT: Yale University Press.

Renzulli, J. S., Reis, S. M., Hebert, T. P., & Diaz, E. I. (1995). The plight of high-ability students in urban schools. In M. C. Wang & M. C. Reynolds (Eds.), *Making a difference for students at risk: Trends and alternatives* (pp. 61-89). Thousand Oaks, CA: Corwin.

Riew, J. (1986). Scale economies, capacity utilization, and school costs: A comparative analysis of secondary and elementary schools. *Journal of Educational Finance, 11,* 433-446.

Rivera, J., & Poplin, M. (1997). Listening to voices on the inside: Beyond the conservative-liberal-radical debate to a common vision for schools in our multiethnic society. In E. Clinchy (Ed.), *Transforming public education: A new course for America's future* (pp. 97-110). New York: Teachers College Press.

Roderick, M., & Stone, S. (1998, August). *Changing standards, changing relationships: Building family-school relationships to promote achievement in high schools* (Research Brief). Chicago: University of Chicago, School of Social Service Administration, Student Life in High Schools Project.

Rogers, R. G. (1987, Fall). Is bigger better? Fact or fad concerning school district organization. *ERS Spectrum, 5*(4), 36-39.

Romo, H. D., & Falbo, T. (1996). *Latino high school graduation: Defying the odds.* Austin, TX: University of Texas Press.

Rorty, R. (1979). *Philosophy and the mirror of nature.* Princeton, NJ: Princeton University Press.

Rosenbaum, J. E. (1976). *Inequality: The hidden curriculum of high school tracking.* New York: Wiley.

Rosenbaum, J. E. (1980). Track misperceptions and frustrated college plans: An analysis of the effects of track and track perceptions in the NLS. *Sociology of Education, 53,* 534-562.

Rosenholtz, S. J. (1989). *Teachers' workplace: The social organization of schools.* White Plains, NY: Longman.

Rothstein, S. W. (1994). *Schooling the poor: A social inquiry into the American educational experience.* Westport, CT: Bergin & Garvey.

Roueche, J. E., & Baker, G. A., III, with Mullin, P. L., & Boy, N. H. O. (1986). *Profiling excellence in America's schools.* Arlington, VA: American Association of School Administrators.

Russell, J. S., Mazzarella, J. A., White, T., & Maurer, S. (1985). *Linking the behaviors and activities of secondary school principals to school effectiveness: A focus on effective and ineffective behaviors.* Eugene: University of Oregon, Center for Educational Policy and Management.

Rutter, M., Maughan, B., Mortimore, P., Ouston, J., & Smith, A. (1979). *Fifteen thousand hours: Secondary schools and their effects on children.* Cambridge, MA: Harvard University Press.

Sadker, M., & Sadker, D. (1994). *Failing at fairness: How America's schools cheat girls.* New York: Scribner.

Schools need answers to rising dropout rates. (1997, October 14). *USA Today,* editorial page.

Sedlak, M. W., Wheeler, C. W., Pullin, D. C., & Cusick, P. A. (1986). *Selling students short: Classroom bargains and academic reform in the American high school.* New York: Teachers College Press.

Shanahan, T., & Walberg, H. J. (1985, July-August). Productive influences on high school student achievement. *Journal of Educational Research, 78*(6), 357-363.

Shore, R. (1995, February). How one high school improved school climate. *Educational Leadership, 52*(5), 76-78.

Shulman, L. S. (1984). Foreword. In L. Cuban, *How teachers taught: Constancy and change in American classrooms 1890-1980* (pp. vii-ix). New York: Longman.

Siskin, L. S. (1995). Subject divisions. In L. S. Siskin & J. W. Little (Eds.), *The subjects in question: Departmental organization and the high school* (pp. 23-47). New York: Teachers College Press.

Siskin, L. S. (1997, December). The challenge of leadership in comprehensive high schools: School vision and departmental divisions [Special Issue]. *Educational Administration Quarterly, 33,* 604-623.

Sizer, T. R. (1964). *Secondary schools at the turn of the century.* New Haven, CT: Yale University Press.

Sizer, T. R. (1984). *Horace's compromise: The dilemma of the American high school.* Boston: Houghton Mifflin.

Smith, J. B., & Lee, V. E. (1996, February 16). *High school restructuring and the equitable distribution of achievement* (Rev. Ed.). Madison, WI: Center on Organization and Restructuring of Schools.

Sonnenberg, W. C. (1993). Elementary and secondary education. In T. D. Snyder (Ed.), *120 years of American education: A statistical portrait* (pp. 25-61). Washington, DC: United States Department of Education, National Center for Educational Statistics.

Spade, J. Z., Columba, L., & Vanfossen, B. E. (1985, April). *Effective schools: Characteristics of schools which predict mathematics and science performance.* Paper presented at the annual meeting of the American Educational Research Association, Chicago, IL.

Spady, W. G. (1988, October). Organizing for results: The basis of authentic restructuring and reform. *Educational Leadership, 46* (2), 4-8.

Spears, H. (1941). *Secondary education in American life.* New York: American Book.

Spring, J. (1990). *The American school 1642-1990: Varieties of historical interpretation of the foundations and development of American education* (2nd ed.). New York: Longman.

Steinberg, L. (1997). *Beyond the classroom: Why school reform has failed and what parents need to do.* New York: Simon & Schuster.

Steinberg, L., (with Brown, B. B., & Dornbusch, S. M.) (1996). *Beyond the classroom: Why school reform has failed and what parents need to do.* New York: Teachers College Press.

Steinberg, L., Elmen, J. D., & Mounts, N. S. (1989). Authoritative parenting, psychosocial maturity, and academic success among adolescents. *Child Development, 60,* 1424-1436.

Steinberg, L., Lamborn, S. D., Dornbusch, S. M., & Darling, N. (1992). Impact of parenting practices on adolescent achievement: Parenting, school involvement, and encouragement to succeed. *Child Development, 63,* 1266-1281.

Steinberg, L., & Silverberg, S. B. (1986). The vicissitudes of autonomy in early adolescence. *Child Development, 57,* 841-851.

Stevenson, D. L., Kochenek, J., & Schneider, B. (1998). Making the transition from high school: Recent trends and policies. In K. Borman & B. Schneider (Eds.), *The adolescent years: Social influences and educational challenges* (pp. 207-226). Chicago: University of Chicago Press.

Stiles, L. J., McCleary, L. E., & Turnbaugh, R. C. (1962). *Secondary education in the United States.* New York: Harcourt Brace.

Stringfield, S., Ross, S. M., & Smith, L. (1996). *Bold plans for school restructuring: The new American schools design.* Mahwah, NJ: Lawrence Erlbaum.

Swanson, D. P., Spencer, M. B., & Peterson, A. (1998). Identity formation in adolescence. In K. Borman & B. Schneider (Eds.), *The adolescent years: Social influences and educational challenges* (Ninety-seventh yearbook of the National Society for the Study of Education, pp. 18-41). Chicago: University of Chicago Press.

Sweeney, T. E. (1992). *The mastery of public speaking skills through sociodrama techniques: Attitudes and ability development.* New York: National Arts Research Center.

Talbert, J. E. (1992). *Constructing a school-wide professional community: The negotiated order of a performing arts school.* Center for Research on the Context of Secondary School Teaching.

Talbert, J. E. (1995). Boundaries of teachers' professional communities in U.S. high schools: Power and precariousness of the subject department. In L. S. Siskin & J. W. Little (Eds.), *The subjects in question: Departmental organization and the high school* (pp. 68-94). New York: Teachers College Press.

Taylor, L. O., McMahill, D. R., & Taylor, B. L. (1960). *The American secondary school.* New York: Appleton-Century-Crofts.

Taylor, R. D. (1994). Risk and resilience: Contextual influences on the development of African-American adolescents. In M. C. Wang & E. W. Gordon (Eds.), *Educational resilience in inner-city America—challenges and prospects* (pp. 119-130). Hillsdale, NJ: Lawrence Erlbaum.

Taylor-Dunlop, K., & Norton, M. (1995). *Suffer the children. . .and they do* (Technical Report). (ERIC Document Reproduction Service No. ED 402 524)

Tewel, K. J. (1995). *New schools for a new century: A leader's guide to high school reform.* Delray Beach, FL: St. Lucie.

Texas Education Agency. (1992, October). *One student at a time: Report of the state board of education task force on high school education.* Austin, TX: Author.

Trow, M. (1961, September). The second transformation of American secondary education. *International Journal of Comparative Sociology II,* 144-166.

Tschannen-Moran, M., Hoy, A. W., & Hoy, W. K. (1998, Summer). Teacher efficacy: Its meaning and measure. *Review of Educational Research, 68*(2), 202-248.

Tyack, D. (1978). *The one best system.* New York: Teachers College Press.

Tyack, D. (1993). School governance in the United States: Historical puzzles and anomalies. In J. Hannaway & M. Carnoy (Eds.), *Decentralization and school improvement* (pp. 1-32). San Francisco: Jossey-Bass.

Tyack, D. B. (1974). *The one best system: A history of American urban education.* Cambridge, MA: Harvard University Press.

Tye, B. B. (1985). *Multiple realities: A study of thirteen American high schools.* Lanham, NY: University Press of America.

Vinovskis, M. A. (1985). *The origins of public high schools: A reexamination of the Beverly High School controversy.* Madison, WI: University of Wisconsin Press.

Walberg, H. J., Fraser, B. J., & Welch, W. W. (1986, January/February). A test of a model of educational productivity among senior high school students. *Journal of Educational Research, 79* (3), 133-139.

Wang, M. C., & Gordon, E. W. (1994). *Educational resilience in inner-city America: Challenges and prospects.* Hillsdale, NJ: Lawrence Erlbaum.

Wang, M. C., & Reynolds, M. C. (1995). *Making a difference for students at risk: Trends and alternatives.* Thousand Oaks, CA: Corwin.

Wehlage, G. G., Rutter, R. A., Smith, G. A., Lesko, N., & Fernandez, R. R. (1989). *Reducing the risk: Schools as communities of support.* New York: Falmer.

Welch, W. W., Anderson, R. E., & Harris, L. J. (1982, Spring). The effects of schooling on mathematics achievement. *American Educational Research Journal, 19*(1), 145-153.

Wells, A. S., Lopez, A., Scott, J., & Holme, J. J. (1999, Summer). Charter school as postmodern paradox: Rethinking social stratification in an age of deregulated school choice. *Harvard Educational Review, 69*(2), 172-204.

Westbury, I. (1988). How should we be judging the American high school? *Journal of Curriculum Studies, 20* (4), 291-315.

Wigfield, A., Eccles, J. S., & Rodriguez, D. (1998). The development of children's motivation in school contexts. In P. D. Pearson & A. Iran-Nejad (Eds.), *Review of Research in Education: Vol. 23* (pp. 73-118). Washington, DC: American Educational Research Association.

Wiggins, G. (1989, April). Teaching to the (authentic) test. *Educational Leadership, 46* (7), 41-47.

Williams, J. E. (1996, April). *Promoting rural students' academic achievements: An examination of self-regulated learning strategies.* Paper presented at the annual meeting of the American Educational Research Association, New York, NY.

Willing, M. H. (1942). From 1890 to 1930 American educators changed the purpose and practice of high schools. In P. B. Jacobson, R. Lindquist, G. N. Mackenzie, H. Spears, & B. L. Johnson (Eds.), *General education in the American high schools* (pp. 41-81). Chicago: Scott Foresman.

Wilson, B. L., & Corcoran, T. B. (1988). *Successful secondary schools: Visions of excellence in American public education.* New York: Falmer.

Wilson, B. L., Webb, J., & Corbett, H. D. (1995). Restructuring and policy research: Connecting adults to students. In W. T. Pink & G. W. Noblit, (Eds.), *Continuity and contradiction: The futures of the sociology of education* (pp. 279-303). Cresskill, NJ: Hampton.

Wilson, K. G., & Daviss, B. (1994). *Redesigning education.* New York: Henry Holt.

Wise, A. E. (1989). Professional teaching: A new paradigm for the management of education. In T. J. Sergiovanni & J. H. Moore (Eds.), *Schooling for tomorrow: Directing reforms to issues that count* (pp. 301-310). Boston: Allyn & Bacon.

Witmer, J. T. (1992, May). Teachers as advisers. *The Executive Educator, 14*(5), 41-42.

Witte, J. F., & Walsh, D. J. (1990, Summer). A systematic test of the effective schools model. *Educational Evaluation and Policy Analysis, 12*(2), 188-212.

Wolf, D., Bixby, J., Glenn, J., III, & Gardner, H. (1989). To use their minds well: Investigating new forms of student assessment. *Review of Educational Research, 46*(7), 31-74.

Wood, G. H. (1992). *Schools that work: America's most innovative public education programs.* New York: Dutton.

Wraga, W. G. (1994). *Democracy's high school: The comprehensive high school and educational reform in the United States.* Lanham, MD: University Press of America.

Wynne, E. (1980). *Looking at schools: Good, bad and indifferent.* Lexington, MA: D. C. Heath.

Index

CORWIN
PRESS

The Corwin Press logo—a raven striding across an open book—represents the happy union of courage and learning. We are a professional-level publisher of books and journals for K–12 educators, and we are committed to creating and providing resources that embody these qualities. Corwin's motto is "Success for All Learners."